W9-DAO-631

Theatre Profiles 7

Theatre Profiles 7

THE ILLUSTRATED GUIDE TO AMERICA'S NONPROFIT PROFESSIONAL THEATRES

Edited by Laura Ross with John Istel

THEATRE COMMUNICATIONS GROUP · NEW YORK · 1986

ACKNOWLEDGEMENTS

TCG gratefully acknowledges the generous support of its individual contributors, and the following foundations, corporations and government agencies:

Actors' Equity Foundation
Alcoa Foundation
Atlantic Richfield Foundation
AT&T Foundation
Chevron, U.S.A.
Citicorp/Citibank
Columbia Pictures Industries
Consolidated Edison of New York
Dayton Hudson Foundation
Equitable Life Assurance Society of the United States
Exxon Corporation
The Ford Foundation
The William and Mary Greve Foundation
Home Box Office
The Andrew W. Mellon Foundation
Mobil Foundation
The Mabel Pew Myrin Trust
National Broadcasting Company
National Endowment for the Arts
New York Life Foundation
New York State Council on the Arts
The Rockefeller Foundation
The Scherman Foundation
Time, Inc.
The Xerox Foundation

Copyright © 1986 by Theatre Communications Group, Inc. Essays appearing in this book are copyrighted © 1986, respectively, Zelda Fichandler, James Reston, Jr., W. McNeil Lowry, Robert Brustein, Gerald Weales, John Dillon, Robert Marx, Gordon Davidson and Des McAnuff. "Things to Come" by Alan Schneider, copyright © 1985, Eugenie R. Schneider, executrix of the estate of Alan Schneider.

Design by Joe Marc Freedman

ISBN 0-930452-52-6

First Edition

CONTENTS

FOREWORD

Peter Zeisler

With this volume in our biennial *Theatre Profiles* series, we have decided to celebrate the first quarter-century of the nonprofit theatre, along with TCG's own twenty-fifth anniversary. In some ways, it's an artificial designation—a few American theatres have been around much longer. But milestones afford opportunities for reflection, and the following pages contain the observations and wisdom of some of the people who were central to the development of that theatre: those who made it happen and those who observed it firsthand.

From their widely various viewpoints, these commentators agree that we've come a long way in twenty-five years—and that we have even further to go. For the purposes of this volume, then, an anniversary is merely a moment in a continuing history, elevated to a vantage point from which to look both backward and ahead, to celebrate achievement and come to terms with looming challenges, to place our most recent efforts (which are thoroughly documented in words and pictures in the latter portions of this book) within their historical context.

As I look through these pages I am awed by the degree of change that has taken place within our theatre over twenty-five years. Any art form that changes—and is changing—with the rapidity of the theatre need not worry unduly about its vitality. When I think about what both artists and audiences had at their disposal in 1961 and what is now available (and taken for granted), it becomes clear that the only way we can truly grasp the magnitude of our progress is over the arc of time that the following essays encompass. Only time will tell what we will have to look back on when the year 2011 rolls around.

Simply scanning the theatre profiles in the back of this volume is a revelation: Opportunities for artists have increased immeasurably; playwrights, directors and actors have widespread access to theatres committed to producing new work, and designers can expect to work with staffs capable of executing sophisticated and demanding productions in many theatre shops. The repertoires listed point out opportunities for artists that simply did not exist twenty-five years ago. I well remember interviewing more than 800 actors for the first season of the Shakespeare Festival at Stratford, Conn. in 1955. It was not possible to find actors with extensive professional experience in the classic repertoire then because, with rare exceptions, Shakespeare simply was not produced professionally in the United

States. Today it is difficult to find a working actor who is not continually confronted with, and challenged by, the classics.

The fact that theatregoers now have that repertoire available to them on a continuing basis additionally serves to develop our critical standards. Just as local audiences across the country are now exposed to most new work before it receives national media coverage, that new work needs to be placed in context. As in all art forms, that context—that base—is the classic repertoire. We have, in twenty-five years, developed a depth and richness of repertoire throughout the country that never before existed.

Now that these theatres exist, what are we going to do with them? Zelda Fichandler points out that we never set out to build institutions twenty-five years ago, and she's absolutely right. We were simply trying to find an effective method of working. With the initiation of arts funding in this country, institutions were built, perhaps because physical plants were regarded as essential to change the previous perception of theatre as an evanescent, non-continuing art; perhaps because it's easier to allocate funds for buildings than ideas; and perhaps simply because there was no other way. So, like Mount Everest, they are *there*. How we use, exploit and bend them to our purposes is a central issue of the day. And, even given the problems that dance companies constantly confront because they lack strong bases (i.e., institutions), I'm not sure the problem of exploiting the institution creatively is less pressing than the problems inherent in the nomadic life of the dance community.

The matter of the "institution" is part of the "whose theatre is this?" issue, and related to the debate about governance that is currently being enjoined by all arts organizations. The debate centers on the degree of income that organizations are expected to generate—an extraordinarily volatile subject for the theatre community. Historically, theatres created profit, and to this day many theatre trustees question why their nonprofit theatre can't be more self-sufficient. Because of the absence of role models, our theatres, when organized, assumed the governance structure of other nonprofit organizations, with a professional staff responsible to a board of trustees. In the first flush of development, costs were contained and trustees were asked primarily to be cheerleaders, not fund-raisers. In today's much-changed funding climate, the issue of how these institutions are to be maintained as they grow at an astounding rate—and by whom—becomes urgent.

A related problem is that of accessibility. As theatres are charged with earning more money, ticket prices are rising with alarming rapidity. For twenty-five years we have tried to encourage younger audiences, but that prospect becomes dimmer as prices soar. Without constantly replenishing an audience with young people—and making it possible for them to attend regularly—one wonders where our audiences will come from in another twenty-five years. The theatre is being automatically thrown back to "privileged" ticket holders, but not necessarily to those who want, or are willing, to be challenged and provoked, two of the theatre's unique capabilities.

In our boundless expansion and concomitant decentralization, one very precious condition has suffered, and has been the focus of TCG's most vigorous efforts: collegiality. All art forms have taken quantum leaps when artists could exchange ideas and view one another's work on a continuing basis. One thinks of the composers centered in Paris in the 1930s, or that astounding group of playwrights and directors in London in the 1950s who reshaped the English theatre. In an effort to overcome the scarcity of the kind of work-center that encourages collegiality, our artists seem to be finding a singular American solution to the problem: they are creating semi-formal arrangements with their peers, and communities of associated artists are attaching themselves to theatres in a variety of ways. From La Jolla, Calif. to Cambridge, Mass., continuing relationships are being forged among directors, designers and actors who use particular theatres as "home bases." In a sense these loose affiliations are a new form of "portable collegiality."

Perhaps most important of all, we need—we must find—ways to nurture our artists through that creative gestation period known as rehearsal. We have to find a way to make "process" not a buzz word but an accepted method of operation. In a society increasingly geared to instant gratification, we seem perilously close to forgetting that creation can't be achieved by popping something into a microwave oven. Simmering and a great deal of basting are necessary. Time is essential, and creativity can't be made cost-effective.

So it is within the context of these thoughts, and the ensuing ruminations of my respected colleagues, that we place our most recent theatre history, the past two seasons of work at 199 diverse theatres across the country. Perhaps this volume's dual purposes—to examine a large piece of history, and to record the most recent events and statistics—will coalesce to provide some new insights in TCG's twenty-fifth anniversary year.

I cannot close without mentioning how the memory of Alan Schneider infuses every aspect of this book. Even without his funny but provocative article, which seems even more pertinent now than when he wrote it for the inaugural issue of TCG's *American Theatre* magazine in April 1984, it is impossible not to "hear" Alan in the essays of his peers and in the lists of artists in these pages, many of whom he served as mentor and confidant. It is that sense of Alan that remains such a palpable force in our theatre and is his continuing legacy.

HIGHLIGHTS

Twenty-five Years in the American Theatre

Although the early sixties were a turning point in the American theatre, the seeds of three alternatives to Broadway's commercial activities had been planted prior to 1960. The Off Broadway movement, which had been established with the success of several companies including an early nonprofit theatre—Circle in the Square (founded 1951)—faced escalating costs, prompting the rise of what inevitably became known as Off-*Off* Broadway. This energetic offshoot encompassed the efforts of such pioneering groups as The Living Theatre (1951) and Caffe Cino (1958). Elsewhere in the U.S., what was coming to be known as the "regional theatre movement" had taken hold in such cities as Cleveland (The Cleveland Play House, 1915), Chicago (Goodman Theatre, 1925), Abingdon, Va. (Robert Porterfield's Barter Theatre, 1933), Houston (Alley Theatre, 1947), Dallas (Margo Jones's Theatre 47, 1947), Washington, D.C. (Arena Stage, 1950) and San Francisco (Actors Workshop, 1952).

In addition to these regional or resident theatres, a number of Shakespeare festivals dotted the American landscape, including the Oregon Shakespearean Festival in Ashland (1935), Old Globe Theatre in San Diego (1937), New York Shakespeare Festival (1954) and American Shakespeare Theatre in

Stratford, Conn. (1955). It was from these roots—the early regional companies along with a vital Off-Off Broadway movement—that the full-fledged non-commercial theatre sprang, spreading, through the seventies, to the furthest reaches of the nation.

1961—The Living Theatre presents Kenneth Brown's *The Brig*, following its influential 1959 production of Jack Gelber's *The Connection*. Tennessee Williams's last widely acclaimed play, *Night of the Iguana*, appears on Broadway. The Judson Poets' Theatre, under the direction of Al Carmines, opens in lower Manhattan's Judson Church. The Bread and Puppet Theatre is born in New York with a production of *Totentanz*. Ford Foundation trustees appropriate an initial $9 million to begin "strengthening the position of resident theatre in the U.S." along with $244,000 for the establishment of Theatre Communications Group. In addition, Ford vice president for the humanities and arts W. McNeil Lowry engages Danny Newman, through TCG, as a subscription consultant, sparking enormous audience growth throughout the nation.

1962—Edward Albee's *Who's Afraid of Virginia Woolf?* opens on Broad-

way, directed by Alan Schneider. New York Shakespeare Festival's 2,300-seat, open-air Delacorte Theatre opens in Central Park. Arthur Kopit's *Oh Dad, Poor Dad . . .* premieres Off Broadway. Ellen Stewart creates Cafe La Mama Off-Off Broadway, beginning with Tennessee Williams's *One Arm*. The Great Lakes Shakespeare Festival opens in Cleveland.

1963—The Guthrie Theater, the first institutional theatre in the U.S. built solely with community support and dedicated to a classical repertoire, opens in Minneapolis with *Hamlet*. Joseph Chaikin, along with Peter Feldman and a group of artists, founds the Open Theatre in New York. The Seattle Repertory Theatre and Center Stage in Baltimore begin operations. Gilbert Moses and John O'Neal open the Free Southern Theatre at Mississippi's Tougaloo College, in response to the Civil Rights movement.

1964—The first two plays of budding playwright Sam Shepard, *Cowboys* and *Rock Garden*, are produced at New York's Theatre Genesis. The Lincoln Center Repertory Theatre is established with Elia Kazan and Robert Whitehead at the helm. The Phoenix and APA theatres merge, and for four years produce plays in repertory on Broadway. The American Place Theatre opens Off Broadway with a production of Robert Lowell's *The Old Glory*. Adrian Hall founds Trinity Square Repertory Company in Providence. Among other theatres to begin operation are Actors Theatre of Louisville and Hartford Stage Company. Ming Cho Lee designs sets for a production of *Electra* in Central Park, forging a new, sculptural design style. The Living Theatre begins two decades of exile in Europe and South America.

1965—San Francisco's American Conservatory Theatre, the first company to operate a professional conservatory, opens under the artistic direction of William Ball. Luis Valdez founds El Teatro Campesino to entertain California's striking farm workers. Robert Kalfin founds the Chelsea Theater Center in Manhattan. The O'Neill Theater Center holds its first National Playwrights' Conference in Waterford, Conn. President Lyndon B. Johnson signs legislation creating the National Endowment for the Arts. Long Wharf Theatre opens in New Haven.

1966—The Twentieth Century Fund publishes the first book to study in depth the subject of economics and the arts, *Performing Arts—The Economic Dilemma*, by William J. Baumol and William G. Bowen. The NEA receives its first funds from Congress: $2.5 million to be spread among all the arts throughout the country. Robert Brustein establishes the Yale Repertory Theatre, to operate in conjunction with the Yale School of Drama. Jules Irving and Herbert Blau bring members of their Actors Workshop from San Francisco to found a new company at New York's Lincoln Center. Megan Terry's *Viet Rock* is born out of an Open Theatre workshop. Ronald Ribman's *Journey of the Fifth Horse*, featuring Dustin Hoffman, premieres at the American Place Theatre. The first League of Resident Theatres contract comes into being.

1967—Sir Tyrone Guthrie directs the *Oresteia* at the Guthrie, with designs by Tanya Moiseiwitsch. John Houseman's Theatre Group, in residence at UCLA since 1959, is invited to move into the Los Angeles Music Center and becomes the Mark Taper Forum; Gordon Davidson is appointed artistic director. Barbara Garson's *MacBird* is first performed at New York's Village Gate. Edward Albee's *A Delicate Balance* wins the Pulitzer Prize for Drama. The New York Shakespeare Festival moves into its new facility, the Public Theater on Lafayette Street, opening with the rock musical *Hair*. Richard Schechner founds The Performance Group in New York along Grotowski-inspired lines. The San Francisco Mime Troupe (founded in 1959 by Ronnie Davis) comes to national prominence with a cross-country tour of anti-war scenarios. Douglas Turner Ward, Robert Hooks and Gerald S. Krone found the Negro Ensemble Company in New York, opening with Peter Weiss's *Song of the Lusitanian Bogey*. Eugene Lee designs his first set for Trinity Square, *The Threepenny Opera*, beginning a long association with the theatre and with director Adrian Hall. A group of theatre artists, psychologists and social scientists found the National Theatre of the Deaf. Joe Cino commits suicide and Caffe Cino closes its doors.

1968—The Open Theatre presents Jean-Claude van Itallie's *The Serpent*, and The Performance Group opens *Dionysus in 69*. The Living Theatre returns to the U.S. briefly to present *Paradise Now and Frankenstein* at the Yale Repertory Theatre and the Brooklyn Academy of Music. *Hair* brings Broadway its first nude scene. The Arena Stage production of *The Great White Hope* opens on Broadway, winning the Pulitzer. Richard Foreman founds the Ontological-Hysteric Theatre.

1969—Gilbert Moses directs the Chelsea Theater Center production of Amiri Baraka's *Slave Ship* at the Brooklyn Academy of Music, with an elaborate environment designed by

Eugene Lee. Robert Wilson founds the Byrd Hoffman School of Byrds. Marshall W. Mason, Lanford Wilson and colleagues found Circle Repertory Company in New York. Gerald Freedman's production of *The Taming of the Shrew* at the New York Shakespeare Festival uses American farce techniques inspired by Chaplin, Keaton and the like. Romanian director Andrei Serban arrives in the U.S. and begins directing at La Mama. Broadway's ANTA Theatre hosts the first showcase of work from the nation's resident theatres, including the American Conservatory Theatre, the American Shakespeare Theatre Trinity Square Repertory Company and the National Theatre of the Deaf.

1970—A collective of performing artists founds Mabou Mines, and Lee Breuer presents the first of his "Animations." Daniel Berrigan's *The Trial of the Catonsville Nine*, directed by Gordon Davidson, premieres at the Mark Taper Forum. Lyn Austin founds the Music-Theatre Group/Lenox Arts Center in Massachusetts to nurture dynamic collaborations among music and theatre artists. Andre Gregory and his Manhattan Project premiere their landmark *Alice in Wonderland* in New York.

1971—Peter Brook and the Royal Shakespeare Company return to New York with their *Midsummer Night's Dream*. The Negro Ensemble Company produces *The River Niger* and takes it on tour. David Rabe's *The Basic Training of Pavlo Hummel* premieres at the New York Shakespeare Festival. Playwrights Horizons, dedicated to new work, is founded by Robert Moss in New York City. The Rockefeller Foundation launches its Fellowships for American Playwrights program.

1972—In collaboration with composer Elizabeth Swados, Andrei Serban directs his adaptation of *Medea* at La Mama, the first play in a classical trilogy that will later be presented collectively as *Fragments of a Trilogy*. John Houseman and Margot

Harley found The Acting Company, a national touring theatre, with members of the first graduating class of the Juilliard School's Drama Division. A bill of four Beckett plays including *Krapp's Last Tape* and *Happy Days* opens at Lincoln Center, directed by Alan Schneider and featuring Hume Cronyn and Jessica Tandy. A Richard Foreman/Stanley Silverman collaboration entitled *Dr. Selavy's Magic Theatre* bows at Music-Theatre Group.

1973—Joseph Papp assumes direction of theatre at Lincoln Center. The Ridiculous Theatrical Company, founded by Charles Ludlam in 1967, presents *Camille* with Ludlam in the title role. *Candide*, directed by Hal Prince, premieres at the Chelsea Theater Center. Adrian Hall and Richard Cumming's *Feasting with Panthers* premieres at Trinity Square and is then televised nationally in the first season of WNET's "Theatre in America" series. Arena Stage is chosen by the U.S. State Department to be the first American company to tour the Soviet Union, and they take *Our Town* and *Inherit the Wind*. The Open Theatre disbands. TCG publishes the inaugural edition of *Theatre Profiles*, covering 89 theatres.

1974—*A Chorus Line* debuts at the New York Shakespeare Festival's Public Theater, after a long workshop period (later going on to Broadway and the 1976 Pulitzer). Liviu Ciulei directs his first play in the U.S., Buchner's *Leonce and Lena*, at Arena Stage. Miguel Pinero's *Short Eyes* opens at the Theatre at the Riverside Church. The Yale Repertory Theatre produces a musical version of Aristophanes' *The Frogs* in the university swimming pool.

1975—Edward Albee wins his second Pulitzer for *Seascape*. The New Federal Theatre production of Ntosake Shange's *For Colored Girls . . .* opens, then moves to the New York Shakespeare Festival. Gregory Mosher directs the world premiere of David Mamet's *American Buffalo* at the Goodman's Stage 2 in Chicago. The Los Angeles Actors' Theatre is founded by Ralph Waite. Richard Foreman directs *The Three-penny Opera* at Lincoln Center. Mabou Mines adapts and produces two Beckett works, *Cascando* and *The Lost Ones*, featuring music by Philip Glass.

1976—Robert Wilson's *Einstein on the Beach* premieres at France's Avignon Festival, and is subsequently produced at the Metropolitan Opera in New York. Lynne Meadow stages David Rudkin's *Ashes* at the Manhattan Theatre Club. *Annie* premieres at the Goodspeed Opera House in Connecticut. David Rabe's *Streamers* premieres at Long Wharf Theatre, directed by Mike Nichols. Fired after a controversial season at Trinity, Adrian Hall in turn fires his board of trustees and remains at the helm. Actors Theatre of Louisville, under the artistic direction of Jon Jory, presents its first Festival of New American Plays. The Alaska Repertory Theatre is founded and is the 50th state's first professional performing arts institution. TCG holds its first National Conference at Yale University, bringing the national nonprofit theatre community together for the first time.

1977—Richard Maltby, Jr. directs his Fats Waller revue, *Ain't Misbehavin'*, at Manhattan Theatre Club. Christopher Durang's *A History of the American Film* enjoys a triple opening at Arena Stage, the Mark Taper Forum and Hartford Stage Company. Michael Cristofer's *The Shadow Box*, born at the Mark Taper, wins the Pulitzer after a run on Broadway. Andrei Serban's production of Chekhov's *The Cherry Orchard* opens at Lincoln Center.

1978—The Oregon Shakespearean Festival completes the entire Shakespeare canon for the second time (having completed it once in 1959). The American Place Theatre inaugurates its Women's Project. Ernest Thompson's *On Golden Pond* bows at the Hudson Guild Theatre. D.L. Coburn's *The Gin Game*, which had premiered at American Theatre Arts in Los Angeles in a different production, wins the Pulitzer. *Zoot Suit* by Luis Valdez is produced at the Mark Taper. Sam Shepard's *Buried Child*, directed by Robert Woodruff, premieres at the Magic Theatre in San Francisco, forging an alliance between the writer, the director and the theatre. (The play will go on to net the Pulitzer the following season.) Arthur Kopit's *Wings* is produced at the Yale Repertory Theatre and moves on to Broadway.

1979—Mark Medoff's *Children of a Lesser God* premieres at the Mark Taper Forum under Gordon Davidson's direction. John Hirsch is hired by the Seattle Repertory Theatre as consulting artistic director. The BAM Theater Company, dedicated to a "company approach to the classics," opens at the Brooklyn Academy of Music under the direction of David Jones, but survives only two seasons. Lloyd Richards is appointed to head both the Yale Repertory Theatre and Yale School of Drama, and institutes a new play festival entitled Winterfest.

1980—Richmond Crinkley and an artistic directorate take over operation of the theatre at Lincoln Center and produce one season. Robert Brustein founds the American Repertory Theatre at Harvard University. Wilford Leach breathes new energy into Gilbert and Sullivan's *Pirates of Penzance*, and it soon transfers from the New York Shakespeare Festival's Delacorte Theater to Broadway. The Yale Repertory Theatre's production of Athol Fugard's *A Lesson from Aloes*, directed by the playwright, begins Fugard's fruitful association with Lloyd Richards and the theatre. Lanford Wilson's *Talley's Folly*, which originated at his theatrical "home base," Circle Repertory Company, under Marshall W. Mason's direction, wins the Pulitzer. The Denver Center Theatre Company is founded as a component of the Denver Center for the Performing Arts.

1981—Liviu Ciulei is appointed artistic director of the Guthrie and opens with an acclaimed production of *The Tempest*. The Phoenix Theatre closes after a number of moves around New York City. Tennessee Williams turns to the noncommercial theatre to premiere his *Something Cloudy, Something Clear* at New York's Cocteau Repertory, and his *A House Not Meant to Stand* at the Goodman Theatre. Charles Fuller's *A Soldier's Play* opens at the Negro Ensemble Company, going on to win the Pulitzer for 1982 and tour extensively. The Wooster Group's *Route 1 & 9* opens at New York's Performing Garage to a flurry of controversy over what some feel is its racist content. Bill Irwin brings his *The Regard of Flight* to the American Place Theatre after its appearance at the New Theatre Festival in Baltimore, introducing the "new vaudeville" movement.

1982—The Eureka Theatre Company in San Francisco commissions Emily Mann to write a play that is to become *Execution of Justice*. *Torch Song Trilogy*, born sequentially at La Mama, lands on Broadway. *Little Shop of Horrors*, the Howard Ashman/Alan Menken musical based on a low-budget horror film, opens at New York's WPA Theatre.

1983—The Brooklyn Academy of Music holds its first Next Wave Festival, featuring Lee Breuer's *Gospel at Colonus* and *The Photographer*, a collaboration of David Gordon, JoAnne Akalaitis and Philip Glass. Marsha Norman's *'night, Mother*, first produced at the American Repertory Theatre, wins the Pulitzer. *In the Belly of the Beast*, adapted by Adrian Hall from Jack Henry Abbott's book, opens at Trinity Square. The Theatre Project Company of St. Louis stirs up the community and jeopardizes its state funding with a production of *Sister Mary Igna-*

tius . . . which some brand "anti-Catholic." *Sunday in the Park with George* begins life as a workshop production at Playwrights Horizons. Mabou Mines and Interart Theatre collaborate on a production of Franz Xaver Kroetz's *Through the Leaves*. Alan Schneider directs his last play in America, Pinter's *Other Places*, at the Manhattan Theatre Club. *The Ballad of Soapy Smith* by Michael Weller opens the Seattle Repertory Theatre's new Bagley Wright Theatre complex. Two productions from Chicago's Steppenwolf Theatre Company, *True West* and *And a Nightingale Sang . . .*, introduce New York audiences to the energetic "Steppenwolf style."

1984—The Goodman Theatre production of David Mamet's *Glengarry Glen Ross*, directed by Gregory Mosher, transfers to Broadway and wins the Pulitzer, while its production of *Hurlyburly*, directed by Mike Nichols, travels from the Goodman to Off Broadway and Broadway. Berkeley Repertory Theatre, under newly appointed artistic director Sharon Ott, produces *Kingdom Come*, a drama about Norwegian pioneers in the Midwest, using black, Hispanic and Asian-American actors. Robert Wilson produces his first full-scale work in this country since *Einstein on the Beach*, *The CIVIL warS*, at the American Repertory Theatre. The first Olympic Arts Festival is held in Los Angeles, presenting such international artists as Ariane Mnouchkine's Théâtre du Soleil, Pina Bausch's Wuppertaler Tanztheater, Tadashi Suzuki's SCOT Theatre and Giorgio Strehler's Piccolo Teatro. James Reston Jr.'s *Jonestown Express* premieres at Trinity Square. Peter Sellars is appointed artistic director of the American National Theatre at the Kennedy Center. Milwaukee Repertory Theater artistic director John Dillon stages *Death*

of a Salesman in Japan with an all-Japanese cast. After several visa denials, Dario Fo is finally permitted into the U.S., not to perform but to attend the Broadway opening of his *Accidental Death of an Anarchist*, which originated at Arena Stage. *Garden of Earthly Delights* by Martha Clarke and Richard Peaslee premieres at Music-Theatre Group/Lenox Arts Center. *American Theatre*, a national monthly magazine, begins publication.

1985—The new Los Angeles Theatre Center opens its four-theatre performing arts facility, and the Alabama Shakespeare Festival's new $21.5 million theatre begins operation in Montgomery. Former Goodman artistic director Gregory Mosher is appointed artistic director and Bernard Gersten managing director of the new Lincoln Center Repertory Company. Liviu Ciulei resigns from The Guthrie, directing *A Midsummer Night's Dream* as his final production. *Big River*, the Roger Miller/William Hauptman musical developed at American Repertory Theatre and the La Jolla Playhouse, moves to Broadway in a production staged by Des McAnuff, salvaging an indifferent commercial season and sweeping the Tonys. Wooster Group member Spalding Gray continues his exploration of the autobiographical monologue with his most ambitious work, *Swimming to Cambodia*, taking it on national and international tour after performances in New York. Circle Repertory Company tours Japan with two productions, launching a ten-year project initiated by the Japan-United States Friendship Commission. The Joyce Theater inaugurates an annual American Theatre Exchange, inviting the Mark Taper Forum, the Yale Repertory Theatre and the Alley Theatre to bring productions to New York.

IN RETROSPECT

INSTITUTION-AS-ARTWORK

by Zelda Fichandler

We shall not cease from exploration
And the end of all our exploring
Will be to arrive where we started
And know the place for the first time.

I start to write on August 16, Arena Stage's thirty-fifth birthday. I have brought my notes with me, they are spread out on the big bed in a smallish hotel room on the Strand in London. I have already seen two plays at the National Theatre, one at the RSC, another at Stratford-on-Avon and got here just in time to enjoy, though jet-lagged, the opening of John Houseman's production of *The Cradle Will Rock* at the newly done-up Old Vic. The rain outside closes in my thoughts of companies, beginnings, economics, governance, the endlessness of the tasks, the nature of growth and change, leadership, the problems ahead, the distance come, signaled by the number thirty-five. The lines from T.S. Eliot's *Four Quartets* are fresh in mind, for I used them in my opening remarks to the new/old acting company, which, on year-round contracts for the first time, assembled at Arena on July 2 to begin a summer of exploratory work before rehearsals late in August.

The words of Eliot move me. They seem to pierce the exact moment of this birthday and pin it down. They speak not only to me personally, but to the nature and needs of a movement that began over three decades ago and now, middle-aged and in some turmoil, seeks redefinition, seeks to "know the place." I hear them—in a way that is both inspiring and practical—urge all of us who are a part of this movement, first, to get on with it and second, to go back to find it.

With curiosity, I reread the program note for our opening production, Oliver Goldsmith's *She Stoops to Conquer*, August 16, 1950. I want to check out what was on our minds then, to test the present against the past:

> Arena Stage plans to bring to its audiences the best of plays both old and new as well as worthwhile original scripts on a permanent year-round repertory basis. Local in origin, it was founded in the belief that if drama-hungry playgoers outside of the ten blocks of Broadway are to have a living stage, they must create it for themselves. Arena Stage was financed

by Washingtonians—students, teachers, lawyers, doctors, scientists, government workers, housewives—who love theatre and who want to see it flourish in the city in which they work and live. Its permanent staff of distinguished actors and technicians, many of whom have come to Arena Stage via the stages of other cities, now all call Washington their home.

Arena Stage invites your participation in the excitement of the first production of Washington's playhouse-in-the-round.

We (Tom Fichandler, my drama professor Edward Mangum and I) had raised, via a series of meetings with like-minded community members, $15,000 for stock in a regular profit-making corporation, set up a Voting Trust arrangement to be sure we retained artistic control, collected a cadre of actors and helpers through auditions and interviews and from among friends, and converted an old movie house in a slum area of Washington to a 247-seat theatre-in-the-round. (We wanted the symbolic intimacy of that form and to save money on scenery.) With our "investors," we scraped the chewing gum off the seats, hung the lights, laid the carpet, painted the walls, scrubbed the johns, and on a budget of $800 a week set out to achieve our goals. I ran the publicity campaign to open the theatre, designed the sets that were built in the alley, helped in the box office, directed seven out of seventeen shows we did that first year, slept many nights on the carpeted stage floor and, along with Mangum, made sixty-five dollars a week. The actors made fifty-five dollars, and from there the pay scaled to zero.

We put on fifty-five productions—nonstop, without a break—in the five years at that first location, had many successes and sometimes played to under a dozen people, on several occasions had a bank balance of under $100 and ended up the five-year period with $25,000 more than we started with. The actors doubled in brass as well as brought forth new roles every two or three weeks in a range and variety that remains vivid for me still. The rest, as they say, is history.

A recent interviewer asked me what made me think it would work and I said, truthfully, "I was young, I had no doubts, I was sure people would respond. Believe me, we didn't do any marketing surveys." In the early fifties, I read Margo Jones's book called *Theatre-in-the-Round*, in which she outlined her dream of a nation with forty (sic!) resident, professional companies performing new plays and classics and I knew that she, the mother of us all, could not be dreaming in vain.

This is not only "My Story." It is the story of several of us who began theatres way back there when. Most importantly, it is the story of our heritage, even those of us who began life later, on a grander scale. I do think we were the only theatre to experience life—for seven years—as a so-to-speak "profit organization," an experience I have never regretted, and the only theatre to pay its own way, on box office income alone, for fifteen years. That gives me a special edge when I have to explain to newcomers why our theatres have to be nonprofit.

When I read our initial program remarks—to be called in a later, more evolved time a "mission statement"—I am astonished that they prefigured most of the potential as well as the pitfalls that our movement was (is) to achieve and would encounter, is encountering. Most of the themes and, implicitly, the counter-themes are there: "audiences"; "local in origin"; "plays old and new and original scripts"; "permanent"; "repertory"; "outside of Broadway"; "create it themselves"; "financed by the community"; "where they live and work"; "permanent staff"; "distinguished actors and technicians"; "Washington their home"; "participation"; "excitement". And when I reach back through the years to our initial organizing principles and the labor of the earliest years, I find some real wisdom there: the need for artistic control; the need to take responsibility for one's own vision; the value of an ongoing collective; the centrality of an acting company; the fundament of contact between play and playgoer, of a continuing dialogue with the audience; each individual theatre being a part of a whole theatre; the ever-presence of budgetary tension and of the success/failure see-saw; the primitive yet sophisticated power of selflessness and faith in the dream. In our innocence, in our knowing yet not-knowing—Eliot's

> Quick, now, here, now, always—
> a condition of complete simplicity
> (costing not less than everything)

we sketched in with fairy-tale boldness the outline of the whole story, the principal characters and the underlying themes.

How far we have come! We should allow ourselves our amazement and our pride, if only for a moment. The size of the achievement is not diminished for me even here in London, across the bridge from the National Theatre with its three stages (although the Cottesloe is now closed for budgetary reasons), its five companies each with about seventeen actors, its elaborate and for the most part splendiferous physical productions held in repertory and brought back at will, its heavy subsidies and affordable ticket prices, its bars and buffets and bookstalls, its intense and responsive audience queued up in the hopes of a returned ticket at the last moment. Progress is a snail that jumps. Our growth has seemed to us slow, so very slow, as fretfully, sometimes exhaustedly, we have hung on to existing circumstances and waited for the next transformation to occur, either *to* us (private foundation support in 1957, the coming of the NEA in 1966) or, aggressively, with our own hands (building theatres, devising subscription plans, forming companies). But, in objective truth, ours has been the fastest-growing art form in history.

Thirty-five years ago there was Broadway and the Road. Today, there are more than 250 theatres (What would Margo think?) of varying shapes and sizes and styles, and our national theatre no longer operates within ten blocks of Broadway but across 3,000 miles of melting-pot America. While the level of work and the extent of enterprise and courage vary greatly from theatre to theatre, and no single theatre as yet stands as a pinnacle of artistic achievement, the overall sense is of individuality, energy, quest and growth. Our many theatres now offer more employment weeks to actors than does Broadway, gradually year-by-year realigning work patterns away from New York and changing the way actors can lead their lives and make their living. Community after community has had its hunger for live theatre responded to or even awakened for the first time; taste has been elevated, discrimination sharpened, life itself enriched through the perception of life-made-into-art. People have come to want their theatres and their arts and will pay money—in taxes, at the box office and in contributions—to have them. A career in the theatre, though hardly a sure thing, has come to seem plausible (even noble, to certain enlightened parents). In these few decades the arts as a profession, and theatre high among them, have lost some—not all, but certainly some—of their historic aura of aberration, dropout-ness, illogic.

The proof has been in the pudding: most of the gifted actors in the country have come the resident theatre route and could not have evolved without the continuity and stretching that years of on-the-boards experience provided; many of them come back from films and television to stretch some more and test themselves against the demands of a classic role and a breathing audience. And where would our writers be, and our directors and designers, without these congeries of work places, these sites for experimentation and development? Would we, indeed, even *have* this enviable pool of American talent without these places? One wonders where these artists would have gone to see their work evolve, to become who they are. For Broadway has been priced out of the market for risk-taking and, irony of ironies, has come to take so for granted its dependence on regional theatre "product" and talent that it points the finger at us when we don't come up with enough of it.

I clipped a front-page article from the May 20 *New York Times* headlined, "Broadway Economic Season Is Called Worst in a Decade," to keep as a symbol and a sign of the times. One of the producers, asked for an explanation for the slump, cited the high cost of road tryouts of musicals and, then, the failure of the non-commercial theatres—which have been able to "provide Broadway with a stream of notable plays"—to do the same in the area of musicals, Broadway's staple money-maker. "The nonprofit theatres have never paid attention to developing musicals," the spokesman said. "There's no place for young directors, young songwriters, young singers to learn. In addition, few non-commercial theatres can afford the stagecraft demanded for contemporary Broadway musicals." Do you hear the gigantic turn-around, the wad of social history stuffed into that complaint??

The achievements that I list are obvious and well-known and have been listed before. I list them here again on this birthday, as a taking-off point and a surround for other thoughts. And as an admonition (to myself, first of all) that we not take for granted the *fact* of it, the very *existence* of it, and the transformation it—this movement—*we* have made in our cultural landscape. Our theatrical world will never be the same again. The changes were radical, we committed a revolution that is irreversible, and attention should be paid to that.

What is particularly remarkable to me, looking back for one moment more, is that it took place without models, from within. We had no teachers except the environment, our own mistakes and each other. We *did* have each other (Mac Lowry put us together twenty-five years ago and TCG has kept us there). And we had some good gleanings from the outside that were crucial. I recall how astonished I was in the mid-fifties by the craft level at the Shakespeare Festival in Stratford, Ontario and how deeply our production standards were influenced by my visit there. And also how much we learned from the Berliner Ensemble's trip to London in the mid-sixties—both about the repertory actor (Ekkehard Schall as both Coriolanus and Arturo Ui) and about the physical aesthetic—Brecht's "Reality is concrete." I can still visualize the long, silent moment at the beginning of the Moscow Art Theatre's production of *The Cherry Orchard* as the family, back from Paris, re-embraces the house. As a director and a producer, I was opened to a totally new level of possible stage behavior. It changed our work.

But chiefly, and especially in our organizational forms and institutional development, we had no models. We taught ourselves out of our own impulses which, made into deeds and thus objectified, taught us back what to do next so that we could stay alive and progress. It has been a revolution made of many and diverse feelings and viewpoints, all discharged more-or-less simultaneously (in the eye of history, thirty-five years is but a blink!)—a kind of collective artwork, like a quilt, a "something" truly surprising, truly unique. As we grapple with current ambivalences and try to solve our problems, we should not forget where we started and not diminish what we made.

We experience and read about "artistic deficits," a term which evidently first appeared in a report by the National Endowment for the Arts last year. An artistic deficit represents the distance between what one would want to do in one's theatre and should do there, and what one can afford to do; it is the shadow between intention and reality. The term has come into wide acceptance very rapidly as a term whose time has come. It names our disease. It seems to explain our feelings of dissatisfaction and longing for something better. It says what ails us.

And, of course, it is true that our theatres are underfunded and our artists underpaid. And it is true that in order to remain solvent some theatres pull in their horns in terms of predictability of repertoire, size of casts and production costs, and channel funds into fund-raising rather than onto the stage. And the art itself suffers and we fail to meet our own standards and, feeling that it is time for a ripening, we rail against our fate or become weary and say, "If not now, when?!?" And surely there is a positive correlation between Art and Money and our complaints are justified ("Art needs comfort, even abundance," wrote Tolstoy). The current episode of our national story, told in numbers, is discouraging indeed. With expenses up seventy-one percent over the past five years and, despite record attendance and box office income, a doubling of the economic deficit last year alone, is it any wonder that we have this sense of our reach forever exceeding our grasp, and seek to find our salvation somewhere in that interlocking system of economic/artistic deficit? It is logical to do that and it feels right.

Without minimizing in any way the seriousness of our economic situation and its direct effect on our power to produce art at the highest level, I think we must look into other areas of our being, where the problems may be less immediate, less visible, less easily identified, but potentially even more corrosive. For while poverty of means can, of course, lead to poverty of ends—and often does—still, courage within can sometimes prevail over negative forces without, passion over penny-pinching and "four boards" over an extravagant set. At least for the time being. And over the longer haul, who knows? Times change. Someone may come to rescue us or we may think of something on our own. Artistic deficits have been with us from the beginning. They seem more painful today because we are older and feel we should be "There" by now. But what if there is no "There"—at least in our lifetime???

Be that as it may, no theatre can ultimately survive the dry rot of institutionalization, the absence of versatile and committed actors, timid and visionless leaders or a troubled, unresolved relationship with its forces of governance. Let's speak about these four hazards of our middle years.

What our early, innocent "mission statement" omits is any reference to the fact that we were about to create an "institution" or, indeed, that such a mechanism might be necessary to do the things we intended to do. We simply didn't think about it. I suppose we knew about institutions (schools, prisons, families, museums), but we didn't think we were one of those. We thought we were a theatre, something else again. Who could have imagined thirty-five years ago how elaborated all this would become—that one day we would live in our own building, make five-year plans(!), have a budget hovering around $7 million, write grant applications and hardly know ourselves for all the baggage we had collected.

At the time, we proceeded very simply and directly: "What needs to be done?" was followed by the direct doing of it, preferably by someone who knew how but, if necessary, by someone who learned it as he/she went along. It is not that we were naive. We were tough and smart and painstaking and we would not be stopped. We set up a box office and ran it well, informed and enticed a public, paid our bills and wrote our contracts, selected and hired actors and directors and designers, put together a repertoire that was exactly the one we wanted and made a myriad of difficult decisions—both artistic and managerial. But out of poverty and out of our early evolutionary position we saw a simpler connection between needs and filling them. And from these needs to "each according to his ability" seemed a logical and direct route. Such evolved concepts as job descriptions or even discrete jobs, departments of this, that and the other, tables of organization, etc. could then not even be projected. And while this was a hectic, often misshapen and, in the end, impermanent way of doing things, it did, I must confess, hold its own kind of magic.

There was never any question of what was of primary concern, which way the arrows of energy were directed; the work on the stage was central and we lived, breathed and slept (no, we rarely slept!) with that in mind. And there were surely no communication problems—all you had to do was stick your head out and yell. Also, although everyone suffered overwhelming fatigue, for about the first ten years (until we moved into the newly built Arena building) we felt that we could hold the whole animal in the palm of our hands and touch it directly. I remember the sensation of knowing—both empirically and philosophically— everything at once: the sentence and the story, the pebble and the beach, every corner of our little world. When I speak of "institution-as-artwork," I find that my clearest image comes from these earliest years when things were most frantic and yet most whole. They serve as a reference point for maintaining a sense of unity within the theatre as it is today—175 people; three stages; the divesting, sharing, delegating that is essential for running a large, theatrical institution.

Unless we get it right, this "institution business" is going to kill us. Something began to feel uncomfortable around the end of the sixties, but by that time the thing had already happened to us; by the time we looked up and noticed, it had been done to us, we had already been institutionalized. No, I'm not saying that right: I exaggerate the degree of passivity involved. In point of fact, we were not force-fed. We wanted what we got, we just didn't realize where it was taking us.

We vigorously, implacably tracked down our subscribers, making a kind of fetish of the yearly subscription brochure; feverishly raised money for new buildings and, using ingenuity, skill and new knowledge, built them; with zealous alacrity we developed and engaged administrators, P.R. people and business managers; we added the concept of production managers as our artistic leaders got more involved in fund-raising and the like (still later, we added the concept of associate directors and literary managers/dramaturgs as theatres grew and artistic directors got still more involved in fund-raising and the like); we created development departments to meet economic deficits (later they were, in some instances, to grow as large or larger than the artistic staff); and, in general, we poured a lot of money away from art and into making more money in order to make art. Quite recently, we computerized. Computer technology, someone said at a recent staff meeting, holds all our operations together. I suppose he's right. . . .

In 1967, I spoke about our mood on a panel called "The Future of the Resident Professional Theatre in America":

> Push, promote, maneuver, advertise, finagle, operate. The story of our lives. "Getting and spending we lay waste our powers" . . . . I think we will not be overwhelmed only if we refuse to give ourselves up, only if we can experience ourselves as autonomous. For me this means leaving the wheeling and dealing to others and going back to where I came from, to the theatre as an art. And we may be overwhelmed anyway. But, then, let them take us while we are doing our own work and not at a fund-raising dinner. It is not a personal thing at base. It is a matter of whether

we are, after all, to be theatres or constructions that put on plays as against ones that manufacture washing machines.

We must achieve a sense that some real power resides in us within the very art we make, and not altogether within the techniques of manipulation, marketing and promotion with which we tend, in the battle for survival, to become over-absorbed.

Later, in 1969, in an article entitled "Theatres or Institutions," I articulated a personal feeling that I believe was shared:

> In my own mind now these two words exist in a kind of uneasy tension, a kind of dialectic opposition, where once they seemed to me to be one and the same word. It seemed to me until quite recently that when a theatre finally stopped being on the way to what it was supposed to become and actually became it, then it would be an institution. . . . But it has not turned out this way. A seduction is what it really was, a leading-from-the-self. I wonder why.

The artistic director of a large regional theatre wistfully, ironically remarked to me a few months ago, "They wouldn't even notice if I disappeared—the administrative machine would go on grinding. No one would stop to see that there was nothing in the grinder."

But I am speaking too negatively. I should not leave this idea with so sullen a view. Our institutional structures are necessary to us. Compartmentalization, specialization, clear and clean procedures and good personnel policies, a strong middle as well as top management structure, the best of promotional and development techniques, budgets that define and defend values and provide guidelines for growth as well as survival are all absolutely essential to us. It isn't 1950 anymore, and our budgets aren't $800 a week; we have heard other voices and lived in other rooms since that time. You can't go home again and no one wants to.

On the other hand we do want, do we not, to avoid the tail wagging the dog or—a worst-case situation—the tail *becoming* the dog? We do want our institutions to organize themselves around the spiritual/aesthetic life they exist to nurture and not have that life made subservient to the demands of institutional paraphernalia. We are acquainted with the notions of foreground and background and first things first.

A theatre is the enclosing, the enfolding of an idea—a vision—something imagined that has the possibility of finding concrete embodiment. It is simultaneously an imaginative act and a place. When the institutional machine ceases to support the imaginative act and begins to encroach upon the place; when it constricts rather than releases the flow of creative energy by its labyrinthine demands, its busy-ness; when the accumulation of resources, the dissemination of information, and the marketing of the "product" take more focus and absorb more power than what we are making and the conditions under which we make it, then the institution must be dismantled and reconceived along better lines. An institution cannot have a life of its own, be a thing in itself. Its life is derived from the animating Idea, and each and every one of its actions must flow from this Idea and contain a piece of it. When we say that "the business of art is art and not business," we don't mean that there is no business in making art (surely, there is!) but that the function and purpose of the business is not *itself*, but the making of this art. If we fail to get this crystal clear, the institutions we created will become blind mechanisms (the trend is already clear in a number of theatres) instead of sentient organisms, and eventually they will petrify and crumble due to the absence of living tissue. An active recollection of our origins can help us to "know the place" in a new way.

> And all shall be well and
> All manner of things shall be well
> When the tongues of flame are in-folded
> Into the crowned knot of fire
> And the fire and the rose are one.

I write now from New York. My apartment overlooks Washington Square. From the windows facing East I can just see Broadway where the new building for the Tisch School of the Arts is located. I'm currently chairing the graduate department of acting there. I have had a longstanding interest in the American actor: the growth and development of the professional actor and the training of the young actor. I am interested in their inner technique (how to produce living behavior), their physical technique (voice, speech, movement), and no less in their mind, psyche and how they see themselves and the part they are to play in shaping the American theatre, for worse or, hopefully, for better. And I'm interested in the connections among these three aspects. I'm grateful for the fresh outlook this new post is providing me.

"See that the players are well bestowed." Indeed, we must. The actor stands at the center of the art of theatre and always has. Before there were literary forms at all, when there were only rituals and embodied myths, it was the actor—the en-actor—who performed the deeds, represented the human situation and stood in for those who, like himself, were seeking to find out who and why. The theatre is and always will be a special place—a differentiated, imagined, moral place— that a society sets aside in order to examine all that fascinates it and all that it seeks to understand. We are endlessly curious about our world, and especially about ourselves. It seems a biologic necessity, a means of survival even, that we ask the questions and act out even what is unanswerable. A society without a theatre is a society that is in the process of disintegration.

Theatre: *Teatron*: a place for seeing. Camus wrote, "If the world were clear, art would not exist. Art helps us pierce the opacity of the world." In his struggle for his own truth, in trying to pull away the life-mask, the actor lets us see ourselves. Through his ability to be himself and yet walk in the footsteps of another, to show himself and still be faithful to the truth of another, the actor teaches us who we are. The theatre can make do without anything but the actor.

So why do we deal with him or her in so desultory a fashion? The theatre of our beginning took for granted that the actor came first and therefore that the company came first, because the company is the natural habitat of the actor. No one taught us that. It seemed to be simple, organic knowledge and we just acted on it. Perhaps it came from what we knew of the Berliner Ensemble, the Moscow Art Theatre, Shakespeare's company or Molière's, or from our own idealistic attempts—Eva Le Gallienne's Repertory Company and the Group Theatre of the thirties, for example.

In the early years of the fifties we chose plays that suited our particular company, assigned roles with the growth and development of our individual actors in mind, cast to the furthest, not the nearest, limits of an actor's talents (with very little "cosmetic" casting from the outside) and looked upon our companies as our greatest asset. While some of this might have been adventitious (we wanted the productions to "look good" and we were short of money), I recall our choices as being more purely motivated. The fact that young actors played older characters and that so-and-so who "just wasn't the right type for the role" played it anyway proved itself out. At least for us at Arena. And not only were major, individual talents developed by these choices but later, when actors moved on to other work, the whole American theatre became enriched. I have carefully checked myself out. I'm not looking at the past through the blur of revisionist remembering.

The output of a theatre is always more than the sum of its parts. Its level of expressiveness (I prefer this phrase to that other one, "professional standards," which I find elusive) depends most of all on releasing the energy and creativity of a whole group: on shaping and sending out a collective consciousness, in a general sense, as in "the spirit of the collective," as well as specifically, in an interpretation, a viewpoint toward any single production. Since a play is its own world and since the chief ingredient of any world (fictive or real) is the pattern and timbre of its human interrelationships, the interior meanings of the play stand a better chance of being revealed by a group whose members know each other, relate well to each other and have found a way of thinking together, playing together (a play is play) and approaching their tasks in a mutually understood way, have a common vocabulary. That is to say, by an acting company. At the same time, the individual actor always develops best within a continuing group. It is sometimes quite astonishing to see the flowering that can take place when failures can be outlived, successes are not blown up out of proportion to what life can consistently offer, continuity is assured, casting is sometimes offbeat— for the benefit of the actor not the management—and friendly faces permit experimentation, a "what-the-hell" attitude towards work that everyone really knows is very serious, and a de-emphasis on quick results.

I wrote an open letter to Robert Prosky in 1978, the anniversary of his twentieth consecutive year as a company member at Arena Stage. I spoke about his achievements, about the roles he had played, about the way that he worked. Then I spoke about his personal life, his wife and three sons, and about other sources for his evolution over the two decades into a major American actor. Here is something from this letter that relates to the development of the actor within a permanent, company situation:

> Since it is life that we show in the theatre (sometimes I think we play variations on only one theme: that we are all more simply human than otherwise), life is what the actor has to know about. And no actor can show more than is in him to show. The actor's talent is fed by his life or it dries up and grows thin. You have grown fuller and fuller with your life. You say you came to Arena with three suitcases, intending to stay eight weeks. Your stay expanded into twenty years, and there aren't enough suitcases to hold what has happened to you, what you "own." . . .
>
> I think you have evolved into who you are because you have had a creative home and the opportunity for the continuous exercise of your skill. . . . You have been able consciously to structure and layer your abilities in a way not given to many actors in this country. . . .
>
> From play to play, from season to season, it has been possible for you to experience and to examine the building blocks of your craft—its laws of inner technique, aspects of physical embodiment, and the relationship between the two—in a systematic and progressive way. And not

only to experience and examine, but also to incorporate and use—immediately, not later, when the learning has already cooled. You have had the privilege to be the continuous and conscious maker of your own instrument. What is so destructive about discontinuity in an actor's life is not simply that it eats away at his sense of self, his ego, which is the raw material from which all else is made, but that he is prevented from "getting it all together." His body forgets from one experience to another what it has found out. And it is hard, if not impossible, for him to accumulate enough knowledge about himself and about his work to reach the peak of his powers and stay there. His creative bursts tend, then, to be sporadic and in mid-career one wonders what he could do if he had the chance. You have avoided the waste of discontinuous creative work.

Despite the advantages to the actor (and therefore the art) of continuous, creative work, all kinds of justifications came forward over our long, middle years for the virtual abandonment—except in a few key places—of the company idea: the audience got tired of the same faces; actors just wouldn't stay, the lures of TV and film were too overpowering; productions were shortchanged by limited casting possibilities; it was cheaper to job in actors for each production, and money was needed to build up the administrative machine and especially to raise funds for sheer survival. All were justifications with some truth to them. The Devil can cite Scriptures. But whenever a real commitment was made to the idea of company and to the individual actor, the actors stayed. (Christopher Morley once said, "There is only one success—to spend your life in your own way." There are numbers of actors who agree.) And because they stayed, the work of that theatre gathered momentum and opened up, expanded beyond itself. Again, the proof is in the pudding.

The best move the National Endowment for the Arts ever made was its recent Ongoing Ensembles program which seeks to retrace an earlier time when work centered on an acting company and, by extension, the artists—playwrights, directors, designers, trainers, artist/administrators—who surround that center. Like monogamy, the acting company is now "in." The terms of the grant were stringent, yet fifty-one applications were received in the first round and another largish number (I think around twenty-eight) in the second. Something was bothering the folk out there about the nature of the work and the feeling-tone of their work/lives. The Theatre Program picked up on this negative national mood, or helped to spotlight it, turned it around and made a change in the dominant method of production in this country a real possibility. That's good.

More must be done to weave our past creatively into our present and on into the future. The kind of training program we had in the late sixties, for which our actors were not ready but now are, needs reinstituting at several theatres; actors need to have more involvement in the running of their artistic lives—at Arena they already have a large say in the roles they play (often choosing one over another that runs concurrently), and the right to refuse any role, but they should have increased input into what plays are done. Guaranteed year-round salaries (just instituted here, thanks to the Ongoing Ensembles grant) should become more the rule than the exception. Actors are observant and they care about their institutions in an overall way. With some creative thought, they could and should be brought more fully into the working operation of the theatre, even beyond those areas that management might at first think appropriate or of concern to them. I recommend periods of exploration and sheer process, freed from focus on a specific production, as enormously enlivening to a company. The Arena

Stage just spent six weeks of summer in this way, three of those weeks in residence at Colorado College both teaching and on our own group search, and now, back in rehearsals, the benefits can be felt in the more improvisational, more open nature of the work.

Twelve years ago our company took two productions to Moscow and Leningrad on a three-week tour. It's not the only tour we've taken, but it was special because of the company tradition of the Russian theatre. It was (Would you believe it?) in Moscow and then Leningrad that we first saw ourselves as we imagined we might be, where we were first recognized as an ensemble of artists with our own style, our own viewpoint. And there has never been that same kind of acknowledgement since. Perhaps in the next twelve years, if there are enough companies and they are strong enough and speak loudly enough in their own voices, America will catch on and catch up. It is a consummation devoutly to be wished.

I said that the theatre can make do without anything but the actor. I don't want to retract that statement, but I must confess it to be a more ideological than practical truth. In the complex theatre world we live in, someone has to chart the course and steer the ship. We call the person who does that by various names, the most frequent being "artistic director." It is a title that can send a shudder through the body of any gifted, sensitive, insightful, responsive, politically minded, knowledgeable, curious, growing, searching, young (or middle-aged?) director who is exactly the right candidate for the job, but who really wants to spend time on the stage with a group of actors evolving the life of a play and not dissipate physical and psychic energy planning one season after the other, gathering up and retaining artists, overseeing the work and developing the talents of others, informing, educating, exhorting and stimulating a board, and representing a theatre to its own members, its community, its world. Gather together a group of artistic directors, succumbed personal artists, all of them, and you have gathered together a group of weary, tormented humans who suffer from the Jimmy Durante syndrome: "Did you ever have the feeling that you wanted to go and yet you wanted to stay and yet you wanted to go . . . ?"

Stay, some of us do. Although there has been of late such a fever of movement into and out of and among theatres that the American theatre scene has come to resemble a South American country living out its political destiny! I happen to have on my desk the June and September issues of *American Theatre* magazine, and under the heading "Entrances and Exits," one can perceive at one fell swoop the contemporary theatre scene in all of its uneasiness, shifting patterns and causes of complaint. This is surely not the way it was in the old days. In the old days, the theatre *was* its artistic director. It was the artistic director, propelled by a vision of burning (and blinding; it was not the time of farsighted five-year plans!) intensity, who brought the theatre into being, assembled the meager economic and physical resources (in our case the theatre was a $1.98 cardboard file-box for many months), persuaded into existence a small board, and collected or already had available a group of artists ready to set out on a journey of undetermined length to a vaguely determined destination. The artistic director had no contract as such, only one with him/herself and that was unwritten and, therefore, binding, more-or-less until death do us part. "Poetry attaches its emotions to the idea; the idea *is* the fact," wrote Matthew Arnold. In that sense, our theatres were poetic.

There are still a few theatres left of that original kind. But the more typical situation is that a second or even third generation of leadership heads the theatre, and that he or she has been brought there by a board of directors and has been commissioned, as it were, to create an artwork for the community. Commissions, we know, are a viable way to bring artworks into being—history shows us that —but for many reasons the analogy tends to break down in the instance of theatres/institutions. In the first place, the new artistic director usually doesn't begin with a clean canvas; there is usually a sketch, there may even be a fairly elaborate design inherited from the past, and a number of clear-cut expectations as to pattern and shape. Since an artwork has to start from an internal impulse, a personally held view of a portion of reality, the commissioned artist begins the labor already at a disadvantage.

In the second place, any artist needs a clear run on the artwork and needs to follow his own nose as it develops. Renewing a contract every two or three years, "evaluations" by the board as the artwork progresses, input coming from all over the place (in one instance, a publicity department sent a memo to an artistic director criticizing the proposed list of plays and suggesting alternate titles that would better suit seasonal needs and the interests of group sales, and look better on the brochure), and kibitzing along the unending route to completion of this piece of art (about subscribers: don't lose them; about money: take in more, spend less; about repertoire: be daring but hang on to audiences; about failures: by all means have them, but only two out of eight)—none of this is conducive to a sure hand or a free play of instinct, both necessary to the creative process. And in the third place (which may be the first place), the board, despite its care and concern, might have selected someone from the wrong genre altogether; they may have picked an action painter when what they really meant to have was an abstract expressionist or a representational artist whose specialty was landscapes. After a while, the discrepancies and divergencies become obvious either to one party or the other or to both, and separation, usually very painful, becomes the only way out.

I am describing the nature of things, how things are. The pressures are real on both sides. However, since the artist is primary to the artwork, which is to say, we can't have a theatre without an artistic director and, indeed, the theatre derives its life from within him or her, it seems that we should scrutinize with great care and revamp where necessary this "commissioning" process, starting from its inception and following it all along the way. I think there is no going back to our beginnings here. Because of current economic pressures, I doubt that there will be many new theatres starting up from scratch with the old insistence, the old do-or-die. And because of the very fertility of the field, born out of the success of the movement over the past decades, there are so many seductive opportunities out there that turnover in leadership is bound to remain the prevailing mode and a persistent problem. The closest we can come to perpetuating our personal visions, those of us who came down on the side of "feeling that you wanted to stay," is to train our successors from within the institution we are still making.

I received a letter from a distinguished management consultant firm outlining the criteria for selecting an artistic director for one of our major theatres:

1. Appropriate scale of work
2. Commitment to, and experience with, classics
3. Ability to develop a resident ensemble of artists
4. Long-range planning and vision and ability to lead the board
5. A personality and style suitable to institutional leadership, especially as it relates to developing the ensemble and community support.

I think these are excellent criteria and I wish with all my heart that they are met by an available visionary who will leap forward to take up the challenge. I hope it is not inappropriate or too forward of me to add to these five points, or to flesh them out. With this man or woman, young or older, American or from the world at large, I would like to share these suggestions, born from my own long journey.

People have more power over their own lives and the lives of others than they think. This power is not necessarily theirs but comes from the idea that inhabits them. (Margo Jones put it this way: "If you have a million-dollar idea, you can raise a million dollars!") The world has more cracks in it than substance; more-or-less everything and more-or-less everybody are constantly slipping through them. If you marshal your ideas clearly, know as much as you can know about what you want, your foothold will be strong. Until you are sure enough, put up with the pangs of aloneness. If you have a friend or two with whom you can share your doubts, you are blessed. Boards, foundations, the community at large will not be smitten by your doubts (to them, they will look like more cracks in the universe), even though they may be the most creative thing about you. Know your position inside and out; when it is ripe, share it.

Also, know your territory. Incorporate into your vision deep, experiential knowledge of its tastes, hungers, presences and absences, past, dreams, pocketbooks, proclivities and, of course, its theatre board and especially the president of it. If the knowledge, when incorporated, despoils the vision, don't go to that place, go somewhere else or do something else. There won't be time to change things very profoundly. The long run doesn't exist anymore.

Hang on to your obsession for dear life. If they pry it loose from you with their caution and precautions, you have lost and become a functionary. In order to lead you have to be a leader, which is to say, someone obsessed with a vision that propels you over and under all obstacles and through the inevitable periods of despair and fatigue. If "other considerations" begin to tip the scales away from the permeating vision (except, perhaps, in the very, very short term), the battle has been lost; you just haven't gotten word.

Be a genius. If you aren't a genius, try harder. No board would dare encroach upon Picasso, Frank Lloyd Wright, Stanislavski or Balanchine. If you try and still can't be a genius, be a strong, committed working artist. If your work is original enough, *yours* enough, it is unassailable. But even this won't be sufficient. You must also stand firm with it. You must hold to your point of view, your way of seeing things, and compromise only in the scheme, in the details. If you permit open spaces around the center of the impulse, other forces will rush in and occupy them.

A necessary though seemingly antithetical demand is that you make your own all the conditions and circumstances that other people see and that, indeed, are there. The constrictions of budget must be felt as your constrictions; only then will you not resent them and retain the power to burst them open. The recalcitrance of the audience; the difficulty of assembling a repertoire that satisfies both you and your associated artists, as well as your audiences; the hazards of limited time for rehearsal and contemplation; the unending demands made on you as the head of an institution—you must feel them as coming not from outside yourself but from within, or they will deplete you to the point where you are powerless to manipulate or change them. Claim the place, with all its problems, as your own. Face up to the fact that you don't have five years to prove yourself, the world is moving too fast and things cost too much. You have to deliver the goods—pro-duce—in the present tense. In an interview this summer in *The Washington Post* by drama critic David Richards, Liberace was quoted as saying, "Without a show, there's no business." That's tough, but it's real. Artistic directors should not expect coddling because that expectation won't be fulfilled.

And, if you possibly can, come in with collaborators, artistic associates with whom you have worked before and who share your vision. The job is now too complex to be a one-person show. And learn to plan. Live in the moment, as if you are an actor on stage, and plan as if you were the director of an opera company. Rub your belly while you pat your head.

"These things being subscribed to, you may, by degrees, dwindle into——an artistic director."

Given an inclination to take it on, plus the requisite touch of fire, artistic leadership can be taught and learned. It's no longer a mystery. I have been urging for twenty years that a training center be organized for artistic directors, funded by a foundation and probably based at a university. A combination of study and apprenticeship could provide us with six or a dozen people groomed for the hazards and, yes, the exhilaration of making an artwork of an institution. As it is now, we are doing too much reshuffling of our existing leadership resources and dampening the possibility of reaching the highest artistic achievement in any one place, or, one can hope, any two or three places. Or four.

Back in Washington now, I look for the July/August issue of *American Theatre* which contains Peter Zeisler's editorial entitled "A National Agenda." I am interested in reading again what he has to say about the increasingly important role of the board of trustees over recent years in view of greater responsibilities both for fund-raising and for hiring artistic and managing directors for the next generation of their theatres. Zeisler states that participants at a recent meeting of representatives from the various arts disciplines unanimously identified the relationships between staff and trustees as the most pressing problem facing arts institutions today, and notes that we are still exploring the role of trustees in their governance. He also lays the groundwork for a project to develop a "national artistic agenda" for the nonprofit theatre: to hammer out goals and examine the ways in which barriers to artistic growth can be overcome. In the September issue of the magazine, trustee Suzanne Pestinger is quoted: "Share with us your ideas, beliefs, visions. Educate us so we can help."

I am moved by this sincere and heartfelt request, and it should be responded to in full measure. And I empathize with the heavy burdens placed on the shoulders of theatre trustees who volunteer their time and concern, often at the expense of their own work and private pleasure, for an endeavor that, after all, does not stand at the center of their lives as it does ours whose profession it is. I salute and thank them. The demand, again and yet again, for more and yet more money for expanding artistic needs must be wearying indeed. And holding in one's hands the very definition of a theatre institution through the choice of an artistic or managing director must surely be experienced as awesome.

But the responsibility to raise money and the responsibility to find new leaders do not take care of describing the relationship between staff and trustees or the increasing importance that relationship is coming to have. Underneath these responsibilities, and affecting them, lie other matters—questions of attitude and feeling that should be probed and illuminated. If we can do this creatively, perhaps we can improve upon what exists. Perhaps a deeper understanding of our separate positions would lighten the burden on both staff and trustees. My remarks are made in the spirit of exploration and not final wisdom since I, too, am in changing waters.

Arena does not have a "money board," and given the choice of that kind of board and the other, I prefer it this way. The board, many of its members hard-working and deeply caring, has limited fund-raising capacities in a city notorious for its lack of philanthropic yield; the development department of the theatre has always borne the main responsibility for closing the deficit gap. We chafe at this a little and wish the board could do more. And so do they. But both Tom Fichandler and I believe that a theatre is most artistically free in this society when it can earn as much as possible by its own devices—box office on the regular season, special events, interest on reserves and investments, royalties and the like. We account for seventy-five percent of our expenses in this manner. For years the theatre management, with only one or two minor exceptions, has balanced the budget and showed a surplus, sometimes quite a hefty one. We have been for-tunate enough and, yes, insistent enough to do the repertoire of our choice and although, because of enormous competition in the city, we don't have as many subscribers as a number of other theatres around the country, we play, fairly consistently, to around ninety percent of capacity. From the trustee point of view, the theatre has not posed a lot of problems, it pleases me to say.

Tom and I have been the sole leaders from the beginning, so the question of continuity has not been a weight upon the board. Indeed, we both feel it our responsibility to provide choices for our own successors in order to maintain the Arena tradition to which both board and staff subscribe, and that was recently elaborated on, in joint deliberation, in our mission statement. Further, we have been, if anything, over-assiduous in sharing our "ideas, beliefs, visions." If nothing else, I am a talker. If talking can do it, the board knows what Arena stands for, what it needs and means to do further and how much it will cost. The staff has also provided the future thrust of the theatre: our five-year plan contains motion and intentionality, it is not just a chart of numbers concocted to satisfy one funding instrumentality or another; it is ours, the theatre's, and it is subscribed to by the board, which has taken shared responsibility for its fulfillment.

Where, then, is the rub?

In 1959, Jacques Barzun wrote, in *The House of Intellect*:

> Many directors of corporate foundations and some university trustees handle money for research and education not as if they were engaged in a nonprofit enterprise, but as if they were engaged in an enterprise that was failing to make a profit.
>
> In other words, they do not see where the actual profit lies. It being intellectual, and they not, it is to them invisible.

Replace the terms "corporate foundations" and "universities," and note that Barzun says "many" and "some" (we all have trustees who *are* intellectual), and that's a statement worth pondering. I suggest that, still, after decades of empirical proof, it has not been accepted—viscerally accepted—by boards of trustees, how-ever much it has been hammered at, however much it is intellectually "under-stood," that "Not-for-Profit" is really a benign and affirmative idea and not a negative and death-dealing one. And that to be *not* for profit is less defining than to be *for* something else: something more transcendent than economic profit and in another category altogether; a mode of human transaction entirely other than the one about money. I wonder if this attitude can ever be dug out from the subconscious of our governors—lawyers, doctors, accountants, builders, businessmen—whose daily lives are lived elsewhere and in another way. "As a man lives, so is he." (One does not want to typecast here: There can be skinny butchers, homely lovers, left-wing millionaires, and politicians who write poetry. Nonetheless, I share what I have experienced.)

I would be overjoyed to find a trustee (am I not sending out strong enough signals?) who, on some one issue, would position himself on the other side so that we could switch and have a fresh look at things. I am able to take his position and often do; why is he not able to take mine? I wait expectantly, hopefully, for that Special One who will plead with me to consider lowering ticket prices, or raising salaries of underpaid technicians or non-competitively paid middle managers, or prod me to expand our playwrights' wing or our advertising budget, or to take the company on tour, or to spend more on the artistic product. But the pressures back and forth are always predictable, they never surprise. The tug-of-war is played over and over again in just the same way. Art against money, how much nonprofit is too much?, us against them, our eyes raised up in aspiration, theirs cast down to the bottom line in anxiety and imminent dismay. They are for us and for our dreams. And in locked combat over the Good, they often come over to join us. But why will they not embrace the First Principle: that it is the Art that makes the Money (earned income at the box office and "unearned" income in more intangible ways)? Does it not feel to them, in the deepest places of their hearts, that—when all is said and done—the Nonprofit really costs too much??

We use the term "partnership." Can we truly be partners across this philosophical divide?

I admire greatly the statement made by Chloe Oldenberg, trustee from the Cleveland Play House, at a TCG national conference in Costa Mesa last spring: "If we can't raise questions of ethics and aesthetics with you, we might as well go out and raise money for the American Cancer Society, where everybody agrees that it's a good thing to cure cancer." I admire it because it shows involvement in the deeper issues, a concern for the things that even money can't buy. However, I understand, a bit sadly, the limitations in such an exchange of thought. For aesthetics is our business, our profession (ethics, I suppose, are a shared concern). Surely we are open to discuss them with you and even to be affected by what you say—all subjects should be open to discussion. But trustees must understand that while we can come together for a time on such issues of our profession, ultimately we must become separate. Just as we cannot, in this brief lifetime, understand the ins and outs of your particular profession, ours, too, has its special province. And after we discuss aesthetics, we must go back to the theatre and put them to work, following our own way, often a lonely and blundering way, but one with its own underlying laws and interior logic.

Taking this a step further: We need help and advice on many things—the law, investments, buildings, contracts, many things. Finally, though, a theatre is a self-contained organism, a creature in its own right. And by now, usually an effectively adaptive one. For survival, our work must be tough-minded and precise, both in its artistic and its managerial aspects, both with time and with money. Boards must trust our competency, for it is there, and demonstrate that trust by not taking on responsibilities that they need not take on. The idea that artists are playful children, whimsical creatures of the night, has long outlived itself.

To go back to Chloe Oldenberg's statement: curing cancer is certainly a priority. But would it not be helpful if each trustee felt that "everyone agrees it's an (equally) good thing" to know ourselves and our world through the formal constructions of art? Please support us because we matter in the abstract—matter extravagantly and immeasurably—in the long, evolutionary process of mankind; support us because we are an instrument of civilization; and for no smaller or more personal reason.

A board tends to think more of the future of the institution and to be terrified of its death. A theatre tends to think more of its present and that it will only die because it is ready for it and should. This is another great philosophical as well as psychological divide. The board wants to squirrel away resources against the winter. The theatre wants to use them now, thinking that if they are used well, there is a chance of a perennial spring. I suggest that the board's way of thinking is contradictory to the world's oldest wisdom, which teaches us that if we are not fully alive in this very instant, there is no life at all. I say to our board that risk-taking is not a line item in the budget but a style, an attitude toward living, but no one hears me and that makes me sad. Perhaps I am not saying it well enough.

A 1965 Rockefeller Board Report on *The Performing Arts: Problems and Prospects* states:

> Good business brains and performances are essential to the successful operation of these organizations, but more than these are required, for the problems are unique. Artistic judgments defying business calculations enter at every step.

Bottom-line thinking doesn't always get to the bottom of things. An artistic director lives in dread of getting out of touch with his/her subconscious sources. An institution is a work of art: feats of deliberation, strategy, craft and cunning derive from powerful, unconscious motives. I have said what I think artistic directors should do. If boards of trustees could offer up their trust, especially on key forward moves and, of course, totally on artistic choices, perhaps the great divide would narrow.

Bertolt Brecht tells us in *The Caucasian Chalk Circle*:

> Everything should belong to whoever is
> best for it—
> Children to the motherly, so that they shall
> thrive,
> Wagons to good drivers, to be well driven,
> And the valley to those who will water it
> and make it fruitful.

The board must be accountable to the community for the honesty and integrity of its theatre, for the perpetuation of its leadership, for its overall policies in the broadest sense and for resources of all kinds, including funds, to assist it in its stability and growth. But "the sand takes lines unknown." The board must also support the elusiveness of the creative enterprise. If there is to be a partnership, it must be one of the spirit as well as of the pocketbook.

How we, at thirty-five, resolve these four questions—the one about institutions, the one about artists and especially actors, the one about artistic leadership and the one about staff/trustee relationships—will determine how we will look five years from now. After forty, someone said, a man is responsible for his own face.

In the thirty-five years since Zelda Fichandler co-founded the Arena Stage, where she continues to serve as producing director, she has directed many plays, including The Three Sisters, Death of a Salesman, An Enemy of the People, Six Characters in Search of an

Author *and the American premieres of new Eastern European works,* Duck Hunting, The Ascent of Mt. Fuji *and* Screenplay. *Her* Inherit the Wind *toured to Moscow and Leningrad in 1973, and in 1980 the company performed her* After the Fall *in Hong Kong. She also serves as chair of the Acting and Directing Department at New York University's Tisch School of the Arts. Numerous awards granted to her and to Arena Stage under her tenure include the first Antoinette Perry ("Tony") Award given to a company outside of New York, the Margo Jones Award for "significant contribution to the dramatic art through the production of new plays," The Brandeis University Creative Arts Citation in Theatre, the Acting Company's John Houseman Award for "commitment and dedication to the development of young American actors" and, most recently, the 1985 Common Wealth Award for distinguished service to the theatre.*

THEATRE IN THE TURBULENT YEARS

James Reston, Jr.

In 1960, Chapel Hill, North Carolina, where I was in college, was a pleasant little village on the edge of a revolution. It had one block, Franklin Street, which seemed to have everything a brazen, somewhat arrogant freshman needed. There was a drugstore with a soda fountain where one could get a lemonade made with real lemons; a rathskeller in a sunken alley where the beer and the hamburgers were prime; preppy clothing stores; and a place called Harry's, where we intellectuals and the bohemians from the PlayMakers Theatre across campus gathered to debate hotly the events of the world around us.

We had, in those days (I say in all modesty), a true world view. This was the liberal oasis in the South which was intensely aware of its mission to enlighten its benighted, strife-torn region. The eyes of the nation were turned our way. This was the year when John Kennedy announced his bid for the Presidency by raising the question of how to give direction to our traditional moral purpose, awakening every American to the dangers and the opportunities that confronted the nation. That was a challenge we took seriously.

The international opportunities at the beginning of that year would turn to dangers before our eyes. Nineteen-sixty began with the Soviet Union promising to stop atomic tests unilaterally, just as, in 1985, it has promised once again. In the spring, Prime Minister Hendrik Verwoerd of South Africa was shot in the head by a white who opposed his apartheid policies, plunging that society into a chaos not unlike what we are now seeing nightly on our television. Also in that spring, Israel captured Adolf Eichmann in Argentina but it missed Josef Mengele in Paraguay. Francis Gary Powers was shot down over the Soviet Union in March, which led to the May collapse of the Paris summit between Khrushchev and Eisenhower. A second American spy plane, the RB 47, was shot down several-months later and the vituperation between the superpowers then was far more intense than it ever got over the downing of the Korean jumbo jet in 1983. We would be shocked by the unforgettable performance of Khrushchev at the United Nations, banging his shoe on the desk and calling the Filipino speaker at the rostrum "a jerk." Toward the end of that year, as somewhere the dream of a regional theatre movement was taking shape, the Russians were rumored to have developed something called "the neutron bomb." But their satellites and dogs in space were no rumors.

Before graduation I would experience the week of the Cuban missile crisis, when we looked to the sky and watched the contrails of military jet planes streaming south to Florida. During that week we had every good reason to feel, as former Secretary of Defense Robert McNamara (who was dispatching those planes) has just revealed that he also felt, that we had just enjoyed our last Saturday night. Since the vast majority of us were virgins in those days—the revolution we knew was racial rather than sexual—we pondered sadly meeting our Maker without ever knowing worldly ecstasy. Some, I was fascinated to learn later, did more than simply bemoan this sorry fact. Not I, of course.

Also on Franklin Street there was a movie house called the Carolina. Unlike many southern cinemas, it happened not to have a balcony for blacks, and this turned out to be an unfortunate oversight. For some ill-conceived reason, the owner of the Carolina decided to bring the film *Porgy and Bess* to town. It was one of the first plays I had ever seen on the stage as a child and I went gleefully to see it again. But not everyone could go. In 1960, there were no black undergraduates at the University of North Carolina but there were a few black law students. They went to the Carolina's owner and pleaded, not in petulance or in anger (not yet anyway), to be able to see just this one movie. It had, after all, an unforgettable black cast that included Sidney Poitier, Dorothy Dandridge, Sammy Davis, Jr., Pearl Bailey and Diahann Carroll. The students were turned down.

Some months before, sixty miles away in Greensboro, blacks "sat in" at a lunch counter at Woolworth's; in Chapel Hill the movie house rather than the five-and-dime became our focus. It symbolized segregation itself. We looked up and down our main street and saw that here, in our precious enclave of enlightenment, all the restaurants except Harry's were segregated. The civil rights stories that the nation read in its newspapers—ninety-four percent of southern schools segregated six years after the Supreme Court's decision, interminable filibusters in the U.S. Senate, the Governor of Georgia threatening to deny state funds to any Georgia school that integrated in accordance with the Supreme Court's ruling—all of that had a direct application down the street and around the corner. The movie house as an institution moved to center stage and a black play recorded on film, accentuating the pathos of it all, was the catalyst for a town's reconstruction.

A picketing movement began and it went on for a year. To this day I remember vividly those pacings in front of the theatre, that sense of exalted nobility mixed with visceral fear. Even in Chapel Hill we had our night riders who hurled objects and epithets at us from slow-moving vehicles. I distinctly remember the night I picketed in my letter jacket, for it warms me now to recall that then I was something of a minor soccer star on campus. (This was before the masses discovered the game.) I had worn the jacket deliberately, knowing it would be provocative to some—but that was simply what one did in those days. In costume the crusader postured, daring the bigot to reveal himself. My tame version of street theatre did not seem tame at the time.

Predictably, several hours into my shift, a car pulled up in front of the theatre and a monster of a tackle on the football team got out, wearing an identical letter jacket. He came directly at me and there ensued a terrific argument. He loomed over me, shouting, berating me for sullying the athletic program in this deplorable public fashion. I was scared, very scared indeed, but at least I could hold my own with him verbally. As I did, the crowd swelled around us. I did not think he would attack me physically because I knew him casually, knew him to be decent enough.

In due course he left, satisfied, I suppose, that he had made his point—and I, too, was satisfied. I even remember his name, for apart from his activities on the playing field and in front of the theatre, he was involved in the Air Force ROTC. Several years later I got an announcement about him from the alumni office. He had been killed when his jet fighter was shot down over North Vietnam. I was genuinely sad.

Somewhere, very far from my knowledge at that time, the acorns for an American national theatre were being planted and the saplings and the trees had begun to grow. It might be attractive now to think that this genesis of regional theatre was spawned by the ferment and the danger of the early sixties, but I doubt it. While others in this collection have a far better grasp of that history than I, the dream of a national theatre seems to me to be the work of a few enthusiastic individuals who were in love with the stage and quite separate from the turbulence of the age.

It was not until quite recently that I made much of a distinction between the movie house and the live theatre, especially as they exist outside of New York. It goes back to that year of pacing in front of the Carolina, I suppose, for that showed what the theatre as an institution could mean to a community. I would like to see a live theatre today engender the same passions as the Carolina did. For the institution can be at the center. People could argue and even quarrel about its fare and its policies. They could love it as an institution or hate it. They could love or even hate its manager. But they could not be indifferent to it, for it was so much a part of the texture of the community's life.

I can say that, even as a callow but very earnest youth, I never hated the manager of the Carolina, bigot though he was. If anything, I felt a little sorry for him, for he was caught up in something much larger than himself or his institution. A year later we broke him economically with that picket line, and he was forced to desegregate. The movement had begun with *Porgy and Bess*, but shortly after our brave pickets were gone and blacks and whites could sit together, by God, in the darkness of the theatre, *Gone with the Wind* was re-released. (The year 1960 was also when Clark Gable died.) It amused me to think that if only that theatre owner had brought Scarlett's southern fantasy three months earlier, he would have swamped us. What southerner, regardless of lofty principle, can resist *Gone with the Wind*?

If the regional theatre as an institution was more the work of individuals than the times, the times shaped the sensibilities of some playwrights who are now taking advantage of it. It is my particular bias to wish that the theatre had been more fertile ground in the last twenty-five years for the *potential* playwright. If one was young and passionate and wanted to be a writer in the sixties, the stage was scarcely the first forum one chose to vent those passions. Rather, the novel seemed like the highest star to shoot for, a novel which would capture the ardent dialogue and emotions of the day, just as it told a human and moving story. Those over at the PlayMakers Theatre seemed to us intellectuals in the back booth at Harry's to be indulging in some strange and irresponsible form of escape, sinking their alienation into sterile soil. To perform remote period pieces while the world exploded all around us seemed like a totally curious enterprise.

The blossoming of the theatre in the sixties was institutional rather than substantive. It soared from its society in a headlong flight from realism and naturalism, and now protests that the advent of television necessitated the flight into precious irrelevance. "Art" suddenly had to be something separate from society.

Consequently, the theatre lost a whole generation of writers who might otherwise have gravitated to it. (Is it any different today?) The body of American plays written in the last twenty-five years, taken together, cannot be said to tell us very much about the society (the Vietnam plays are a possible exception). The theatre was far more preoccupied with nudity, eroticism and homosexuality as it pressed the outer limits of the subsequent sexual revolution. That's okay, but it can be carried only so far before it traverses into pornography and triviality.

It pains me now to think of what sensational material existed then for dramatic molding. We had all the ingredients: great stories, great energy, abundant anger and alienation, big questions and, very often, victory. Our material was every bit as good then as South African playwright Athol Fugard's material is today. The year after I left Chapel Hill the focus there shifted from the Carolina Theatre to the Watts Motel. It was time to move to basics, from the place of entertainment to the place where people—all kinds of people—made love. For sex, and especially interracial sex, is, as everyone knows, at the core of racial hatred.

The Watts Motel was an ugly little redneck lair on the edge of town and the meanness of the struggle, just like the earnestness of our purpose, seems hard to remember now. Before that motel owner, too, broke under pressure, his wife squatted over the leader of the protest, limp and immobilized as he was by the principles of nonviolence, and she urinated on him.

When the conflicts outside the theatre are that elemental, the theatre has a choice. It can stand aside or it can become involved. Like no other form, the theatre seemed to separate itself all too willingly, and then make this separation part of its credo about its "art." The stage could not compete with the realism of television, nor could it top the inherent sensationalism of real events. In tempestuous times, social and political drama paled before reality. Now, in peaceful times (albeit times with many big subjects and questions that television will not dare to touch), we hear that abrasive drama is "not entertaining." It is not appetizing.

Recently a well-known playwright who has taken ample advantage of this magnificent network of regional theatres in America said to me, "This is not a country that especially respects the playwright." I was not sure where he lodged his blame. In the audiences? In the critics? In the society at large? Or in the theatre itself? On the face of it, I do not see why a playwright should be any less respected in this society than its novelists or its journalists or its poets. Respect flows to the artist or his genre when he has something to say and his institution is anxious to serve it up whether or not the society wants to hear it. Perhaps it is true to say that the society does not *respect* its pure entertainers. For them, we reserve a different emotion, a bit of fleeting thanks for lightening our day, or something of that kind.

If theatre unplugged itself from its society and discouraged many young writers from exploring its possibilities, it seems now, in certain places, to be groping in the dark for a reconnection. Here and there, theatres are beginning to realize how they can demand attention. Some are realizing that survival lies in boldness rather than in caution. Television and the movies have revealed their shortcomings. The screen does not come off as the great monster threat to live theatre that it once appeared to be, simply because those forms have truly become a *reflection* of the times. The theatre's calling is quite different, nearly the opposite. It can—it should—operate, and occasionally it *is* operating, on the cutting edge.

The system is healthy. A redefinition of its place in the society is under review. It is beginning to rethink what it should be as an institution and what its material should be and who *else* besides its small cadre of natural devotees should be involved in its glorious process. It will be even more healthy by using this twenty-fifth year to take stock.

Born in New York City in 1941, James Reston, Jr. graduated in philosophy from the University of North Carolina in 1963. He is the author of two novels, To Defend, To Destroy *and* The Knock at Midnight, *and of several nonfiction books including* The Amnesty of John David Herndon, The Innocence of Joan Little *and* Our Father Who Art in Hell *(Times Books, 1981), which recounts the life and death of Jim Jones. Reston is the creator of the award-winning documentary* Father Cares: The Last of Jonestown, *and has written two plays,* Sherman, the Peacemaker, *first produced at PlayMakers Repertory Company, and* Jonestown Express, *first produced at Trinity Repertory Company and published in December 1984 as part of TCG's Plays in Process series. His latest book is* Sherman's March and Vietnam, *published in 1985 by Macmillan.*

A MOVEMENT COMES OF AGE

W. McNeil Lowry

In 1957, when I had been at the Ford Foundation for three-and-a-half years, the trustees first authorized a program in support of the arts. As director and later vice president of the new program, I and a small staff began working with professionals in each area of the arts to develop objectives for organized philanthropy, the first such undertaking in American history on a national scale.

The Ford Foundation's aim in nurturing the theatre was to offer American artists a clean slate, to encourage them to build companies devoted to process; in other words, to foster the coming together of American directors, actors, designers, playwrights and others beyond a single production and beyond commercial sanction. This motive intrinsically contained the seeds of a plan, which came into sharper focus through the staffwork of the Program in Humanities and Arts; the exploratory phase of that work was launched in the spring of 1957. Fieldwork concentrated on the baker's dozen of "winter stock" companies outside New York, as well as community and academic theatres, but it also included consultation with theatre professionals and critics in New York City.

Aside from a handful of actors who had ventured out of the city for one or more productions in winter stock, very few New Yorkers in the fifties could envision a future for the American theatre that was an alternative to Broadway, nor could they relate what was going on, for example, Off Broadway or in Central Park under Joseph Papp's aegis to this alternative future. One who could was *New York Times* critic Brooks Atkinson, who had ventured as far as Nina Vance's and Margo Jones's theatres, both in Texas. Another was the director Alan Schneider who, in addition to his work at Arena Stage in Washington, D.C., at the Alley and at two other Houston theatres, and at numerous universities besides his Catholic University base, had also begun his long preoccupation with Samuel Beckett by directing the first American production of *Waiting for Godot* in Miami.

Atkinson believed that the only actors capable of handling the classical style were those self-taught young people coming out of colleges and the newer winter stock companies, those attempting to create their own theatre and to become professional artists at the same time. What New York's Actors' Studio turned out may have been perfectly suited to Broadway, he reasoned, but it was simply not adequate preparation for the experimental modern repertoire or the classics. Off

Broadway, which Atkinson had steadily encouraged, sometimes provided a place for these young people to be seen, but it was really only a reflection of what Jones, Vance, Papp, Zelda Fichandler at Arena, Group 20 in Wellesley, Mass. and others were doing outside of New York.

Schneider felt that the standards of Off Broadway were very uneven, generally vastly inferior to the Alley's, sometimes even inferior to the best university theatres. Yet he could not figure out how to get a two-way flow started between New York professionals and the best regional companies.

In Cleveland in 1958, Schneider, Papp and producer Roger Stevens took part in joint auditions of young actors, along with nine directors I invited from winter stock, community and academic theatres. The twelve participated in two days of Ford Foundation planning sessions whose purpose was the launching of pilot programs for actors, playwrights and directors. But the first planks in the resident theatre movement were laid down in an April 1959 conference in New York, comprised almost totally of seasoned New York professionals. The following are a few random quotes from a meeting which, in hindsight, takes on an historic cast:

> There is a greater ability and willingness to experiment outside of New York commercial conditions. There is also a limit to how far you can experiment behind a proscenium. But it is not a solution to strip the stage of scenery and say you can do anything; it is an expression of bankruptcy.
>
> The important goal is the opportunity to go wrong, to *try out* some things, which is practically impossible in New York.
>
> All over America, it seems that people are feeling some kind of stir, some need for theatre. . . . How can we put together theatre artists responsible to each other as artists, supported by the Ford Foundation, without commercial penalties?
>
> How does all this differ from Off Broadway now? It is different in its very roots. Even in the most idealistic aims Off Broadway, it always backs down to commercial exploitation. If there is some way to help professional actors work together through even two productions, we will have broken through. And this is exactly what a commercial producer will not subsidize.
>
> When the Ford Foundation in September 1957 published its statement that theatre in America was an artistic resource like music and the visual arts and should not be regarded as commerce and entertainment, it made a "crack in the wall" which theatre artists could now exploit.

It was only the parochialism of the New York theatre professionals that obscured the fact that a few existing companies outside New York already struggled to devote themselves, with high standards, to the artistic process (if only with as much continuity as they could afford). A prerequisite to change, as the 1958 Cleveland conference had also concluded, was effective communication among the various segments of theatre. For a meeting of twenty-three persons from around the country in December 1959, the Ford Foundation set an explicit agenda for the first time: "One of the most obvious factors revealed by [our] staffwork in the American theatre," we noted, "is the inadequacy of communication or the absence of common objectives. . . . Truly professional resident theatres outside New York exist in only a very limited number." How were the directors of any additional companies to be enabled to "go through the experience of those few persons who have developed voluntary community activities into permanent professional companies?" And beyond that, we determined that "improving communication among the segments of the American theatre is worth worrying about only if we can conclude that doing so will practically assist the American theatre to reach its main goal—the higher development of the theatre art in the United States."

Among the people engaged in that 1959 conference were the directors of three companies for which the Foundation was subsidizing half the costs of acting ensembles, ten actors each, for the first time under seasonal contracts of $200 a week: Fichandler, Vance and Jules Irving of the Actor's Workshop in San Francisco. By the second day's discussion, the possible means of "practical assistance" had been fairly well sketched. "If it works out," Irving said, "six people are going to Zelda Fichandler's theatre for experience. If it works out for Miss Vance, then some company that wants to become an Equity company can work at it, not by reading about it, but by seeing how Miss Vance has done it."

No design of an actual program had been solicited by the end of the two days, but a few key elements were obvious: the use of two or more existing companies as models for others in their developmental or planning stages; visitations by directors and other staff members of one theatre to another for periods as prolonged as could be managed; annual central auditions of young actors before nonprofit producers who offered paying jobs; exchange of company directors and managers with key university department heads in order to help focus training programs and facilitate the recruiting of apprentices.

In late 1960, I drafted a grant for a four-year program to establish something called "Theatre Communications Group," to be administered through the Goodman School of the Art Institute of Chicago and controlled by an advisory board of professional and academic theatre people. (The administering body was later shifted to Carnegie Tech when the Art Institute raised objections about the grant money being earmarked solely for theatre objectives.)

In 1959, while theatre and better theatre communications continued to be the focus of its staffwork, the Ford Foundation took pilot steps toward strengthening and creating resident companies. I have already mentioned the underwriting of annual contracts for actors. In 1959, there were also individual awards of $10,000 to ten directors nominated and selected from the field, and fully staged productions of works by ten playwrights similarly selected. In 1960, a program was established whereby twenty-six of America's leading novelists and poets got seasonal residencies in nonprofit theatre and (in three cases) opera companies.

On May 17, 1960 I came as close as I ever did to forecasting the shape that the resident theatre movement would take in this country, in a letter to Jules Irving:

> There is, as you know, an increasing pessimism among theatre people about the prospects in the New York theatre, both on and Off Broadway. The number of commercial failures, the attenuation of any cultural repertoire by the efforts to hit theatre party audiences and numerous other trends felt Off Broadway as well as on—all these particularly affect the actor who is more serious about the nature of the parts he can play.
>
> I have asked the people making these characterizations whether they were more hopeful that talented actors would leave New York for Houston and San Francisco and Washington to take part in the new resident ensembles. The answer has been somewhat optimistic, but the qualification is made that an important question for each actor will be the exact repertoire planned for the year . . . and whether you would have the time,

under existing pressures [in your theatre], to plan such a repertoire . . .
at *least* by late summer.

I went on to relate to Irving a personal experience of my own, which came after having spent three years helping to evolve some kind of model for the development of resident theatre. I told him that I had had a long talk with the French painter André Girard, who, in the twenties and thirties, had been a scenic designer in Paris for Pitoeff, Baty, Dullin, Jouvet and other directors. Girard thought that the hope for attracting the talents of U.S. poets and novelists to the stage was the same as in France and Britain: namely, support for resident theatres producing a large number of plays in one year, offering the actor at least minimal economic security, meeting his interests in a higher-quality repertoire and proving to writers, designers, composers and painters that enough plays are produced in enough theatres, then artists would turn their attentions to the stage.

The actual design of Theatre Communications Group was worked out with individual theatre professionals and with TCG's first advisory board, which included a number of people from the 1959 conference—Vance, Fichandler, Irving, Theodore Hoffman of Carnegie Tech, John Reich of the Goodman Theatre School, Lowell Lees of Utah, Mack Scism of the Mummers in Oklahoma City and Newell Tarrant of the Erie Playhouse—as well as Roger Stevens, Alan Schneider, actresses Nan Martin and Geraldine Page, Pat Brown of the Magnolia Theatre in Long Beach and Michael Ellis of the Bucks County Playhouse. Sixteen theatres and eight drama departments were involved in the first network, and the traffic of artists was charted by Pat Brown, as a field director working out of New York.

Under the chairmanship of Ted Hoffman, with Carnegie Tech the nonprofit intermediary, TCG's first meeting thereafter was held in Washington, where the decision was made to engage, part-time, Danny Newman of the Chicago Lyric Opera, whose work as a subscription consultant has had such a lasting impact on the performing arts. Two years later, the Foundation asked the TCG Advisory Board to seek its own separate incorporation, making it directly controlled by theatre professionals. New recruits included Peter Zeisler and Oliver Rea from the Guthrie Theater.

The seeds of the resident theatre movement had been planted after World War II by a very few driven persons seeking to professionalize themselves and their developing companies. Their efforts were linked together and crystallized through exchanges created by the Ford Foundation in its explorations of all the arts, beginning in 1957. In December 1961, the Foundation trustees approved in principle an appropriation of $9 million to begin "strengthening the position of resident theatre in the United States."

In the first formal grants from this appropriation in 1962, Foundation staff said that they were "convinced that the solid development here of what Europe knows as 'repertory theatres' can have historic importance to the future of the American culture. . . . The resident theatre company is the chief hope for theatre as an artistic resource." Within five years there would be more Equity actors engaged in nonprofit companies than on Broadway and on the road combined.

The Foundation had its most sweeping effect in its first five years (1962–67), when twenty-six companies were established (exclusive of those which could be better characterized as part of the growing Off-Off Broadway movement). Moreover, several companies that had been in existence before 1962 became caught up in the movement during these years, including the Cleveland Play House, Studio Arena Theatre in Buffalo, the Barter Theatre, Virginia Museum Theatre, the Oregon Shakespearean Festival and the Old Globe in San Diego.

Six companies among those receiving the earliest Foundation grants were at or near the core of the movement: the Alley, Arena Stage, the Actor's Workshop, the Guthrie, the Theatre Group at UCLA (known after 1967 as the Mark Taper Forum) and the Fred Miller (later renamed the Milwaukee Repertory Theater). All exist today, save the Actor's Workshop which was liquidated in 1966, a short time after the departure of Jules Irving and Herbert Blau for the Lincoln Center Repertory Theatre in New York. Looking back for a moment: the increased communication we had stimulated among directors and managers of theatres, and their sharing of services through Theatre Communications Group, had helped to focus a resident theatre movement in the United States. But its potential became evident to patrons and to the press largely as a result of the actions taken by the Foundation in 1962. Press reactions were often excessive, or at least premature. *The Wall Street Journal* advised business leaders around the country that if they did not have a resident professional company in their communities, they were behind the times. *Time* magazine reported that every actor who could crawl through the Holland Tunnel was on his way to a "regional" theatre, a trend which, over the next few years at least, almost every actor's agent would seek to restrain.

In 1964 and 1965, the TCG Board faced the fact that the organization's services were now sought by an increasing number of theatres at widely varying stages of development. Should they cope with this trend by giving more time to the larger or more fully developed companies? Nina Vance found this tactic extremely disquieting, since it could again leave in isolation a number of artistic leaders determined to professionalize their companies.

Zelda Fichandler wrote to Oliver Rea of the Guthrie, then president of the TCG Board, "What has really caused the flowering of our own work this year has been the discovery of a few creative talents. How long and hard that search was, and how much easier, given the context of today's world, it will be to solve the problem of economic support . . . than it was to discover and engage the imagination and commitment of two major talents!" Later, Rea wrote to Nina Vance, "What unites us also tears us asunder; namely, the fact that we are all hanging by our thumbs and are never far away from being hastily extinguished. I feel that many of the problems have been caused by our theatre here in Minneapolis. We didn't grow into what we are progressively. . . . We emerged full-grown, haughty, with the tar brush of Broadway still visible down the small of our back."

There was much truth in this characterization, which sharply distinguished the Guthrie from the steady, stubborn evolution of an Alley or an Arena Stage. ("I clawed this theatre out of the ground," Vance said of the Alley.) And yet there were two sides to the coin. If the Alley, the Arena, the Actor's Workshop, the Theatre Group and the Fred Miller were identifiable models for expansion of the resident theatre, planting the Guthrie full-blown in a Midwest landscape, for many corporate and lay patrons, gave credibility to new efforts in other communities.

The momentum reached its peak by 1966, before the first efforts of the new program of the National Endowment for the Arts. "Hinterland Legits Top Broadway," proclaimed *Variety* (March 19, 1966). In 1963, the year of the opening seasons of both the Guthrie and the short-lived Actors' Studio Theatre in New York, came also Center Stage in Baltimore, the Seattle Repertory Theatre, the Theatre Company of Boston (also short-lived) and the movement to Equity status of the Goodman Theatre in Chicago, founded as a school back in 1925. In 1964 were added Actors Theatre of Louisville, Trinity Square, Hartford Stage Company and the Theatre of the Living Arts in Philadelphia; the last did not survive the decade. The year 1965 included the openings of the American Conservatory Theatre in San Francisco and the Long Wharf Theatre in New Haven.

Today it may be necessary to remind ourselves that the American Conservatory Theatre, which had its first temporary base in Pittsburgh and went on to tour to Ann Arbor, Westport, Palo Alto and Ravinia Park before it settled in San Francisco, carried the potential of being a world-class theatre company. Critic Walter Kerr commented in the June 9, 1968 *New York Times*, "It is just possible that ACT may revolutionize American theatre practice not merely because it has found a practical way to mount a bewildering number of productions in a hurry and so to force repertory two or three giant steps forward without any irremediable loss of quality, but because with its schooling program it is in a position to give back to the contemporary actor the lost half of his craft. Our actors have been good at feeling what they are doing. Under this system they may become adroit at doing what they are feeling."

Of the roughly $60 million given by the Foundation in assistance to companies, $20 million went to eight: $4.4 million to the American Conservatory Theatre, $3.6 million to the Alley, $3.3 million to the Arena, $1.8 million to the Guthrie, $1.8 million to the Mummers Theatre of Oklahoma City, $1.7 million to the American Shakespeare Festival in Stratford, Conn., $1.6 million to the Center Theatre Group of Los Angeles and $1.5 million to the New York Shakespeare Festival.

But the enormous promise of these gifts was sometimes hamstrung by the lack of a sustained focus. Four months before Kerr's panegyric, I had written to ACT general director William Ball, "It should be understood by you and your associates that [our latest payment] carries clear recognition of the plain and hard truth that neither the Ford Foundation nor any other outside agency, even one so deeply involved as we are in the theatre, can help to run ACT from a distance or help you to the important decisions. . . . I see no way for ACT to survive except through your willingness to take all your responsibilities and to act on them with the greatest sense of realism."

As theatre outside New York was developing, New York was experiencing a new infusion of energy in the form of Off Broadway. And it is not inappropriate, as Brooks Atkinson did, to relate these developments to what Vance, Fichandler and others were doing in the regions. At first, Off Broadway was not primarily dedicated to avant-garde or experimental work, or even to the new playwright. In 1956, for example, the Off Broadway season included around a hundred plays, two-thirds of which were classic and one-third contemporary. The concessions by the unions worked as well for Shakespeare, Shaw and Ibsen as for Brecht, Ionesco and Sartre—but only for a while. Within a few years, Off Broadway production budgets were inflated to a point at which concern over margins of profit again became dominant. But already in the early fifties there were Off Broadway producers who did not remotely think of theatre as a means of economic livelihood. They had philosophical, aesthetic or vaguely sociological goals (only in the sixties did the goals of some of them become political), or they were dedicated to the new playwright while remaining eclectic in their philosophy. However various their concepts were, they all felt themselves to be in the advanced guard and sought to cultivate techniques of acting and directing which expressed particular or personal visions. They wanted not only to confront the audience but to disturb its sense of values. Jarry and Artaud were their progenitors; Ionesco and

Beckett helped to confirm their view of the present; the emergence of the "happening" (through the work of such artists as Cage, Kaprow, Dine and others) told them that they had allies in the musical and visual arts.

An easily identifiable source of conceptual theatre in America was what much later was to become known in Europe as "*le Living.*" Julian Beck and Judith Malina often let the force of events change their original goal of "challenging plays using vital stage techniques." It would take too much space to chart their course from 1947 to the present; for the purposes of this essay it is, however, necessary to recall Jack Gelber's *The Connection* (1959) and Kenneth H. Brown's *The Brig* (1961), which was repeated in 1963 when the Living was still refusing to pay federal withholding and entertainment taxes. Not paying the rent did not strike the group's landlord as mere "civil disobedience," however, and he moved in to close their operations.

The Living Theatre was a collective more than a company, but many actors were glad to work for the Becks for the $45-a-week maximum, including two who were to influence the avant-garde theatre in New York, Joseph Chaikin and Peter Feldman.

In the winter of 1963, these two met in a loft on 24th Street with Gordon Rogoff, Richard Gilman, Megan Terry, Maria Irene Fornes, Jean-Claude van Itallie, Arthur Sainer, Michael Smith, Barbara Vann and Jerry Ragni. The series of workshops they planned were dubbed The Open Theatre, to distinguish them from the "closed" theatre of Broadway. The most advanced of the workshops continued to be those of Chaikin and Feldman, joined from time to time by Sam Shepard and other writers. In 1966, two one-acts by van Itallie previously produced at La Mama E.T.C. were combined with a third and produced at the Pocket Theatre as *America Hurrah*. That production, like Peter Brook's New York staging of *Marat/ Sade* the year before, became a landmark in avant-garde theatre. Another influential production of that year was the Open Theatre workshop of Megan Terry's *Viet Rock*, also first produced at La Mama.

But there were other roots of Off-Off Broadway that were anything but ideological. Ellen Stewart's simple objective in 1962, when she opened La Mama E.T.C. in a Greenwich Village cafe, was to offer initial productions of the work of unknown playwrights. Improbably, this was the start of a catalytic and proliferating enterprise which would intersect with or draw together almost the whole of the experimental theatre internationally, and ultimately make Stewart the nexus of original work from both the advanced and underdeveloped worlds.

La Mama staged twenty-eight new scripts before the Off Broadway critics gave it much public attention, and when they did, the City inspectors moved in to close an operation that could not justify a club license. When Stewart moved into a Second Avenue loft and attempted to sell a few tickets, she was closed again, this time by Actors' Equity, because she could not afford minimums. (To this point Stewart's earnings as a dress designer had been La Mama's only steady resource.) In her third location, also on Second Avenue, Stewart made an agreement with Equity that she would neither sell tickets nor advertise. In its first five years, La Mama developed playwrights, actors and directors who won a significant majority of the awards open to Off Broadway artists, and La Mama writers had more of their works published than all of their contemporaries. In 1967, a La Mama troupe performed *America Hurrah* in London, and a play written for La Mama was Britain's own entry in the Edinburgh Festival. By this date, scrounging on the land in a minibus, La Mama actors had played throughout Western Europe and also in Poland, Czechoslovakia, Romania and Yugoslavia, presenting works by van Itallie, Paul Foster, Lanford Wilson, Rochelle Owens, Megan Terry and

Sam Shepard. When an article in *The New York Times* prompted Stewart's landlord to raise her rent to $475 a month, both West Germany and Sweden offered La Mama a permanent subsidy if she would abandon New York. Stewart's answer was a plan to renovate and mortgage a four-story building on East 4th Street, with a down payment from the Ford Foundation.

In 1968 the Foundation began awarding a series of grants for Off-Off Broadway workshops and staged performances of new works, and these continued to be available as a part of the Foundation's efforts to encourage new playwrights. Between 1968 and 1975 La Mama received almost $1.2 million; Chelsea Theater Center about half that; and the Open Theatre, Theatre Genesis and New Theatre Workshop less. Because Joseph Chaikin felt that short Off Broadway runs of Open Theatre workshops were seductive and divisive, one of the Ford grants to the Open was directed toward internal experimentation rather than the development of public performances.

Perhaps the only indispensable further example of the Foundation's contributions Off and Off-Off Broadway is the establishment of Peter Brook's International Center of Theatre Research in Paris. Founded with the generous collaboration of the Anderson Foundation, the Center's purpose was the training of actors and directors from every part of the world in new techniques and approaches to theatrical texts. It is probably no accident that six of Brook's thirteen actors chosen for the first year were from La Mama, and that the only director he admitted was Andrei Serban, a Romanian brought to La Mama on a Foundation travel and study grant at the prompting of Ellen Stewart.

By the early sixties, blacks of talent and perseverance had managed to find their way into theatre and film; black parts were played by blacks and in some of the resident companies, classical parts traditionally played by whites were given to blacks. But there were few opportunities for young blacks to find training, and almost none for professional apprenticeship. Nor was the struggle for integration in the theatre totally relevant so long as the black experience was recreated by white dramatists, however motivated. Opening the theatre profession to blacks was to depend on the black consciousness of a few writers. But first of all it depended on the motivation of a few potential artistic producers.

The growth, even the survival, of a black theatre company required both a committed audience and financial resources which could share the ideas and objectives among potential producers. Realistically, there were only two possible sources for the money required: private foundations on the one hand and the variety of community action programs created during the Kennedy and Johnson years on the other. And there was an interesting, often a delicate problem to overcome: the black entrepreneur might harbor a psychological necessity to assault or repudiate any representative of the largely white American "establishment," *including* the foundation officer or community official attempting to give him support.

I lived with this, more successfully than not, for fifteen years. The bearer of philanthropic gifts to black separatists could, of course, understand how the gifts would be received and either accept that or ignore it. But it was harder for the receiver. In the most extreme case he managed by convincing himself that the grant constituted "reparations" for the blacks' rightful use. In the less extreme, indeed most usual case, the black entrepreneur rewrote his own history to omit the role of his philanthropic partner. This worked very well, except in a brief period when the New York State Council on the Arts required a note about its role to be made public. One of the first moves toward separatist black theatre was an example of the extreme case, and it failed to find its own roots. The writer LeRoi Jones (later Imamu Amiri Baraka), in Off Broadway productions of *The Slave* and *The Toilet*, assailed not only the audience but the white actors required to play some of the roles. In the period before he immersed himself in the community action politics of Newark, Baraka sought to discourage other potential leaders of the black theatre in New York who, though political in their radical objectives, were not seeking a personal political career in the ghettos.

Early in 1964, a group of black theatre professionals with other goals in mind met on their own initiative at the Ford Foundation to discuss the possibility of recreating an "American Negro Theatre," which, with inadequate funds and little continuous support between 1940 and 1950, had nevertheless proved significant to their own careers. They included Osceola Archer, Sidney Poitier, Ruby Dee, Alice and Alvin Childress, Hilda Simms and Frederick O'Neal, then vice president of Actors' Equity. They were somewhat troubled about backing a "Negro" theatre when complete integration was the dominant objective of most blacks. But, given the absence of professional training opportunities for younger blacks, they believed that waiting for complete integration of the American theatre might mean that another whole generation would go untrained.

The Foundation agreed to provide funds for the study and design of a repertory company and a professional apprenticeship program without commitment to the study's recommendations, but again history proved the improbability of planning a theatre by committee. It was the summer of 1967 before a report was produced, and even then, there was no concurrence among the black professionals involved.

A year before that, however, the black actor, director and playwright Douglas Turner Ward wrote a *New York Times* essay. Ward's two short plays, *Happy Ending* and *Day of Absence*, were running at the St. Mark's Theatre on 8th Street. His thesis was that what both the Negro theatre artists and Negro audience (his words) required was material that, by speaking directly to blacks' sense of identity, could also speak to audiences of any race or nationality. Further, Ward said, only in a theatre center in which this material, however unpolished, was utilized, could the young black actor, director, playwright or designer become a professional worthy of the name. In short, Ward's separatist drive was not political but professional and psychological.

Invited to pursue this subject with me, Ward brought with him actor Robert Hooks and Off Broadway manager Gerald Krone. Here began a long and difficult collaboration which resulted in the establishment of the Negro Ensemble Company, using over $2 million in Ford funds through 1975. The company would face repeated financial crises in the seventies (when, as Ward expressed it, "black was no longer beautiful" so far as lay white patrons were concerned). The main problem was that aggressive black producers never really accepted responsibility for widening the base of their financial support. Had not the Ford Foundation established the NEC? Then let the Ford Foundation ensure its permanence.

But these were second thoughts. In the climate of 1967 the Negro Ensemble Company was an instant phenomenon. Announcement of its establishment brought charges from some Civil Rights leaders, reputedly including Martin Luther King, Jr. and the NAACP's Roy Wilkins, that the Ford Foundation had retreated from its integrationist policies. Howard Taubman of *The New York Times*, in an interview with Dr. Esther Jackson—professor of drama in a North Carolina Negro college—supported this conclusion without discussing with Ward or Hooks the rationale of their training program. But the real pressures came from the black activists with an exactly contrary view. They approved Ward's objective of building a repertoire of plays by blacks, but his concentration on training, his toleration of integrated audiences and his use of the word "Negro" were apolitical in character and allegedly designed to curry favor with the Ford Foundation, whatever he had independently expressed in the *Times* article of 1966.

But the momentum with which the company went into production changed the subject. Before it could complete the first cycle in its training program or work on unproduced scripts thrust upon it, the NEC was hailed by the critics as the first full-fledged black repertory company, when it opened with Weiss's *Song of the Lusitanian Bogey*. Ward, actor Moses Gunn and the company won all the prizes given to Off Broadway theatres, young black trainees—often after only a few weeks—found employment by using the NEC label, the Aldwych and various European theatre festivals invited the group abroad, and French, British, German and Italian television networks featured members of the company. After four productions and only one year of existence, the NEC was accepted as a permanent addition to professional theatre in America; there was no time for growth. Within the first three seasons even apprentices being trained backstage and in lighting were pulled away to jobs elsewhere, yet when the NEC was forming there was not one black stage electrician qualified by the union in New York.

Three months after the NEC's establishment, black actor and playwright Robert Macbeth made plans to convert one wing of the old Lafayette Theatre in Harlem into workshop and performance spaces for another all-black company. Macbeth had very different aims from Ward; though, like Ward, he resisted the anarchist course of LeRoi Jones, he was not tolerant of mixed audiences, as Ward was. He saw the New Lafayette as a recreation, in dramatic form, of the life Harlem blacks knew on the streets—and this was the only audience he wanted. And Macbeth had what Ward and other black producers needed: the allegiance of the most noted and prolific black playwright of the sixties, Ed Bullins.

While the New Lafayette existed, it was rare that a Bullins play was performed anywhere else; Bullins himself was, for a number of years, extremely ambivalent in his relationships with white producers or with white patrons. In Macbeth, a vigorous, articulate and attractive man, Bullins found a natural leader. In turn, his plays brought into the New Lafayette that sense of Harlem street life Macbeth sought. If the New Lafayette had continued on its original course, the history of the black theatre movement would have been markedly different.

As it was, after four seasons Macbeth turned the New Lafayette in another direction: It was to become a black arts center devoted to all media. In truth, the company was turning in on itself and becoming less devoted to serving its audience, which had been non-paying in the first two years before reaching a top of $2 per ticket. NYSCA and private foundation grants were gradually being withdrawn, but nothing affected Macbeth's fantasy that, through this charming and talented man, the Ford Foundation was repaying society's debts to blacks. By 1971–72, our support hit $500,000, including the underwriting of a proposed film of Bullins's *Goin' a Buffalo*. The film project was abandoned in favor of making a film about the New Lafayette itself. By 1974, after spending $1.4 million in Ford Foundation money, Macbeth's enterprise collapsed.

The work of Ed Bullins continued to inform the black theatre movement for a time, and provided encouragement to other playwrights. Woodie King, Jr. used the Henry Street Settlement as a site for the New Federal Theatre and particularly as a service to new writers. Joseph Papp gave much attention to black playwrights from the time he established the New York Shakespeare Festival, and arranged cooperative productions with King at New Federal of Bullins's *The Taking of Miss Janie* and Ntozake Shange's *For Colored Girls. . . .*

Most of the Ford Foundation's attention to the opportunities of young blacks outside New York was for their training or apprenticeship in the performing arts. But two continuing series of grants supported both training and production. One, between 1968 and 1976, went to the Free Southern Theatre, created by Gilbert Moses and John O'Neal out of Tougaloo College in response to the Civil Rights movement; the other went to one of the most comprehensive ethnic programs ever devised in the performing arts, the Inner City Cultural Center of Los Angeles, inspired by C. Bernard Jackson.

Over the decades of the sixties and seventies, professional theatre in this country burgeoned. It used as its vehicle both traditional and non-traditional material, classics and the newest texts and performance techniques, and employed for the first time the voices and talents of America's minorities. Using the initiative of the Ford Foundation's program in the creative and performing arts, I was privileged to be near the center of the resident theatre movement and the development of both the avant-garde theatre and the black theatre. Theatre as an American art form has greatly matured over the past generation, but the depth and richness of its resources have only begun to be plumbed. The unceasing battle will continue to be over standards. Too often we accept novelty or ambition as substitutes.

W. McNeil Lowry has been a university instructor, writer, lecturer and Washington correspondent in addition to his twenty-three years at the Ford Foundation where he was Director of Education, Director and Vice President, Humanities and the Arts, and Vice President, Policy and Planning. His latest book is The Arts and Public Policy in the United States *(Prentice-Hall, 1984). In his Ford Foundation career, the resident theatre movement was one dominant theme. Others included the transformation of performance and training resources in ballet, the evolution of new opera companies from the level of "civic operas," the expansion of seasons and services of sixty-one American symphonic orchestras, and the renaissance of the American lithograph, along with the reestablishment of professional conservatories of music and of independent schools of art.*

AMERICA AND THE CLASSICS

Robert Brustein

The post-World War II classical theatre in America was initially a sort of English impersonation, despite some scattered early efforts to evolve a native approach to Shakespeare. One reason for this was training—or the lack of it: not until the sixties did our drama schools recognize a need to relate classical acting to the American experience rather than some mannered imitation of scratchy English recordings. Before that, young Americans serious about classical training usually went directly to England, the Old Vic School in particular, and inevitably drew their models from the great English actors of that era—Laurence Olivier, Ralph Richardson, Peggy Ashcroft, John Gielgud, Michael Redgrave, Joyce Redman. I began my own career as a classical character comic actor aping Robert Newton's flamboyant Pistol in Olivier's *Henry V* (though John Barrymore's snorting cadences also sounded in my ears when playing Shakespeare). Some of us had sailed over on Fulbright scholarships (William Ball was one of our companions on shipboard) to saturate ourselves in British theatre. Thus, while the Method training then in vogue emphasized working from the self in naturalistic roles, classical acting in this country began as a form of following the leader.

One of the earliest American classical companies—Group 20's Theatre on the Green in Wellesley, Massachusetts—was largely a creation of English influences. As a member of this group from 1950 until 1957 (we turned Equity in 1953 after moving to Wellesley's outdoor amphitheatre from a town hall in Unionville, Connecticut), I can testify personally to its Anglophile qualities. Our director was Alison Ridley, daughter of M. R. Ridley, the British Shakespeare scholar; most of us were graduates of Ivy League schools, followed by training in England; and although we brought an irrepressible American brashness to our Shakespeare, Shaw and Sheridan productions, we were essentially trying to plant the Old Vic, the Nottingham Playhouse or the Bristol Old Vic in the soil of New England.

The merging of Group 20 with members of Cambridge's Brattle Theatre in the mid-fifties extended this process, which was further spread when some people associated with the merger went off to found their own theatres in various parts of the country: Ellis Rabb the touring APA; Bill Ball the American Conservatory Theatre in San Francisco; and Jack Landau a training unit loosely associated with the Phoenix Theatre Company in New York, significantly called the Young Vic.

Most of these companies circulated the same small blood-group of classically trained actors: Fritz Weaver, Peter Donat, Jerry Kilty, Nancy Wickwire, Rosemary Harris, Gerry Jedd, Donald Moffat, Frederick Warriner, Frances Sternhagen, Clayton Corzatte, Patricia Falkenhain, Ray Reinhardt, Larry Gates, John Heffernan, Richard Dysart, Jacqueline Brooks. But except for Ball's unorthodox production of *Six Characters in Search of an Author* and a few other impressive aberrations, most of the early classical companies had few ambitions beyond speaking clearly, parading costumes elegantly and observing the reigning tradition.

That is, until Joe Papp stepped into the breach with the New York Shakespeare Festival. Papp's initial productions were erratic, but they provided us with our first glimpse of indigenous classical theatre since Orson Welles's productions of *Julius Caesar* and *Doctor Faustus*. I remember auditioning for the lead in *Richard III* along with a horde of other hopefuls, only to be beaten out for the role by an unknown actor named George C. Scott. Scott's performance in the part was riveting, and it was followed by equally powerful performances in *The Merchant of Venice* and (opposite Colleen Dewhurst) *Antony and Cleopatra*. But the Papp production that really opened our eyes to the possibility of an American classic theatre was the 1969 *Taming of the Shrew*, directed by Gerald Freedman. With admirable daring, this show flipped tradition on its back, substituting an exuberant farce style which drew on the Marx Brothers, Mack Sennett, Chaplin, Keaton and animated cartoons—utilizing, in short, a native American comic tradition enacted by inspired clowns who made the play our own.

Two other companies with classical ambitions were functioning around the same time: the American Shakespeare Theatre at Stratford, Connecticut, and the Living Theatre in New York. Under its successive directors, and even with the distinguished Mercury Theatre alumnus John Houseman at the helm, the Stratford Shakespeare company was rarely more than a stopover for tourists, picnicking indoors and out. Largely inspired by Tyrone Guthrie's work in England and at the Stratford Festival in Canada, the most adventurous thing this theatre was able to do with Shakespeare was update him. We had *Twelfth Night* set in Brighton during the Napoleonic Wars, *Much Ado About Nothing* in Spanish Texas, *Measure for Measure* in 19th-century Vienna—to no other detectable purpose than to redesign the costumes, scenery and props (Guthrie called this "jollying up" the classics—similar techniques, with similar motives, are now being used in operas, Handel and Mozart in particular). There was nothing then (or now) particularly offensive about this approach, except that it so rarely involved any compelling confrontation with the text. Instead, "jollying up" was usually a matter of cosmetic invention doing the work of the intellect or the imagination, with directorial cleverness upstaging dramatic intention. The audience invariably left the theatre neither moved nor enlightened nor challenged. If they talked about the show, they usually discussed its visual gimmicks and scenic novelty.

At the Living Theatre, on the other hand, the audience was never held at arm's length; it remained at all times an involved participant in the play. I am referring to the period prior to the group's exile in Europe and subsequent affliction with self-inflated notions of its revolutionary, messianic mission. Before that prolonged psychotic episode, still in New York functioning in a small theatre on 14th Street, the Living Theatre was always intriguing and serious, even when its productions floundered. That period of the company's life is largely remembered today for new works—Jack Gelber's *The Connection*, Kenneth Brown's *The Brig*, plays by Paul Goodman and Jackson MacLow and William Carlos Williams—but it was also a vital center for reinterpreted classics, mostly modern: Pirandello's *Tonight We Improvise*, Brecht's *In the Jungle of Cities* and *Man Is Man*, even an

Ezra Pound *Women of Trachis*. What the Living Theatre brought to all these works was a passionate belief, largely influenced by Pirandello, that the theatre was not just an expensive pastime or amusement center, but a place where the spectator was co-extensive with the characters on stage, his destiny equally at stake. The Living Theatre was distinguished by an early effort to challenge the concept of theatre as "show," with the classics functioning as metaphors vital to our lives rather than hollow displays of histrionic posturing.

Not long after the Living Theatre went into European exile, there were signs that the baton of classical theatre was beginning to pass from New York. Ellis Rabb's APA seasons at the Lyceum could not survive Broadway economics. The Phoenix, after changing its location, abandoned its classical policy, then closed. Successive regimes at Lincoln Center were unable to satisfy demands, by press and public alike, for instant classical theatre companies, even when Herbert Blau and Jules Irving tried to reproduce at the Vivian Beaumont the groundbreaking work they had done at the Actor's Workshop in San Francisco. Two attempts to build a company by the Brooklyn Academy of Music—both with proven English directors—quickly succumbed to the same impatience. And even Papp began to mix his summer Shakespeare offerings with a variety of musicals aimed towards Broadway. Soon Lincoln Center would be plunged into darkness for six years and the appetite for classical theatre in New York would subside.

It remained very much alive, though, in the resident theatre movement from its very beginnings—and in both manifestations. While the Guthrie Theater in Minneapolis and the American Conservatory Theatre in San Francisco were trying to extend, often effectively, the English classical tradition in this country, other resident theatres around the country were trying to build with the native bricks first baked in the kilns of the New York Shakespeare Festival and the Living Theatre. Settling in San Francisco after efforts to start a company in Pittsburgh and Chicago, Ball designed an institution modeled on the symbiotic relationship between the Old Vic and the Old Vic School—a conservatory of acting connected to a functioning professional theatre and staffed by many of its members. It was a new idea for training in this country, though George Balanchine and Lincoln Kirstein had already created a similar institution at the New York City Ballet and School. The result of Ball's efforts are debatable. There are those, including myself, who believed that his technically oriented approach to acting and training resulted in a product too supine before English traditions. But his conservatory structure proved an extremely valuable model for those few resident theatres devoted to training, and it certainly influenced our work at Yale.

Still, the two major classical companies in this country in the early sixties—the Guthrie and ACT—however technically accomplished, were failing to develop anything radically new in dramatic interpretation, much less indigenous to American culture, and as a result, they were perceived by many to be retrograde and conservative. The first few seasons at the Guthrie had been accomplished; yet, even with fine designers, talented actors and Guthrie himself guiding the enterprise, "I rarely sensed," as I wrote after its first season, "that it was native, and to our manner born." When Guthrie left, even that initial energy evaporated, as the energy of the Old Vic had disappeared under Michael Benthall. As for ACT, after a promising start, it became afflicted with what I called "cuckoo-clock" acting, featuring absolute precision in the bows and fan work and considerable vacancy in the vision. For awhile, even though critics applauded the elegance of these English-influenced classical productions (as they continue to praise the high gloss of visiting English companies), it seemed as if the engines of classical theatre in this country were running out of steam.

There were some vestigial spasms, however, little twitches resembling those of the shattered broom in the Disney-Dukas *Sorcerer's Apprentice*, which suggested that the movement might reconstitute itself again and start to dance. First, there was Andre Gregory's work at the Theatre of the Living Arts in Philadelphia, particularly an outrageous *Endgame* set in a cage where Hamm and Clov broke into numbers from vaudeville and early movie comedies; then, there was Papp's garbled, irreverent 1967 *Hamlet* at New York's Public Theater; and, finally, there was Barbara Garson's politically irresponsible but highly volatile reworking of *Macbeth* as *MacBird*, an allegory of the Kennedy assassination (Richard Schechner's *Dionysus in 69* fell into the same category, though I liked it a lot less). These were extreme productions which inspired equally aggressive reactions. But whatever their failings, they shared a common premise: that classical theatre was a continuum of images and experiences and not simply an event frozen in the past.

The vitality of these productions encouraged me, overcoming professorial scruple, to write a manifesto called "No More Masterpieces"; it called for "no more piety, no more reverence, no more sanctimoniousness in the theatre." The secret agenda of this piece was an appeal for liberation from the shackles of the English tradition which now seemed artificially imposed and inhibiting to American talents. We needed the freedom to approach the most sacred text as though it had just been written, and that meant recreating not so much the original environment of the work as the original excitement which first informed it. Naturally, there were dangers inherent in this position, particularly in the area of directorial narcissism, but I assumed that the risks were worth it if the energies of classical plays were ever to be opened to American audiences.

This impulse motivated many of our classical attempts at the Yale Repertory Theatre in the late sixties and seventies, as well as finding expression in other pockets of the country. Classical plays were being reconstructed, metaphorized, rewritten, adapted and relocated with varying degrees of success. In a follow-up essay, "No More Masterpieces Revisited," I described the inevitable excesses, but it was nonetheless clear that people were groping towards a whole new form of classical reinterpretation. With Andrei Serban's imagistic adaptation of three Greek dramas, *Fragments of a Trilogy*, acted in a babel of languages including ancient and modern Greek and Swahili, the American theatre finally had a classical event that was freshly imagined, yet faithful to the impulses of the plays.

Serban was a Romanian, later a naturalized American. Soon other Romanians, including Liviu Ciulei (Serban's mentor), Andre Belgrader, and Lucian Pintilie, not to mention the brilliant Polish director, Andrzej Wajda, were to begin work in this country, resulting in a revolutionary approach to dramatic classics that is still reverberating throughout our theatre.

Critic Mike Steele wrote about the impact of these directors on our theatrical consciousness in an essay published in *American Theatre* called "The Romanian Connection." Their goals can be summed up by Pintilie's remark: "But even when I express an ostensibly radically different point of view about a play, I believe I remain faithful to it. The worst thing is to kneel before a lot of sacrosanct prejudices." It is this capacity to stand a classical work of art on its head without losing justification in the text that makes these directorial essays so dazzling and so powerful. Bringing an entirely original vision to hallowed works of literature, exhuming metaphors and themes that were never seen in the plays before, these directors have restored a high theatricality to the classics that keeps them vigorous and fresh.

The question arises, why should East European methods be considered any more relevant to American theatre than the reigning English conventions? Perhaps the answer is that the Romanians have been more responsive to the explorations of postmodernism. While British culture is essentially insular, postmodernism is international, indeed a powerful presence in our own country: Americans such as Robert Wilson, Richard Foreman, Lee Breuer, Joseph Chaikin, Laurie Anderson, Meredith Monk, among others, have all made important contributions to its aesthetic which have been absorbed in Europe (including Romania). True, our theatrical heritage has strong English roots which continue to be fed through visits by the Royal Shakespeare Company and Broadway's open door to English plays and actors. But our polyglot culture also includes theatre people who have European blood in their veins, which may account for the parallel influence of Stanislavsky and Meyerhold and Brecht. Thus, if Britain still holds sway over Establishment theatre (and public television), the alternative theatre is now using an international idiom. I believe it is in that postmodernist language that the most important classical interpretations are currently being written.

Admittedly, this language is essentially non-verbal—or at least, it tends to subordinate speech to visual concepts, music, projections, puppetry, rituals and emblematic acting. Since these are the traditional devices of experimental performance groups, it suggests that the development I have been describing is really a new union between the avant-garde and the classical theatre. And, as a matter of fact, around the same time that the counterculture finally made peace with the culture, experimental theatre directors began to collaborate with the resident theatre movement on an unprecedented number of classical projects.

For example, following his *Fragments of a Trilogy* at La Mama, Serban directed his controversial *Cherry Orchard* at Lincoln Center's Vivian Beaumont—the first of four directorial essays on Chekhov; then, between opera assignments abroad, he tried his hand at Strindberg's *Ghost Sonata*, Molière's *Sganarelle* and Gozzi's *The King Stag*, the latter three at the Yale Repertory and American Repertory Theatres. Ciulei, during his brief but brilliant stay in Minneapolis, transformed the Guthrie into a postmodern rather than British-influenced classical theatre, directing seminal productions of *The Tempest*, *Peer Gynt* and *A Midsummer Night's Dream*, after his productions of *Leonce and Lena* at the Arena Stage and *Spring's Awakening* at Juilliard. He also imported Pintilie to stage a revolutionary *Sea Gull* at the Guthrie, and to follow this with a trans-historical interpretation of *Tartuffe* which later went to the Arena. Around the same time, Lee Breuer of Mabou Mines, who had already made his reputation with startling Beckett productions, did a controversial production of *Lulu* at the American Repertory Theatre and, at the Brooklyn Academy of Music, a black version of *Oedipus at Colonus* renamed *Gospel at Colonus*. His Mabou Mines colleague, JoAnne Akalaitis, created a post-nuclear *Endgame* at the ART which (illustrating the pitfalls of reinterpreting living classical dramatists) provoked Beckett's agents enough to try to close it down; she is now preparing Genet's *The Balcony* for the coming season. Richard Foreman produced a version of Molière's *Don Juan* at the Guthrie and restaged it later for the New York Shakespeare Festival. And Robert Wilson, inspired by his collaboration on *the CIVIL warS* with the East German dramatist Heiner Müller—a postmodernist deeply influenced by Shakespeare and the Greeks—has been turning more and more towards the classics for his material. He has done a workshop version of *King Lear* at UCLA planned for full production later, and this season he staged Euripides' *Alcestis* at the ART, with additional material by Heiner Müller and Laurie Anderson.

This represents a tremendous richness of inspiration and imagination invested in classical plays which is certain to have a profound effect on classical theatre in America. It also suggests a unique merging of tradition and the individual talent that will unquestionably prove a significant challenge to Establishment Anglophilia. Of course, Shakespeare will always be an English dramatist, and one would no more want the theatre to abandon virtuoso acting than to see opera lose its divas. But given the fact that our own major actors have not been particularly faithful to the stage, much less to classical companies, and that our theatre impulses are both more conceptual and more emotional than those of Britain, this represents an important alternative approach which meets our current needs superbly. It demythologizes classical plays so that they can be seen afresh; it acknowledges the current theory that dramatic works are more than verbal constructs; it subordinates elocution and style (never American strengths) in favor of imaginative ensemble playing; it challenges the audience to think and feel rather than sit back passively in awed admiration; it exploits our native genius for music, movement and design; and it relates these plays to the myths and mysteries of our own historical experience. British theatre methods will probably remain central to certain strains in the American theatrical heritage, and British polish and dazzle will always be admired. But this new merging of inspirational directors, imaginative designers and resident theatre acting ensembles—of classical theatre and the avant-garde—is one of the most promising developments in the history of our stage, and augurs an exciting, unpredictable future.

Robert Brustein is the founder and artistic director of the American Repertory Theatre in Cambridge, Mass. He was dean of the Yale School of Drama from 1966 to 1979, where he founded and served as artistic director of the Yale Repertory Theatre. He has been the theatre critic of The New Republic *since 1959 and is the author of seven books on the theatre, the most recent being a memoir of his Yale years,* Making Scenes. *Brustein has worked in the theatre as a director, actor and writer for over 35 years, and is the recipient of the George Jean Nathan Award in criticism and the Elliott Norton Award for excellence in theatre.*

PLAYWRIGHTS' VOICES

Gerald Weales

By 1960, most of the pre-World War II playwrights had fallen into silence—had died or withdrawn from the theatre. There were new plays from S. N. Behrman, Lillian Hellman, Sidney Kingsley and Irwin Shaw in the early 1960s, but they were largely unsuccessful works, aesthetically and commercially. Tennessee Williams and Arthur Miller were generally accepted as America's most important practicing playwrights, although Miller, a little out of practice, had not been heard from since the publication of his *Collected Plays* in 1957. He would return to the theatre with two plays in 1964, *After the Fall* and *Incident at Vichy*, which seemed to grow as much from a generalized concept of human guilt as from observation (even though *Fall* was heavily autobiographical).

Since then, Miller has written, somewhat fitfully, for the stage, but later plays lack the force and the immediacy of his early work. *The Price* (1968) is the exception, not so much for the central conflict between the brothers—an echo of so many Miller works—as for what seems to me a major theme of the play: the failure of talk as therapy. It is also notable for the figure of the aged furniture dealer, a beautifully conceived comic character unlike anything else in the Miller canon. Miller's best and most moving writing of the past few years is in *Salesman in Beijing* (1984), his prose account of the production of *Death of a Salesman* in China, but that is a work *about* the theatre and not for it.

Tennessee Williams's last widely acclaimed play, *The Night of the Iguana*, was produced in New York in 1961. During the following two decades, despite the constant prospect of physical or spiritual collapse, Williams continued to write new plays and rewrite old ones (as in the 1974 revision of *Cat on a Hot Tin Roof*). He experimented with new forms in *Slapstick Tragedy* (1966) and *The Two-Character Play* (1967), and turned again to his own past in *Vieux Carré* (1978) and *A Lovely Sunday for Crève Coeur* (1979). Sometimes, as in *Something Cloudy, Something Clear* (1981), he did both at once. At his death in 1983, he left a vast body of post *Iguana* work—much of it developed at a distance from Broadway, at such theatres as New York's Cocteau Repertory and Chicago's Goodman Theatre—which deserves careful critical reconsideration.

Other celebrated playwrights of the 1940s and 1950s, such as William Inge, Robert Anderson, Arthur Laurents, Garson Kanin, Paddy Chayefsky, William Gibson, found, as Miller and Williams did, that the American theatre was changing. With a few exceptions, such as Anderson's 1967 evening of one-act comedies entitled *You Know I Can't Hear You When the Water's Running*, Broadway success eluded this group in the 1960s, and they turned to Off Broadway and the newly burgeoning regional theatres, to musicals, to movies, to fiction.

There was a new generation of playwrights at their heels. Neil Simon quickly became a staple on Broadway with his oddly bleak comedies and, more recently, with his sentimental reconstructions of his own past, *Brighton Beach Memoirs* (1983) and *Biloxi Blues* (1985). An even more revealing indication of the changing structure of our theatre was the emergence in the early sixties of Off Broadway playwrights, including Edward Albee, Jack Gelber, Jack Richardson, Arthur Kopit, Arnold Weinstein, Murray Schisgal, William Hanley and Frank D. Gilroy. Not all of them had staying power (Richardson, one of the most interesting voices among them, has had no plays produced since the 1960s), and some of their once highly praised plays have lost a bit of their luster over the years. Yet, the initial reception of their work indicated that the phrase "American dramatist" was no longer synonomous with "Broadway playwright." Many of them went on to Broadway but, like those who would later emerge from tiny Off-Off Broadway houses, they worked on or Off Broadway, in or out of New York as the occasion demanded.

Albee, whose *Zoo Story* reached New York by way of Berlin in 1960, became the most famous of the group, particularly after the Broadway production of *Who's Afraid of Virginia Woolf?* opened in 1962. "Miller and Williams," the thumbnail version of postwar American drama, became "Miller, Williams and Albee." Like his older colleagues, Albee became a victim of his early success. *Virginia Woolf*, which is probably still his best play, haunts his substantial output of the past twenty years as Miller's *Salesman* and Williams's *A Streetcar Named Desire* do their later work. Albee's most recent plays have been too casually dismissed. *The Man Who Had Three Arms* (1983), for example, is more than a display of the playwright's anger at being a victim of critical nostalgia; it has something substantial to say about celebrity in the United States.

If Albee is the most celebrated of these Off Broadway graduates, Arthur Kopit is proving the most interestingly unpredictable. The New York success of *Oh, Dad, Poor Dad, Mama's Hung You in the Closet and I'm Feelin' So Sad* in 1962 gave him a reputation for facile wit that took a long time to shake. It is now obvious that his odd amalgam of farce, parody and deep seriousness, best exemplified in *Indians* (1968) and *End of the World* (1984), marks him as one of the most imaginative political playwrights of the period. And his *Wings* (1978) is an exquisitely made reminder, if one is needed, that there is no easily recognizable Kopit formula.

While Albee and company were solidifying or abandoning their positions in the American theatre, yet another crop of new playwrights was attracting attention, this time Off-Off Broadway and in the regional theatres. The early one-act plays of Sam Shepard, one of the best and most prolific of the second wave of the 1960s, were performed at Theatre Genesis, the Albee-Barr-Wilder Playwrights Unit, Caffe Cino and the Judson Poets' Theatre in New York. As his *Red Cross* (1966) so beautifully indicates, these were attempts to create dramatic events without the conventions of plot and characterization, holding on only to the suspense and the intensity of received drama. With *La Turista* (1967) at the American Place Theatre and *Operation Sidewinder* (1970) at Lincoln Center, Shepard began to reach larger audiences. After spending a few years in England in the early seventies, where *The Tooth of Crime* (1972) and *Geography of a Horse Dreamer* (1974) were first performed, Shepard established a fruitful and continuing relationship with the Magic Theatre in San Francisco. In collaboration with its artistic director John Lion and director Robert Woodruff, most of his recent work originated there. His newest work, *A Lie of the Mind*, premiered in December 1985, not at the Magic but back on the East Coast.

Plot and character have come back into his work, somewhat obliquely, in *Buried Child* (1978), *True West* (1980) and *Fool for Love* (1983), and he has become a staple of the American theatre, widely performed around the country, as attractive to conventional producers as to experimental ones. His preoccupation with automobiles, movies, popular music and the myths of the American West give continuity to his work. Throughout his early and late plays he has displayed a remarkable verbal ingenuity, creating both aria-like set speeches and word combats more powerful than physical confrontation.

Although very different in style and theatrical technique, Ronald Ribman, most of whose works originated at the American Place Theatre in New York, is Shepard's equal in eloquence and inventiveness. His plays are richly allusive, as good poetry is, his verbal and visual images echoing and playing off of one another within each individual work. His thematic preoccupation, from *Harry, Noon and Night* (1965) to *Buck* (1983), has been with the way in which people are trapped by situations that, in most cases, they help create. *Cold Storage* (1977) is unusual among the Ribman plays because it is a song of life rising out of the terminal ward of a hospital; it is a fine example of the way in which Ribman manages to mesh form and content. The voices in *Cold Storage*, particularly that of the dazzlingly articulate Parmigian, become the response of life to death. It is the wholeness of *Cold Storage*, art subsuming idea, that allows the play to avoid the sentimentality that infects so many death-acceptance plays, even those as ambitious as Michael Cristofer's *The Shadow Box* (1975) and William M. Hoffman's *As Is* (1985).

There is such variety among the playwrights of which Shepard and Ribman here stand as examples that they can be considered a group only by their having been first performed in the same decade. They range from the high camp of Michael McClure and Ronald Tavel to the more serious playfulness of Maria Irene Fornes and Jean-Claude van Itallie. They are often political, either overtly (Megan Terry) or subtly (A.R. Gurney, Jr.). They appeal to audiences as wide as the one Lanford Wilson reaches and as special as that served by Murray Mednick. Julie Bovasso, Rosalyn Drexler, Tom Eyen, John Guare, Israel Horovitz, Romulus Linney, Terrence McNally, Mark Medoff, Leonard Melfi, Michael Weller—the list is as long as it is various.

The stage has always been tempting to writers in other genres, as the trials and tribulations of Henry James as playwright indicate. The 1960s were particularly rich in interlopers and some of them, like cartoonist Jules Feiffer, settled down and became part of the resident population. Feiffer, who has never abandoned his drawing board, began with short plays that resembled his cartoons. From *Little Murders* (1966) to *Grownups* (1981), he has retained his satirical impulse, his ear for social and psychological cliches and his itchy sense of both the small and the cosmic indignities visited on us daily. Historian Martin Duberman turned to the stage with *In White America* (1963), using documentary material to chronicle the history of racial prejudice in this country and, having once tested the boards, he stayed to write plays on more personal themes. Poets as various as Robert Lowell, Kenneth Koch, Edwin Honig (who has also done fine translations of Calderon), James Schevill and William Alfred were attracted to the theatre; Lowell's trilogy *The Old Glory* (1964) proved—particularly in *Benito Cereno*—that historical settings and borrowings from Hawthorne and Melville could speak directly to audiences in a troubled decade. Among the transplanted novelists, who included Bruce Jay Friedman, Joseph Heller and Mark Harris, the most interesting were Saul Bellow, with his disheveled and very plummy philosophical farce *The Last Analysis* (1964), and John Hawkes, whose enigmatic *The Questions* (1966) is the most intriguing of his handful of plays.

One of the most important developments in American theatre in the 1960s was the emergence of the black playwright as something more than an anomaly on the American stage. Lorraine Hansberry's *A Raisin in the Sun* had appeared and won a Pulitzer Prize in 1959, but it was in 1964, with James Baldwin's *Blues for Mister Charlie* and LeRoi Jones's *Dutchman* that black playwrights announced unequivocally that they would voice the concerns and—in that decade—the militancy of the American black. Black theatre had barely become visible when it began to divide between those artists, like the founders of the Negro Ensemble Company, who hoped to reach as wide an American audience as possible and those, like Jones (newly named Imamu Amiri Baraka), who saw black theatre as a separatist operation, black art for the black community. Whatever the value of the latter for blacks themselves, it has been companies like the Negro Ensemble Company that have fed American drama not only by bringing black playwrights into mainstream theatre but by introducing black playgoers into audiences that were once almost exclusively white.

The black label, which the dramatists wear proudly, is misleading because it suggests a sameness that cannot apply in a group that has produced Adrienne Kennedy's allusive *Cities in Bezique* (1969), Negro Ensemble artistic director Douglas Turner Ward's funny *Day of Absence* (1965), Ed Bullins's sadly celebratory *In the Wine Time* (1968) and Ntozake Shange's sometimes lyrical, sometimes declamatory *For Colored Girls who have Considered Suicide/When the Rainbow is Enuf* (1976). Add names like Alice Childress, Lonne Elder, III, Ossie Davis, Melvin Van Peebles, Joseph A. Walker, Richard Wesley, Ron Milner, Philip Hayes Dean, Leslie Lee and Samm-Art Williams, and the variety becomes even more impressive. Charles Fuller's development as a dramatist is an indication of the way not only black theatre in general, but its individual playwrights, have grown in the past fifteen years. Fuller's talent was obvious in his play *The Rise*, which Ed Bullins included in his 1969 anthology *New Plays from the Black Theatre*. But that early account of the Marcus Garvey movement, in which black protest and character development mixed uncomfortably, scarcely hinted at the complexity and dramatic power that his later plays, *Zooman and the Sign* (1980) and the Pulitzer-winning *A Soldier's Play* (1981) would have. These plays were nurtured in and first performed by the Negro Ensemble Company, which toured the latter play extensively before it was transformed into a well-received movie featuring many of the NEC actors in their original roles.

The 1970s saw a growing interest in women's theatre, gay theatre and—more recently—Asian-American theatre. Insofar as these movements are the occasion to explore themes and milieus insufficiently treated in American drama, they can enrich the American repertoire; insofar as they are excluding mechanisms, separatist in intent, they can be of value only to special audiences. The former seems generally to be the case in practice. The playwrights included in an anthology like Honor Moore's *The New Women's Theatre* (1972)—women like Tina Howe, Ruth Wolff and even Myrna Lamb (the co-founder of the New Feminist Repertory Theatre)—do not write for a sexually segregated audience. When Harvey Fierstein's schmaltzer, *Torch Song Trilogy*, born sequentially at La Mama E.T.C., arrived on Broadway in 1982, it made gay life so acceptable a subject for conventional audiences that serious plays like William Hoffman's *As Is*, originally produced at Circle Repertory Company, and Larry Kramer's *The Normal Heart*, first seen at the New York Shakespeare Festival, could present gayness matter-of-factly and get on with their real concerns: the political implications of the AIDS epidemic and the anguish of learning to accept death.

Among Asian-American playwrights, David Henry Hwang has deservedly received critical approbation for his dance-drama *The Dance and the Railroad* (1981), and he should have had it as well for the underappreciated *Family Devotions*, produced later that same season. Both plays premiered at the New York Shakespeare Festival which, over the years, has served as a home for the work of many minority artists, among them the Puerto Rican playwright Miguel Piñero. There is a kind of continental divide in Hispanic theatre; Piñero's *Short Eyes* proved more successful on the East Coast while Luis Valdez's *Zoot Suit*, which grew out of the Mexican-American experience in Los Angeles, reached an audience at the Mark Taper Forum that it failed to find on Broadway.

Many more American dramatists emerged during the 1970s and '80s. Although such playwrights as Thomas Babe, Tom Cole, Christopher Durang, Amlin Gray, Beth Henley, Albert Innaurato, Wendy Kesselman, Emily Mann, Dennis McIntyre, John Ford Noonan, Ted Tally and Wendy Wasserstein have their admirers (and sometimes I am in their number), the three playwrights who most interest me from this period are David Rabe, David Mamet and Marsha Norman. Rabe made his name with *The Basic Training of Pavlo Hummel* and *Sticks and Bones*, first produced at Joseph Papp's New York Shakespeare Festival. This pair of plays earned the limiting label "anti-war" when they were produced in 1971, just as the sentiment against the war in Vietnam was beginning to build rapidly. They *are* anti-war plays, of course, but as they and his later *Streamers* (Long Wharf Theatre, 1976) indicate, their primary thematic concern is the ways in which people perceive, and how their misperceptions—dictated by individual and group rigidities—lead to personal, social and political disaster. More recently, in *Hurlyburly* (1984), Rabe has shown again what the sergeants in *Streamers* indicated: that he can use sardonic comedy to very serious ends.

Hurlyburly made its way first to Off Broadway and then to Broadway from the Goodman Theatre in Chicago, which has also served as an artistic home base for David Mamet in recent years. A Chicago native, Mamet's works and his life in the theatre have remained closely connected to that city. If ways of seeing define Rabe's characters, then ways of talking dictate the actions of Mamet's. Although one might be tempted to reduce plays like *American Buffalo* (1975) and *Glengarry Glen Ross* (1983) to overt criticism of the American business ethic, the most interesting thing about them (and about *Sexual Perversity in Chicago* [1974] and *Edmond* [1982]) is Mamet's understanding of how patterns of language become patterns of thought, which in turn become patterns of action.

Marsha Norman, the most celebrated discovery in the Actors Theatre of Louisville's continuing search for new playwrights, does not have the body of work that Rabe and Mamet have, but in the plays she has written, particularly *Getting Out* (1977) and *'night Mother* (1982), she demonstrates remarkable technical skills and a deep concern with the human need to survive or escape the traps—the lives—imposed by self or society.

It is a commonplace of American theatre history that Eugene O'Neill got his start in Provincetown, that Tennessee Williams often worked out his plays in early productions in Italy or Florida, and that even the most conventional Broadway playwrights used the pre-Broadway road tours to polish their products. Yet these playwrights did not really find their place in our national repertoire until they had received the imprimatur of Broadway. That is no longer the case. American playwrights are truly American these days, establishing reputations in once un-likely corners of the country. Broadway now offers very few new plays and almost no serious ones. New York is still the richest theatre city in the country, but it is a marketing center now, and not a manufacturing one. American drama seems to me healthier for the change.

Gerald Weales, who teaches drama in the English Department of the University of Penn-sylvania, won the George Jean Nathan Award for Dramatic Criticism, 1964–65, for his reviews in Drama Survey. *Formerly the drama reviewer for* The Reporter, *he is currently critic for* Commonweal *and contributes an annual American Theatre Watch to* The Georgia Review. *His books on American theatre include* American Drama Since World War II; The Jumping-Off Place, American Drama in the 1960s; *the University of Minnesota Press pam-phlet* Tennessee Williams; *and* Clifford Odets, Playwright, *recently reissued by Methuen. He is editor of the Viking critical editions of* Death of a Salesman *and* The Crucible. *His most recent book, published in fall 1985 by University of Chicago Press, is* Canned Goods as Caviar, American Film Comedy of the 1930s.

'HOW A THEATRE MEANS'

John Dillon

It's a street that looks more like a battle zone in Beirut than a thoroughfare in a Midwest metropolis. But this section of Detroit's Woodrow Wilson Avenue is mostly populated with gutted buildings and boarded-up windows. An exodus has left behind scars, but in the midst of the rubble stands hope turned into brick and mortar. The graceful new facade that looks out of place here is probably meant to, for the building is the visible symbol of the faith the Detroit Repertory Theatre has that its community will be reborn. Its new construction stands as firm as the company's commitment to color- and gender-blind casting.

The theatres in this volume are the blood and muscle of the American theatre. As artists, we say what we have to say first and foremost through the quality and immediacy of our work. As professionals that's the judgment we invite. But the work itself is not the limit of our meaning or our impact, as the Detroit Rep demonstrates.

The Oregon Shakespearean Festival is, like its fellow in Detroit, an act of faith in its community, this time a small town hundreds of miles from a major metropolis. But the enterprise has been so successful, its program so full, its audience so large that Ashland now defines *its* identity as much by the Festival as the other way around. Here's a rural Oregon town that for fifty years has immersed itself in Shakespeare without needing the name "Stratford" to inspire its theatre's invention.

Most of our society's new images are manufactured by the mass media, and that leads to the homogenization of our culture. The episode of *Dynasty* seen in Sarasota is the same one aired three hours later in Seattle. But in creating *Zoot Suit* in the late seventies, Luis Valdez and the Mark Taper Forum brought forth a drama that examined racial conflict in their own L.A. community during World War II. The play took a style of dress, the zoot suit of the forties, and made it a theatrical image to illuminate the prejudice against—and the pride of—that city's Chicanos. The production expanded the Forum's Hispanic audience while entering into the dialogue that is necessary if Los Angeles is to understand its past and present. And *Zoot Suit* is only one of many such projects commissioned by theatre companies in an effort to explore the special historical, social and/or spiritual roots of their regions.

When San Francisco's Eureka Theatre asked Emily Mann to write a play about the tragic murder of that city's mayor George Moscone and its first openly gay city supervisor Harvey Milk by ex-policeman and ex-councilman Dan White, they saw the creation of a theatre piece that could help explain a community's pain while raising larger issues about gay rights and our legal system. The result, *Execution of Justice*, transforms daily headlines into pattern and metaphor. By immersing herself in the life and history of one community, Mann created a play that has gone on to move audiences in communities from coast to coast.

Many would prefer to call themselves "resident" or "experimental," or most anything other than "regional." A work by a Manhattan playwright about Manhattan and presented by a Manhattan theatre wouldn't be attacked for being provincial, though a similar project in Little Rock or Los Angeles might be. But this is a nation that gathers its strength from its diversity, and plays like *Zoot Suit* or *Execution of Justice* can help reflect that which is different (for good or ill) about their own communities while speaking to audiences elsewhere.

By recruiting minority actors living in the Bay Area for her production of *Kingdom Come*, Berkeley Repertory Theatre artistic director Sharon Ott transformed Amlin Gray's drama about Norwegian pioneers in the Midwest into a metaphor for the immigrant experience that created the Bay Area's own rich racial mix. Some audience members might have been jolted to see black, Hispanic and Asian actors portraying blonde, blue-eyed Norwegian settlers, but the point of Ott's casting was to remind us of the play's larger meaning: that the experiences my grandparents had in coming to these shores are probably not all that dissimilar from those of your forebearers, or even from those of people arriving here today from the world's troubled corners. All this, of course, raises a bigger issue: Does a play like *Our Town* portray only the emotional life of White New Englanders? The answer, of course, is "no," but how can we truly reflect the wonderful multicultural nature of our society if we don't embrace that fact in our art?

Productions, then, like plays themselves, can become mirrors of their communities. And sometimes, angry controversy reminds us of how different regions can be. Christopher Durang's *Sister Mary Ignatius Explains It All for You* and Lanford Wilson's *Hot l Baltimore* have been produced often, and successfully, around the country. Yet when *Sister Mary* was performed in St. Louis and *Hot l* in Anchorage, furor engulfed both productions. Charges of "anti-Catholic" in Missouri and "obscene" in Alaska captured headlines and threatened the respective theatres' public funding. A play's acceptance in one city is no guarantee of its acceptance anywhere else. A "safe" choice in one city can bring down the wrath of lawmakers and would-be censors in another.

In the world of dance it's not uncommon for the identity of a company to be synonymous with its choreographer. But even though Adrian Hall's style is as much a part of the identity of the theatre company he founded as is that of Twyla Tharp to the dance company bearing her name, Hall's theatre is called "Trinity Repertory" and not "The Adrian Hall." In fact, I know of only one U.S. troupe named after its founder (The Guthrie), while dozens, including my own, have embraced the names of their communities in their monikers. But then most of us *chose* to locate outside of New York, to fill the countryside with theatre companies. Decentralization was part of the original game plan, after all.

One measure of the success of the not-for-profit theatre movement (though by no means the crucial one) is its longevity, symbolized by TCG's 25th birthday. That survival has led, inevitably, to the passing of the torch to a new generation, a second generation of artistic directors that has been dubbed "the inheritors." As we walk into our new theatres (new only to us, of course), we also walk into a history and a set of expectations. If the community cherishes its theatre as an important cultural institution, then its survival, no matter what, is an important local issue. Of course, *we're* not cherished—in fact we're not even known yet— and there's some proving to be done before our personal survival resembles anything like a local issue. Further, the new artistic director is often greeted by a board of directors, a managing director and a staff with long associations and a style of working together. And we're rarely natives to the town to which we've been called. What this theatre is to the community, how it's helped (or failed to help) that community understand itself may be unfamiliar to us. How then are we to remake this institution, to forge for it an identity as unique as that created by its founder? What, in short, are the inheritors inheriting? Do we inherit a corporate name, an empty building, a group of artists, a tradition? Are we being asked to remodel or just rearrange the furniture? And if we take too long trying to figure out if the new sofa should go by the window or the door, will we find ourselves out on the street? We *expect* Merce Cunningham's work to differ from Twyla Tharp's, but what should be the differences among the MRTs in Massachusetts, Misssouri and Wisconsin? Will the board of directors need convincing that the theatre company even *ought* to have an individual identity, be guided by a vision? Such a vision may seem just so much excess baggage to the "main" task of getting six popular plays mounted each year. (We all know the season: a Shakespearean comedy; a cheerful small-cast musical; a rib-tickling New York hit; a sweet old American chestnut; a lighthearted, Broadway-bound, small-cast, single-set, to-be-announced new play; and of course *A Christmas Carol*.) Are "the inheritors" to be the great homogenizers?

A friend of mine once had lunch with Picasso. As they talked, Picasso restlessly fiddled with paper napkins and doodled on his paper placemat. The activity seemed random and incidental. But when the lunch was over, my friend observed that the great artist had transformed the whole table into one big original Picasso! Great artists will always create with whatever is at hand, and the future of the American theatre will stand or fall on the strength and originality of the work itself. But there are, nevertheless, other ways "how a theatre can mean," that are also potent sources of dramatic impact. How we mean can be a function of where and when, as well as what. How well "the inheritors" wrestle with that issue will form part of the judgment that someday must be made as to whether the longevity of the theatres in this volume has provided a great opportunity or an artistic dead end.

But in the meantime, where to put that new sofa?

John Dillon has served as artistic director of the Milwaukee Repertory Theater since 1977. He started his career as a member of Joseph Chaikin's Open Theatre and has directed in a score of the country's not-for-profit theatres. Internationally, Dillon has staged Death of a Salesman *in Tokyo,* Detective Story *in Manchester and will soon direct* Our Town *in Singapore.*

THE EXPERIMENTERS

Robert Marx

In the 1960s a new generation of American theatre artists broke away from the traditional Broadway mold. This radical change had its most visible sign in the emergence of professional regional theatres, but those newborn, essentially mainstream organizations were not the only elements of a national theatrical rebellion. During that same turbulent decade there also appeared a whole landscape of original experimental performance ensembles and artists. These were companies rooted largely but not exclusively in New York City's Off-Off Broadway realm, and this avant-garde community—a wildly disjointed, fragile, passionate and imaginative field—eventually developed into the most internationally significant and influential arena in the whole of the American theatre.

Even a partial laundry list of artists, companies and productions still conjures the images of a new, vital and entirely American kind of theatricality: The Becks and the Living Theatre, Ellen Stewart's La Mama E.T.C., the Actor's Workshop in San Francisco, Caffe Cino, Andre Gregory's Manhattan Project, the Open Theatre, Second City, Judson Poet's Theatre, Bread and Puppet Theatre, El Teatro Campesino, San Francisco Mime Troupe, Free Southern Theatre, Sam Shepard, Maria Irene Fornes, Al Carmines, Joseph Chaikin, Lanford Wilson, Megan Terry, Jean-Claude van Itallie, Luis Valdez, Richard Schechner, Mabou Mines, Robert Wilson, *The Connection, Paradise Now, Dionysus in 69, Deafman Glance, Viet Rock, Dynamite Tonight!, The Mutation Show, La Turista, MacBird, Promenade, In Circles, Slaveship, Alice in Wonderland, The Serpent, America Hurrah.*

That's scarcely the tip of the iceberg and admittedly, it's a most arbitrary selection. But even though so many of these plays and productions do not form an American repertoire in the sense of possible revival, collectively they are the aesthetic foundation for much of what gives today's American theatre its most indigenous and contemporary forms.

"Experimental" is a relative term. The play choices of Herbert Blau and Jules Irving at the Actor's Workshop in San Francisco, which in the early 1960s were a model of adventurousness, would seem fairly conventional today: *The Caucasian Chalk Circle* and *The Birthday Party* have long since moved into the modern classic category. But at a time when most regional theatres were doing the certified Great Plays, the experimental groups established a beachhead in the USA for the largely unknown works of Beckett, Genet and Ionesco, as well as the new generation of American playwrights. When the Actor's Workshop took its production of *Waiting for Godot* to San Quentin prison, both the event and the play were on the very fringe of our theatrical culture.

In the beginning, there was the Living Theatre. No matter how one chooses to trace a history of the recent American avant-garde, all roads lead back to the Becks. Julian Beck and Judith Malina had been producing new and unusual plays in various lofts, apartments and Off Broadway theatres since the early 1950s, when on July 15,1959, they opened Jack Gelber's *The Connection*. A play with jazz concerning drug addiction, Gelber's unnerving script and the nightmare realism of Beck's staging set a new standard for graphic American social drama. Working in repertory with a company of unknown actors, the Becks continued to thrive as this country's most adventurous theatre—one of intellectual force and influential style—until the IRS shut them down for tax evasion in 1964. After this came two decades of exile, mostly in Europe and South America, mixed with a few controversial American tours.

The Living came to define theatrical daring and guts. Although the Off Broadway movement in New York was already thriving with the growth of such organizations as Circle in the Square, it was the Living Theatre that served as the experimental lodestone. After leaving the USA in 1964, the company's work changed into something much more improvised and political—its new style ignited a hugely controversial American tour in 1968—but in its original form, the Living Theatre established the notion of a distinctly American experimental performance ensemble. This was something quite different from the Actor's Studio naturalism that dominated our mainstream theatre, and the Living moved American drama forward as a political/social force in ways that had not been seen since the time of *Waiting for Lefty*. The Becks also used all forms of progressive performance in their productions. They engaged the most vital choreographers, painters, poets and composers of the New York arts world for collaborative projects that would have no ongoing counterpart again until the Brooklyn Academy of Music's Next Wave Festivals were launched in the 1980s.

This very freewheeling environment that embraced the whole of New York's avant-garde extended far beyond the walls of the Living Theatre's Greenwich Village loft: The Caffe Cino was only the most successful of many coffee houses where new plays were staged; Theatre Genesis emerged at St. Mark's Church-in-the-Bouwerie, while Al Carmines (newly appointed minister of the Judson Memorial Church) founded the Judson Poets Theatre; La Mama, "dedicated to the playwright and all forms of the theatre," as Ellen Stewart still announces before each performance, also began its nomadic existence in and out of New York City basements and storefronts. Before long, the legendary Off-Off Broadway movement was in full swing.

As with regional theatres in the early stages of their growth, there was a steady drive for ensemble technique. If the regional houses pursued a basically Anglophile view of the classics (one encouraged by the beacon of the Guthrie Theater), the experimentalists were prompted by the Living Theatre and further inspired by the essays of Artaud (*The Theatre and Its Double*) and Grotowski (*Towards a Poor Theatre*). Those books, along with Peter Brook's *The Empty Space* were required 1960s reading for the theatre community.

Soon, the drive for ensemble acting in scripted drama led to the performer-based, company-created theatre piece. These became an almost universal norm, led once again by the Living Theatre when it returned to America in 1968 with anarchic productions of *Paradise Now* and *Frankenstein*.

Even before the Living's controversial return, the Open Theatre had emerged as the most significant of the new ensembles. Under Joseph Chaikin's direction (Chaikin was a former Living Theatre actor), the Open Theatre developed its own company style based upon specific acting techniques that Chaikin later explored in his book *The Presence of the Actor*. With productions using only minimal props or settings, the focus was always on the actor's fluid body and a physical matrix of human sound and movement. Founded in 1963, the company's early work covered a range of literary styles encompassing Brecht, T. S. Eliot, Ionesco, and others, but there were also resident playwrights like Jean-Claude van Itallie (*America Hurrah*) and Megan Terry (*Viet Rock*) who were responsible for the texts of some of the group's most important productions. Even so, the Open Theatre's major impact was its deployment of the actor as creator; it continually explored the psyches of company members in such pieces as *The Mutation Show*.

Both the artistic achievement and theatrical fashion of performer-based ensembles led to the birth of other idiosyncratic companies. In 1967, Richard Schechner founded the Performance Group along Grotowski-inspired lines, with a strong directorial emphasis on environmental theatre. The mercurial Andre Gregory launched regional theatres in Philadelphia and Los Angeles, but it was with the New York-based Manhattan Project that he came into his own element. His *Alice in Wonderland* became a celebrated example of classic material reinterpreted through actor improvisations. The company's subsequent production of Beckett's *Endgame* pointed the way towards the kind of directorial revisionism that embraces the script as a "found object."

In the 1960s, Gregory was the only artist rooted in the experimental community who also served as a bridge to the regional theatres (and—briefly—to Broadway). But Andre Gregory, like so many of his colleagues, tended to avoid scripted plays in favor of theatre pieces dominated almost entirely by conceptualist directors and actor improvisations. Playwrights usually emerged elsewhere, either in regional theatres or in new playwrights' institutions such as the New York Shakespeare Festival's Public Theater. There were always exceptions, like the New York premiere of Sam Shepard's *The Tooth of Crime* staged by Richard Schechner with the Performance Group. But more and more, the idea of experimental theatre came to be associated with the concept of collective performance ensembles.

Some of the most celebrated groups were specifically political theatres. The San Francisco Mime Troupe redefined the whole idea of American street theatre in its sharp satires against the Vietnam war. Also in California, Luis Valdez founded El Teatro Campesino as a company dedicated to the heritage and lives of Hispanic farm workers. With the direct support of Cesar Chavez, the Campesino has helped bring national attention to the experiences of migrant workers. The peace imagery and anti-war pageants of the Bread and Puppet Theatre were probably New York's most overtly moving and emotional artistic response to all the political upheavals of the 1960s.

Much of the initial recognition for this entire range of experimental work came from Europe. Overall, the American critical reception was uncomprehending or condescending and there was little acceptance beyond the core Off-Off Broadway audience and the pages of the *Village Voice*. But the Living Theatre had already enjoyed a successful European tour as early as 1961. *The Connection* appeared in Paris about the same time as an official State Department tour of *The Skin of Our Teeth* starring Helen Hayes, and the French embraced "*le Living*" as both an artistic and anti-establishment hit.

The triumph of *The Connection*'s European tour not only led the way for the

Living Theatre's own exile, but for a steady flow of American experimental theatre and dance out of the USA and into the European festival circuit. By the mid-1970s, hardly any American experimental company would plan a season without including a European residency, and the cream of the American roster (Robert Wilson, Richard Foreman, Merce Cunningham, Meredith Monk and others) were given direct subsidies—or even their own theatres—through various European ministries of culture.

La Mama went abroad for the first time in 1965 with a repertoire that included *America Hurrah*. Despite efforts by American officialdom to shut the production down, European sponsors kept the tour alive and, in subsequent years, Ellen Stewart emerged as a major international force. La Mama became this country's only two-way street for theatre. It was (and is) not only a home for American experimental companies and a sponsor of their foreign tours, but a welcome American base for theatres from all over the world. Only at La Mama can one experience contemporary European, African, Latin and Asian work side by side with the Americans, and it was at La Mama that we had our first look at the work of such directors as Tadeusz Kantor, Tadashi Suzuki and Andrei Serban.

Serban arrived at La Mama in 1969, and stayed for most of the next decade. With Elizabeth Swados as his composer/collaborator, Serban grew from strength to strength. In particular, their adaptations of *Medea*, *Elektra*, and *The Trojan Women* (which were eventually staged consecutively as *Fragments of a Trilogy*) became a new high water mark for mythic interpretation and sheer directorial invention.

At La Mama, Serban had an ongoing repertory of productions. (*Medea* was kept alive in one version or another for almost five years.) Drawing actors from many of New York's experimental companies, Serban assembled the virtuoso Great Jones Repertory Company. The group was named after the location of La Mama's rehearsal hall on Great Jones Street, and few people who were there for those seasons will ever forget Priscilla Smith's shattering performances in the Greek plays, Brecht, Shakespeare and Chekhov. Serban has moved on now to a distinguished career as a director of both plays and operas. Among his assignments have been productions at the New York Shakespeare Festival, American Conservatory Theatre, Yale Repertory Theatre, the Guthrie Theater and American Repertory Theatre, but the La Mama period was his most inventive and inspiring.

By the 1970s, when American experimental theatre became a steady presence in Europe, no artist had more impact than Robert Wilson. Born in Texas, Wilson studied art in New York and became attracted to the theatre. One of his first theatre jobs was designing the puppets for *America Hurrah* at La Mama. He soon branched out into his own surrealistic style, a painterly theatre reminiscent of the French surrealists. The monumental productions of the seventies (*Deafman Glance*, *The Life and Times of Sigmund Freud*, *The Life and Times of Josef Stalin*) were dominated by massive stage images, choreographed movement, light, sound and mysterious texts that seemed like Gertrude Stein prose filtered through modern American vernacular. Unlike the intimate, rigorously physicalized performance ensembles, Wilson's work was loose and spectacular. With scores of actors—sometimes hundreds—his productions could last for hours or days, and he required vast proscenium stages for his *tableaux vivants*.

Like many others who gravitated towards the realm of experimental dance and fine art, Wilson found a home at the Brooklyn Academy of Music. BAM remains our most adventurous theatre for large-scale, visionary and collaborative performance projects. But even BAM could not offer Wilson sufficient financial support, and with massive subsidies offered from France, Italy, and Germany,

Wilson began to create his pieces in Europe. Since the Avignon Festival's premiere of *Einstein on the Beach* in 1976, he has been essentially an emigre artist. The situation may change, though. He has always returned here for smaller shows, and he is now reviving some major European productions in New York and Boston.

The impact of Wilson and his American colleagues abroad has been profound. A production such as Patrice Chereau's centennial staging of Wagner's *Ring* cycle at the Bayreuth Festival (seen here on Public Television) would have been inconceivable without the precedent of Robert Wilson. The Royal Shakespeare Company's *Nicholas Nickleby* was almost a compendium of American experimental technique, most notably Paul Sills's "story theatre." David Edgar, the playwright/adapter of the Dickens novel, once said at a New York press conference that *Nickleby* wasn't pathfinding or "the first great play of the 1980s." Instead, he called it the last great play of the 1960s, using the styles of American experimental theatre and adapting them for the needs of an established, mainstage theatre event.

American experimentalists have not been without influence upon mainstream American theatre but, unlike the situation in Europe, the effects have been random and mostly achieved through osmosis: *Hair* as a blockbuster commercial musical that originated at the Public Theater and surfaced on Broadway with La Mama talent; the Harold Prince staging of *Candide*, which was one of the first to gut a Broadway theatre for environmental effects; *A Chorus Line*, which used the collaborative workshop techniques of performance ensembles and even employed a famous moment of stage business from the Open Theatre's *Mutation Show*.

Apart from those commercial instances, the exchange between the nonprofit, institutional theatres and the experimentalists was limited to a few organizations. Brooklyn's Chelsea Theater Center, which originated the Harold Prince *Candide*, used environmental techniques to extraordinary effect for Amiri Baraka's *Slaveship* and created an elaborate video installation for Peter Handke's *Kaspar*. Joseph Papp was loyal to many experimental artists in the late 1970s, including Chaikin, Lee Breuer, Richard Foreman and Serban. He also provided both a home and direct subsidy for Mabou Mines—probably this country's most outstanding experimental ensemble at that time. For a few seasons at Lincoln Center, Papp had a policy of offering experimental directors the "large canvas" of the Vivian Beaumont Theatre. It was a successful approach that resulted in the Foreman/Stanley Silverman production of *The Threepenny Opera* (which ran a year), as well as important Serban stagings of *The Cherry Orchard* and *Agamemnon*.

The Brooklyn Academy of Music continued to be a loyal home for the avant-garde on a festival basis, but experimentalists remained apart from the regional theatres. In that realm, the only artistic director who regularly engaged these artists for classic and new plays was Robert Brustein.

First at the Yale Repertory Theatre and later at the American Repertory Theatre in Boston, Brustein hired Paul Sills, Gregory, Breuer, Serban and Peter Sellars to stage productions and sometimes teach classes. Brustein also sponsored tours by ensembles such as the Open Theatre, Mabou Mines, Philadelphia's Theatre of the Living Arts, and was actively involved (with much regret afterwards) in the Living Theatre's first return to America in 1968. Since 1984 Brustein has fully absorbed the approach first used successfully by Papp at the Beaumont. Under his aegis, Breuer, JoAnne Akalaitis, Wilson, and Serban have been tackling plays by Gozzi, Wedekind, Genet, Beckett, Euripides and other classic playwrights.

Outside the Northeast, Liviu Ciulei's appointment as head of the Guthrie Theater signaled a major change: For the first time, an important American theatre was placed in the hands of a director whose self-defined mission was to bridge the gap between regional theatres and the American avant-garde. Foreman, Sellars and Serban came to Minneapolis, as did Lucian Pintilie from Romania. For a variety of reasons, Ciulei resigned in 1985, but one hopes that his adventurous artistic policies will have a national life beyond his tenure in the Midwest.

For many American theatre people, there are strong memories attached to this merging of the avant-garde with established companies, and they center on the long American shadow of Peter Brook's work with the Royal Shakespeare Company in the 1960s. His productions of *King Lear*, *Marat/Sade* and *A Midsummer Night's Dream* stay in the mind as prime examples of what can be done with experimental technique in traditional surroundings. Brook drew freely from Polish, French and Chinese theatre, as well as American influences. At the time, he seemed to alter the art form itself, and he still serves as a model for theatrical inventiveness. But despite the recent activity of Minneapolis and Boston, a potential merging of the experimental and the traditional in our regional theatres remains untested. Its limits have not been defined or reached.

In general, there continue to be more opportunities abroad than at home for the American avant-garde. Even European opera houses are more responsive to American experimentalists than our own theatres. Foreman has staged *Die Fledermaus* for the Paris Opera, and Wilson is preparing *Tristan und Isolde* for Paris and *Parsifal* for Milan's La Scala. (Serban and Ciulei also work regularly in opera.)

One wonders about the future of American experimental theatre. Cities like Chicago and Seattle, which have generated thriving theatrical cultures, have no experimental companies. The work in those communities—good as it is—exists almost entirely in traditional forms. San Francisco is home to a few experimental theatre artists like George Coates, Chris Hardman and his Antenna Theatre and Laura Farabough's Nightfire, but they are not part of a national alternative community equal to what there was even a decade ago. The idea of bringing progressive directors into opera houses is an old approach that goes back at least to Weimar Germany, when artists from the Bauhaus and the Berlin theatre were active at Otto Klemperer's Kroll Opera. Overall, it seems that despite the huge national growth of theatre, the experimental wing has remained largely a phenomenon of New York City and Europe.

Experimentation must be rebellion. It reacts against an established object like Newton's law of motion. In that sense many of the changes in American experimental theatre may just be part of an organic evolution. As Richard Schechner once wrote:

> My generation effectively destroyed the idea that the playwright is the only, or main originator of a theatrical event; the generation after me did the same to the director. . . . In America at least, the director's dominance didn't so much end as it was challenged by the assertion of performers in their own right. Just as directors said that writers should not control the creative strings, so performers said that directors should let go, too. With the advent of performer-led theatre came solo work, the monologue, the story-teller; the eminence of Spalding Gray, Stuart Sherman . . . Jeff Weiss.

The soloist—performance art—has taken root as the new focus of experimental theatre, and the ensemble seems to have faded from the scene. Despite the popularity of an extraordinary performer/writer like Spalding Gray, the great era in

American experimental theatre may be over. Most of the important performance ensembles have dissolved, or continue under compromised circumstances. The Living Theatre is today a dated parody of itself. The Open Theatre is no more, and its successors (Chaikin's Winter Projects and The Talking Band) have not achieved equivalent artistic distinction. The individual artists of Mabou Mines stay together as an administrative entity, but they no longer perform as a collective ensemble. Serban's Great Jones Repertory Company is also gone. Only the Wooster Group (successor to the Performance Group) holds on as a regular producing organization, along with the veteran political companies: Bread and Puppet Theatre (now based in Vermont), El Teatro Campesino and the San Francisco Mime Troupe.

But some elements in the current experimental landscape are promising. The most significant is that a few "post-ensemble" directors have emerged—notably Peter Sellars, Anne Bogart and Robert Woodruff—who have absorbed the heritage of the American avant-garde and can translate the best of it into mainstage work. And there are still the veterans (Chaikin, Breuer, Foreman, Wilson, et al.) whose talents have not been exhausted. One may be concerned that a truly vital experimental theatre cannot have, to use Richard Schechner's phrase, "a set of stars who have been fixed as Polaris for more than ten years," but that mature talent can still be routed into unexplored channels by imaginative producers.

Beyond the questions concerning performance ensembles, there is also the exciting development of experimental music theatre. A generation of theatre composers is coming into its own, including such artists as Philip Glass, Richard Peaslee, Elizabeth Swados, Stanley Silverman, Meredith Monk, Laurie Anderson, Bob Telson and Peter Gordon. Works like *Einstein on the Beach, Gospel at Colonus, The Garden of Earthly Delights* and *Dr. Selavy's Magic Theater* are real contributions to both American musical theatre and opera. Much of this work has been encouraged by institutions created specifically for the development of new musical theatre. The most important of these has been the Music-Theatre Group/ Lenox Arts Center where—among many other projects—almost all the Foreman/ Silverman collaborations began.

These music theatre artists are based primarily in the New York world of alternative dance, music, theatre and performance art but, as with their stage director colleagues, they are becoming known in mainstream environments. Glass is now writing for opera houses, Swados is produced on Broadway and Anderson has received orchestral commissions. As with experimental work in general, the new commissions are more likely to come from Europe than the USA, but this new music theatre has the potential to develop an extraordinary creative momentum in America. These are the first new theatre pieces in some time that relate directly to today's popular music. It should surprise no one that for many younger audiences, music theatre productions have the same immediate appeal, communicative style and sheer entertainment values that the great American musicals had for another generation.

Perhaps any overview of American experimental theatre must now be historical. The field has changed radically since the 1960s. New talent of the kind that breaks barriers, definitions and expectations may now gravitate toward other arts. In a larger sense, theatre itself might no longer be a form of real communication for Americans. We live in a society dominated by media images and the technical perfections of film and television. The very unpredictable and uninhibited qualities that make live performance unique have become something of a liability in an American context. Are environmental rock clubs a new form of non-narrative theatre? Is music video America's new musical theatre? It is entirely possible that potential theatre talent—along with new audiences—has gone in another direction, one not prepared for by the theatrical avant-garde of the previous generation. In any event, only continued live performance can answer such questions. In theatre, at least, we'll all find out soon enough if there are new worlds to conquer.

Robert Marx writes about theatre and opera for a wide variety of publications. He is a producer of the international theatre festival scheduled for New York during 1987-88, and is an associate artist of the Music-Theatre Group/Lenox Arts Center. In recent seasons he has been artistic associate of the Mark Taper Forum, a consultant for theatre programming at the Los Angeles Olympic Arts Festival and director of the Rockefeller Foundation's Bellagio Conference on International Exchange in the Performing Arts.

A SIMPLE LIGHT AND A RETURNING LIGHT

Gordon Davidson

At a time when an empty theatre can be as common a sight as people sleeping in boxes in the streets of the world's great cities, when dark marquees on Broadway herald productions that have closed months, sometimes years, before, the Mark Taper Forum has been blessed by growth and good fortune. On a recent Monday night, as an audience gathered for a special mainstage event, it occurred to me that out of 365 days-a-year for nineteen years, except for changeovers and occasional maintenance work, the Taper has rarely been dark. From our inaugural thirty-seven-week season of four plays, we have expanded to become a year-round operation encompassing not only mainstage activity and numerous workshops and special projects, but a second stage, a newly renovated proscenium theatre, a literary cabaret, a touring theatre for youth and a burgeoning television and film division.

My theatre, and the remarkable regional theatre movement of which it is a part, have flourished. But like many other resident theatres, the Taper is continually threatened by a kind of darkness, a darkness resulting from economic constraint and artistic deficit. As the initial, vital impulse behind the regional theatre movement begins to fade, the lights of our "collective marquee" may flicker and grow uncertain.

When a theatre goes dark, the resulting damage amounts to more than a lull in restaurant business or neighborhood street activity. The loss of a theatre means that the life taking place in those restaurants or on those streets is not being recreated, *investigated*, onstage. I have always believed that it is the responsibility and unique privilege of the theatre to illuminate the life around it, to disclose the danger or beauty of the landscape with the fidelity and urgency of a lighthouse. Theatres are, or can be, the beacons by which we experience truth.

"When one speaks to one's fellows, there goes out a simple light and a returning light." This is a line from Barbara Myerhoff's *Number Our Days*, one of a series of plays the Taper commissioned to examine the social, cultural and political history and identity of Los Angeles. This empathy, "a simple light and a returning light," is more than mere collaboration. It occurs between actors onstage as well as between artists and audiences. And it's because of this empathy, this light, that theatre enables us to learn about one another; it offers us another way of experiencing what we know.

In this way, a theatre may reveal and respond to the community in which it resides. My work has helped to acquaint me with many of the communities to which Los Angeles is home, and the city's racial, ethnic and cultural diversity has continually challenged and enriched the Taper. Ours is not an easy constituency to identify, let alone to represent. But we are listening to the city's voices, learning to recognize its faces and trying to make its spirit and special character live on our stages.

As TCG celebrates its twenty-fifth anniversary and my theatre approaches its twentieth, I find that the most urgent challenge is to keep discovering ways for the theatre to *breathe.*

The ongoing experiment in rotating repertory, engaged in by a few of America's resident theatre including the Taper, offers artists and audiences yet another kind of critical perspective, by calling attention to the kinship between our world and Shakespeare's, say, or Arthur Schnitzler's. It is the special ability of repertory to reach across centuries, to create a context that enables us to see our own. The performance in repertory of the classic library dispels the misconception that we live in neighborless isolation from other cultures and eras, and it confirms the longevity of certain beliefs or aspirations in the changing face of experience.

By building a repertory company to undertake both modern and classical work, we invite a growing ensemble of actors, directors and designers to investigate the theatre's most demanding texts. But the Taper's project, now in its sixth year, has confronted us with perhaps our most complex and frustrating challenge. I believe that Taper Rep has yet to find its own character, its own distinct vision. While we are continually fighting less lofty battles, trying to convince funding sources, critics—and even audiences—that the undertaking is worthwhile and artistically profitable, the aesthetic questions remain the most taxing. How, for example, can we present the living library in new and provocative ways? Our answer is to bring together the forces of new and old, not by using motorcycles or a "new wave" score, but by inviting contemporary artists to *re-imagine* the possibilities and achievements of time-honored texts.

There is another approach to repertory, more infrequently taken and even riskier, perhaps. Like opera and ballet, the theatre can conjure up another world in its entirety: its manners and mores, its beliefs and prejudices. This approach is rarely taken; when it is, the result is often stuffy or bloodless. But we do enjoy the encompassing sense of time and place that museums create, and we resent the intrusion of fluorescent lights and drinking fountains. A theatre, like a museum, can be a repository of cultural values and idiosyncrasies.

Each new generation may seem to come to the theatre without a history, but the theatre—and the society it depicts and scrutinizes—*has* a history. This history demands recreation or retelling; such is the responsibility of repertory.

The questions which attend repertory work are sometimes thematic: Should we produce plays that share concerns, or even settings? The issues can also be philosophical, as when we consider how best to serve and stretch the talents of an ensemble company. Other considerations involve the funding and scheduling of sustained repertory activity. Although Rep is still a seasonal endeavor at the Taper, my hope is that the company of actors, directors and designers will eventually work year-round, housed in its own theatre. Ideally, its schedule would allow for two phases. The first would be a laboratory period of research and training, for the purpose of exploring all the special considerations (of language and imagery, movement and style) that lead to performance. The second would be a production phase leading to the actual presentation of a season. I'm convinced that the profile of our theatre must combine a vigorous investigation of the existing library with the discovery and development of new work.

In its commitment to that new work, the Taper has continued to seek new constituencies of both artists and audiences. Taper Media Enterprises, now in its third year, has been a key factor in that search, as it reaches into homes across the country for both its viewers and its subject matter. Most of the work resulting from the project has been documentary in nature, including an hour-long celebration of Eleanor Roosevelt, a play by and about the disabled called *Tell Them I'm a Mermaid* and a series, *Starring . . . the Actors*, which provides a library of conversations with actors on their art. The real test of the enterprise will be its ability to generate and develop works of pure imagination.

This foray into television and film has confirmed my idea that theatre can share certain goals and values with other media. Indeed, the initial impulse behind the department's inception was my belief that today's creative pool is made up of the children of many disciplines; our world is influenced by a range of interpretation and presentation. My desire was to build bridges, to open doors, so that those of us who work in theatre might find new access to television and film, and those who traditionally think of themselves as working in other media could explore the possibilities of the stage. The resulting cross-fertilization has been invigorating, and it has encouraged the belief that our creative life can embrace many forms of collaboration and expression. Whatever the medium, the underlying intention is the same: to provide audiences with *access*, a spiritual and imaginative access, and a fighting chance to see something that might transform their lives.

Our exploration of other media and our work in repertory return us to the central questions governing any form of expression: How can we make aggressive use of our talents in the revelation of the human soul? How can we tell the truth? Both artists and audiences know when they're in the presence of a lie. Unfortunately, that doesn't make the truth any easier to get hold of.

The milieu of the theatre is darkness, and it is in the dark that stories—and truths—are shared. The communal dark of the theatre is a mystical, even revelatory place, for it is haunted (enhanced is a better word) by the sounds and gestures and passions of the artists who inhabit it. "Actors exert pressure against the outer darkness," Father Daniel Berrigan told the company incarnating his own story in the 1970 *The Trial of the Catonsville Nine*. (Berrigan spoke to us from the darkness via a tape he'd recorded while seeking refuge underground.) "They communicate light around their bodies, the light of the spirit of man." Like mine canaries, artists penetrate the unknown, test its depths and re-emerge to share their discoveries.

The work we do is, by its very nature, highly perishable; the theatrical event consists only of moments written in sand. Yet these "abstract and brief chronicles of the time" can be astonishingly enduring and universal. Given the diversity of opinion and experience that characterizes an audience, it is amazing that there are *any* common links in love or aspiration. What's more, the theatre can locate these bonds, etch these truths, embody these longings. That's why we must ask ourselves: What are the dangers to the community of artists and audiences if theatres go dark? And what are the costs and risks of keeping theatres lit?

It's my belief that the theatre must find a new, but perhaps ancient, definition of its role. The reasons for which we make theatre probably haven't changed considerably over the centuries. But in the past few years, I've sensed a change in the people who sit in the seats, particularly in the critical audience. As a result, another kind of darkness threatens, a darkness ensuing from the lack of common understanding on which any form of collaboration relies.

Today, reviewers seem to bestow on plays a kind of consumer rating, and blessed few productions are anointed as a "critic's choice" or a "best bet of the week." This approach misconstrues the intention, the act of theatre. But it also maligns the relationship between the theatrical event and the audience. People are encouraged to see only that which is recommended, and a good or bad mark often determines whether or not a vast number of people encounter a production. The audience seems to have surrendered its right to judge a review, then disregard it and see for themselves.

The price of theatre tickets, the infrequency with which people get to the theatre, the appeal of a good meal or movie—all have contributed to the power of the consumer rating. But this kind of "quality control" has another damaging, even dangerous aspect. Those making the judgments are saying not only that they don't like a given play or production but that, in effect, it doesn't *belong*. It has no place in the theatre. Very few plays can survive, let alone resist, *that* kind of judgment.

Harold Clurman once said that "the history of the theatre is the history of bad plays." His observation wasn't an invitation to fail or an excuse to make bad theatre. It was a recognition that bad plays are a part of the landscape. They provoke thought, affect judgment, stimulate feeling and debate. Plays, all plays, help artists and audiences alike to refine their sense of what the theatre might be.

"Good" or "bad" ballets or paintings often remain accessible; they don't disappear from view. The art form sustains them either through continuity or repetition. Such work either continues to evolve and mature, or something changes in the eyes and ears of the viewer. We find something to admire in such work, some accomplishment or intention, or we enjoy simply being in a performance hall or gallery. Similarly, we'll go to a ballgame for the sheer pleasure of watching the sport. Yes, it's more fun to see a well-played game and a winning team, but our presence in the stands is also an act of support, a show of faith in the sport itself and in its possibilities.

The theatre can flourish only if people accept the *idea* of theatre and embrace their roles of witness *and* participant. We often think of productions as being somehow "right" or "wrong," but we must also consider what a play or performance attempts and what it accomplishes. We must seek, in every theatrical event, what Berrigan calls "the light of the spirit of man." It's the way for theatre, those who make it and those who watch it, to stand against the dark.

In his nineteen years as artistic director of the Mark Taper Forum in Los Angeles, Gordon Davidson has guided more than 100 major productions to the stage. He himself has directed such plays as The American Clock, In the Matter of J. Robert Oppenheimer, The Trial of the Catonsville Nine, Savages, The Shadow Box, Terra Nova, Getting Out, Black Angel, Children of a Lesser God, The Lady and the Clarinet, The Hands of Its Enemy *and* Traveler in the Dark, *many in their world premieres. He was executive producer of the film version of* Zoot Suit *and the director of the film version of* The Trial of the Catonsville Nine, *the television versions of* Who's Happy Now? *and* It's the Willingness. *Davidson was honored with the first annual Harold Clurman Theatre Achievement Award, in addition to a Tony and an Obie.*

THE NEXT GENERATION

Des McAnuff

I began my professional career fourteen years ago, as a playwright and composer. In Toronto where I grew up, due to an abundance of liberal government funding, there were suddenly twenty Equity theatres run by artists in their mid- to late-twenties, with the grandfather of the scene being at that time younger than I am now. I was therefore led to believe at an early age that the theatre was for my generation, and indeed most of the audience was comprised of students and young people—and most of the subject matter was topical and pertinent—addressing issues that concerned my friends and peers and the world we lived in. It never occurred to me that the theatre was a place to escape to; it was, rather, a place to congregate.

By the time I was twenty-three, I became disillusioned with the Toronto theatre scene and left for New York. I was disenchanted with the theatrical hierarchies that had quickly established themselves in Toronto: systems of organization had become the obsession, and the quality of the work suffered. The best advice I ever got about working in the theatre was that theatre was first and foremost collaborative, and that whatever you do, you must find your people. I set out to look for my people.

In the U.S. I discovered that the generation which had founded the institutional theatres was still very much in place and was made up of individual producing directors like Joe Papp, Adrian Hall, Zelda Fichandler and Gordon Davidson—leaders who had created their own boards of directors in response to a commercial theatre that was becoming less culturally relevant—leaders who took responsibility for both the business and the art. It was quite possible to flit around from theatre to theatre relying on these producing directors to maintain the forums that one's work could flourish or fail in. The professional schools such as Yale, Juilliard, Southern Methodist University, the University of California in Los Angeles and San Diego, and Carnegie-Mellon were for the most part just beginning, and for directors there was more opportunity than competition. The American theatre scene had been galvanized to some extent by the Vietnam War, and there was energy aplenty and experimentation on many fronts in many genres, from Mabou Mines and Joe Chaikin to Robert Wilson in the avant-garde;

from Stephen Sondheim and Michael Bennett to Richard Foreman and Stanley Silverman in the American musical, to the dramatic works of Sam Shepard, David Rabe and John Guare. I basked in these influences and assumed that the state of the American theatre would simply steadily improve. That's a natural assumption when you're young and naive and in the middle of something vibrant. I didn't realize at that point that by the end of the decade our theatres would begin to suffer funding problems and would dwell more on the politics of running theatrical institutions than on the politics and affairs of the world—just as they had in Toronto. Orson Welles said that an actor is either getting better or getting worse—perhaps this applies to the theatre at large. it was not until the early 1980s that I realized with a certain amount of horror that I was dependent to some extent on the quality of work going on around me; and it was only then that I sought out more responsibility and decided to play a leadership role beyond that of a freelance director for a given production.

The not-for-profit theatre scene in America is approaching late adolescence. When I was eighteen, I was surprised to find that I was not nearly as good a chess player as I'd been when I was twelve. It's always disturbing to find that you've gotten worse at something. Upon looking into it, I discovered that this was not unusual. Children are natural chess tacticians and can sometimes see brilliant combinations that allude the eyes and minds of adults. Adult chess players must become strategists and have an overall understanding of the principles of chess; they must study chess history and come to appreciate the innovations of Lasker and Steinitz, Nimsovich and Capablanca. These principles are not recipes, but simply ways of looking at the chess board and taking a larger view that children cannot appreciate. This view comes only with hard work, experience and diligent study.

The American theatre is at a point where it needs more strategy and fewer tactics. When I started running a theatre I started to become a strategist, and I now find myself more interested in the state of the American theatre than I've ever been before. This interest is largely selfish, and founded on frustration as much as on love, but I recognize that we are all, to some extent, interdependent. If I am to grow I must try to provide opportunities for other directors, writers and artists. A vacuum is being created in the area of leadership in our theatre, as the founding producer-directors approach retirement. This is a dangerous moment. Somewhere along the line, systems were created to fill this vacuum. These systems, up until recently, have gone largely unquestioned. The founding producer-directors are being replaced by a peculiar panel consisting of artistic director, managing director, production manager and sometimes dramaturg, in some weird relation to a board of trustees which is supposedly protecting a statement of purpose created by someone who is no longer around. Our theatres are passing from a generation of leaders who began institutions out of a sense of need to a generation that is inheriting them.

The La Jolla Playhouse gave some colleagues and me an opportunity—perhaps one of the last opportunities for the time being—to start a LORT theatre from scratch. By 1982 it was clear that there were many traps in the theatrical assembly-line blueprint that had been employed across our country. We were doing, ironically, exactly what television had done. After twenty years of American television, network executives turned to marketing surveys and program formulas, and the brilliant, naive inspiration of "The Honeymooners" was lost forever. Those executives had enough data to talk Ibsen and Molière into accepting thirty-minute time slots. The very same pattern had been followed in the American motion picture industry when it developed enough of a history to look over its shoulder and become bureaucratized with a few sure fire recipes for developing popular product.

The not-for-profit American theatre today has reached the critical point of consciousness, just as film and television did, where artistic values threaten to be drowned in a sea of industry information, and where wisdom turns to cynicism; where the lobe of the brain that is responsible for institutional conservation takes over from the lobe that is responsible for inspiration and innovation. The conservative lobe determines which slot you should put your Brecht in and how long you must run a musical. It is not a very generous lobe—but sometimes it lets the other lobe operate between the cracks, jamming risks between recreations of yesterday's successes. Unfortunately, this is the lobe of the brain that kept us from falling out of trees when we slept in them, and so it is not particularly enlightened. It doesn't know that its recipes for success or survival are short-sighted, and that there is no magic formula or guarantee for success in the theatre.

It has been my experience that when it occurs, successful theatre comes from the imaginations of artists—not from subscription formulas and telemarketing surveys. Following trends and predicting fashions is a full time occupation, as anyone who works on Madison Avenue will tell you. Being a serious artist is also a full time occupation. I've been constantly amazed by the amount of impact a group of serious artists can have on theatregoers when those artists are passionate about what they are doing. I believe that it is important to do away with the notion of one or two people choosing a season and then finding hirelings to execute it, unless those people are geniuses—and I don't know many geniuses. I've observed that great theatre comes from a kind of collective genius, but that it is more likely to happen when some of the artists involved in a particular project have initiated it.

I've been fortunate enough to do four Shakespeare plays over the last four years. I've been shocked by the universality of these plays, and by the extent to which they apply to our own lives and times. It's interesting that we have no idea how Shakespeare's company was organized or who was in charge. I've got to believe that if it were important, somehow we'd know. Every individual human being is unique and every company must look for the most effective way of organizing its gathering of unique human beings. Some chains of command may be more eccentric than others, and in some cases the term "chain of command" might not apply at all. Ultimately, all that is important is the work. A structure must be created that supports the work, and while that structure might employ certain principles, it cannot follow recipes or it will deny the individual artists the necessary freedom it takes to create. One thing is certain: The creation of these structures must be left to artists and professionals, and they in turn must constantly be looking for new and more effective ways of organizing themselves.

The "formula" system of regional theatre programming has been fed by the decentralization of theatrical talent in America. In some ways this has been a good thing; it has helped to bring theatre to communities across the nation and provided work for all those theatre school graduates. Serving a community's desire to see particular plays is perhaps a decent enough reason for a theatre to exist, but it places severe restrictions on the passions of artists. The American talent pool is perilously close to being 3,000 miles wide and one-eighth of an inch deep. Many of the major institutions that were operating in New York when I first arrived are no longer in existence due to funding cutbacks, and the talent has simply gone elsewhere. New forums must be created across America where leading theatre talents can gather. Recently, it has come to feel as if the commercial theatre has been waiting for the regional theatre to develop product, while the regional theatre has been waiting to recreate last season's commercial hits—which reminds me of the children's story that ends with the lines: "Who will help me eat the cake? 'I will,' said the pig. 'I will,' said the goat.'" We have reached the point in the theatre where even the new American musical must turn away from New York if it hopes to be developed.

We must provide for the needs of theatre artists in all of our institutions across the country, and not simply feed audiences what we think they want. We must put our best artists out front and let the audiences judge for themselves. God knows it is not easy for the nonprofit theatre in this country. True artistic integrity is not a sometimes thing, and integrity can be easily compromised for a whole host of expedient reasons, particularly when the survival of an institution is at stake. The commercial theatre existing side by side with the not-for-profit theatre creates an abundance of public confusion. It is sometimes hard to explain that the goal of making profits for investors is very different from the goal of creating works of art. Unfortunately, it would not be unheard of in our nation's theatre to do *Two Gentlemen of Verona* with Pete Rose and Howard Cosell in order to pave the way for production of a commissioned work by Bill Hauptman or Emily Mann. We live in a nation where a 1988 candidate for President may be a former football star, and where Conan the Barbarian has his eyes on the governorship of California. Who can blame the public for mistaking Las Vegas-style musicals for the real thing?

The Greeks considered actors sacred beings, priests who had great souls passing through their beings. Harming an actor was a great sin. We call almost anyone an actor—even our President—and with all due respect, Ronald Reagan is to acting what bull-baiting was to Shakespeare. It is not easy to keep our sights straight. It is easy to forget that the theatre has for 2,500 years been an important social, political and moral platform for all civilized societies. It is easy to forget that traditionally, the most gripping work on history's stages—whether comedy, tragedy, melodrama or even performance art—has been work of serious intent.

In the midst of this confusion many theatres have adopted two artistic policies, one that encourages vital work, the other that allows for the production of anything short of dog fights and public executions to get bottoms in seats. It is little wonder that our young audiences are confused and impatient. They, unlike my generation in Canada fifteen years ago, have not laid claim to this arena. They do not congregate in our theatres. The commercial and the not-for-profit blend together before their eyes. Further confusion is added by the fact that the nonprofit and the commercial theatres are grouped together under the umbrella of the so-called "entertainment industry"—which is 2,450 years younger than the theatre.

We in the American theatre have become aware that we've got problems. Just attend any conference and you'll hear all about them. There's a new term being bandied about, the "artistic deficit." I've yet to meet a single artist who admits to suffering from the artistic deficit, but nonetheless we think we have one. So the first thing we do is look for a new system to solve our problems. The National Endowment for the Arts, in our nation's capital, has decided to reward theatres that have "companies." Britain's Royal Shakespeare Company is frequently cited as an example of what we could have here in America. Apparently it has no artistic deficit. But the RSC employs up to 150 actors, which creates more of a theatre *scene* than a theatre company. If you travel to West Germany you can see some horrible examples of what "company" can come to mean: mediocre actors trapped in a kind of theatrical purgatory, destined to live out their lives in undistinguished productions in front of bored audiences. The American situation for theatre artists is unique; importing foreign methods of organization will not solve our problems. We need to find our own way.

I have no pat or easy solutions to propose; if only I did. But I can end by sharing my personal "wish list" for the American theatre over the next quarter-century:

1. That our theatre absorb the innovations of the visual poets and return to a concentration on words and texts. The pursuit and execution of important texts can lead to a theatre that emphasizes content above style and form.
2. That we bring together artists who have experimented in various genres over the last two decades and promote the creation of new forms and styles.
3. That the American theatre live up to its responsibility as part of the cultural fabric and conscience of the mightiest superpower the world has ever known; that theatre artists develop the ability to look at the world situation from points of view other than our own, and particularly from the point of view of the Third World.
4. That our theatre encourage collaboration and, while allowing for genius, discourage troupes from waiting around for the Messiah to arrive to tell everyone what to do. Even Brecht started the Berliner Ensemble on the assumption that two heads were better than one.
5. That we involve young people in our theatre and even encourage them to take it over as their own. That we welcome them into a theatre that is concerned with reality—which isn't to say that we need to do plays that are realistic in style—but rather, plays that deal with the real world in whatever style is most effective.
6. That we break down the habits of our funding bodies, which tend to reward security over excellence.
7. That we try to reach a wider audience by making theatre as inexpensive and accessible as possible for all our people.
8. That we turn to a length of rehearsal time that is consistent with international standards—a rehearsal period that is appropriate to a particular project.
9. That we enable new leaders to create their own mandates at the institutions they inherit from the leaders who founded them.
10. That we establish a theatre that is representative in its membership—talent, leadership and audience—of the entire spectrum of America's people in matters of age, race, class, language, sex, sexual preference and so on.
11. That we open the theatre up to other artists, from visual artists to pop musicians; that we avoid snobbery and elitism, and demystify the making of theatre so others can join us.
12. That we encourage our artistic leaders to be creative, wise and knowledgeable; and that we encourage them to use the theatre as a means of viewing the world we live in.

An American citizen raised in Toronto, Des McAnuff co-founded New York's four-member Dodger Theater Company in 1978, for which he directed Gimme Shelter, Mary Stuart *and*

How It All Began. *Also in New York, he staged* The Crazy Locomotive *at the Chelsea Theatre Center,* Henry IV *at the Delacorte Theater in Central Park and his own* The Death of Von Richthofen as Witnessed from Earth *at the New York Shakespeare Festival. McAnuff has been artistic director of the La Jolla Playhouse in San Diego since 1982, where he has directed* A Mad World My Masters, Romeo and Juliet, As You Like It, The Seagull *and* Big River. *His Broadway restaging of* Big River *netted seven Tony awards including Best Director. This essay is adapted from remarks McAnuff made at two conferences in fall 1985: FEDAPT's Theatre/Dance Management Conference and The American Dramaturg: Stage Two, sponsored by the Literary Managers and Dramaturgs of America.*

THINGS TO COME

Alan Schneider

Like the fortune-teller lady in *The Skin of Our Teeth* says, telling the future is no problem. Especially the future of the American theatre. Telling the past—including the theatre's past—is something else again. Why was last season as bad as it turned out to be? What happened to that old dream of repertory with a company? Where is that wonderful new talent from two seasons ago? The past is tough to see into. But telling the future? The lady said it: "Nothing easier."

The shorter the time span, of course, the less easy the job of seeing ahead. Tomorrow is the hardest to predict—it's too close to yesterday. We all think we know what Frank Rich will say in the morning light, but will he? Will tomorrow's rehearsal go well or badly? Who is next week's artistic director?

Further ahead, the road becomes increasingly visible. In the next couple of seasons on Broadway, for example, there'll be thirty to forty productions, mostly musicals, comedies and a growing number of both imports and revivals. The season will start out being "the best in years," and end up not as good as the year before. Production and operating costs will go up (as well as the number of seats in each theatre); and quality, artistic and vocal, will go down (as well as the number of available theatres). Lobbies—and stages—will be smaller, auditoriums larger. More will be taken in at the box office and by various Administrative Personnel, and less by ordinary working actors, directors, playwrights, designers and stage managers.

Fewer people will be going to the theatre in more places. The dominant form of playwriting will continue to be realism—mixed with surrealism. British plays will continue to dominate our marquees, brought in alternately from the repertoires of the National Theatre and the Royal Shakespeare (which in London are largely supported by American theatregoers).

In Samuel Beckett's newest and most minimal masterpiece, titled *Untitled*, the first act will open on an empty stage, no actors visible. The play will be composed of simple forms and fundamental sounds (in the words of the author, "no pun intended"). It will run approximately seven to eleven minutes, depending on the director's interpretation of the pauses. In the second act, the curtain will not rise at all. It will be a very short act. Actors' Equity—ever vigilant and alert

—will react by passing a new rule requiring a minimum of roles for its members per act, properly proportioned by sex, race and national origin.

Everyone will blame the playwrights, the producers, the unions, the system. And there will be no new American plays, no decent directors, no trained actors and lots of extraordinary designers, mostly from Yale, capable of making the scenery move up and down and from side to side. Especially in overtime.

What will happen in about five years is even clearer. A musical version of *King Lear* (set in Houston in 1984 and renamed *Lear!* in order to save on ad space) will star Richard Burton and Angela Lansbury, alternating in the title role. *Lear!*'s production budget will be a relatively modest $17.5 million; its producers (Alexander H. Cohen, the Messrs. Barr and Woodward, and the Msses. Nugent and McCann, in association with the Shuberts, the Nederlanders, the Minskoffs, the Feld Brothers and Lee Iacocoa together with Neil Simon, who was called in to work on the last act) will announce that fact proudly in a full-page ad. The Broadway season will have twenty to thirty productions, mostly musicals, comedies and an alarming number of imports and revivals. British plays will continue to dominate, including several hauled out of the RSC's and National's warehouses. The dramatization of the Warren Commission report, *Oswald!*, will arouse much debate and controversy, as well as riots in the grand ballroom of the new Portman Hotel. What Barnes says about it will be a rave; what Simon says will not be.

The "Tony" Award committee, newly reconstituted to make sure that no one on it is involved in any way with the theatre (to avoid charges of prejudice), will be hopelessly split over its Best Play award between a new and sensitive work, originally presented off-off-off Broadway in a telephone booth, about a blind, deaf and one armed mute who has difficulty expressing himself—and the regional theatre's candidate: a four-hour epic drama about a maladjusted transvestite electrician unable to cope with the strain of existence in Omaha, Neb.

The Actors Studio Theatre, now under Shelley Winters' artistic leadership in a well-equipped living room overlooking the Pacific in Malibu, will decide that no audiences are to be allowed to see their performances. (People watching tend to disturb the actors.) Undaunted, Joseph Papp—President-for-life of the New York International Shakespeare and Gilbert and Sullivan Festival (now performing Boucicault on various sidewalks of New York)—will decide not to disturb his audiences every evening by doing things on stage. His favorite director-in-exile, Andrei Serban, will be on hand to direct the audience in and out of the theatre.

In the nation's resident repertory theatre movement—its actual numbers ranging from 500 to 5,000 depending on which mimeographed letter one reads—only one theatre will continue to retain an acting company, that being The Acting Company, whose one-night stands on the road will give the term "resident" an even more extended meaning. Its producing artistic director, John Houseman, will have completed the ninth volume of his memoirs. The Pulitzer Prize in Drama will be shared by Robert Wilson for the longest play and Richard Foreman for the one most lacking in clarity.

Everyone will blame the playwrights, the critics, the unions, the system. And there will be no new American plays, no decent directors, no trained actors and lots of extraordinary designers, mostly from Yale, with fascinating and highly workable ideas about scenery composed entirely of computerized holograms, thereby cutting down considerably on production costs. The producers and theatre owners will be especially interested.

The situation even further down the road, say fifteen years from now, is obvious. Only a carefully selected and screened number of non-musical plays will be permitted on Broadway (ten to twenty productions, mostly musicals, comedies, imports and revivals) by order of the Mayor's Central Tourist Bureau. British plays will continue to dominate, presented by the National Royal Shakespeare, Ltd. All Broadway theatres will be required to have a minimum of 5,000 seats, built-in invisible microphones and a closed-circuit television screen so that the people sitting in the back half of the auditorium will be able to see the stage. In return, all regional theatres (some 15,000 by now) will be expected to present a Shakespeare, a Chekhov, a Neil Simon, a Stoppard or a Beckett (choose one), and one original script in order not to lose their good standing as a member of LORT. As theatre board members in such places as Washington, D.C. and Tulsa have always stated, "We want art, but we have to break even."

Off Broadway, of course, will continue to operate as an antidote to rising costs and expectations on Broadway. Its average budget will be a relatively low $2 million. The Lincoln Center Permanent Revolving Committee of Artistic Directors (now numbering seven) will announce a season to be announced. And the avant-garde theatre will continue to be as experimental as ever, with such pioneers as Lee Breuer, Ellen Stewart and Richard Schechner still trying to come through with a successor to *A Chorus Line*. With the growing use by designers of three-dimensional projections, laser beams and ballistic missiles, advancing theatre technology will literally flash across the horizon: Instant Theatre, Total Instant Theatre and Instant Multiplex Theatre (triggered by the recent publication of Peter Brook's new opus, *The Empty Vacuum*) will replace Gordon Craig's old-fashioned notions about the Temporary Theatre and the Permanent Theatre as starting points for discussions of theatrical aesthetics.

There will be such evolving forms as the Structuralist Theatre (which will stress the "Barthes Method" of acting and directing), the Semiotic Theatre, the anti-Semiotic theatre (Anti-defamation League, please note spelling), the Theatre of Frenzy, the Theatre of Paroxysm, the Theatre of Ecstasy and the You-Know-What Theatre.

Everyone will blame the playwrights, the critics, the unions, the system. And there will be no new American plays, no decent directors, no trained actors and a flock of new, talented designer-engineers, mostly from Yale, to whom verticality rather than horizontality will be paramount. In some cases, theatre stage houses will have to be rebuilt to accommodate their advanced ideas.

Finally, a period of time as long ahead as, say, fifty years, is more predictable still. Broadway will, of course, continue to be the fabulous invalid, although perhaps a trifle less energetic than previously (five to ten productions, mostly musicals, comedies, imports and revivals). Tickets for those lucky enough to buy in will be relatively inexpensive—a top price on weekends of $888.88, including all taxes and penalties. Seats bought at the TKTS Booth atop the World Trade Center will still go for half-price. All ticket holders, including those who buy their tickets via Think-It, will be somatically sensitized during the performance, and wired for National Cable-Vis and isotape transmission if they specify.

In spite of translation difficulties, an Odets revival will sweep the country in 2034, resulting in 25,000 simultaneous hundredth anniversary productions of *Awake and Sing!* Especially worth noting will be an outdoor version of the play, performed in sign language by a group of Hopi Indians in New Mexico (their unique interpretation of "Twice, I weighed myself in the subway" will be considered especially moving). The Stanislavski System, once known as "The Method," will now be referred to as "The Thing" (from Inner Space). Together with the Old

Actors Studio, which had to go underground around the turn of the century because of extreme pressure from the growing number of British artistic directors running American theatres, "The Thing" will eventually emerge stronger than ever as its followers rediscover O'Neill, O'Casey, Sam Shepard and Israel Horovitz.

In towns across the U.S., most theatregoers will also have the opportunity to watch televised 3-D performances of the Royal National Company, or the I Am a Berliner Ensemble Theatre on do-it-yourself micro-chip cable. Robert Brustein's most recent collection of his half-century's most significant reviews, *The Theatre: What Was It?*, will hit the bestseller lists briefly, before being filmed in empathetic "feelies" by Federico Fellini.

Everyone will blame the playwrights, the critics, the unions, the system. And there will be no new American plays, no decent directors, no trained actors. Talented youthful designers will, of course, continue to emerge, mostly from Yale, self-propelled lasers in hand and trajectories trailing. There will always be a theatre, albeit not necessarily on 45th Street, New York, NY 10036.

In contrast to such clear-cut certainty, let me postulate a few less provable fantasies.

As the American theatre moves into the twenty-first century—if we're all lucky enough to make it that far—the institution of "Broadway" will become, increasingly, the appendix of the body theatric. That body in the meantime will continue to spread far, wide and—hopefully, in some cases—handsomely. Whatever its artistic virtues, theatregoing outside Manhattan, in such places as Minneapolis and Washington and Denver and Louisville, will be more pleasant, more convenient, more possible, safer and perhaps even less expensive. The structures, the mechanisms and the talent will exist and persist in a growing number of locations remote from Shubert Alley. That process of dispersal will be irreversible in spite of what the National Endowment or the foundations do or don't do. And the network of regional theatres will finally get that name for which they have always been searching: the American National Theatre.

In that same period, our plays will continue their gradual shift from trying to portray the surfaces of life—"human interest stories," as critic Mary McCarthy so aptly characterized them back in the '40s and '50s—to suggesting in varied styles and degrees "the essence of being human." We will finally realize that with electronic closeups of "reality" available as well as disposable at the touch of a fingertip, only some sort of magnification, intensification, penetration and rearrangement of that "reality" will succeed in holding us in our twelfth-row seats.

The theatre of the future, if it is to hold us, will have to shake off a belief it has held only a relatively short time—the belief that it is showing us "a real room with real people." For the theatre's role is to present life not in its literal exactness but rather through some kind of poetic vision, metaphor, image—the mirror held up as 'twere to nature. Only such a mirror can present us with the "grand crash and glitter of life," in Robert Edmond Jones's classic phrase.

Once our stages and our plays shake off the proscenium's delusion about illusion and return to the more familiar ritual of theatricality, our manner of performing and the nature of our performers will also change—as it is already changing. The actors in our future theatre will be not only truthful but interestingly expressive, physically and vocally. They will seek to present life as it might be as well as to represent it as it is. The American actor and actress, no less than his or her British or Continental counterpart, has the equipment to do that. All that he or she must do is replace the concept of acting as "just playing oneself in imaginary circumstances" with the larger concept that acting is actually transforming oneself, utilizing both truth and craft, into someone else.

The American actor has, in addition, an emotional aliveness and a physicality not always inherently present in other societies or cultures. That's why our musicals remain so popular worldwide. The demands made on the actor by the musical theatre, where our national rhythms and tones have long been dominant, will be more and more matched by the technical demands of our non-musical theatre of the future. From all this will come a larger and more powerful theatre of images and truth, a theatre concerned with the pulsations of life, not just its breathing.

The specifics of that future theatre will be, as always, unpredictible. Who will be the next new playwright, post-Beckett, post-Shepard, post-Durang? What new forms will replace the old ones? What shape will the new avant-garde take? The theatre must always be "new," always "experimental," always seeking to renew itself—from within and under the influence of outside nontheatrical forces—and always coming back to its older self. A great portion of what we hailed in the sixties and seventies, the work of a vast array of real and ersatz artists, individual gurus and group gurus, was blown up out of all proportion to its worth. Many of the works we once called masterpieces have turned out to be doodles.

The eighties and nineties of our turbulent end-of-the-century will be equally full of theatrical sound and fury, signifying not very much. And our problem will be, as before, to fasten onto the few genuine forces and talents, and to separate them from the fool's gold whose glitter will always attract and distract our attention. Who will be our Peter Brook of 1999? Peter Sellars . . . ? Who will follow where J. Grotowski left off? J. Chaikin . . . ? Who will go beyond Sam Beckett? Sam Shepard . . . ?

No one can predict the exact nature and locus of the future theatre. We *do* know that it will continue to stress the performer's image and three-dimensionality. It will return more and more to a dependence on and a respect for the text, for language itself, for the power and beauty of the human voice. Music and dance, from both primitive and contemporary sources, will more and more share the performer's freer vocal and physical expressiveness. Finally, and perhaps more vitally, the theatre of the future will depend more and more on accepting the living presence of the spectator-auditor—not in the superficial sense of the actors running up and down the aisles and touching the audience physically, but in the sense of the entire theatrical event happening only because the audience is there, because the audience and the event truly touch each other at the moment of performance.

The theatre, in whatever form or manifestation, can never be more than a minority preoccupation. But as there has already been a transition from a theatre of personal and private truths to a theatre of more public and communal awareness, so the theatre of purely private gain is gradually giving way to a theatre of public benefit. The transition is slow but steady. More people would go to the theatre if they were only stimulated to do so—and if they could afford to go. There are entire sections of our population who do not go because the subject matter or the process—in addition to the prices—do not suit them. But that caring minority which still depends on the theatre for at least a portion of its sensuous and emotional sustenance is gradually growing, and will continue to grow—if only the theatre does what it alone can do: make its audiences experience the essential nature of the living of life.

Along with the rest of our society, the theatre will go the way the world goes, with a bang or a whimper. Presumably, it is still the theatre which can suggest to us, a few minutes ahead of the journalist or the politician, which way that is going to be. The theatre is fundamentally poetry, not prose. And our playwrights are poets who can read the shapes in the sands ahead of the rest of us and form the tremors we don't even know we're feeling into sentences and speeches. We can stop saying that theatre as art is dead or passé—and admit that it is only our own fault, the fault of those who are working in it, that theatre happens to be less important or effective than it used to be.

I'd like to live long enough to see the demise of words like "hit" and "flop," "revival," "show business." Do we "revive" Mozart or Modigliani? Is Isaac Stern in the "music business"? And I'd like to see the day when audiences pay more attention to their own responses than to what the critics said. And the evening when an airplane pilot, while he's landing, tells me what's playing that night at the Arena Stage or the Beaumont (if anything!) as well as what the Yankees or the Redskins did that afternoon. Sometimes I agree with Brecht that if a theatre ticket cost no more than a pack of cigarettes, we'd have the greatest theatre in the world—without needing any artistic changes or *pronunciamentos*.

Someday I'd like to feel that actors—and directors, and the rest of us who labor in the theatre's chaotic landscape—might be provided some semblance of stability and sanity in their artistic lives instead of the hit-and-miss madness with which they daily have to cope. I'm dreaming of a day when I can actually go to a "repertory theatre" in New York City—or anywhere else in these United States—that's actually playing more than one show at a time, and changing the bill each night on purpose.

In spite of the playwrights, the critics, the unions, the system.

In the meantime, I'm keeping my eyes open for more Zelda Fichandlers and more Adrian Halls and more Jon Jorys and more Lloyd Richardses.

The system, we've got to remember, is us.

In the course of his active career in the theatre, Alan Schneider directed more than 180 productions on Broadway, Off Broadway, Off-Off Broadway and in regional theatre. He is known chiefly as a director of new and experimental works, having staged the original American productions of plays by Samuel Beckett, Harold Pinter, Edward Albee, Robert Anderson, Joe Orton and Michael Weller. He had a long association with Arena Stage in Washington, D.C., later serving as artistic director of New York's Acting Company, head of the Juilliard School's Theatre Center and head of the directing program at the University of California, San Diego. Schneider wrote this essay, which first appeared in American Theatre *magazine, shortly before his tragic death in 1984.* Entrances, *a volume of Schneider's memoirs, was published posthumously in January 1986 by Viking.*

THEATRE PROFILES (1983-84, 1984-85)

Academy Theatre

FRANK WITTOW
Producing Artistic Director

MARGARET FERGUSON
Managing Director

MARTIN C. LEHFELDT
Board Chairman

Box 77070
Atlanta, GA 30357
(404) 873-2518 (business)
(404) 892-0880 (box office)

FOUNDED 1956
Frank Wittow

SEASON
September-June

FACILITIES
1137 Peachtree St.
Mainstage
Seating capacity: 412
Stage: thrust

First Stage
Seating capacity: 90
Stage: arena

FINANCES
August 1, 1984-July 31, 1985
Operating expenses: $445,056

AUDIENCE
Annual attendance: 210,000
Subscribers: 2,200

TOURING CONTACT
Pamela Turner

BOOKED-IN EVENTS
Theatre, music, dance

PRODUCTIONS 1983–84

Productions	Directors	Sets	Costumes	Lights
I'm Getting My Act Together and Taking It on the Road Gretchen Cryer and Nancy Ford	Barbara Lebow	Michael Halpern	Judy Winograd	
A Christmas Carol adapt: John Stephens, from Charles Dickens	John Stephens	Rick Hammond	Judy Winograd	Bruce Bailey
Hedda Gabler Henrik Ibsen; trans: Rolf Fjelde	Margaret Ferguson	Michael Halpern	Anita Beaty	Cullen Clark
Playboy of the Western World John Millington Synge	Frank Wittow	Michael Halpern	Sandra Rood	Charley Rickett
Dula Frank Wittow	Frank Wittow	Mark Loring	Sandra Rood	Cullen Clark
Three Brass Monkeys Bonnie Pike	Margaret Ferguson	Kerrie Osborn	Amy Hare	Staff
The War Brides Terri Wagener	John Stephens	Bruce Bailey	Cast	Bruce Bailey
City of Cells Michele Rubin	Michele Rubin	Gregg Wallace	Cast	Gregg Wallace
Crock of Gold John Stephens	John Stephens	John Stephens	Karen Whipple	Charley Rickett
Calamity Jane Judith Shotwell	Judith Shotwell	Judith Shotwell	Linda Kesler	Bruce Bailey
Pig Tale Tom Marquardt	Rosemary Newcott	Chris Brinkley	Mark Schneider	Charley Rickett
Changing Beats company-developed	Judith Shotwell			

PRODUCTIONS 1984–85

Productions	Directors	Sets	Costumes	Lights
The War Brides Terri Wagener	John Stephens	Bruce Bailey	Judy Winograd	Charley Rickett
A Christmas Carol adapt: John Stephens, from Charles Dickens	John Stephens	Rick Hammond	Judy Winograd and Anita Beaty	Jerry Woolard
The School for Wives Molière; trans: Richard Wilbur	Eddie Lee	Michael Stauffer	Anita Beaty	Bruce Bailey
The Member of the Wedding Carson McCullers	John Stephens	Tom Brown	Judy Winograd	S. R. Johnson
The Hothouse Harold Pinter	Frank Wittow	Bruce Bailey	Anita Beaty	Jerry Woolard
Decameron adapt: Frank Wittow, from Boccaccio	Frank Wittow	Charley Rickett	Judy Winograd	S. R. Johnson
Flint and Roses Jim Peck	Frank Wittow	Natasha Laughrun	Linda Kesler	Andrea Alexander

Productions	Directors	Sets	Costumes	Lights
The Wishing Place Beverly Trader	Kenneth Leon	Staff	Staff	Staff
A Shayna Maidel Barbara Lebow	Barbara Lebow	Michael Halpern	Judy Winograd	S. R. Johnson
Starship Rock & Roll John Stephens	John Stephens	Chris Kayser	Linda Kesler	Charley Rickett
The Other End of the Island Judith Shotwell	Judith Shotwell	Bruce Bailey	Linda Kesler	Bruce Bailey
Another Voyage of Gulliver Tom Marquardt	Rosemary Newcott	Katherine Rickett	Linda Kesler	Jerry Woolard
Boss Baby Blues company-developed	Judith Shotwell			

A Contemporary Theatre

GREGORY A. FALLS
Producing Director

PHIL SCHERMER
Producing Manager

SUSAN TRAPNELL MORITZ
Administrative Manager

RICHARD C. CLOTFELTER
Board President

Box 19400
Seattle, WA 98109
(206) 285-3220 (business)
(206) 285-5110 (box office)

FOUNDED 1965
Gregory A. Falls

SEASON
Mainstage
May-November

Young ACT Company
January-April

FACILITIES
100 West Roy St.
Mainstage
Seating capacity: 454
Stage: thrust

Backstage
Seating capacity: 100
Stage: flexible

FINANCES
January 1, 1984-December 31, 1984
Operating expenses: $1,691,480

AUDIENCE
Annual attendance: 140,292
Subscribers: 9,394

TOURING CONTACT
Polly Conley

BOOKED-IN EVENTS
Theatre, music

*AEA LORT (C) and Theatre for Young
Audiences contracts*

Productions	Directors	Sets	Costumes	Lights
Not Just Kidstuff book and lyrics: Liza Nelson and Charles Abbott; music: Michael Fauss	Anne-Denise Ford	Gilbert Wong	Josie Gardner	Lee DeLorme
The Persian Princess Gregory A. Falls	Anne-Denise Ford	Shelley Henze Schermer	Shelley Henze Schermer	Jody Briggs
Amadeus Peter Shaffer	Jeff Steitzer	Shelley Henze Schermer	Sarah Nash Gates	Phil Schermer
Top Girls Caryl Churchill	Sharon Ott	Robert Dahlstrom	Alexandra B. Bonds	Jody Briggs
Angels Fall Lanford Wilson	Fred Chappell	Karen Gjelsteen	Josie Gardner	Rick Kennedy-Paulsen
Thirteen Lynda Myles	Gregory A. Falls	Bill Forrester	Sally Richardson	A. W. Nelson
Fool for Love Sam Shepard	Gary Gisselman	Shelley Henze Schermer	Shelley Henze Schermer	Donna Grout
The Communication Cord Brian Friel	Mel Shapiro	Bill Forrester	Sarah Nash Gates	James Verdery
A Christmas Carol adapt: Gregory A. Falls, from Charles Dickens; music: Robert MacDougall	Anne-Denise Ford	Bill Forrester	Nanrose Buchman	Jody Briggs

PRODUCTIONS 1985

Productions	Directors	Sets	Costumes	Lights
Beauty and the Beast Gregory A. Falls; music: Chad Henry	Gregory A. Falls	Shelley Henze Schermer	Anne Thaxter Watson	Jody Briggs
Step on a Crack Susan Zeder	Anne-Denise Ford	Bruce Jackson	Sheryl Collins	Donna Grout
The Odyssey adapt: Gregory A. Falls and Kurt Beattie, from Homer	Jeff Steitzer	Scott Weldin	Rose Pederson	Jennifer Lupton
What's in It for Me? company-developed	Brucy Sevy	Patti Henry and Wendy Ponte	Mary Ellen Walter	Peter Allen
King Lear William Shakespeare; music: Robert Davidson	Arne Zaslove	Shelley Henze Schermer	Julie James	Phil Schermer
True West Sam Shepard	John Dillon	Michael Olich	Liz Covey	Jody Briggs
Maydays David Edgar	Jeff Steitzer and Anne-Denise Ford	Bill Forrester	Liz Covey	Bill Forrester
Other Places Harold Pinter	Gregory A. Falls	Bill Raoul	Rose Pederson	Donna Grout
End of the World Arthur Kopit	Jeff Steitzer	Scott Weldin	Sally Richardson	Rick Kennedy- Paulsen
Quartermaine's Terms Simon Gray	Gregory A. Falls	Shelley Henze Schermer	Ann Thaxter Watson	A. L. Nelson
A Christmas Carol adapt: Gregory A. Falls, from Charles Dickens; music: Robert MacDougall	Anne-Denise Ford	Bill Forrester	Nanrose Buchman	Jody Briggs

The Acting Company

JOHN HOUSEMAN
Producing Artistic Director/Board
   Chairman

MICHAEL KAHN
Artistic Director

MARGOT HARLEY
Executive Producer

EDGAR LANSBURY
Board President

Box 898, Times Square Station
New York, NY 10108
(212) 564-3510

FOUNDED 1972
John Houseman, Margot Harley

SEASON
August-May

FINANCES
July 1, 1984-June 30, 1985
Operating expenses: $1,799,835

AUDIENCE
Annual attendance: 105,000

TOURING CONTACT
Gina Willens

AEA LORT (B) and (C) contracts

PRODUCTIONS 1983–84

Productions	Directors	Sets	Costumes	Lights
The Cradle Will Rock Marc Blitzstein	John Houseman and Christopher J. Markle	Mark Fitzgibbons	Judith Dolan	Dennis Parichy
The Merry Wives of Windsor William Shakespeare	Michael Kahn	Douglas Stein	Judith Dolan	Dennis Parichy
Pericles William Shakespeare	Toby Robertson	Franco Colavecchia	Judith Dolan	Dennis Parichy
Pieces of 8 Jules Feiffer, Harold Pinter, Ring Lardner, Edward Albee, Tom Stoppard, Samuel Beckett, Eugene Ionesco, Robert Anderson	Alan Schneider	Mark Fitzgibbons	Carla Kramer	Richard Riddell

Productions	Directors	Sets	Costumes	Lights
A New Way to Pay Old Debts Philip Massinger	Michael Kahn	Michael Kahn	John Kasarda	Dennis Parichy
The Skin of Our Teeth Thornton Wilder	Gerald Freedman	Joel Fontaine	Jeanne Button	Dennis Parichy
As You Like It William Shakespeare	Mervyn Willis	Stephen McCabe	Stephen McCabe	Dennis Parichy
Pieces of 8 Jules Feiffer, Harold Pinter, Ring Lardner, Edward Albee, Tom Stoppard, Samuel Beckett, Eugene Ionesco, Robert Anderson	Alan Schneider and Charles Newell	Mark Fitzgibbons	Carla Kramer	Richard Riddell

Actors Theatre of Louisville

JON JORY
Producing Director

ALEXANDER SPEER
Administrative Director

FRANK P. DOHENY, JR.
Board President

316-320 West Main St.
Louisville, KY 40202
(502) 584-1265 (business)
(502) 584-1205 (box office)

FOUNDED 1964
Richard Block, Ewel Cornett

SEASON
September-June

FACILITIES
Pamela Brown Auditorium
Seating capacity: 637
Stage: thrust

Victor Jory Theatre
Seating capacity: 159
Stage: thrust

Starving Artist Cabaret
Seating capacity: 100
Stage: cabaret

FINANCES
June 1, 1984-May 31, 1985
Operating expenses: $3,470,000

AUDIENCE
Annual attendance: 242,000
Subscribers: 18,000

TOURING CONTACT
Marilee Hebert-Slater

AEA LORT (B) and (D) contracts

PRODUCTIONS 1983-84

Productions	Directors	Sets	Costumes	Lights
A Midsummer Night's Dream William Shakespeare	Laszlo Marton	Miklos Feher	Karen Gerson	Paul Owen
Holy Ghosts Romulus Linney	Patrick Tovatt	Paul Owen	Marcia Dixcy	Jeff Hill
A Christmas Carol adapt: Barbara Field, from Charles Dickens	Frazier Marsh	Paul Owen	Marcia Dixcy and Kurt Wilhelm	Jeff Hill
Shorts Festival:				
Flickers, Robert Spera and Becky Mayo	Robert Spera	Sandra Strawn	Katherine Bonner	Geoffrey L. Korf
The Death of King Philip, Romulus Linney	Ray Fry	Paul Owen	Marcia Dixcy	Karl Haas
Couvade, Sallie Bingham	Frazier Marsh	Paul Owen	Marcia Dixcy	Karl Haas
A Gothic Tale, John Pielmeier	John Pielmeier	Paul Owen	Marcia Dixcy	Karl Haas
Businessman's Lunch, Michael David Quinn	Larry Deckel	Paul Owen	Marcia Dixcy	Karl Haas
Graceland, Ellen Byron	Ken Jenkins	Paul Owen	Marcia Dixcy	Karl Haas
Husbandry, Patrick Tovatt	Jon Jory	Paul Owen	Marcia Dixcy	Karl Haas
Trotsky's Bar Mitzvah, Max Apple	Frazier Marsh	Paul Owen	Marcia Dixcy	Karl Haas
Cheek to Cheek, John Pielmeier	Robert Spera	Paul Owen	Marcia Dixcy	Karl Haas
Cuffs, Lee Eisenberg	Robert Spera	Paul Owen	Marcia Dixcy	Karl Haas
Arts and Leisure, Paul Rudnick	Frazier Marsh	Paul Owen	Marcia Dixcy	Karl Haas
Sweet Sixteen, David Bradley	Frazier Marsh	Paul Owen	Marcia Dixcy	Karl Haas
Five Ives Gets Named, Roy Blount, Jr.	Robert Spera	Paul Owen	Marcia Dixcy	Karl Haas
American Tropical, Richard Ford	Frazier Marsh	Paul Owen	Marcia Dixcy	Karl Haas
Shasta Rue, Jane Martin	Jon Jory	Paul Owen	Marcia Dixcy	Karl Haas

PRODUCTIONS 1983–84

Productions	Directors	Sets	Costumes	Lights
Coastal Waters, Corey Beth Madden	Ken Jenkins	Paul Owen	Marcia Dixcy	Karl Haas
Girl in Green Stockings, Kenneth Pressman	Larry Deckel	Paul Owen	Marcia Dixcy	Karl Haas
What Comes After Ohio?, Daniel Meltzer	Vaughn McBride	Paul Owen	Marcia Dixcy	Karl Haas
Approaching Lavendar, Julie Beckett Crutcher	Robert Spera	Paul Owen	Marcia Dixcy	Karl Haas
The Renovation, Susan Sandler	Adale O'Brien	Paul Owen	Marcia Dixcy	Karl Haas
Well Learned, Andrew J. Bondor	Larry Deckel	Paul Owen	Marcia Dixcy	Karl Haas
Creative Pleas, Fred Sanders	Robert Spera	Paul Owen	Marcia Dixcy	Karl Haas
The Gift of the Magi adapt, music and lyrics: Peter Ekstrom, from O. Henry	Robert Spera	Paul Owen	Karen Gerson	Karl Haas
Of Mice and Men John Steinbeck	Adale O'Brien	Paul Owen	Marcia Dixcy	Paul Owen
The Three Sisters Anton Chekhov	Jon Jory	Paul Owen	Marcia Dixcy	Jeff Hill
A Coupla White Chicks Sitting Around Talking John Ford Noonan	Barnet Kellman	Paul Owen	Marcia Dixcy	Jeff Hill
Humana Festival:				
Danny and the Deep Blue Sea, John Patrick Shanley	Barnet Kellman	Paul Owen	Marcia Dixcy	Geoff Cunningham
Independence, Lee Blessng	Patrick Tovatt	Paul Owen	Marcia Dixcy	Geoff Cunningham
The Octette Bridge Club, P. J. Barry	Robert Spera	Paul Owen	Marcia Dixcy	Geoff Cunningham
Courtship, Horton Foote	Frazier Marsh	Paul Owen	Marcia Dixcy	Jeff Hill
Execution of Justice, Emily Mann	Oskar Eustis and Anthony Taccone	Paul Owen	Marcia Dixcy	Jeff Hill
Lemons, Kent Broadhurst	Kent Broadhurst	Paul Owen	Marcia Dixcy	Jeff Hill
The Undoing, William Mastrosimone	Jon Jory	Paul Owen	Marcia Dixcy	Jeff Hill
007 *Crossfire*, Ken Jenkins	Jon Jory		Marcia Dixcy and Sandra Strawn	Jeff Hill
Husbandry, Patrick Tovatt	Jon Jory	Paul Owen	Marcia Dixcy	Karl Haas and Jeff Hill
Dial M for Murder Frederick Knott	Larry Deckel	Paul Owen	Marcia Dixcy	Jeff Hill
The Middle Ages A. R. Gurney, Jr.	Ray Fry	Paul Owen	Marcia Dixcy	Jeff Hill

PRODUCTIONS 1984–85

Productions	Directors	Sets	Costumes	Lights
True West Sam Shepard	Patrick Tovatt	Paul Owen	Marcia Dixcy	Jeff Hill
The Caine Mutiny Court-Martial Herman Wouk	Ray Fry	Paul Owen	Marcia Dixcy	Jeff Hill
Shorts Festival:				
Summer, Jane Martin	Jon Jory	Paul Owen	Marcia Dixcy	Jeff Hill
The American Century, Murphy Guyer	Jon Jory	Paul Owen	Marcia Dixcy	Jeff Hill
The Black Branch, Gary Leon Hill and Jo Hill	Jackson Phippin	Paul Owen	Marcia Dixcy	Jeff Hill
That Dog Isn't Fifteen, Roy Blount, Jr.	Alan Duke	Paul Owen	Marcia Dixcy	Jeff Hill
My Early Years, Charles Leipart	Robert Spera	Paul Owen	Marcia Dixcy	Jeff Hill
The Person I Once Was, Cindy Lou Johnson	Robert Spera	Paul Owen	Marcia Dixcy	Jeff Hill
I'm Using My Body for a Roadmap, Patrick Tovatt	Jackson Phippin	Paul Owen	Marcia Dixcy	Jeff Hill
The Love Suicide at Schofield Barracks, Romulus Linney	Frazier Marsh	Paul Owen	Marcia Dixcy	Jeff Hill
The Root of Chaos, Douglas Soderberg	Larry Deckel	Paul Owen	Marcia Dixcy	Jeff Hill
Private Territory, Christopher Davis	Frazier Marsh	Paul Owen	Marcia Dixcy	Jeff Hill
The Cool of the Day, Wendell Berry	Robert Spera	Paul Owen	Marcia Dixcy	Jeff Hill
Advice to the Players, Bruce Bonafede	Larry Deckel	Paul Owen	Marcia Dixcy	Jeff Hill
The Dining Room A. R. Gurney, Jr.	Thomas Bullard	Paul Owen	Ann Wallace	Paul Owen
The Gift of the Magi adapt, music and lyrics: Peter Ekstrom, from O. Henry	Robert Spera	Paul Owen	Katherine Bonner	Geoffrey L. Korf

Productions	Directors	Sets	Costumes	Lights
A Christmas Carol adapt: Barbara Field, from Charles Dickens	Frazier Marsh	Paul Owen	Kurt Wilhelm and Marcia Dixcy	Jeff Hill
The School for Wives Molière; trans: Richard Wilbur	Laszlo Marton	Miklos Feher	Marcia Dixcy	Paul Owen
Uncle Vanya Anton Chekhov; trans: Stark Young	Alexa Visarion	Paul Owen	Marcia Dixcy	Jeff Hill
'night, Mother Marsha Norman	Kathy Bates	Paul Owen	Marcia Dixcy	Jeff Hill
Humana Festival:				
Available Light, Heather McDonald	Julian Webber	Paul Owen	Marcia Dixcy	Jeff Hill
Tent Meeting, Rebecca Wackler, Larry Larson and Levi Lee	Patrick Tovatt	Paul Owen	Marcia Dixcy	Jeff Hill

The Very Last Lover of the River Cane, James
    McLure
	Ray Fry and
	    Steve Rankin
		Paul Owen	Marcia Dixcy	Jeff Hill

War of the Roses, Lee Blessing	Bill Partlan	Paul Owen	Marcia Dixcy	Jeff Hill
Days and Nights Within, Ellen McLaughlin	Jon Jory	Paul Owen	Marcia Dixcy	Jeff Hill
Ride the Dark Horse, J. F. O'Keefe	Robert Spera	Paul Owen	Marcia Dixcy	Jeff Hill
Two Masters (The Rain of Terror and *Errand of Mercy)*, Frank Manley	Jackson Phippin	Paul Owen	Marcia Dixcy	Geoffrey L. Korf
Wait Until Dark Frederick Knott	Frazier Marsh	Paul Owen	Marcia Dixcy	Jeff Hill
K2 Patrick Meyers	Ken Jenkins	Paul Owen	Marcia Dixcy	Jeff Hill

Actors Theatre of St. Paul

MICHAEL ANDREW MINER
Artistic Director

JAN MINER
Managing Director

ROBYN HANSEN
Board President

28 West Seventh Pl.
St. Paul, MN 55102
(612) 227-0050

FOUNDED 1977
Michael Andrew Miner

SEASON
October-May

FACILITIES
Seating capacity: 350
Stage: proscenium

FINANCES
July 1, 1984-June 30, 1985
Operating expenses: $565,000

AUDIENCE
Annual attendance: 36,000
Subscribers: 2,400

TOURING CONTACT
Andrew Brolin

BOOKED-IN EVENTS
Theatre, dance, music, film

AEA LORT (D) contract

Productions	Directors	Sets	Costumes	Lights

The Grand Hunt
    adapt: Suzanne Grossmann, from Gyula Hernadi
	David Ira
	    Goldstein
		Dick Leerhoff	Nayna Ramey	Chris Johnson

Translations Brian Friel	Michael Brindisi	Chris Johnson	Chris Johnson	Nayna Ramey

The Hothouse
    Harold Pinter
	David Ira
	    Goldstein
		Tom Butsch	Chris Johnson	Doug Pipan

My Sister in This House Wendy Kesselman	George C. White	Chris Johnson	Nayna Ramey	Chris Johnson

Nice People Dancing to Good Country Music
    Lee Blessing
	James Cada	Dick Leerhoff	Christopher
			    Beesley
				Nayna Ramey

The Woods David Mamet	Jeff Steitzer	Chris Johnson	Nayna Ramey	Nayna Ramey

Pygmalion
    George Bernard Shaw
	Michael Andrew
	    Miner
		Chris Johnson
		    and Michael
		    Andrew Miner
			Christopher
			    Beesley
				Chris Johnson

PRODUCTIONS 1984–85

Productions	Directors	Sets	Costumes	Lights
Awake and Sing! Clifford Odets	D. Scott Glasser	Chris Johnson	Chris Johnson	Chris Johnson
Season's Greetings Alan Ayckbourn	David Ira Goldstein	Dick Leerhoff	Nayna Ramey	Doug Pipan
Faith Healer Brian Friel	Michael Andrew Miner	Chris Johnson	Chris Johnson	Chris Johnson
We Won't Pay! We Won't Pay! Dario Fo	Jeff Steitzer	Dick Leerhoff	Nayna Ramey	Chris Johnson
Careless Love John Olive	David Ira Goldstein	Tom Butsch	Karen Nelson	Nayna Ramey
Bully Paul D'Andrea	Michael Andrew Miner	Mary Helen Horty and Michael Andrew Miner	Nayna Ramey	Chris Johnson
Scapin Molière	Jeff Steitzer	Nayna Ramey	Nayna Ramey	Chris Johnson

Alabama Shakespeare Festival

MARTIN L. PLATT
Artistic Director

JIM VOLZ
Managing Director

PHILLIP A. SELLERS
Board Chairman

Box 20350
Montgomery, AL 36120-0350
(205) 272-1640 (business)
(205) 272-2273 (box office)

FOUNDED 1972
Martin L. Platt

SEASON
December–August

FACILITIES
1 Festival Dr.
Festival Theatre
Seating capacity: 750
Stage: modified thrust

The Octagon
Seating capacity: 225
Stage: flexible

FINANCES
January 1, 1984-December 31, 1984
Operating expenses: $792,677

AUDIENCE
Annual attendance: 165,000
Subscribers: 8,000

TOURING CONTACT
Carol Ogus

BOOKED-IN EVENTS
Theater, music, dance

AEA LORT (B) contract

PRODUCTIONS 1984

Productions	Directors	Sets	Costumes	Lights
Love's Labour's Lost William Shakespeare	Martin L. Platt	Michael Stauffer	Susan Rheaume	Michael Stauffer
Macbeth William Shakespeare	Martin L. Platt	Michael Stauffer	Susan Rheaume	Michael Stauffer
She Stoops to Conquer Oliver Goldsmith	Martin L. Platt	Michael Stauffer	Susan Rheaume	Michael Stauffer
Billy Bishop Goes to War John Gray and Eric Peterson	Charles Abbott	Mark Morton	Susan Mickey	Paul Ackerman
Oh, Mr. Faulkner, Do You Write? John Maxwell and Tom DuPree	William Partlan	Jimmy Robertson and Jack Stevens	Martha Wood	Paul Ackerman
Arms and the Man George Bernard Shaw	Martin L. Platt	Mark Morton	Susan Rheaume	Julie Richardson

Note: Alabama Shakespeare Festival did not produce in 1985, due to construction of a new facility.

Alaska Repertory Theatre

ROBERT J. FARLEY
Artistic Director

PAUL BROWN
Producing Director

ROBERT KLEIN
Board President

705 West Sixth Ave., #201
Anchorage, AK 99501
(907) 276-2327 (business)
(907) 276-5500 (box office)

FOUNDED 1976
Alaska State Council on the Arts

SEASON
June-February

FACILITIES
Fourth Avenue Theatre
620 West Fourth Ave.
Seating capacity: 650
Stage: modified thrust

Fine Arts Theatre
University of Alaska/Fairbanks
Seating capacity: 481
Stage: proscenium

Grant Hall
Seating capacity: 226
Stage: modified thrust

FINANCES
June 1, 1984-May 31, 1985
Operating expenses: $3,005,390

AUDIENCE
Annual attendance: 60,000
Subscribers: 11,303

TOURING CONTACT
Bennett E. Taber

BOOKED-IN EVENTS
Theatre

AEA LORT (B) contract

PRODUCTIONS 1983–84

Productions	Directors	Sets	Costumes	Lights
All My Sons Arthur Miller	Robert J. Farley	Karen Gjelsteen	Cathleen Edwards	Judy Rasmuson
Wings Arthur Kopit	Robert J. Farley	Michael Stauffer	Michael Olich	Michael Stauffer
The Philadelphia Story Philip Barry	John Going	David Potts	William Schroder	Dennis Parichy
Tartuffe Molière	Walton Jones	Kevin Rupnik	Dunya Ramicova	Donald Thomas

PRODUCTIONS 1984–85

Productions	Directors	Sets	Costumes	Lights
Noises Off Michael Frayn	Robert J. Farley	Connie Lutz	Cathleen Edwards	Spencer Mosse
Translations Brian Friel	Michael Murray	Karl Eigsti	Mariann Verheyen	Neil Peter Jampolis
Brighton Beach Memoirs Neil Simon	Clayton Corzatte	Karen Gjelsteen	Sally Richardson	Judy Rasmuson
Pantagleize Michel de Ghelderode	Robert J. Farley	Michael Olich	Deborah Dryden	Bob Peterson
Billy Bishop Goes to War John Gray and Eric Peterson	Robert J. Farley	Connie Lutz	Jennifer Svenson	Lauren MacKenzie Miller
Pump Boys and Dinettes John Foley, Mark Hardwick, Debra Monk, Cass Morgan, John Schimmel and Jim Wann	Robert J. Farley	Connie Lutz	Jennifer Svenson	Lauren MacKenzie Miller

Alley Theatre

PAT BROWN
Artistic Director

TOM SPRAY
Managing Director

HUGO V. NEUHAUS, JR.
Board President

615 Texas Ave.
Houston, TX 77002
(713) 228-9341 (business)
(713) 228-8421 (box office)

FOUNDED 1947
Nina Vance

SEASON
October–September

FACILITIES
Large Stage
Seating capacity: 798
Stage: thrust

Arena Stage
Seating capacity: 296
Stage: arena

FINANCES
October 1, 1984-September 30, 1985
Operating expenses: $4,350,000

AUDIENCE
Annual attendance: 255,399
Subscribers: 30,065

BOOKED-IN EVENTS
Theatre

AEA LORT (B) and (C) contracts

PRODUCTIONS 1983–84

Productions	Directors	Sets	Costumes	Lights
The Dresser Ronald Harwood	Josephine R. Abady	Michael Holt	David Toser	Richard W. Jeter
Donkey's Years Michael Frayn	Pat Brown	Dale F. Jordan	Ainslie G. Bruneau	Richard W. Jeter
Cloud 9 Caryl Churchill	Joan Vail Thorne	Keith Belli	Ainslie G. Bruneau	Richard W. Jeter
All My Sons Arthur Miller	Pat Brown	Dale F. Jordan	Ainslie G. Bruneau	Richard W. Jeter
True West Sam Shepard	George Anderson	Keith Belli	Fotini Dimou	Richard W. Jeter
Crimes of the Heart Beth Henley	Cliff F. Baker	Keith Belli	Fotini Dimou	Richard W. Jeter
Angels Fall Lanford Wilson	John Vreeke	Dale F. Jordan	Fotini Dimou	Richard W. Jeter
Uncle Vanya Anton Chekhov; trans: Michael Henry Heim	John Going	Dale F. Jordan	Ainslie G. Bruneau	Dale F. Jordan
Amateurs Tom Griffin	George Anderson	Keith Belli	Fotini Dimou	Richard W. Jeter
'night, Mother Marsha Norman	Pat Brown	Dale F. Jordan	Ainslie G. Bruneau	Richard W. Jeter
Angel Street Patrick Hamilton	John Vreeke	Dale F. Jordan	Ainslie G. Bruneau	Richard W. Jeter
Winnie-the-Pooh adapt: Beth Sanford, from A. A. Milne	John Vreeke	Michael Holt	Fotini Dimou	Richard W. Jeter

---

PRODUCTIONS 1984–85

Productions	Directors	Sets	Costumes	Lights
The Sorrows of Frederick Romulus Linney	Pat Brown	Michael Holt	Fotini Dimou	Richard W. Jeter
Season's Greetings Alan Ayckbourn	Pat Brown	Dale F. Jordan	Fotini Dimou	Dale F. Jordan
Starry Night Monte Merrick	George Anderson	Mo Holden	Ainslie G. Bruneau	Richard W. Jeter
Quartermaine's Terms Simon Gray	Neil Havens	Dale F. Jordan	Ainslie G. Bruneau	Richard W. Jeter
Extremities William Mastrosimone	Beth Sanford	Byron A. Taylor	Mo Holden	Richard W. Jeter
Finding Home book and lyrics: Michael Bigelow Dixon and Jerry Patch; music: Diane King and Jan Cole	John Vreeke	Byron A. Taylor	Joanie Canon	
Sweet Bird of Youth Tennessee Williams	Joan Vail Thorne	Dale F. Jordan	Ainslie G. Bruneau	Dale F. Jordan
Fool for Love Sam Shepard	Lee Shallat	Dale F. Jordan	Mo Holden	Dale F. Jordan

Productions	Directors	Sets	Costumes	Lights
Much Ado About Nothing William Shakespeare	Mervyn Willis	Charles Stanley Kading	Ainslie G. Bruneau	Richard W. Jeter
Open Admissions Shirley Lauro	George Anderson	Mo Holden	Ainslie G. Bruneau	Richard W. Jeter
Sizwe Bansi Is Dead Athol Fugard	Jim O'Conner	Mo Holden	Ainslie G. Bruneau	Richard W. Jeter
And a Nightingale Sang . . . C. P. Taylor	Beth Sanford	James Franklin	Fotini Dimou	Richard W. Jeter
A . . .My Name Is Alice Joan Micklin Silver and Julianne Boyd	Charles Abbott	James Franklin	Ainslie G. Bruneau	Richard W. Jeter
Tales from the Arabian Nights book and lyrics: Michael Bigelow Dixon; music: Jan Cole	John Vreeke	Michael Holt	Fotini Dimou	Richard W. Jeter
Pecos Bill Rides Again book and lyrics: Michael Bigelow Dixon and Valerie Smith; music: Art Yelton	James Gardner	James Franklin	Ainsley G. Bruneau	Richard W. Jeter
Kind Lady Edward Chodorov	Cliff F. Baker	Byron A. Taylor	Fotini Dimou	Dale F. Joran

Alliance Theatre Company/ Atlanta Children's Theatre

KENT STEPHENS
Associate Director

EDITH H. LOVE
Managing Director

BENJAMIN T. WHITE
Board President

1280 Peachtree St., NE
Atlanta, GA 30309
(404) 898-1132 (business)
(404) 892-2414 (box office)

FOUNDED 1969
Atlanta Arts Alliance

SEASON
September–June

FACILITIES
Alliance Theatre
Seating capacity: 826
Stage: proscenium

Studio Theatre
Seating capacity: 200
Stage: flexible

FINANCES
August 1, 1984–July 31, 1985
Operating expenses: $3,450,000

AUDIENCE
Annual attendance: 271,194
Subscribers: 20,688

TOURING CONTACT
Debbie Shelton

BOOKED-IN EVENTS
Theatre, music, dance

AEA LORT (B), (D) and Theatre for
Young Audiences contracts

Productions	Directors	Sets	Costumes	Lights
A Streetcar Named Desire Tennessee Williams	Fred Chappell	Phillip Jung	Susan Hirschfeld	Michael Stauffer
In the Sweet Bye and Bye Donald Driver	Kent Stephens	Mark William Morton	Susan Mickey	William B. Duncan
The Music Man book, music, and lyrics: Meredith Willson	Edward Stone	Mark William Morton	Susan Hirschfeld	Jason Kantrowitz
Crimes of the Heart Beth Henley	Fred Chappell	Mark William Morton	Susan Hirschfeld	Paul Ackerman
The Threepenny Opera book and lyrics: Bertolt Brecht; music: Kurt Weill; trans: Marc Blitzstein	Kent Stephens	Michael Stauffer	Susan Hirschfeld	Cassandra Henning
Julius Caesar William Shakespeare	Robert Woodruff	Mark William Morton	Susan Hirschfeld	Paulie Jenkins

PRODUCTIONS 1983–84

Productions	Directors	Sets	Costumes	Lights
The Boys in Autumn Bernard Sabath	Fred Chappell	Johnny Thigpen	Judy Winograd	Paul Ackerman
True West Sam Shepard	Kent Stephens	Nancy Margaret Orr	J. Thomas Seagraves	P. Hamilton Shinn
Cloud 9 Caryl Churchill	Jeff Steitzer	Johnny Thigpen	J. Thomas Seagraves	David Brewer
The Dining Room A. R. Gurney, Jr.	Skip Foster	Johnny Thigpen	Joyce Andrulot	Jeff Margolin
The Arkansaw Bear Aurand Harris	Fred Chappell	Mark William Morton	Joyce Andrulot	Paul Ackerman
The Adventures of Tom Sawyer adapt: Timothy Mason, from Mark Twain	Kent Stephens	Nancy Margaret Orr	Joyce Andrulot	P. Hamilton Shinn
The Grubb Chronicles Eddie Lee and Lee Larson	Kent Stephens and Skip Foster		Joyce Andrulot	

PRODUCTIONS 1984–85

Productions	Directors	Sets	Costumes	Lights
Cyrano de Bergerac Edmond Rostand; adapt: Emily Frankel	Arthur Storch	Victor A. Becker	Jennifer von Mayrhauser	Marc Weiss
Foxfire Hume Cronyn and Susan Cooper	Skip Foster	Paul Wonsek	J. Thomas Seagraves	Gregg Marriner
She Loves Me book: Joe Masteroff; music: Jerry Bock; lyrics: Sheldon Harnick	Fred Chappell	Mark William Morton	Susan Hirschfeld	Jason Kantrowitz
And a Nightingale Sang... C. P. Taylor	Kent Stephens	Richard Hoover	J. Thomas Seagraves	Gregg Marriner
Cat on a Hot Tin Roof Tennessee Williams	Fred Chappell	Michael Stauffer	Joyce Andrulot	Paulie Jenkins
The Tempest William Shakespeare	Kent Stephens	Mark William Morton	Susan Hirschfeld	William B. Duncan
Master Harold...and the boys Athol Fugard	Stephen Hollis	Mark Loring	Yvonne Lee	Dante Cardone
High Standards Tom Huey	Skip Foster	Johnny Thigpen	J. Thomas Seagraves	Liz Lee
Painting Churches Tina Howe	Malcolm Morrison	Thomas R. Lee	J. Thomas Seagraves	Liz Lee
So Long on Lonely Street Sandra Deer	Kent Stephens	Mark William Morton	Joyce Andrulot	David Brewer
The Emperor and the Nightingale adapt: Kent Stephens and Sandra Deer, from Hans Christian Anderson	Kent Stephens	Nancy Margaret Orr	Joyce Andrulot	Gregg Marriner
The Prince and the Pauper adapt: John Vreeke, from Mark Twain	Bill Crowe	Mark William Morton	Susan Mickey	Gregg Marriner
The Beast Skip Foster	Skip Foster		Joyce Andrulot	
The Land Between Elizabeth Sams	Skip Foster		Joyce Andrulot	

AMAS Repertory Theatre

ROSETTA LeNOIRE
Artistic Director

GARY HALCOTT
JERRY LAPIDUS
Administrators

DON ELLWOOD
Board Chairman

1 East 104th St.
New York, NY 10029
(212) 369-8000

FOUNDED 1968
Rosetta LeNoire, Gerta Grunen, Mara Kim

SEASON
October-August

FACILITIES
Experimental Theatre
Seating capacity: 99
Stage: modified thrust

Eubie Blake Children's Theatre
Seating capacity: 75
Stage: proscenium

FINANCES
July 1, 1984-June 30, 1985
Operating expenses: $275,000

AUDIENCE
Annual attendance: 16,000

AEA Funded Non-Profit Theatre code

PRODUCTIONS 1983-84

Productions	Directors	Sets	Costumes	Lights
I Can Still Hear and See Them book: Rosetta LeNoire; music and lyrics: various	Bob Brooker		Cindy Boyle	
The Buck Stops Here! book: Norman J. Fedder; music and lyrics: Richard A. Lippman; additional lyrics: Norman J. Fedder	Regge Life	Kalina Ivanov	Eiko Yamaguchi	Gregg Marriner
Sing Me Sunshine! book: Robert E. Richardson; music and lyrics: Johnny Brandon	Jack Timmers	Robert Lewis	Gail Cooper-Hecht	Paul Sullivan
Blackberries book: Joseph George Caruso; sketches: Billy K. Wells	Andre DeShields	Edward Goetz	Mardi Philips	Deborah Tulchin
Godspell conceived: John Michael Tebelak; music and lyrics: Stephen Schwartz	Fred Tuso	Kieran Kelly	Linda Taoka	Deborah Tulchin
On the Town book: Betty Comden and Adolph Green; music and lyrics: Leonard Bernstein	Jonathan Failla	Janice Davis	Lewis Wilkes	Dan Kotlowitz

---

PRODUCTIONS 1984-85

Productions	Directors	Sets	Costumes	Lights
I Can Still Hear and See Them book: Rosetta LeNoire; music and lyrics: various artists	Bob Brooker		Robert Locke	
Anonymous book, music and lyrics: Vincenzo Stornaiuolo; additional music: Giancarlo de Marreis; additional lyrics: Jack Everly	Vincenzo Stornaiuolo	Janice Davis	Robert Locke	William H. Grant, III
Northern Boulevard book: Kevin Brofsky; music and lyrics: Carleton Carpenter	William Martin	Tom Barnes	Judy Dearing	Deborah Tulchin
Manhattan Serenade conceived and arranged: Karen Cotterell and Alfred Heller; music: Louis Alter; lyrics: various	Bob Rizzo	Mina Albergo	Christina Giannini	Gregg Marriner
Oliver! book, music and lyrics: Lionel Bart	Fred Tuso	Janice Davis	Robert Locke	Deborah Matlack
Showboat book and lyrics: Oscar Hammerstein, II; music: Jerome Kern	Fred Tuso	Michael DeSouza	Anita Ellis	Deborah Matlack

---

American Jewish Theatre

STANLEY BRECHNER
Artistic Director

LEDA GELLES
Managing Director

MRS. ROBERT RUBIN
Board President

1395 Lexington Ave.
New York, NY 10128
(212) 427-6000, ext. 220 (business)
(212) 427-4410 (box office)

FOUNDED 1974
Stanley Brechner

SEASON
September-June

FACILITIES
American Jewish Theatre
Seating capacity: 125
Stage: flexible

Kaufmann Concert Hall
Seating capacity: 945
Stage: proscenium

FINANCES
July 1, 1984-June 30, 1985
Operating expenses: $300,000

AUDIENCE
Annual attendance: 18,000
Subscribers: 3,500

TOURING CONTACT
Norman Golden

AEA Off Broadway contract

PRODUCTIONS 1983–84

Productions	Directors	Sets	Costumes	Lights
Made in Heaven Edward Belling	Stanley Brechner	Jeffrey Schneider	Barbara Weiss	Jenny Ball
I Am a Camera John van Druten	Geoffrey Sherman	Paul Wonsek	Don Newcomb	Sid Bennett
It's Hard to Be a Jew Sholem Aleichem; trans: Isaiah Sheffer	Dan Held	John Kenny	Barbara Blackwood	Greg Chabay
Andorra Max Frisch; trans: Michael Bullock	Martin Fried	Kalina Ivanov	Muriel Stockdale	Greg Chabay

PRODUCTIONS 1984–85

Productions	Directors	Sets	Costumes	Lights
Jesse's Land Ernest Joselovitz	Jeff Martin	George Tsypin	Stephan Rotandro	Amy Richards
Enter Laughing Joseph Stein	Dan Held	Dan Conway	Arnold S. Levine	Amy Richards
The Rachel Plays Leah K. Friedman	Susan Einhorn	Audrey Hemenway	Karen Gerson	Victor En Yu Tan
My Old Friends book, music and lyrics: Mel Mandel and Norman Sachs	Philip Rose	Paul Wonsek	Don Newcomb	Dennis Size
A Broadcast Baby Isaiah Sheffer	Dan Held	Eugene Gurlitz	Karen Hummel	Robert Bessoir

The American Place Theatre

WYNN HANDMAN
Director

JULIA MILES
Associate Director

ALBERT BILDNER
Board Chairman

111 West 46th St.
New York, NY 10036
(212) 246-3730 (business)
(212) 247-0393 (box office)

FOUNDED 1964
Wynn Handman, Michael Tolan,
    Sidney Lanier, Myrna Loy

SEASON
September-June

FACILITIES
Mainstage
Seating capacity: 299
Stage: flexible thrust

Subplot Cabaret
Seating capacity: 74
Stage: flexible

First Floor Theatre
Seating capacity: 74
Stage: flexible

FINANCES
July 1, 1984-June 30, 1985
Operating expenses: $640,000

AUDIENCE
Annual attendance: 20,200
Subscribers: 1,000

TOURING CONTACT
Julia Miles

BOOKED-IN EVENTS
Theatre, music, dance

AEA Special Production contract

PRODUCTIONS 1983–84

Productions	Directors	Sets	Costumes	Lights
The Vi-Ton-Ka Medicine Show		Marco A. Martinez-Galarce		Marco A. Martinez-Galarce
The Danube Maria Irene Fornes	Maria Irene Fornes	Maria Irene Fornes	Gabriel Berry	Anne Militello
Do Lord Remember Me James de Jongh	Regge Life	Julie Taymor	Judy Dearing	Sandra L. Ross
Terra Nova Ted Tally	Gerald Gutierrez	Douglas Stein	Ann Emonts	Paul Gallo
American Humorist Series: *Pay Attention*, Doug Skinner	Doug Skinner			
Breakfast Conversations in Miami, Reinhard Lettau	Gordon Edelstein	Neil Peter Jampolis	David C. Woolard	Jane Reisman
Women's Project: *A . . . My Name Is Alice*, Joan Micklin Silver and Julianne Boyd	Joan Micklin Silver and Julianne Boyd	Adrianne Lobel	Mimi Maxmen	Ann Wrightson
Special Family Things, Ara Watson and Mary Gallagher	Page Burkholder	Johniene Papandreas	Mimi Maxmen	Jane Reisman
The Only Woman General, Lavonne Mueller	Bryna Wortman			
Old Wives Tale, Julie Jensen	Alma Becker			
Aye Aye Aye I'm Integrated, Anna Deavere Smith	Billie Allen		Judy Dearing	
Candy and Shelley Go to the Desert, Paula Cizmar	Carey Perloff			
The Longest Walk, Janet Thomas	Claudia Weill			
To Heaven in a Swing Katherine Houghton	Joan Vail Thorne	Rosaria Sinisi	David Toser	Anne Militello

PRODUCTIONS 1984–85

Productions	Directors	Sets	Costumes	Lights
Rude Times Stephen Wylie	Gordon Edelstein	Patricia Woodbridge	David C. Woolard	John Gisondi
Jubilee! A Black Theatre Festival: *M. L. K.: The Life and Times of Martin Luther King*, Al Eaton	Larry Coen	Patrice Macaluso	Patrice Macaluso	Ernest Baxter
Celebration, Shauneille Perry	Shauneille Perry		Judy Dearing	Ernest Baxter
Love to All, Lorraine, Elizabeth Van Dyke	Woodie King, Jr. and Elizabeth Van Dyke			Ernest Baxter

PRODUCTIONS 1984–85

Productions	Directors	Sets	Costumes	Lights
American Humorist Series:				
What's a Nice Country Like You Doing in a State Like This?, music: Cary Hoffman; lyrics: Ira Gasman	Miriam Fond	Neil Peter Jampolis	David C. Woolard	
Doings of Gotham: The Wit and Humor of *Edgar Allan Poe*, adapt: Conrad Pomerleau			Marcy Grace Froehlich	Anne Militello
Women's Project:				
Four Corners, Gina Wendkos	Gina Wendkos			Anne Militello
Paducah, Sallie Bingham	Joan Vail Thorne	Karen Schulz	Mimi Maxmen	Anne Militello

American Repertory Theatre

ROBERT BRUSTEIN
Artistic Director

ROBERT J. ORCHARD
Managing Director

BARBARA W. GROSSMAN
Board Chairman

64 Brattle St.
Cambridge, MA 02138
(617) 495-2668 (business)
(617) 547-8300 (box office)

FOUNDED 1980
Robert Brustein

SEASON
November–July

FACILITIES
Loeb Drama Center
Seating capacity: 556
Stage: flexible

Hasty Pudding Theatre
12 Holyoke St.
Seating capacity: 353
Stage: proscenium

FINANCES
July 1, 1984-June 30, 1985
Operating expenses: $2,897,600

AUDIENCE
Annual attendance: 123,170
Subscribers: 10,365

TOURING CONTACT
Robert J. Orchard

BOOKED-IN EVENTS
Theatre, music, dance

AEA LORT (B) contract

PRODUCTIONS 1983–84

Productions	Directors	Sets	Costumes	Lights
Measure for Measure William Shakespeare	Andrei Belgrader	Douglas Stein	Kurt Wilhelm	Jennifer Tipton
A Moon for the Misbegotten Eugene O'Neill	David Leveaux	Brien Vahey	Brien Vahey	Donald Edmund Thomas
Traveler in the Dark Marsha Norman	Tom Moore	Heidi Landesman	Robert Blackman	James F. Ingalls
Big River book adapt: William Hauptman, from Mark Twain; music and lyrics: Roger Miller	Des McAnuff	Heidi Landesman	Patricia McGourty	James F. Ingalls
Six Characters in Search of an Author Luigi Pirandello; adapt: Robert Brustein	Robert Brustein	Michael H. Yeargan	Michael H. Yeargan	Jennifer Tipton
Angel City Sam Shepard	David Wheeler	Kate Edmunds	Elizabeth Perlman and Lynn Jeffery	Thom Palm
Holy Wars Allan Havis	Gerald Chapman	Kate Edmunds	Elizabeth Perlman and Lynn Jeffery	Thom Palm
Strokes Leslie Glass		Kate Edmunds	Elizabeth Perlman and Lynn Jeffrey	Thom Palm
Sganarelle Molière; trans: Albert Bermel	Andrei Serban	Michael H. Yeargan	Dunya Ramicova	James F. Ingalls
The School for Scandal Robert Brinsley Sheridan	Jonathan Miller	Patrick Robertson	Rosemary Vercoe	Jennifer Tipton

Productions	Directors	Sets	Costumes	Lights
The King Stag Carlo Gozzi; trans: Albert Bermel	Andrei Serban	Michael H. Yeargan	Julie Taymor	Jennifer Tipton
Endgame Samuel Beckett	JoAnne Akalaitis	Douglas Stein	Kurt Wilhelm	Jennifer Tipton
Jacques and His Master Milan Kundera; trans: Michael Henry Heim	Susan Sontag	Douglas Stein	Joan Greenwood	Jennifer Tipton
the CIVIL warS: a tree is best measured when it is down, Act III, Scene E; Act IV Scene A and Epilogue Robert Wilson and Heiner Müller	Robert Wilson	Robert Wilson and Tom Kamm	Yoshio Yabara	Jennifer Tipton
Love's Labour's Lost William Shakespeare	Jerome Kilty	Michael H. Yeargan	Connie Wexler	Spencer Mosse
Gillette William Hauptman	David Wheeler	Karen Schulz	Lynn Jeffrey	Thom Palm
Claptrap Ken Friedman	Robert Drivas	Karen Schulz	Karen Eister	Thom Palm
Sganarelle Molière; trans: Albert Bermel	Andrei Serban	Michael H. Yeargan	Dunya Ramicova	James F. Ingalls
Six Characters in Search of an Author Luigi Pirandello; adapt: Robert Brustein	Robert Brustein	Michael H. Yeargan	Michael H. Yeargan	Jennifer Tipton

The American Stage Company

VICTORIA HOLLOWAY
Artistic Director

JOHN BERGLUND
Managing Director

JAMES REICHLE
Board President

Box 1560
St. Petersburg, FL 33731
(813) 823-1600 (business)
(813) 822-8814 (box office)

FOUNDED 1979
Richard Hopkins, Bobbie Seifer

SEASON
October-June

FACILITIES
211 3rd St. South
Seating capacity: 120
Stage: arena

FINANCES
July 1, 1984-June 30, 1985
Operating expenses: $178,000

AUDIENCE
Annual attendance: 14,000
Subscribers: 1,100

AEA Guest Artist contract

Productions	Directors	Sets	Costumes	Lights
Nuts Tom Topor	Victoria Holloway	Lloyd Greenwood	Joyce Peterson	Lloyd Greenwood
Mass Appeal Bill C. Davis	Michael Hoffman	Paul Eppling	Hugh Slack	Brian Anstedt
Come Back to the 5 and Dime Jimmy Dean, Jimmy Dean Ed Graczyk	John Berglund	David Bewley	David Bewley	Brian Anstedt
Kennedy's Children Robert Patrick	Victoria Holloway	Paul Eppling	Hugh Slack	Brian Anstedt
El Grande de Coca Cola Ron House, John Neville-Andrews, Alan Shearman, Diz White and Sally Willis	John Berglund	Sandy Eppling	Victoria Holloway	Brian Anstedt

PRODUCTIONS 1984–85

Productions	Directors	Sets	Costumes	Lights
What I Did Last Summer A. R. Gurney, Jr.	Victoria Holloway	Sandy Eppling	Hugh Slack	Brian Turner
A Midsummer Night's Dream William Shakespeare	Victoria Holloway	Sandy Eppling	Sandy Eppling, Joanne Johnson and Nancy Lee	Michael Newton-Brown
Same Time, Next Year Bernard Slade	Paul Frellick	Sandy Eppling	Nancy Lee and Claudia Benbow	Paul Gralen
Agnes of God John Pielmeier	John Berglund	Paul Eppling	Hugh Slack	Michael Newton-Brown
Close Ties Elizabeth Diggs	David Lee-Palmer	Sandy Eppling	Claudia Benbow	Brian Turner
The Wake of Jamey Foster Beth Henley	John Berglund	Sandy Eppling	Hugh Slack and Peter Massey	Brian Turner

American Stage Festival

LARRY CARPENTER
Artistic Director

SYLVIA S. TRAEGER
Managing Director

KAY A. MARCUS
Board President

Box 225
Milford, NH 03055
(603) 673-1231 (business)
(603) 673-7515 (box office)

FOUNDED 1975
Terry C. Lorden and local citizens

SEASON
June-September

FACILITIES
Route 13N (Mont Vernon St.)
Seating capacity: 480
Stage: proscenium

FINANCES
November 1, 1983-October 31, 1984
Operating expenses: $513,036

AUDIENCE
Annual attendance: 50,000
Subscribers: 3,500

TOURING CONTACT
Sylvia S. Traeger

BOOKED-IN EVENTS
Children's theatre, popular and classical music

AEA Council on Resident Stock Theatre contract

PRODUCTIONS 1984

Productions	Directors	Sets	Costumes	Lights
The Man Who Came to Dinner Moss Hart and George S. Kaufman	Nagle Jackson	John Falabella	David Murin	Frances Aronson
She Stoops to Conquer Oliver Goldsmith	Larry Carpenter	Scott Bradley	Gail Brassard	John Gisondi
Sally's Gone, She Left Her Name Russell Davis	Tony Giordano	Richard Hoover	David Murin	Dennis Parichy
Greater Tuna Jaston Williams, Joe Sears and Ed Howard	Larry Carpenter	Scott Bradley	C. L. Hundley	John Gisondi
You Never Know Siegfried Geyer and Karl Farkus; book adapt: Roland Leigh; music and lyrics: Cole Porter	Paul Lazarus	James Joy	John Falabella	Craig Miller

Productions	Directors	Sets	Costumes	Lights
The Unexpected Guest Agatha Christie	Larry Carpenter	Dennis Bradford	Gail Brassard	David Lockner
Billy Bishop Goes to War John Gray and Eric Peterson	John Henry Davis	John Falabella	John Falabella	Stuart Duke
Rosencrantz and Guildenstern Are Dead Tom Stoppard	Munson Hicks	Lowell Detweiler	Gail Brassard	John Gisondi
Opera Buffa Kenneth Ludwig	Larry Carpenter	John Falabella	David Murin	John Gisondi
Pump Boys and Dinettes John Foley, Mark Hardwick, Debra Monk, Cass Morgan, John Schimmel and Jim Wann	Debra Monk	Christopher J. Schriver	Deborah Shippee- O'Brien	John Gisondi

American Theatre Arts

DON EITNER
Artistic Director

JAMES HILDEBRANDT
Executive Director

EDITH M. LASHLEY
Honorary Board Chairman

JUDITH SEELIG
Board President

6240 Hollywood Blvd.
Hollywood, CA 90028
(213) 466-2463 (business)
(213) 466-2462 (box office)

FOUNDED 1976
Don Eitner

SEASON
September-August

FACILITIES
Borelli Theatre
Seating capacity: 70
Stage: flexible

Thornton Theatre
Seating capacity: 60
Stage: proscenium

FINANCES
January 1, 1984-December 31, 1984
Operating expenses: $227,600

AUDIENCE
Annual attendance: 9,045
Subscribers: 240

AEA 99-seat waiver

PRODUCTIONS 1983–84

Productions	Directors	Sets	Costumes	Lights
Sherlock Holmes book adapt: William Gillette, from Arthur Conan Doyle; music: Bruce Ewen	Ken Letner	W. Lansing Barbour	Elena Del Rio	Robert Smitherman
Twelfth Night William Shakespeare; American sign language trans: Lou Fant, Tom Henschel, Lois Foraker and Gary Sanderson	Don Eitner	Betty G. Miller	Armand Coutu	Tom Coffey
How We Lived Yale Gould	Bette Ferber	Alex Stewart	Marianna Elliott	Ilya Mindlin
The Country Wife William Wycherly	Tom Henschel	Robert Green	Armand Coutu	Magda Gonzalez
Inner/Inter Changes—a one-act repertory: *The Rooming House*, Conrad Bromberg	Sue Wolfe	N. J. Benedetti	Reve Richards and Susanne L. Holland	Geoffrey Rinehart

PRODUCTIONS 1983–84

Productions	Directors	Sets	Costumes	Lights
Animal, Oliver Hailey	Armand Coutu	N. J. Benedetti	Reve Richards and Susanne L. Holland	Geoffrey Rinehart
Rats, Israel Horovitz	Ron Ames	N. J. Benedetti	Reve Richards and Susanne L. Holland	Geoffrey Rinehart
Jew, Harvey Perr	Armand Coutu	N. J. Benedetti	Reve Richards and Susanne L. Holland	Geoffrey Rinehart
Momma as she became—but not as she was . . ., John Rechy	Armand Coutu	N. J. Benedetti	Reve Richards and Susanne L. Holland	Geoffrey Rinehart
The New Quixote, Michael Frayn	Howard Penn	N. J. Benedetti	Reve Richards and Susanne L. Holland	Geoffrey Rinehart
Chinamen, Michael Frayn	Jim Drake	N. J. Benedetti	Reve Richards and Susanne L. Holland	Geoffrey Rinehart
Black and Silver, Michael Frayn	Ron Ames	N. J. Benedetti	Reve Richards and Susanne L. Holland	Geoffrey Rinehart

PRODUCTIONS 1984–85

Productions	Directors	Sets	Costumes	Lights
Blood Relations Sharon Pollock	Don Eitner	Dan Dryden	Elena Del Rio	Geoffrey Rinehart
The Diary of a Madman Nikolai Gogol; adapt: Don Eitner and Tom Troupe; trans: Rodney Patterson	Don Eitner	Owen Williams		Geoffrey Rinehart
The Scarecrow Percy Mackaye; adapt: Rico Peterson; trans: Bob Daniels and Freda Norman	Ed Waterstreet	Armand Coutu	Armand Coutu	Paul Mitchell
A Scrap of Paper Victorien Sardou; trans: Leonie Gilmour	Tom Henschel	Robert Green	Suzanne Cranfill	Magda Gonzalez
Rules of the Game Luigi Pirandello; trans: William Murray	Don Eitner	Margaret Perry	Sonya Haney	Scott M. Stipetic

American Theatre Company

KITTY ROBERTS
Artistic/Producing Director

DEWEY F. BARTLETT, JR.
Board Chairman

Box 1265
Tulsa, OK 74101
(918) 747-9494 (business)
(918) 592-7111 (box office)

FOUNDED 1970
Kitty Roberts

SEASON
October-June

FACILITIES
Brook Theatre
3403 South Peoria St.
Seating capacity: 483
Stage: proscenium

John H. Williams Theatre
2nd and Cincinnati Sts.
Seating capacity: 429
Stage: proscenium

FINANCES
January 1, 1984-December 31, 1984
Operating expenses: $350,000

AUDIENCE
Annual attendance: 44,356
Subscribers: 3,400

TOURING CONTACT
Bob Odle

BOOKED-IN EVENTS
Theatre, music, dance

AEA Guest Artist contract

PRODUCTIONS 1983–84

Productions	Directors	Sets	Costumes	Lights
Blues Will Bartlett	Kitty Roberts	Richard Ellis	Jo McClelland	Richard Wilson
The Crystal Forest book and lyrics: Kerry Hauger; music: Richard Averill	Kerry Hauger	Bill Motyka	Jo McClelland	Jim Queen
The Diary of Anne Frank Frances Goodrich and Albert Hackett	Scott Rubsam	Richard Ellis	Jo McClelland	Jim Queen
Close Ties Elizabeth Diggs	Steve Ramey	James Queen	Jo McClelland	Jeff Darby
Mass Appeal Bill C. Davis	Scott Rubsam	Richard Ellis	Jo McClelland	Jim Queen
Bullshot Crummond Ron House, Diz White, Alan Shearman, John Neville-Andrews and Sally Willis	Ted Kachel	Jim French	Jo McClelland	Jeff Darby

---

PRODUCTIONS 1984–85

Productions	Directors	Sets	Costumes	Lights
The Best Man Gore Vidal	Scott Rubsam	Richard Ellis	Jo McClelland	Jim Queen
A Christmas Carol book adapt: Robert Odle, from Charles Dickens; music: Richard Averill	David Gately	Richard Ellis	Jo McClelland	Richard Wilson
The Miracle Worker William Gibson	Scott Rubsam	Richard Ellis	Jo McClelland	Dan Cork
Oedipus Rex Sophocles	Ted Kachel	Richard Ellis	Jo McClelland	Jeff Darby
Peter Pan book: James M. Barrie; music: Mark Charlap and Jule Styne; lyrics: Carolyn Leigh, Betty Comden and Adolf Green	Paula Kalustian	Eduardo Sicangco	Eduardo Sicangco	Jeff Darby
'night, Mother Marsha Norman	Bill Fears	Richard Ellis	Jo McClelland	Jim Queen

Arena Stage

ZELDA FICHANDLER
Producing Director

THOMAS C. FICHANDLER
Executive Director

DOUGLAS C. WAGER
Associate Producing Director

LEE G. RUBENSTEIN
Board President

6th and Maine Aves., SW
Washington, DC 20024
(202) 554-9066 (business)
(202) 488-3300 (box office)

FOUNDED 1950
Zelda Fichandler, Thomas C.
   Fichandler, Edward Mangum

SEASON
September-June

FACILITIES
The Arena
Seating capacity: 827
Stage: arena

The Kreeger Theatre
Seating capacity: 514
Stage: modified thrust

The Old Vat Room
Seating capacity: 180
Stage: cabaret

The Scene Shop
Seating capacity: 130
Stage: flexible

FINANCES
July 1, 1984-June 30, 1985
Operating expenses: $6,069,125

AUDIENCE
Annual attendance: 300,000
Subscribers: 18,000

TOURING CONTACT
Catherine Irwin

BOOKED-IN EVENTS
Theatre, musical theatre

AEA LORT (B) contract

PRODUCTIONS 1983–84

Productions	Directors	Sets	Costumes	Lights
The Importance of Being Earnest Oscar Wilde	Richard Russell Ramos	Tony Straiges	Marjorie Slaiman	Frances Aronson
Beyond Therapy Christopher Durang	Gary Pearle	Thomas Lynch	Mary Ann Powell	William Mintzer
As You Like It William Shakespeare	Douglas C. Wager	Thomas Lynch	Marjorie Slaiman	Paul Gallo
The Three Sisters Anton Chekhov; trans: Randall Jarrell	Zelda Fichandler	Alexander Okun	Ann Hould-Ward	Arden Fingerhut
Accidental Death of an Anarchist Dario Fo; adapt: Richard Nelson	Douglas C. Wager	Karl Eigsti	Marjorie Slaiman	Allen Lee Hughes
Quartermaine's Terms Simon Gray	Jacques Cartier	David Jenkins	Marjorie Slaiman	Nancy Schertler
Cloud 9 Caryl Churchill	Gary Pearle	Thomas Lynch	Laura Crow	Paul Gallo
Happy End book and lyrics: Bertolt Brecht; music: Kurt Weill; adapt: Michael Feingold	Garland Wright	John Arnone	Marjorie Slaiman	Frances Aronson

PRODUCTIONS 1984–85

Productions	Directors	Sets	Costumes	Lights
The Tempest William Shakespeare	Garland Wright	John Arnone	Jared Aswegan	Frances Aronson
Gospel at Colonus Sophocles; book adapt: Lee Breuer; music: Bob Telson	Lee Breuer	Alison Yerxa	Ghretta Hynd	Julie Archer
Passion Play Peter Nichols	Elinor Renfield	Loren Sherman	Marjorie Slaiman	Allen Lee Hughes
Man and Superman George Bernard Shaw	Douglas C. Wager	Adrianne Lobel	Marjorie Slaiman	Paul Gallo
Real Estate Louise Page	Christopher Markle	David Jenkins	Marjorie Slaiman	Paul Gallo
Tartuffe Molière; trans: Richard Wilbur	Lucian Pintilie	Radu Boruzescu	Miruna Boruzescu	Beverly Emmons
Isn't It Romantic Wendy Wasserstein	Amy Saltz	Patricia Woodbridge	Mary Ann Powell	Nancy Schertler
Execution of Justice Emily Mann	Douglas C. Wager	Ming Cho Lee	Marjorie Slaiman	Allen Lee Hughes

Arizona Theatre Company

GARY GISSELMAN
Artistic Director

BETSY L. BOLDING
Board President

53 West Congress St., Box 1631
Tucson, AZ 85702
(602) 884-8210 (business)
(602) 622-2823 (box office)

17 East Thomas Road, Suite 15
Phoenix, AZ 85012
(602) 234-2892 (business)
(602) 279-0534 (box office)

FOUNDED 1966
Sandy Rosenthal

SEASON
October-June

FACILITIES
Tucson Community Center Theatre
Seating capacity: 526
Stage: modified thrust

Phoenix College Theatre
1202 West Thomas Road
Seating capacity: 305
Stage: thrust

Scottsdale Center for the Arts
Scottsdale Mall
Seating capacity: 785
Stage: modified thrust

FINANCES
July 1, 1984-June 30, 1985
Operating expenses: $1,800,000

AUDIENCE
Annual attendance: 105,000
Subscribers: 10,600

TOURING CONTACT
Lorraine Glazar

AEA LORT (C) contract

PRODUCTIONS 1983–84

Productions	Directors	Sets	Costumes	Lights
A Streetcar Named Desire Tennessee Williams	Jon Cranney	Don Yunker	Christopher Beesley	James Sale
Billy Bishop Goes to War John Gray and Eric Peterson	Ken Ruta	Jack Barkla	Bobbi Culbert	Donald Darnutzer
The Taming of the Shrew William Shakespeare	Gary Gisselman	Jack Barkla	Jared Aswegan	Donald Darnutzer
Our Town Thornton Wilder	Gary Gisselman	Jack Barkla	Jared Aswegan	Donald Darnutzer
'night, Mother Marsha Norman	Ken Ruta	Don Yunker	Bobbi Culbert	Donald Darnutzer
Quilters book: Molly Newman and Barbara Damashek; music: Barbara Damashek	Gary Gisselman	Don Yunker	Jared Aswegan	Donald Darnutzer

---

PRODUCTIONS 1984–85

Productions	Directors	Sets	Costumes	Lights
And a Nightingale Sang... C. P. Taylor	Gary Gisselman	Don Yunker	David Mickelson	Vivian Robson
Master Harold...and the boys Athol Fugard	Walter L. Schoen, Jr.	Don Yunker	Bobbi Culbert	Don Hooper
The Learned Ladies Molière; trans: Richard Wilbur	Ken Ruta	Vicki Smith	Lewis Brown	Donald Darnutzer
Death of a Salesman Arthur Miller	Gary Gisselman	Vicki Smith	David Mickelsen	Donald Darnutzer
Goodbye Freddy Elizabeth Diggs	Ken Ruta	William Bloodgood	David MIckelsen	Vivian Robson
The Robber Bridegroom book and lyrics: Alfred Uhry; music: Robert Waldman	Gary Gisselman and Myron Johnson	Dahl Delu	Jared Aswegan	Donald Darnutzer

Arkansas Repertory Theatre

CLIFF FANNIN BAKER
Artistic Director

ANDREW C. GAUPP
Managing Director

MIMI DORTCH
Board President

712 East Eleventh St.
Little Rock, AR 72202
(501) 378-0405

FOUNDED 1976
Cliff Fannin Baker

SEASON
July-June

FACILITIES
Seating capacity: 112
Stage: flexible

FINANCES
July 1, 1984-June 30, 1985
Operating expenses: $453,945

AUDIENCE
Annual attendance: 45,000
Subscribers: 1,500

TOURING CONTACT
Guy Couch

BOOKED-IN EVENTS
Theatre, music, dance

AEA Guest Artist contract

PRODUCTIONS 1983-84

Productions	Directors	Sets	Costumes	Lights
Billy Bishop Goes to War John Gray and Eric Peterson	Cliff F. Baker	Robert Smith	Morgan James	David Simmons
Black Coffee Agatha Christie	Cliff F. Baker	Michael Smith	Morgan James	Kathy Gray
A Christmas Carol adapt: Addie Walsh, from Charles Dickens	Cathey Crowell Sawyer	Michael Nichols	Morgan James	Kathy Gray
Side Shows Andrew Johns	Cliff F. Baker	Michael Nichols	Morgan James	Guy Couch
How the Other Half Loves Alan Ayckbourn	Terry Sneed	Don Yanik	Morgan James	Keith Smith
Oh, Coward! music and lyrics: Noel Coward; adapt: Roderick Cook	Cliff F. Baker	Don Yanik	Morgan James	Kathy Gray
Sing for Your Supper music: Richard Rodgers; lyrics: Lorenz Hart; adapt: Richard Lewine and John Fearnley	Cliff F. Baker and Terry Sneed	Don Yanik	Cliff F. Baker	Kathy Gray

PRODUCTIONS 1984-85

Productions	Directors	Sets	Costumes	Lights
That Championship Season Jason Miller	Cathey Crowell Sawyer	John McFadden	Christie Bowles	James W. Hunter
Mass Appeal Bill C. Davis	Cliff F. Baker	Michael Nichols	Christie Bowles	James W. Hunter
Ain't Misbehavin' music and lyrics: Fats Waller, et al.; adapt: Richard Maltby, Jr.	Cathey Crowell Sawyer	Michael Nichols	Christie Bowles	James W. Hunter
Bus Stop William Inge	Cathey Crowell Sawyer	Don Yanik	Christie Bowles	James W. Hunter
Talley's Folly Lanford Wilson	Terry Sneed	Michael Nichols	Christie Bowles	James W. Hunter
Crimes of the Heart Beth Henley	Cliff F. Baker	Michael Nichols	Christie Bowles	James W. Hunter
The Good Woman of Setzuan Bertolt Brecht; trans: Eric Bentley	Cliff F. Baker	Michael Smith	Connie Fails	Kathy Gray

The Ark Theatre Company

BRUCE DANIEL
DONALD MARCUS
LISA MILLIGAN
Artistic Directors

PEGGY O. WILLIAMS
Board Chairman

131 Spring St.
New York, NY 10012
(212) 431-6285 (business)
(212) 226-7682 (box office)

FOUNDED 1978
Donald Marcus, Lisa Milligan

SEASON
October-June

FACILITIES
Seating capacity: 82
Stage: thrust

FINANCES
September 1, 1984-August 31, 1985
Operating expenses: $136,000

AUDIENCE
Annual attendance: 4,800
Subscribers: 350

AEA letter of agreement

PRODUCTIONS 1983–84

Productions	Directors	Sets	Costumes	Lights
Macbeth William Shakespeare	Rebecca Guy	Kalina Ivanov and Loy Arcenas	Donna Zakowska	Betsy Adams
The Man Who Could See Through Time Terri Wagener	Carey Perloff	Loy Arcenas	Martha Kelly	David N. Weiss
The Transposed Heads book adapt: Sidney Goldfarb and Julie Taymor, from Thomas Mann; music: Masa Imamura and Sheila Dabney	Julie Taymor	Atsushi Moriyasu	Donna Zakowska; puppets: Julie Taymor	David N. Weiss and Caterina Bertolotto

PRODUCTIONS 1984–85

Productions	Directors	Sets	Costumes	Lights
Charley Bacon and His Family Arthur Giron	Donald Marcus	Derek Molane	Catherine Zuber	Richard Dorfman
Life Is a Dream Pedro Calderon de la Barca; trans: Edwin Honig	James Simpson	John Arnone	Kurt Wilhelm	Frances Aronson
Chopin in Space Philip Bosakowski	Rebecca Guy	Anne Servanton	Catherine Zuber	Bruce Daniel

Asolo State Theater

JOHN ULMER
Artistic Director

RICHARD G. FALLON
Executive Director

STEPHEN ROTHMAN
Associate Executive Director

WENTON STEWART
Board President

Postal Drawer E
Sarasota, FL 33578
(813) 355-7115 (business)
(813) 355-5137 (box office)

FOUNDED 1960
Arthur Dorlang, Richard G. Fallon,
  Eberle Thomas, Robert Strane

SEASON
December-August

FACILITIES
Ringling Museum
5401 Bayshore Road
Seating capacity: 316
Stage: proscenium

FINANCES
October 1, 1983-September 30, 1984
Operating expenses: $1,764,110

AUDIENCE
Annual attendance: 196,226
Subscribers: 2,572

TOURING CONTACT
Linda DiGabriele

AEA LORT (C) contract

PRODUCTIONS 1983-84

Productions	Directors	Sets	Costumes	Lights
Arms and the Man George Bernard Shaw	Robert Falls	John Doepp	Catherine King	Martin Petlock
Waiting for Godot Samuel Beckett	John Ulmer	Bennet Averyt	Catherine King	Martin Petlock
The Gin Game D. L. Coburn	John Gulley	Bennet Averyt	Catherine King	Martin Petlock
Promenade, All! David V. Robison	John Ulmer	Henry Swanson	Catherine King	Martin Petlock
Death of a Salesman Arthur Miller	John Ulmer	Jeffrey Dean	Catherine King	Martin Petlock
The Drunkard book: Bro Herrod; music and lyrics: Barry Manilow	Cash Baxter	Kenneth Kurtz	Catherine King	Martin Petlock
Rashomon Fay and Michael Kanin	Sheldon Epps	Robert Barnes	Catherine King	Martin Petlock
The Importance of Being Earnest Oscar Wilde	John Ulmer	John Doepp	Catherine King	Martin Petlock

PRODUCTIONS 1984-85

Productions	Directors	Sets	Costumes	Lights
Children of a Lesser God Mark Medoff	Lucy Martin	Jeffrey Dean	Catherine King	Kenton Yeager
Amadeus Peter Shaffer	John Reich	John Ezell	Catherine King	Martin Petlock
And a Nightingale Sang... C. P. Taylor	John Gulley	Jeffrey Dean	Catherine King	Martin Petlock
The Little Foxes Lillian Hellman	John Ulmer	Bennet Averyt	Catherine King	Martin Petlock
Dames at Sea book and lyrics: George Haimsohn and Robin Miller; music: Jim Wise	Neal Kenyon	Peter Harvey	Catherine King	Martin Petlock
A Month in the Country Ivan Turgenev; trans: Emlyn Williams	John Ulmer	Kenneth Kurt	Catherine King	Martin Petlock
You Can't Take It with You Moss Hart and George S. Kaufman	John Gulley	Jeffrey Dean	Catherine King	Martin Petlock
Twice Around the Park Murray Schisgal	Stephen Rothman	Bennet Averyt	Catherine King	Martin Petlock

A Traveling Jewish Theatre

NAOMI NEWMAN
Artistic Director

DEBRA J. CRANE
Administrative Director

Box 421985
San Francisco, CA 94142
(415) 861-4880

FOUNDED 1978
Naomi Newman, Corey Fischer, Albert
  Greenberg

SEASON
Year-round touring

FINANCES
July 1, 1984-June 30, 1985
Operating expenses: $148,000

AUDIENCE
Annual attendance: 10,000

TOURING CONTACT
Debra Crane, Amy Mueller

PRODUCTIONS 1983-84

Productions	Directors	Sets	Costumes	Lights
A Dance of Exile company-developed	Naomi Newman	Jim Quinn	Jane Pollack; masks: Corey Fischer	Jim Quinn
The Last Yiddish Poet: An Incantation Against Woe company-developed	Naomi Newman		Corey Fischer	Jim Quinn
Coming from a Great Distance company-developed	Naomi Newman		Corey Fischer	Jim Quinn

PRODUCTIONS 1984-85

Productions	Directors	Sets	Costumes	Lights
Berlin, Jerusalem and the Moon company-developed	Michael Posnick	Gene Angell, Ron Pratt and Mary Gould	Eliza Chugg; masks and puppets: Corey Fischer	Jim Quinn
Coming from a Great Distance company-developed	Naomi Newman		Corey Fischer	Jim Quinn

At the Foot of the Mountain

PHYLLIS JANE ROSE
Executive Director

ANNE GRIFFITH
Board President

2000 South 5th St.
Minneapolis, MN 55454-1337
(612) 375-9487

FOUNDED 1974
Martha Boesing, Jan Magrane, Paul
  Boesing, Jeff Woodward, Kathy
  Rieves, Jeff Heller

SEASON
Year-round

FACILITIES
Cedar/Riverside People's Center Theatre
Seating capacity: 90
Stage: flexible

FINANCES
July 1, 1984-June 30, 1985
Operating expenses: $180,000

AUDIENCE
Annual attendance: 36,000

TOURING CONTACT
Terri Ziegler

BOOKED-IN EVENTS
Theatre, music, dance

PRODUCTIONS 1983–84

Productions	Directors	Sets	Costumes	Lights
Antigone Too: Rites of Love and Defiance adapt: Martha Boesing, from Sophocles, et al.	Martha Boesing	Carol Wisewomoon	Lisa Stephens	Carol Wisewomoon
Haunted by the Holy Ghost Jan Magrane and company	Jan Magrane	Peg Griffin and Clancy O'Riordan	Lisa Stephens	Elisa River Stacy
Las Gringas Martha Boesing and company	Martha Boesing and Jan Magrane	Elisa River Stacy	Jan Magrane and company	Elisa River Stacy
The Girls Room Jane Magrane and company	Jan Magrane and Erica Tismer	Deb James	Jan Magrane and company	Deb James

PRODUCTIONS 1984–85

Productions	Directors	Sets	Costumes	Lights
Head over Heels: Teenage Rites of Passage Jan Magrane and company	Dawn Renee Jones	Deb James	Jan Magrane and company	Deb James
The Clue in the Old Birdbath book: Kate Kasten and Sandra de Helen; music: Paul Boesing; lyrics: Paul Boesing, Martha Boesing and Kate Kasten	Phyllis Jane Rose	Deb James	Corrine Zala	Elisa River Stacy
Going to Seed Nancy Rawles	Dawn Renee Jones	Deb Hatch	Dawn Renee Jones and company	Elisa River Stacy

LAVINIA MOYER
Artistic Director

ERIC DUEWEKE
Managing Director

JOHN C. SCHERBARTH
Board Chairman

3031 West Grand Blvd., Suite 132
Detroit, MI 48202
(313) 875-8285 (business)
(313) 875-8284 (box office)

FOUNDED 1975
Lavinia Moyer, Herbert Ferrer, Nancy
Shaynes, Divina Cook, James Moran,
Curtis Armstrong

SEASON
Year-round

FACILITIES
New Center Theatre
Seating capacity: 288
Stage: proscenium

FINANCES
October 1, 1983-September 30, 1984
Operating expenses: $348,300

AUDIENCE
Annual attendance: 40,000
Subscribers: 1,200

BOOKED-IN EVENTS
Theatre, music

AEA letter of agreement

PRODUCTIONS 1983–84

Productions	Directors	Sets	Costumes	Lights
How I Got That Story Amlin Gray	Lavinia Moyer	Gary Decker	Katherine Holkeboer	Paul Brohan
Willing Simone Press	Randall Forte	Thomas Aston	Ann Correll	Paul Epton
Awake and Sing! Clifford Odets	Yolanda Fleischer	Samuel Pollack	Ann Correll	Paul Epton
Sea Marks Gardner McKay	Lavinia Moyer	Gary Decker	Ann Correll	Paul Epton
Lydie Breeze John Guare	Laurence Carr	Philipp Jung	Philipp Jung	Ed Zuckerman
True West Sam Shepard	Bill Clyne	Jaye Beethem	Ann Correll	Paul Epton
Strider book adapt: Mark Rosovsky, from Leo Tolstoy; music: Mark Rosovsky, S. Vetkin and Norman L. Berman; lyrics: Uri Riashentsev; trans: Robert Kalfin and Steve Brown	Daniel Yurgaitis	Gary Decker	Barb Oleszczuck	Paul Brohan

PRODUCTIONS 1984–85

Productions	Directors	Sets	Costumes	Lights
Fool for Love Sam Shepard	Daniel Yurgaitis	Tom Macie	Ann Correll	Paul Epton
Kennedy at Colonus Laurence Carr	Laurence Carr	Philipp Jung	Philipp Jung	Gary Decker
Children of a Lesser God Mark Medoff	Lavinia Moyer	Thomas Aston	Ann Correll	Paul Brohan
Wedding Band Alice Childress	Robert Wright	Gary Decker	Ann Correll	Paul Epton
Top Girls Caryl Churchill	Ada Brown Mather	Philipp Jung	Philipp Jung	Gary Decker
The Sunshine Boys Neil Simon	Anthony B. Schmitt	Doug Miller	Ann Correll	Paul Epton
Piaf Pam Gems	Daniel Yurgaitis	Gary Decker	Katharine Holkeboer	Paul Brohan

The Back Alley Theatre

LAURA ZUCKER
ALLAN MILLER
Producing Directors

DAWN SUTTON
Managing Director

VIVIAN FORBES
Board President

15231 Burbank Blvd.
Van Nuys, CA 91411
(818) 780-2240

FOUNDED 1979
Laura Zucker, Allan Miller

SEASON
Year-round

FACILITIES
Seating capacity: 93
Stage: proscenium

FINANCES
January 1, 1984-December 31, 1984
Operating expenses: $197,720

AUDIENCE
Annual attendance: 25,000
Subscribers: 3,000

TOURING CONTACT
Tim Reilly

BOOKED-IN EVENTS
Theatre, performance art, children's theatre

AEA Special Production contract and 99-seat waiver

PRODUCTIONS 1983–84

Productions	Directors	Sets	Costumes	Lights
Cisterns Julie Jensen	Laura Zucker	Jim Billings		Joe Morrissey
Hot & Cold (Plays for All Seasons) David Bennett Carren, Iris Rainer Dart, Terry Kingsley Smith, Brooke David Kofford, Jim McGinn, Maureen McIlroy, Rich Orloff, John Pleshette, Karen Weiss Raskind, Gary Socol, Lee Thomas, Vallie Ullman	Jim Hornbeck, Allan Miller, John Pleshette, Karen Weiss Raskind, Ted Post	Marcia Hinds	Barbara Metzenbaum	Pam Rank
A Woman of Independent Means adapt: Elizabeth Forsythe Hailey, from her novel	Norman Cohen	Marcia Hinds	Garland W. Riddle	Pam Rank
Suburban Romance Richard Caliban	Allan Miller	Don Llewellyn	Barbara Metzenbaum	Pam Rank
East of the Sun: The Fisherman and His Wife and *West of the Moon: Journey to Xibala* adapt: Sally Gordon	Sally Gordon	Hacho Mouhibian	Gail Viola, Susan Tanner and Christina Romo	Dawn Hollingsworth

PRODUCTIONS 1984–85

Productions	Directors	Sets	Costumes	Lights
Are You Now Or Have You Ever Been? Eric Bentley	Allan Miller	George Becket		Dawn Hollingsworth
Slab Boys John Byrne	Bill Castellino	Christopher M. Idoine	Diana Eden	Christine Lomaka
Thin Walls Phoef Sutton	Allan Miller	Christopher M. Idoine	Martha Burke	Christine Lomaka
A Good American Novel and *Having Fun in the Dark* Beth Lapides	Beth Lapides			John Calhoun
Duet for One Tom Kempinski	Ron Satlof	Christopher M. Idoine	Martha Burke	Joseph N. Tawil
In the Sweet Bye and Bye Donald Driver	Donald Driver	Rich Rose	Armand Coutu	Leslie Sullivant

Yale Repertory Theatre. Leonard Jackson, Robert Judd, Joe Seneca and Theresa Merritt in *Ma Rainey's Black Bottom*. Photo: George G. Slade.

The Goodman Theatre, above.
Mike Nussbaum and Joe Mantegna
in *Glengarry Glen Ross*. Photo:
Brigitte Lacombe. Long Wharf
Theatre, right, Maria Tucci and
John Lithgow in *Requiem for a
Heavyweight*. Photo: Gerry
Goodstein.

Theater of the Open Eye, left. Jodi
Long in *The Dream of Kitamura*.
Photo: Ken Howard. The Wooster
Group, below. Willem Dafoe,
Nancy Reilly and Kate Valk in
L.S.D. (Just the High Points).
Photo: Nancy Campbell.

The Clarence Brown
Company, right. Basia McCoy
and William Shust in *Richard
III*. Photo: Nick Myers. Dallas
Theater Center, below. Harold
Suggs, Tom Key, Martin
Rayner and James Werner in
A Christmas Carol. Photo:
Linda Blase.

Great Lakes Theater Festival, top. Kimberly King, Barry Boys, Suzanne Petri and Christine Malik in *Alcestis and Apollo, or The Alcestiad*. Photo: Mary Beth Camp. Folger Theatre, left. Edward Gero and Richard Hart in *A Midsummer Night's Dream*. Photo: Joan Marcus. Court Theatre, above. Ingrid Blekys and John Reeger in *A Midsummer Night's Dream*. Photo: Jennifer Girard.

McCarter Theatre, above. *The Dawns Are Quiet Here.*
Photo: Cliff Moore. Alliance Theatre Company, right. Jay
McMillan and Al Hamacher in *High Standards.* Photo:
Charles Rafshoon.

New York Shakespeare Festival, above. Kevin Kline in *Henry V*. Photo: Martha Swope. The CAST Theatre, right. William Frankfather, Cotter Smith and Jerry Craig in *From the Journal of Hazard McCauley*. Photo: Ed Krieger.

Berkeley Repertory Theatre, right. Paul Santiago and
Charles Dean in *The Tooth of Crime.* Photo: Ken
Friedman. StageWest, below. John Abajian and
Christopher McHale in *True West.* Photo: Carl Bartels.

The Philadelphia Company. Brett Porter, Brenda Wehle and Zach Grenier in *Strange Snow*. Photo: Ken Kauffman.

The Salt Lake Acting Company. Betsy Nagel and Don Glover in *Wave's Home for Hurtin Tammies*. Photo: Jess Allen.

Milwaukee Repertory Theater. Daniel Mooney in *The Devil's Disciple*.

Roadside Theater. Frankie Taylor, Gary Slemp and Don Baker in *Red Fox/Second Hangin'*. Photo: Dan Carraco.

TheatreVirginia, above. Michael McCarty and Trip Plymale in *Greater Tuna*. Photo: Ronald Jennings. New Playwrights' Theatre, right. Kathleen Weber and Stanley Anderson in *Lydie Breeze*. Photo: Doc Dougherty.

The Wilma Theater, above. Doug Schaerer, Odell Conyers, Harry Bennett, Jan Versoza and Richard Boddy in *The Hairy Ape*. Photo: Stan Sadowski. Perseverance Theatre, right. Phil Smith, Kay Smith and Claudia Coyner in *Island of Tears*.

Intiman Theatre, left. James Scales and Gregg Hashimoto in *The Dance and the Railroad*. Photo: Chris Bennion. Old Globe Theatre, below. *Elektra*. Photo: Susan Blanchard.

A Contemporary Theatre,
above. *The Odyssey*. Photo:
Chris Bennion. New Stage
Theatre, right. Ceal Phelan,
Vicky Little Waters and Jane
Reid-Petty in *Agnes of God*.
Photo: Chuck Allen.

Soho Repertory Theatre, left. Tom Crawley, Suzanne Ford, Sybil Lines, and Helen Zelon in *The Crimes of Vautrin*. Photo: Gerry Goodstein. Paper Mill Playhouse, below. John Thomas Waite and company in *Amadeus*. Photo: Jerry Dalia.

La Jolla Playhouse, above. Ben Halley, Jr. and Tuck Milligan in *Big River: The Adventures of Huckleberry Finn*. Photo: Micha Langer. Mark Taper Forum, right. Mare Winningham, Miriam Mayer and Andrew Robinson in *The Genius*. Photo: Jay Thompson.

The Harold Clurman Theatre, above. Alice Drummond, James Greene, Alvin Epstein and Peter Evans in *Endgame*. Photo: Martha Swope. American Repertory Theatre, left. Harry Murphy and company in *King Stag*. Photo: Richard Feldman.

WPA Theatre. John Bedford-Lloyd, Elizabeth Berridge and Jay O. Sanders in *The Incredibly Famous Willy Rivers*. Photo: Ken Howard.

Attic Theatre, above. Glen Allen Pruett and Lavinia Moyer in *Fool for Love*. Photo: Leni Sinclair. Wisdom Bridge Theatre, right. Aidan Quinn in *Hamlet*. Photo: Jennifer Girard.

Actors Theatre of St. Paul. *Awake and Sing!* Photo: Connie Jerome.

Chocolate Bayou Theater Company. Harry Booker and Kathryn Hill in *84 Charing Cross Road*. Photo: John R. Pearson.

Detroit Repertory Theatre. Willie Hodge and Robert Williams-Vogue in *Ceremonies in Dark Old Men*.

Center Stage. Mary Layne, Brenda Wehle and Marek Johnson in *On the Verge or The Geography of Yearning*.
Photo: Richard Anderson.

Philadelphia Drama Guild. Jane Jones, Esther Rolle and Roshi Handwerger in *The Member of the Wedding*. Photo: Ken Kauffman.

Steppenwolf Theatre Company. Terry Kinney, John Mahoney and Kevin Anderson in *Orphans*. Photo: Lisa Ebright.

Pioneer Memorial Theatre, above. *Candide.* Photo: Robert Clayton. The Children's Theatre Company, right. Julie Powell Taylor and Bain Boehlke in *The Legend of Sleepy Hollow.* Photo: George Heinrich.

Seattle Repertory Theatre, left.
Daniel Davis and Kate Mulgrew
in *The Misanthrope*. Photo:
Chris Bennion. Empire State
Institute for the Performing
Arts, below. *The Crucible*.
Photo: Fred Ricard.

East West Players, right. Alberto Isaac and Robert Ito in *A Song for a Nisei Fisherman*. Photo: James Young. Coconut Grove Playhouse, below. *Pump Boys and Dinettes*. Photo: Henry Friedman.

CSC: City Stage Co., top. Charles H. Patterson, Guy Paul, Sheridan Crist and Amy Warner in *The Underpants*. Photo: Gerry Goodstein. A Traveling Jewish Theatre, above. Corey Fischer and Albert Greenberg in *Coming from a Great Distance*. Photo: Marvin Lichtner.

L.A. Theatre Works. Darrell Larson, Norbert Weisser and Christine Avila in *The Coyote Cycle*. Photo: Margaret Von Biesen.

Manhattan Theatre Club. Dianne Wiest and Henderson Forsythe in *Other Places*. Photo: Gerry Goodstein.

L.A. Public Theatre. Meg Foster, Kim Darby, Lauren Hutton and Kario Salem in *Extremities*. Photo: David Hiller.

Studio Arena Theatre. Stephen McKinley Henderson, Basil A. Wallace and David Bottrell in *Master Harold . . . and the boys*.
Photo: K.C. Kratt.

Arena Stage, above. Michael Jeter and Richard Bauer in *Accidental Death of an Anarchist*. Photo: Joan Marcus. Pan Asian Repertory Theatre, right. Tom Matsusaka, Mel Duane Gionson and Tina Chen in *Empress of China*. Photo: Corky Lee.

Circle in the Square Theatre, above. Rex Harrison and Amy Irving in *Heartbreak House*. Photo: Martha Swope. Circle Repertory Theatre, right. Karen Sederholm, Billie Neal and Tanya Berezin in *Balm in Gilead*. Photo: Gerry Goodstein.

Barter Theatre

REX PARTINGTON
Producing Director

FILLMORE McPHERSON
Board President

Abingdon, VA 24210
(703) 628-2281 (business)
(703) 628-3991 (box office)

FOUNDED 1933
Robert Porterfield

SEASON
April-October

FACILITIES
Barter Theatre
Seating capacity: 380
Stage: proscenium

Barter Playhouse
Seating capacity: 138
Stage: modified thrust

FINANCES
November 1, 1983-October 31, 1984
Operating expenses: $848,374

AUDIENCE
Annual attendance: 71,378
Subscribers: 2,772

TOURING CONTACT
Pearl Hayter

AEA LORT (C) contract

PRODUCTIONS 1983–84

Productions	Directors	Sets	Costumes	Lights
The Mousetrap Agatha Christie	Dorothy Marie Robinson	Bennet Averyt	Sigrid Insull	Al Oster
Bus Stop William Inge	Ken Costigan	Lynn Pecktal	Marianne Custer	Al Oster
Fallen Angels Noel Coward	Harry Ellerbe	Lynn Pecktal	Barbara Forbes	Al Oster
Da Hugh Leonard	Ken Costigan	Daniel Ettinger	Barbara Forbes	Al Oster
The Dining Room A. R. Gurney, Jr.	William Van Keyser	John Larrance	Sigrid Insull	Al Oster
Dial M for Murder Frederick Knott	Harry Ellerbe	John Larrance	Sigrid Insull	Al Oster
Side by Side by Sondheim music and lyrics: Stephen Sondheim, et al.; adapt: Ned Sherrin	Pamela Hunt	Rex Partington	Georgia Baker	Al Oster
Relatively Speaking Alan Ayckbourn	Ken Costigan	Daniel Ettinger	Barbara Forbes	Al Oster

PRODUCTIONS 1984–85

Productions	Directors	Sets	Costumes	Lights
Tintypes Mary Kyte, Mel Marvin and Gary Pearle	Pamela Hunt	Lynn Pecktal	Georgia Baker	Al Oster
Crimes of the Heart Beth Henley	Geoffrey Hitch	Daniel Ettinger	Carr Garnett	Al Oster
The Good Doctor adapt: Neil Simon, from Anton Chekhov	Ken Costigan	Dennis Bradford	Martha Hally	Al Oster
Artichoke Joanna M. Glass	Gregory S. Hurst	Daniel Ettinger	Karen Brewster	Al Oster
Mass Appeal Bill C. Davis	Ken Costigan	Jim Stauder	Sigrid Insull	Al Oster
Promenade, All! David V. Robison	William Van Keyser	Daniel Ettinger	Martha Hally	Al Oster
Bell, Book and Candle John Van Druten	Ken Costigan	Lynn Pecktal	Barbara Forbes	Al Oster
Calling on Lou adapt: Larry Richman, from Lou Crabtree	William Van Keyser		Karen Brewster	Al Oster

Berkeley Repertory Theatre

SHARON OTT
Artistic Director

MITZI SALES
Managing Director

EDWIN C. SHIVER
Board President

2025 Addison St.
Berkeley, CA 94704
(415) 841-6108 (business)
(415) 845-4700 (box office)

FOUNDED 1968
Michael W. Leibert

SEASON
September–August

FACILITIES
Mainstage
Seating capacity: 401
Stage: thrust

Second Stage
Seating capacity: 70
Stage: flexible

FINANCES
September 1, 1983–August 31, 1984
Operating expenses: $1,561,445

AUDIENCE
Annual attendance: 118,000
Subscribers: 12,600

BOOKED-IN EVENTS
Theatre

AEA LORT (C) contract

PRODUCTIONS 1983–84

Productions	Directors	Sets	Costumes	Lights
American Buffalo David Mamet	John Dillon	Ralph Funicello	Kurt Wilhelm	Dan Kotlowitz
The Way of the World William Congreve	Albert Takazauckas	Bernard Vyzga	Deborah Dryden	Greg Sullivan
Season's Greetings Alan Ayckbourn	Douglas Johnson	Karen Gjelsteen	Merrily Ann Murray	Derek Duarte
Awake and Sing! Clifford Odets	Joy Carlin	Jesse Hollis	Michael Olich	Derek Duarte
Filumena Eduardo De Filippo	Tony Amendola	Vicki Smith	Sally Richardson	Tom Ruzika
The Margaret Ghost Carole Braverman	Edward Hastings	Mark Donnelly	Jeannie Davidson	Greg Sullivan
Kabuki Medea Euripides; adapt: Shozo Sato	Shozo Sato	Shozo Sato	Shozo Sato	Shozo Sato

---

PRODUCTIONS 1984–85

Productions	Directors	Sets	Costumes	Lights
A Touch of the Poet Eugene O'Neill	Steven Schachter	Jesse Hollis	Jeannie Davidson	Derek Duarte
Otherwise Engaged Simon Gray	Richard E. T. White	William Bloodgood	Debra Bruneaux	Derek Duarte
Tartuffe Molière; trans: Richard Wilbur	Albert Takazauckas	William S. Eddelman	Beaver Bauer	Greg Sullivan
Kingdom Come Amlin Gray	Sharon Ott	Laura Maurer	Colleen Muscha	Dan Kotlowitz
Misalliance George Bernard Shaw	Robert Moss	Karen Gjelsteen	Michael Olich	Steve Peterson
The Tooth of Crime Sam Shepard	Sharon Ott and Richard E. T. White	Kent Dorsey	Susan Hilferty	Kent Dorsey
Execution of Justice Emily Mann	Oskar Eustis and Anthony Taccone	Vicki Smith	Eliza Chugg	Derek Duarte

---

Berkeley Shakespeare Festival

DAKIN MATTHEWS
Artistic Director

JOHN MAYNARD, JR.
Managing Director

RONALD VINCENT
Board President

Box 969
Berkeley, CA 94701
(415) 548-3422

FOUNDED 1974
Bay Area actors

SEASON
July-September

FACILITIES
John Hinkel Park
Southampton and San Diego Roads
Seating capacity: 350
Stage: thrust

FINANCES
January 1, 1984-December 31, 1984
Operating expenses: $334,640

AUDIENCE
Annual attendance: 31,000
Subscribers: 3,500

TOURING CONTACT
Eric Berne

AEA LORT (D) contract

PRODUCTIONS 1984

Productions	Directors	Sets	Costumes	Lights
Othello William Shakespeare	Richard E. T. White	Michael Cook	Eliza Chugg	James Brentano
The Merchant of Venice William Shakespeare	Tony Amendola	Shevra Tait	Patricia Polen	James Brentano
Love's Labour's Lost William Shakespeare	Julian Lopez-Morillas	Eric Landisman	Diana Stone	James Brentano

---

PRODUCTIONS 1985

Productions	Directors	Sets	Costumes	Lights
A Midsummer Night's Dream William Shakespeare	Richard E. T. White	Peggy McDonald	Barbara Bush	Brad Belleville
The Two Noble Kinsmen William Shakespeare and John Fletcher	Julian Lopez-Morillas	Gene Angell and Ron Pratt	Frances Kenney	Brad Belleville
Richard III William Shakespeare	Anne McNaughton	Eric Landisman	Patricia Polen	Brad Belleville

Berkshire Theatre Festival

JOSEPHINE R. ABADY
Artistic Director

JOAN STEIN
Managing Director

JANE P. FITZPATRICK
Board President

Box 797
Stockbridge, MA 01262
(413) 298-5536 (business)
(413) 298-5576 (box office)

FOUNDED 1928
Mabel Choate, Walter Clark, Daniel
  Chester, Austin Fox Riggs

SEASON
June-September

FACILITIES
East Main St.
Mainstage
Seating capacity: 429
Stage: proscenium

Unicorn Theatre
Seating capacity: 100
Stage: thrust

Children's Theatre
Seating capacity: 100
Stage: flexible

FINANCES
September 1, 1983-August 31, 1984
Operating expenses: $744,970

AUDIENCE
Annual attendance: 40,000
Subscribers: 461

*AEA Council on Resident Stock Theatres
  (Y) contract*

PRODUCTIONS 1984

Productions	Directors	Sets	Costumes	Lights

Sabrina Fair
  Samuel Taylor
	Josephine R.
	  Abady
		David Potts	David Tosner	Jeff Davis

A Loss of Roses
  William Inge
	Josephine R.
	  Abady
		John Lee Beatty	David Murin	Jeff Davis

Miss Lulu Bett Zona Gale	Jack Hofsiss	David Potts	Ann Roth	Jeff Davis

High Spirits
  adapt: Timothy Gray and Hugh Martin; music
  and lyrics: Noel Coward
	Randy Hoey	John Lee Beatty	Jennifer von
			  Mayrhauser
				Jeff Davis

American Dreams adapt: Peter Frisch, from Studs Terkel	Peter Frisch	John Iacovelli	Pat Saftner	Tom Sturge
Loose Ends Michael Weller	Peter Frisch	John Iacovelli	Pat Saftner	Tom Sturge
Silver Linings Ted Tally	James Luse	John Iacovelli	Pat Saftner	Tom Sturge
Couplings Michael Wright	Michael Breault	John Iacovelli	Pat Saftner	Tom Sturge
His First Deer Nat Smith	James Luse		Pikke Allen	
The First Bloom Richard Zucco	Eli Simon	John Iacovelli	Pikke Allen	
Big Green Bridge Sean Jost	Eli Simon	John Iacovelli	Pikke Allen	

PRODUCTIONS 1985

Productions	Directors	Sets	Costumes	Lights

The Member of the Wedding
  Carson McCullers
	Josephine R.
	  Abady
		David Potts	Linda Fisher	Jeff Davis

Beyond Therapy Christopher Durang	Richard Ramos	David Jenkins	Bruce Harrow	Jeff Davis

Caught
  Bernard Kahn
	Josephine R.
	  Abady
		David Potts	Carol Oditz	Jeff Davis

Paris Bound Philip Barry	Jack Hofsiss	John Lee Beatty	Julie Weiss	Jeff Davis
Incoming Michael Breault and Dennis Poore	Michael Breault	Jim Noone	Bruce Goodrich	Tom Sturge
The Day They Shot John Lennon James McLure	Eli Simon	Jim Noone	Bruce Goodrich	Tom Sturge
Fifth of July Lanford Wilson	Michael Breault	Jim Noone	Bruce Goodrich	Tom Sturge

Productions	Directors	Sets	Costumes	Lights
The Journey of the Sea Box Rebecca Hoogs	James Luse	Jim Noone	Marla Rice	
The Beach Cat Leslie Fields	James Luse	Jim Noone	Marla Rice	
The Sea Monster Thao Nguyen	James Luse	Jim Noone	Marla Rice	

Bilingual Foundation of the Arts

MARGARITA GALBAN
Artistic Director

SUE WELSH
Executive Director

CARMEN ZAPATA
President/Managing Producer

L. G. TRUJILLO
Board Chairman

421 North Ave. 19
Los Angeles, CA 90031
(213) 225-4044

FOUNDED 1975
Carmen Zapata, Margarita Galban,
Estela Scarlata

SEASON
January-June, September-December

FACILITIES
Seating capacity: 99
Stage: thrust

FINANCES
January 1, 1984-December 31, 1984
Operating expenses: $263,785

AUDIENCE
Annual attendance: 28,000

TOURING CONTACT
Michael Dewell

BOOKED-IN EVENTS
Theatre

*AEA LORT (B) and (D) contracts and
99-seat waiver*

PRODUCTIONS 1983–84

Productions	Directors	Sets	Costumes	Lights
Rosalba Y Los Llaveros Emilio Carballido; trans: Lina Montalvo and Estela Scarlata	Margarita Galban	Paul Ayers	Estela Scarlata	Paul Ayers
Equinox Mario Diament; trans: Simone Z. Karlin and Evelyn Strouse	Margarita Galban	Paul Ayers	Estela Scarlata	Paul Ayers
Maria Cristina Me Quiere Gobernar Jose Gabriel Nunez	Armando Gota	Estela Scarlata	Estela Scarlata	Robert Fromer
El Juego Mariela Romero; trans: Susana Castillo, Carmen Zapata and Joseph Chrzanowski	Margarita Galban	Estela Scarlata	Estela Scarlata	Robert Fromer

---

PRODUCTIONS 1984–85

Productions	Directors	Sets	Costumes	Lights
Blood Wedding Federico Garcia Lorca; trans: Carmen Zapata and Michael Dewell; music: Ian Krouse	Margarita Galban	Estela Scarlata	Ruth Enriquez	Robert Fromer
A La Diestra de Dios Padre Enrique Buenaventura	Jaime Jongil	Estela Scarlata	Estela Scarlata	Robert Fromer
El Animador Rodolfo Santana; trans: Lina Montalvo and Carmen Zapata	Margarita Galban	Estela Scarlata	Estela Scarlata	Robert Fromer

PRODUCTIONS 1984-85

Productions	Directors	Sets	Costumes	Lights
The Young Lady from Tacna Mario Vargas Llosa; trans: Joanne Pottlitzer	Joanne Pottlitzer	Estela Scarlata	Richard Smart	Robert Fromer
Rainbow Red Carmen Zapata and Estela Scarlata	Linda Dangcil	Estela Scarlata	Diane Anderson	Estela Scarlata

BoarsHead: Michigan Public Theater

NANCY-ELIZABETH KAMMER
Artistic Director

CHRISTINE CHERNIS
Executive Director

DAVID T. HAYHOW
Board Chairman

425 South Grand Ave.
Lansing, MI 48933
(517) 484-7800 (business)
(517) 484-7805 (box office)

FOUNDED 1966
John Peakes, Richard Thomsen

SEASON
September-May, July-August

FACILITIES
Lansing Center for the Arts
Seating capacity: 249
Stage: thrust

Overbrook Theater
221 Quarterline Rd., Muskegon
Seating capacity: 322
Stage: proscenium

FINANCES
October 1, 1984-September 30, 1985
Operating expenses: $500,000

AUDIENCE
Annual attendance: 55,500
Subscribers: 2,700

TOURING CONTACT
Melissa Kaplan

*AEA Small Professional Theatre
contract*

PRODUCTIONS 1983-84

Productions	Directors	Sets	Costumes	Lights
Da Hugh Leonard	Patricia K. Smith	Tim Stapleton	Patricia K. Smith	Jeff Guzik
Time Steps Gus Kaikkonen	Richard Thomsen	Tim Stapleton	Patricia K. Smith	George Sherlock
Harvey Mary Chase	Robert Hall	Tim Stapleton	Patricia K. Smith	Jeff Guzik
The Gift of the Magi adapt: Peter Ekstrom, from O. Henry; music and lyrics: Peter Ekstrom	Kyle Euckert	Tim Stapleton	Patricia K. Smith	Dennis Sherman
The Courtship of Carl Sandburg Bob Gibson	Nancy-Elizabeth Kammer	Tim Stapleton	Patricia K. Smith	Dennis Sherman
Tartuffe Molière; adapt: Robert Strane and Eberle Thomas	Kristine Thatcher	Tim Stapleton	Patricia K. Smith	George Sherlock
Taking Comfort Glen Merzer	John Peakes	Tim Stapleton	Patricia K. Smith	George Sherlock
Why Am I Always Alone When I'm with You? Andrew Johns	Barbara Carlisle	Tim Stapleton	Patricia K. Smith	George Sherlock
The Little Prince book adapt and music: Ada Janik, from Antoine de Saint-Exupery	Penny Owen	Tim Stapleton	Patricia K. Smith	George Sherlock
Letters from Bernice Jeanne Michels and Phyllis Murphy	Barbara Carlisle	Tim Stapleton	Patricia K. Smith	Dennis Sherman
The Michigan Play Richard Thomsen and company	Richard Thomsen	Tim Stapleton	Patricia K. Smith	Glen J. Clements
Beyond the Fringe Allan Bennett, Peter Cook, Jonathan Miller and Dudley Moore	John Peakes	Tim Stapleton	Patricia K. Smith	Dennis Sherman
Loot Joe Orton	Mark Klein	Tim Stapleton	Patricia K. Smith	George Sherlock

Productions	Directors	Sets	Costumes	Lights
Crimes of the Heart Beth Henley	Mark Klein	Tim Stapleton	Charlotte Deardorff	George Sherlock
Nice Faces of 1943 Jane Brody, Robert Grusecki and Tom Sherohman	Barbara Carlisle	Fred Engelgau	Charlotte Deardorff	John Eckert
Morning's at Seven Paul Osborn	Kyle Euckert	Tim Stapleton	Charlotte Deardorff	Dennis Sherman
The Gift of the Magi adapt: Peter Ekstrom, from O. Henry	Kyle Euckert	Tim Stapleton	Charlotte Deardorff	Dennis Sherman
Foxfire Hume Cronyn and Susan Cooper	Nancy-Elizabeth Kammer	Tim Stapleton	Charlotte Deardorff	Dennis Sherman
None of the Above Peter D. Sieruta	Claude File	Tim Stapleton and Kyle Euckert	Charlotte Deardorff	Joseph Grigaitis
A Doll's House Henrik Ibsen	John Peakes	Ed Kruis	Charlotte Deardorff	John Eckert
Of Mice and Men John Steinbeck	Nancy-Elizabeth Kammer	Tim Stapleton	Charlotte Deardorff	Dennis Sherman
The Michigan Play Richard Thomsen and company; music: Bob Gibson and company	Barbara Carlisle and Richard Thomsen	Tim Stapleton	Patricia K. Smith	Dennis Sherman and Glen Clements
Hercules and Friends Eric Tull	Michelle Napier	Tim Stapleton	Charlotte Deardorff	Dennis Sherman
Josh Peter Link and Josh White, Jr.	Peter Link	Tim Stapleton	Patricia K. Smith	Dennis Sherman
The Gin Game D. L. Coburn	Barbara Carlisle	Tim Stapleton	Charlotte Deardorff	Dennis Sherman
Fallen Angels Noel Coward	Kyle Euckert	Tim Stapleton	Charlotte Deardorff	Richard Oman
The Michigan Young Playwrights Festival	various	Tim Stapleton	Charlotte Deardorff	Dennis Sherman

Body Politic Theatre

JAMES O'REILLY
Artistic Director

SHARON PHILLIPS
Managing Director

CAROL NIE
Board President

2261 North Lincoln Ave.
Chicago, IL 60614
(312) 348-7901 (business)
(312) 871-3000 (box office)

FOUNDED 1966
Community Arts Foundation

SEASON
February-November

FACILITIES
Seating capacity: 192
Stage: thrust

FINANCES
January 1, 1984-December 31, 1984
Operating expenses: $395,815

AUDIENCE
Annual attendance: 24,000
Subscribers: 1,700

BOOKED-IN EVENTS
Theatre, music

AEA Chicago Area Theatre contract

Productions	Directors	Sets	Costumes	Lights
The Merchant of Venice William Shakespeare	A. J. Morey with Ro Ceballos	James Dardenne	Kerry Fleming	Michael McBride
Volunteers Brian Friel	Pauline Brailsford	Jeff Bauer	Kerry Fleming	Michael Rourke

PRODUCTIONS 1984

Productions	Directors	Sets	Costumes	Lights
Ladies in Retirement Edward Percy and Reginald Denham	James O'Reilly	James Dardenne	Kerry Fleming	Michael Rourke
A Life Hugh Leonard	Tom Mula	Gary Baugh	Kerry Fleming	Michael Rourke

PRODUCTIONS 1985

Productions	Directors	Sets	Costumes	Lights
The Madwoman of Chaillot Jean Giraudoux; trans: Maurice Valency	James O'Reilly and Sheldon Patinkin	Michael Merritt	Kerry Fleming	Mary Badger
All My Sons Arthur Miller	Pauline Brailsford	Jeff Bauer	Kerry Fleming	Michael Rourke
Spokesong book and lyrics: Stewart Parker; music: Jimmy Kennedy	James O'Reilly	Jeff Bauer	Kerry Fleming	Michael Rourke
Season's Greetings Alan Ayckbourn	Pauline Brailsford	Jeff Bauer	Kerry Fleming	Michael Rourke

Caldwell Playhouse

MICHAEL HALL
Producing Director

KENNETH R. MILLER
Board Chairman

Box 277
Boca Raton, FL 33429
(305) 368-7611 (business)
(305) 368-7509 (box office)

FOUNDED 1975
James R. Caldwell

SEASON
November-June

FACILITIES
Boca Raton Mall, 286 North Federal
  Hwy.
Seating capacity: 245
Stage: proscenium

FINANCES
October 1, 1984-September 30, 1985
Operating expenses: $1,000,000

AUDIENCE
Annual attendance: 70,000
Subscribers: 7,000

TOURING CONTACT
Joe Gillie

BOOKED-IN EVENTS
Children's theatre

AEA LORT (C) contract

PRODUCTIONS 1983–84

Productions	Directors	Sets	Costumes	Lights
Lunch Hour Jean Kerr	Joe Warik	Frank Bennett	Bridget Bartlett	Craig R. Ferraro
Cat on a Hot Tin Roof Tennessee Williams	Michael Hall	Frank Bennett	Bridget Bartlett	Laurel Shoemaker
The Bicycle Man Edward Moore	Michael Hall	Frank Bennett		Craig R. Ferraro
The Middle Ages A. R. Gurney, Jr.	Michael Hall	Frank Bennett	Bridget Bartlett	Craig R. Ferraro
Bedroom Farce Alan Ayckbourn	Joe Warik	Frank Bennett	Bridget Bartlett	Craig R. Ferraro
The Deadly Game Friedrich Durrenmatt; adapt: James Yaffe	Michael Hall	James Morgan	Bridget Bartlett	Craig R. Ferraro
The Circle W. Somerset Maugham	Michael Hall	Frank Bennett	Bridget Bartlett	Laurel Shoemaker

Productions	Directors	Sets	Costumes	Lights
The Decline and Fall of the Entire World as Seen Through the Eyes of Cole Porter, Revisited music and lyrics: Cole Porter; adapt: Ben Bagley	J. Randall Hugill	Frank Bennett	Bridget Bartlett	Laurel Shoemaker

PRODUCTIONS 1984–85

Productions	Directors	Sets	Costumes	Lights
Same Time, Next Year Bernard Slade	Michael Hall	James Morgan	Bridget Bartlett	Laurel Shoemaker
Whose Life Is It Anyway? Brian C. Clark	Michael Hall	Laurel Shoemaker	Bridget Bartlett	Laurel Shoemaker
Isn't It Romantic Wendy Wasserstein	Michael Hall	James Morgan	Bridget Bartlett	Craig R. Ferraro
Painting Churches Tina Howe	Michael Hall	Frank Bennett	Bridget Bartlett	Craig R. Ferraro
Bent Martin Sherman	Michael Hall	James Morgan	Bridget Bartlett	Mary Jo Dondlinger
The Play's the Thing Ferenc Molnar; adapt: P. G. Wodehouse	Michael Hall	Frank Bennett	Bridget Bartlett	Laurel Shoemaker
Gershwin Revue music and lyrics: George and Ira Gershwin; adapt: Andrea A. McCullough	Andrea A. McCullough			

California Theatre Center

GAYLE CORNELISON
General Director

MARY HALL SURFACE
Associate Director

RUSS McBRIEN
Board President

Box 2007
Sunnyvale, CA 94087
(408) 245-2979 (business)
(408) 245-2978 (box office)

FOUNDED 1976
Gayle Cornelison

SEASON
October–August

FACILITIES
Performing Arts Center
550 East Remington
Seating capacity: 200
Stage: proscenium

FINANCES
July 1, 1984-June 30, 1985
Operating expenses: $415,000

AUDIENCE
Annual attendance: 125,000
Subscribers: 6,484

TOURING CONTACT
Suzanne Herbert

BOOKED-IN EVENTS
Theatre

AEA Guest Artist contract

PRODUCTIONS 1983–84

Productions	Directors	Sets	Costumes	Lights
Beauty and the Beast Gayle Cornelison	Tom Ramirez	Paul Vallerga	Colleen D. Troy	Deborah Terrell
Summer Is a Time for Growing Gayle Cornelison	Gayle Cornelison	Gayle Cornelison	Colleen D. Troy	Deborah Terrell
The Troubled Waters of Spring Brian Kral	Mary Hall Surface	Ralph Ryan	Mary Hall Surface	Duncan W. Graham
An Old-Fashioned Holiday Gayle Cornelison	Mary Hall Surface	Anders Bolang	Colleen D. Troy	Duncan W. Graham

PRODUCTIONS 1983–84

Productions	Directors	Sets	Costumes	Lights
Jim Thorpe, All-American Saul Levitt	Will Huddleston	Paul Vallerga	Colleen D. Troy	Duncan W. Graham
Dandelion Judith Martin	Mary Hall Surface	Paul Vallerga	Colleen D. Troy	Duncan W. Graham
The Ransom of Red Chief Brian Kral	Jody Johnston	Paul Vallerga	Colleen D. Troy	Duncan W. Graham
A Midsummer Night's Dream William Shakespeare	Will Huddleston	Paul Vallerga	Colleen D. Troy	Duncan W. Graham
The Princess and the Pea Gayle Cornelison	Gayle Cornelison	Bill Breidenbach	Colleen D. Troy	Duncan W. Graham
Cinderella Gayle Cornelison	Gayle Cornelison	Paul Vallerga	Colleen D. Troy	Deborah Terrell
Most Valuable Player Mary Hall Surface and company	J. Steven White	Paul Vallerga	Colleen D. Troy	Duncan W. Graham
The Woolgatherer William Mastrosimone	William Ball and Janice Hutchins	Michael Cook	Dawn Line	Robert J. Stout
Deathtrap Ira Levin	Will Huddleston	Michael Cook	Dawn Line	Robert J. Stout
Five Finger Exercise Peter Shaffer	Janice Hutchins	Michael Cook	Dawn Line	Robert J. Stout

PRODUCTIONS 1984–85

Productions	Directors	Sets	Costumes	Lights
The Emperor's New Clothes Gayle Cornelison	Michael Cook	Paul Vallerga	Colleen D. Troy	Deborah Terrell
Fact or Fancy? Gayle Cornelison and company	Gayle Cornelison	Michael Cook	Gayle Cornelison	Deborah Terrell
Most Valuable Player Mary Hall Surface and company	J. Steven White	Paul Vallerga	Colleen D. Troy	Duncan W. Graham
A Holiday of Times Past Gayle Cornelison	Gayle Cornelison	Michael Cook	Deborah Weber	Deborah Terrell
A Christmas Carol adapt: Mary Hall Surace, from Charles Dickens	Mary Hall Surface	Paul Vallerga	Colleen D. Troy	Michael Cook
The Wizard of Oz adapt: Will Huddleston, from L. Frank Baum	Will Huddleston	Paul Vallerga	Colleen D. Troy	Deborah Terrell
The Changeling Thomas Middleton; adapt: Selma LaGerlof	Finn Paulsson	Tommy Glans	Tommy Glans	Mary Hall Surface
A New Age Is Dawning Will Huddleston and company	Will Huddleston	Paul Vallerga	Colleen D. Troy	Deborah Terrell
The Princess and the Pea Gayle Cornelison	Gayle Cornelison	Michael Cook	Colleen D. Troy	Michael Cook
Maggie Magalita Wendy Kesselman	David Gassner	Paul Vallerga	Colleen D. Troy	Deborah Terrell
The Sleeping Beauty Gayle Cornelison	Mary Hall Surface	Paul Vallerga	Deborah Weber	Deborah Terrell
Hansel and Gretel Gayle Cornelison	Gayle Cornelison	Paul Vallerga	Colleen D. Troy	Deborah Terrell
I Ought to Be in Pictures Neil Simon	Gayle Cornelison	Michael Cook	Colleen D. Troy	Brooke Carlson
Nathan the Wise Gotthold Lessing; adapt: Roy Franklin and Sydney Walker	Sydney Walker	Michael Cook	Colleen D. Troy	Brooke Carlson
Same Time, Next Year Bernard Slade	Will Huddleston	Paul Vallerga	Colleen D. Troy	Brooke Carlson

Capital Repertory Company

BRUCE BOUCHARD
PETER H. CLOUGH
Producing Directors

HERBERT L. SHULTZ, JR.
Board Chairman

Box 399
Albany, NY 12201-0399
(518) 462-4531 (business)
(518) 462-4534 (box office)

FOUNDED 1980
Oakley Hall, III, Michael Van
    Landingham

SEASON
October-May

FACILITIES
Market Theatre
111 North Pearl St.
Seating capacity: 258
Stage: thrust

FINANCES
July 1, 1984-June 30, 1985
Operating expenses: $715,000

AUDIENCE
Annual attendance: 35,725
Subscribers: 3,202

AEA LORT (D) contract

PRODUCTIONS 1983–84

Productions	Directors	Sets	Costumes	Lights
The Glass Menagerie Tennessee Williams	Michael J. Hume	Jeffrey Schneider	Barbara Forbes	Mal Sturchio
Happy End book and lyrics: Bertolt Brecht; music: Kurt Weill; adapt: Michael Feingold	Peter H. Clough	Ray Recht	Lloyd Waiwaiole	Robert Thayer
Translations Brian Friel	Pamela Berlin	Jeffrey Schneider	Barbara Forbes	Lary Opitz
Living Together Alan Ayckbourn	Lynn Polan	Leslie Taylor	Lloyd Waiwaiole	David Yergan
Alice and Fred Dan Ellentuck	Gloria Muzio Thayer	Ray Recht	Lloyd Waiwaiole	Robert Thayer
The Wake of Jamey Foster Beth Henley	Bruce Bouchard	Rick Dennis	Martha Hally	Lary Opitz

PRODUCTIONS 1984–85

Productions	Directors	Sets	Costumes	Lights
And a Nightingale Sang... C. P. Taylor	Gloria Muzio Thayer	Evelyn Sakash	Lloyd Waiwaiole	Mal Sturchio
The Dining Room A. R. Gurney, Jr.	Michael J. Hume	Jeffrey Schneider	Barbara Forbes	Lary Opitz
Who's Afraid of Virginia Woolf? Edward Albee	Peter H. Clough	Leslie Taylor	Susan Hirschfeld	Jackie Manassee
Quilters book: Molly Newman and Barbara Damashek; music and lyrics: Barbara Damashek	Louis Rackoff	Ray Recht	Lloyd Waiwaiole	Todd Lichtenstein
Master Harold... and the boys Athol Fugard	Bruce Bouchard	Rick Dennis	Theresa Inman	Jackie Manassee
The Wonderful Tower of Humbert Lavoignet Lynne Alvarez	Susan Gregg	Dale F. Jordan	Lloyd Waiwaiole	Dale F. Jordan

The CAST Theatre

TED SCHMITT
Producing Artistic Director

RANDY J. CLIFTON
Artistic Director

DWIGHT W. DICKEY
Associate Artistic Director

DORIS KOENIG
Board President

804 North El Centro Ave.
Hollywood, CA 90038
(213) 462-9872 (business)
(213) 462-0265 (box office)

FOUNDED 1976
Kathleen Johnson, Ted Schmitt

SEASON
Year-round

FACILITIES
The CAST Theatre
Seating capacity: 65
Stage: proscenium

The Cast-at-the-Circle
Seating capacity: 99
Stage: proscenium

FINANCES
October 1, 1983-September 30, 1984
Operating expenses: $176,640

AUDIENCE
Annual attendance: 25,000

BOOKED-IN EVENTS
Theatre

AEA 99-seat waiver

PRODUCTIONS 1983

Productions	Directors	Sets	Costumes	Lights
The Wrong Box adapt: Trace Johnson, from Larry Gelbart and Burt Shevelove; songs: Harry Aquado	Richard Gersham	A. Clark Duncan	Madeline Ann Graneto	Russell Pyle
A History of the American Film Christopher Durang	Steve Nevil	Randy J. Clifton	Debbie Saunders	Ilya Mindlin
Key Exchange Kevin Wade	Paula Russell	Dwayne Gardella		Dwayne Gardella
Women Behind Bars Tom Eyen	Ron Link	A. Clark Duncan	Madeline Ann Graneto	Barbara Ling
Strider book adapt: Mark Rozovsky, from Tolstoy; lyrics: Uri Riashentsev and Steve Brown; adapt: Robert Kalfin and Steve Brown; music: S. Vetkin and Mark Rozovsky	Matt Casella	Roger Holzberg	Neal San Teguns	Steve Cuden
Performance Hell Philip-Dimitre Galas	Philip-Dimitre Galas			
The Truth Is Bad Enough Michael Kearns	Gillian Eaton			
She Also Dances Kenneth Arnold	Jules Aaron	Michael Devine	Dorothy Jean Smith	Paulie Jenkins
Pool Play John Morgan Evans	John Morgan Evans	Jim Newton		
Boys Life Donald Kreiger; music: Jack Colvin and Steve Moshier	Donald Kreiger	Ed Woll and Donald Krieger		Ken Fermoyle
Girly Girly Jack Colvin	Jack Colvin	A. Clark Duncan	Lynn Kitzlin	Paulie Jenkins
Three Down, Four Across . . .Love book and lyrics: Randy J. Clifton and Doris Koenig; music: Michael Reno	Randy J. Clifton	Randy J. Clifton	Randy J. Clifton	D. Martyn Bookwalter

PRODUCTIONS 1984

Productions	Directors	Sets	Costumes	Lights
A Night at Harpo's Les Marderosian				
Boys Life Donald Krieger; music: Jack Colvin and Steve Moshier	Donald Krieger	Donald Krieger		Ken Fermoyle
Steaming Nell Dunn	Paul Levine	Bo Welsch	Doug Spesert	Paul Mitchell

Productions	Directors	Sets	Costumes	Lights
Is There Life After High School? book: Jeffrey Kindley; music nd lyrics: Craig Carnella	Gordon Hunt	Bob Breen	Carol Brolaski	Liz Stilwell
1984 adapt from George Orwell	Ethan D. Silverman	Jim Houle	Allen Highfill	D. Martyn Bookwalter
From the Journal of Hazard McCauley Philip Reeves	Randy J. Clifton	Randy J. Clifton	Deborah Bowlus	D. Martyn Bookwalter
Brain Hotel Tony Abatemarco, Bill Castellino, Jane Schoman and Mimi Seton	Tony Abatemarco	Barbara Ling	Barbara Ling	Barbara Ling
Island Donald Krieger and Tim Bennett; music: Steve Moshier and Kristian Hoffman	Donald Krieger	Samuel F. Hale	Bennie Shokouhi	Jim Feldman and Ken Fermoyle
Sightlines Mark Eisman	Dwight W. Dickey	Randy J. Clifton	Randy J. Clifton	Anthony Battelle
Enemy Robin Maugham	Price Coetzee	Steve Wolff	Patrick R. Norris	

Center for Puppetry Arts

VINCENT ANTHONY
Executive Director

ELLIOT L. HAAS
Board Chairman

1404 Spring St. NW
Atlanta, GA 30309
(404) 873-3089 (business)
(404) 873-3391 (box office)

FOUNDED 1978
Vincent Anthony

SEASON
July-June

FACILITIES
Mainstage
Seating capacity: 313
Stage: proscenium

Back Door Theatre
Seating capacity: 77
Stage: flexible

FINANCES
July 1, 1984-June 30, 1985
Operating expenses: $664,685

AUDIENCE
Annual attendance: 250,000
Subscribers: 26,008

TOURING CONTACT
Gail Reid

BOOKED-IN EVENTS
Puppetry

Productions	Directors	Sets	Costumes	Lights
Dracula: Master of the Undead Mitchell Edmonds	Luis Q. Barroso	Michael Stauffer	Fannie Schubert; puppets: Chimera Productions	Liz Lee
Blue Night and Other Works for Puppets Janie Geiser	Janie Geiser	Rick Houdesheldt	puppets: Janie Geiser and Terri Epstein	Diane Kempler
Pinocchio Vincent Anthony and Robyn Sosebee	Robyn Sosebee	Gene Ericson	puppets: Chimera Productions	Gene Ericson
Peter Pan Mitchell Edmonds	Luis Q. Barroso	Thom Coates	Jamie Greenleaf, III; puppets: Ken Wilson, Gary Gue, Frank Skelton	Liz Lee

PRODUCTIONS 1983–84

Productions	Directors	Sets	Costumes	Lights
Uncle Remus Tales Mitchell Edmonds and Jon Ludwig	Jon Ludwig	Michael Stauffer	puppets: Chimera Productions	Liz Lee

PRODUCTIONS 1984–85

Productions	Directors	Sets	Costumes	Lights
An Evening with Bruce D. Schwartz Bruce D. Schwartz	Bruce D. Schwartz	Thomas E. Disbrow	Bruce D. Schwartz	Alice Prussin
Cinderella Mitchell Edmonds and Vincent Anthony	Luis Q. Barroso	Lewis S. Greenleaf, III	Lewis S. Greenleaf, III and Fannie Schubert; puppets: Gary Max	Liz Lee
The Wizard of Oz book adapt and lyrics: Richard Graham, from L. Frank Baum; music: Fred Palmisano	Luis Q. Barroso	Michael Stauffer	puppets: Michael Stauffer, Fannie Schubert and Mark Edlund	Michael Stauffer
Dr. Doolittle adapt: Richard Graham, Luis Q. Barroso and company, from Hugh Lofting	Luis Q. Barroso	James A. Wood, Jr.	puppets: Chimera Productions	Liz Lee

Center Stage

STAN WOJEWODSKI, JR.
Artistic Director

PETER W. CULMAN
Managing Director

JOSEPH M. LANGMEAD
Board President

700 North Calvert St.
Baltimore, MD 21202
(301) 685-3200 (business)
(301) 332-0033 (box office)

FOUNDED 1963
Community Arts Committee

SEASON
September-June

FACILITIES
Seating capacity: 541
Stage: modified thrust

FINANCES
July 1, 1984-June 30, 1985
Operating expenses: $2,420,500

AUDIENCE
Annual attendance: 175,000
Subscribers: 14,855

TOURING CONTACT
Victoria Nolan

AEA LORT (B) contract

PRODUCTIONS 1983-84

Productions	Directors	Sets	Costumes	Lights
Crossing the Bar Michael Zettler	Stephen Zuckerman	Hugh Landwehr	Mimi Maxmen	Richard Winkler
Our Town Thornton Wilder	Jackson Phippin	Tony Straiges	Del W. Risberg	James F. Ingalls, Jr.
The Sleep of Reason Antonio Buero-Vallejo; trans: Marion Peter Holt	Travis Preston	Kate Edmunds	Kate Edmunds	Jennifer Tipton
You Never Can Tell George Bernard Shaw	Stan Wojewodski, Jr.	Hugh Landwehr	Dona Granata	Craig Miller
Another Part of the Forest Lillian Hellman	Irene Lewis	Douglas Stein	Jess Goldstein	Pat Collins
Ohio Tip-Off James Yoshimura	John Pasquin	Hugh Landwehr	Linda Fisher	Judy Rasmuson

PRODUCTIONS 1984-85

Productions	Directors	Sets	Costumes	Lights
Danton 's Death Georg Buchner; adapt: Howard Brenton	Stan Wojewodski, Jr.	Hugh Landwehr	Jess Goldstein	Pat Collins
Henry IV, Part 1 William Shakespeare	Stan Wojewodski, Jr.	Douglas Stein	Lawrence Casey	Stephen Strawbridge
Execution of Justice Emily Mann	Stan Wojewodski, Jr.	Hugh Landwehr	Jess Goldstein	James F. Ingalls, Jr.
On the Verge or The Geography of Yearning Eric Overmyer	Jackson Phippin	Tony Straiges	Del W. Risberg	James F. Ingalls, Jr.
Native Speech Eric Overmyer	Paul Berman	Hugh Landwehr	Jess Goldstein	James F. Ingalls, Jr.
Hedda Gabler Henrik Ibsen	Irene Lewis	Hugh Landwehr	Jess Goldstein	Stephen Strawbridge
Who They Are and How It Is with Them Grace McKeaney	Jackson Phippin	Hugh Landwehr	Jess Goldstein	James F. Ingalls, Jr.
A Flea in Her Ear Georges Feydeau; adapt: Roy Brocksmith	Roy Brocksmith	Nancy Winters	Jim Buff	Pat Collins
Painting Churches Tina Howe	Stan Wojewodski, Jr.	Hugh Landwehr	Del W. Risberg	Judy Rasmuson

The Changing Scene

MAXINE MUNT
ALFRED BROOKS
Co-Producing/Artistic Directors

1527 1/2 Champa St.
Denver, CO 80202
(303)893-5775

FOUNDED 1968
Maxine Munt, Alfred Brooks

SEASON
Year-round

FACILITIES
Seating capacity: 76
Stage: flexible

FINANCES
January 1, 1984-December 31, 1984
Operating expenses: $99,923

AUDIENCE
Annual attendance: 25,000

BOOKED-IN EVENTS
Theatre, music, dance, film, mime,
poetry, visual arts

PRODUCTIONS 1983-84

Productions	Directors	Sets	Costumes	Lights
Mixed Doubles Richard Lore	Richard Lore	Robert Schnautz	Candace Pederson	Van Emden Henson
Le Piege de Meduse and *The Sting of the Jellyfish* book, music and lyrics: Erik Satie; trans: Frieda Sanidas	Frieda Sanidas	Tom Reed	Nicole Kirkpatrick	Peter Nielson
Obstacles company-developed	Alfred Brooks	company	company	George Caffine
Suburban Gothic Jacob Clark	Dennis Bontems	Dennis Bontems	Bethe Allison	Dennis Bontems
Vineyard Haven Bob Cronin	Joan Shields-Kole	Dennis Lockhart		Peter Nielson

---

PRODUCTIONS 1984-85

Productions	Directors	Sets	Costumes	Lights
The Only Woman Awake Is the Woman Who Has Heard the Flute William Borden	Don Malmgren	Don Malmgren		Gus Malmgren
Caverns Doug Smith	Van Emden Henson	Van Emden Henson	Doug Smith	David F. Cautley
Fitness Laura Shames	Dan Hiester	Danny Ionazzi	Don Bill	Danny Ionazzi
D D Dada Denver John S. Wilson	John S. Wilson	John S. Wilson	company	Peter Nielson
A Beautiful World David Jones	Dennis Bontems	Dennis Bontems	Dennis Bontems	Dennis Bontems
Eggman August Baker	John Osburn	Robert Schnautz	Eleanor Glover	Rod Lansberry
L'Orchestre Jean Anouilh	Dan Hiester	Rod Thompson	Nicole Kirkpatrick	Dan Hiester
Fisheggs Jacob Clark	Eric Engdahl	James Lovell	Ginny Rossman	Craig Williamson
Shadows of Canyons and *The Flame* Danny Berwick	Christine MacDonald	Daniel J. Reeverts		Mark Cole
Any Guitar Don Malmgren	Jacob Clark	Don Malmgren	Ginny Rossman	Craig Williamson

---

The Children's Theatre Company

JON R. CRANNEY
Artistic Director

JOHN B. DAVIS, JR.
Executive Director

DENNIS MATHISEN
Board President

2400 Third Ave. South
Minneapolis, MN 55404
(612) 874-0500 (business)
(612) 874-0400 (box office)

FOUNDED 1961
Beth Linnerson

SEASON
September-June

FACILITIES
Mainstage
Seating capacity: 746
Stage: proscenium

Studio Theatre
Seating capacity: 50-90
Stage: flexible

FINANCES
July 1, 1984-June 30, 1985
Operating expenses: $3,110,000

AUDIENCE
Annual attendance: 185,000
Subscribers: 7,800

TOURING CONTACT
Tony Sertich

BOOKED-IN EVENTS
Theatre, dance, music, lectures,
symposia

Note: During the 1983-84 season,
John Clark Donahue served as
artistic director.

PRODUCTIONS 1983-84

Productions	Directors	Sets	Costumes	Lights
The Secret Garden adapt: Thomas W. Olson; music: Hiram Titus	John Clark Donahue	Jack Barkla	Christopher Beesley	Jonathan D. Baker
The Adventures of Babar Thomas W. Olson and Laurent de Brunhoff; music: Steven M. Rydberg	Myron Johnson	Jack Barkla and Robert Braun	Judith Cooper and Barry Robison	Karlis Ozols
Cinderella adapt: John B. Davidson; music: Ted Gillen, Diane Cina, John Gessner and Hiram Titus	Bain Boehlke	Edward Haynes	Gene Davis Buck	Jonathan D. Baker
Frankenstein adapt: Thomas W. Olson; music: Steven M. Rydberg	John Clark Donahue	Jack Barkla	Jack Edwards	Duane Schuler
The Nightingale adapt: Marisha Chamberlain; music: Roberta Carlson and Howard Arthur	Myron Johnson	Nancy Ekholm Burkert and Jack Barkla	Nancy Ekholm Burkert and Gene Davis Buck	Duane Schuler
Pinocchio adapt: Timothy Mason; music: Hiram Titus	Barry L. Goldman	Dahl Delu	Rae Marie Pekas and Gene Davis Buck	Jeffrey W. Bartlett

---

PRODUCTIONS 1984-85

Productions	Directors	Sets	Costumes	Lights
The Legend of Sleepy Hollow adapt: Frederick Gaines; music: Roberta Carlson	Bain Boehlke	Jack Barkla	Gene Davis Buck	David Karlson
Madeline and the Gypsies adapt: John Clark Donahue; music: Hiram Titus	Barry L. Goldman	Jack Barkla	Ricia Birturk	Donald Darnutzer
The Little Match Girl adapt: John Clark Donahue	Myron Johnson	Jack Barkla	Gene Davis Buck	Donald Darnutzer
The Mystery of the Tattered Truck adapt: Thomas W. Olson, Wendy Lehr and Richard Russell Ramos, from Wendy Lehr; music: Hiram Titus	Richard Russell Ramos	Jack Barkla	Jack Edwards	Duane Schuler
The Princess and the Pea adapt: Barbara Field; music: Roberta Carlson	Richard Edwards and Myron Johnson	Jack Barkla	Gene Davis Buck	Donald Darnutzer
Penrod adapt: Thomas W. Olson; lyrics: Thomas W. Olson and Anita Ruth; music: Anita Ruth	Jon Cranney	Tom Butsch	Christopher Beesley	Duane Schuler

---

Chocolate Bayou Theater Company

PAT MILLER
LEONARD T. WAGNER
Co-Producing Directors

S. TEVIS GRINSTEAD
Board President

Box 270363
Houston, TX 77277
(713) 528-0070 (business)
(713) 528-0119 (box office)

FOUNDED 1979
Pat Miller, Leonard T. Wagner

SEASON
October–July

FACILITIES
Mainstage
Brazos at Bremond
Seating capacity: 249
Stage: modified thrust

The Other Performing Space
Seating capacity: 149
Stage: arena

FINANCES
September 1, 1984–August 31, 1985
Operating expenses: $265,000

AUDIENCE
Annual attendance: 20,000
Subscribers: 510

TOURING CONTACT
Clive Carlin

BOOKED-IN EVENTS
music, dance

AEA Guest Artist contract

PRODUCTIONS 1983–84

Productions	Directors	Sets	Costumes	Lights
Harvey Mary Chase	Leonard T. Wagner	Deborah Jasien	Sue Ellen Rich-Pearson	Mo Pitman
Skirmishes Catherine Hayes	John David Etheredge	Deborah Jasien	Roger Gentry	Mo Pitman
84 Charing Cross Road Helen Hanff	Tim Tavcar	Deborah Jasien	Pat Miller	Deborah Jasien
Dogg's Hamlet, Cahoot's Macbeth Tom Stoppard	Cindy Goatley	Deborah Jasien	Deborah H. Boily	Mo Pitman
Plenty David Hare	John David Etheredge	Deborah Jasien	Sue Ellen Rich-Pearson	David Roederer
Years in the Making Glenn Allen Smith	Bob Dowdall	Deborah Jasien	Cindy Goatley	David Marco
The Speckled Band Arthur Conan Doyle	Harry Booker	Deborah Jasien	Paul W. Bannon	Mark Porter
Nice People Dancing to Good Country Music Lee Blessing	John R. Pearson	Deborah Jasien	Sue Ellen Rich-Pearson	Mark Porter
Foxfire Susan Cooper and Hume Cronyn	Tim Tavcar	Deborah Jasien	Sue Ellen Rich-Pearson	Mark Porter
Win/Lose/Draw Mary Gallagher and Ara Watson	Cindy Goatley	Deborah Jasien	Sue Ellen Rich-Pearson	Mark Porter
Last Meeting of the Knights of the White Magnolia Preston Jones	Leonard T. Wagner	Deborah Jasien	Sue Ellen Rich-Pearson	Mark Porter
Man with a Raincoat William Wise	Patti Bean	Deborah Jasien	Bob Shank	Mark Porter

---

PRODUCTIONS 1984–85

Productions	Directors	Sets	Costumes	Lights
The Hothouse Harold Pinter	Tim Tavcar	Deborah Jasien	Deborah Jasien	Mark Porter
The Gift of the Magi book adapt, music and lyrics: Peter Ekstrom, from O. Henry	Barbara H. Hartman	Deborah Jasien	Deborah Jasien	Mark Porter
Zastrozzi George F. Walker	Ed Muth	Deborah Jasien	Deborah Jasien	Mark Porter
Scheherazade Marisha Chamberlain	John R. Pearson	Ken Atwater and Bob Shank	Bob Shank	Bob Shank
Doctors and Diseases book: James Kramer; music and lyrics: Peter Ekstrom	James Kramer	Bob Shank	Pat Miller	Bob Shank
Stage Struck Simon Gray	John David Etheredge	Arch Andrus	Bob Shank	Marvyn Byrkett

Productions	Directors	Sets	Costumes	Lights
To Gillian on Her 37th Birthday Michael Brady	Jo Alessandro Marks	Arch Andrus	Pat Miller	Bob Dowdall
Master Harold . . . and the boys Athol Fugard	Ed Muth	Arch Andrus	Bob Shank	Marvyn Byrkett
Rude Times Stephen Wylie	Mark A. Albright	Arch Andrus	Bob Shank	Marvyn Byrkett
The Lion, the Witch and the Wardrobe adapt: Clanche du Rand, from C.S. Lewis	Eoghan Ryan	Eoghan Ryan	Pat Miller	Bob Shank

Cincinnati Playhouse in the Park

WORTH GARDNER
Artistic Director

KATHERINE MOHYLSKY
Managing Director

CHARLES O. CAROTHERS
Board President

Box 6537
Cincinnati, OH 45206
(513) 421-5440 (business)
(513) 421-3888 (box office)

FOUNDED 1960
Community members

SEASON
October-June

FACILITIES
962 Mt. Adams Circle
Robert S. Marx Theatre
Seating capacity: 629
Stage: modified thrust

Thompson Shelterhouse
Seating capacity: 220
Stage: thrust

FINANCES
September 1, 1984-August 31, 1985
Operating expenses: $2,490,000

AUDIENCE
Annual attendance: 200,000
Subscribers: 19,261

BOOKED-IN EVENTS
Theatre, music, dance

AEA LORT (B) and (D) contracts

Note: During the 1984-85 season,
Robert Kalfin served as artistic
director.

Productions	Directors	Sets	Costumes	Lights
True West Sam Shepard	Don Toner	Alison Ford	Rebecca Senske	Jay Depenbrock
Sweet Bird of Youth Tennessee Williams	Michael Murray	Paul R. Shortt	James Berton Harris	William Mintzer
They Dance to the Sun Leigh Podgorski	Gloria Muzio Thayer	David Ariosa	Rebecca Senske	Jay Depenbrock
Godspell John-Michael Tebelak; music and lyrics: Stephen Schwartz	Darwin Knight	Charles Caldwell	Caley Summers	F. Mitchell Dana
Monday After the Miracle William Gibson	Leonard Mozzi	James Fenhagen	Rebecca Senske	Jay Depenbrock
Julius Caesar William Shakespeare	Michael Murray	Karl Eigsti	Kurt Wilhelm	Neil Peter Jampolis
Translations Brian Friel	Don Toner	David Ariosa	Rebecca Senske	Jay Depenbrock
Hay Fever Noel Coward	Geoffrey Sherman	Paul Wonsek	William Schroder	Paul Wonsek
The Dining Room A.R. Gurney, Jr.	Michael Hankins	David Ariosa	Kurt Wilhelm	William Mintzer
Maybe I'm Doing It Wrong music and lyrics: Randy Newman	David Holdgrive	David Ariosa	Rebecca Senske	Jay Depenbrock

PRODUCTIONS 1984–85

Productions	Directors	Sets	Costumes	Lights
Empress of China Ruth Wolff	Robert Kalfin	Michael Sharp	Andrew B. Marlay	Edward Effron
Shades of Brown Michael Picardie	Joan Kemp- Welch	David Ariosa	Rebecca Senske	Jay Depenbrock
The Big Holiday Broadcast Arne Zaslove, Mary-Claire Burke and the Bathhouse Theatre company	Arne Zaslove	Shelley Henze Schermer	Julie James	Judy Wolcott
The Seagull Anton Chekhov; trans: John Murrell	Robert Kalfin	David Ariosa	Steven Jones	Jay Depenbrock
Amateurs book: Winnie Holzman and David Evans; music: David Evans; lyrics: Winnie Holzman	Mitchell Ivers	Eduardo Sicangco	Eduardo Sicangco and Rebecca Senske	Spencer Mosse
Paradise! book and lyrics: George C. Wolfe; music: Robert Forrest	Robert Nigro	John Yeck	Rebecca Senske	Neil Jenkinson
Have Julius Hay; trans: Peter Hay	Robert Kalfin	Wolfgang Roth	Sam Kirkpatrick	Edward Effron
Amadeus Peter Shaffer	Robert Kalfin	Wolfang Roth	Rebecca Senske	Christopher Popowich
Sleuth Anthony Shaffer	Robert Moss	Rick Dennis	Rebecca Senske	Jay Depenbrock
The Miss Firecracker Contest Beth Henley	Michael Montel	David Ariosa	Rebecca Senske	Jay Depenbrock

Circle in the Square Theatre

THEODORE MANN
Artistic Director

PAUL LIBIN
Managing Director

JOHN RUSSELL
Board Chairman

1633 Broadway
New York, NY 10019
(212) 307-2700 (business)
(212) 307-2735 (box office)

FOUNDED 1951
Theodore Mann, Aileen Cramer,
Edward Mann, Jose Quintero, Emily
Stevens, Jason Wingreen

SEASON
Year-round

FACILITIES
Seating capacity: 600-681
Stage: arena

FINANCES
July 1, 1984-June 30, 1985
Operating expenses: $4,446,000

AUDIENCE
Annual attendance: 221,000
Subscribers: 17,467

AEA LORT (A) contract

PRODUCTIONS 1983–84

Productions	Directors	Sets	Costumes	Lights
The Caine Mutiny Court Martial Herman Wouk	Arthur Sherman	John Falabella	David Murin	Richard Nelson
Heartbreak House George Bernard Shaw	Anthony Page	Marjorie Bradley Kellogg	Jane Greenwood	Paul Gallo
Awake and Sing! Clifford Odets	Theodore Mann	John Conklin	Jennifer von Mayrhauser	Richard Nelson

Productions	Directors	Sets	Costumes	Lights
Danny and the Deep Blue Sea John Patrick Shanley	Barnet Kellman	David Gropman	Marcia Dixcy	Richard Nelson
Design for Living Noel Coward	George C. Scott	Thomas Lynch	Ann Roth	Marc B. Weiss
The Loves of Anatol Arthur Schnitzler; adapt: Ellis Rabb and Nicholas Martin	Ellis Rabb	Lawrence Miller	Robert Morgan	Richard Winkler and James Tilton
Arms and the Man George Bernard Shaw	John Malkovich	Thomas Lynch	Ann Roth	Richard Nelson

Circle Repertory Company

MARSHALL W. MASON
Artistic Director

SUZANNE M. SATO
Managing Director

CIRO A. GAMBONI
Board Chairman

161 Ave. of the Americas
New York, NY 10013
(212) 691-3210 (business)
(212) 924-7100 (box office)

FOUNDED 1969
Marshall W. Mason, Lanford Wilson,
Tanya Berezin, Robert Thirkield

SEASON
October–June

FACILITIES
99 Seventh Ave. South
Seating capacity: 160
Stage: flexible

FINANCES
October 1, 1983–September 30, 1984
Operating expenses: $1,808,552

AUDIENCE
Annual attendance: 57,952
Subscribers: 6,000

BOOKED-IN EVENTS
Theatre, music, dance

AEA Off Broadway contract

Productions	Directors	Sets	Costumes	Lights
The Seagull Anton Chekhov; trans: Jean-Claude van Itallie	Elinor Renfield	John Lee Beatty	Jennifer von Mayrhauser	Dennis Parichy
Full Hookup Conrad Bishop and Elizabeth Fuller	Marshall W. Mason	David Potts	Laura Crow	John P. Dodd
Levitation Timothy Mason	B. Rodney Marriott	David Potts	Laura Crow	Dennis Parichy
The Harvesting John Bishop	John Bishop	Loren Sherman	Ann Emonts	Mal Sturchio
Danny and the Deep Blue Sea John Patrick Shanley	Barnet Kellman	David Gropman	Marcia Dixcy	Richard Nelson
Balm in Gilead Lanford Wilson	John Malkovich	Kevin Rigdon	Glenne Headley	Kevin Rigdon
Fool for Love Sam Shepard	Sam Shepard	Andy Stacklin	Ardyss L. Golden	Kurt Landisman
Who's Afraid of Virginia Woolf? Edward Albee	Marshall W. Mason	David Potts	Laura Crow	Dennis Parichy

Productions	Directors	Sets	Costumes	Lights
Love's Labour's Lost William Shakespeare; music: Norman L. Berman	Toby Robertson	Franco Colavecchia	Laura Crow	Dennis Parichy

PRODUCTIONS 1984–85

Productions	Directors	Sets	Costumes	Lights
Bing and Walker James Paul Farrell	Dan Bonnell	David Potts	Deborah Shaw	Mal Sturchio
Dysan Patrick Meyers	B. Rodney Marriott	Christopher Barreca	Fran Rosenthal	Dennis Parichy
As Is William H. Hoffman	Marshall W. Mason	David Potts	Michael Warren Powell	Dennis Parichy
Balm in Gilead Lanford Wilson	John Malkovich	Kevin Rigdon	Glenne Headly	Kevin Rigdon
Fool for Love Sam Shepard	Sam Shepard and Julie Herbert	Andy Stacklin	Ardyss L. Golden	Kurt Landisman
Who's Afraid of Virginia Woolf? Edward Albee	Marshall W. Mason	David Potts	Laura Crow	Dennis Parichy
Talley and Son Lanford Wilson	Marshall W. Mason	John Lee Beatty	Laura Crow	Dennis Parichy

Clarence Brown Company

WANDALIE HENSHAW
Artistic Director

PETER GARVIE
Producer

KEVIN COLMAN
General Manager

ROBERT WEBB
Board Chairman

Box 8450
Knoxville, TN 37996
(615) 974-6011 (business)
(615) 974-5161 (box office)

FOUNDED 1974
Anthony Quayle, Ralph G. Allen

SEASON
January-June

FACILITIES
1714 Andy Holt Ave.
Clarence Brown Theatre
Seating capacity: 604
Stage: proscenium

Studio Theatre
Seating capacity: 150
Stage: thrust

Carousel Theatre
Seating capacity: 400
Stage: arena

FINANCES
July 1, 1984-June 30, 1985
Operating expenses: $396,724

AUDIENCE
Annual attendance: 20,000
Subscribers: 4,000

TOURING CONTACT
Kevin Colman

BOOKED-IN EVENTS
Theatre

AEA LORT (B) and Theatre for Young Audiences contracts

PRODUCTIONS 1983–84

Productions	Directors	Sets	Costumes	Lights
Arms and the Man George Bernard Shaw	Wandalie Henshaw	Robert Cothran	Connie Furr	Leonard Harman
Engaged W.S. Gilbert	Wandalie Henshaw	Robert Cothran	Marianne Custer	Leonard Harman
A Doll's House Henrik Ibsen	Albert Harris	Robert Cothran	Marianne Custer	Leonard Harman
Let's Get a Divorce Victorien Sardou	Robert Mashburn	Robert Cothran	Bill Black	Leonard Harman

Productions	Directors	Sets	Costumes	Lights

Richard III
    William Shakespeare
	Wandalie
	    Henshaw
		Thomas
		    Struthers
			Marianne Custer	Leonard
				    Harman

The Caretaker
    Harold Pinter
	Robert
	    Mashburn
		Leonard
		    Harman
			Marianne Custer	L.J. DeCuir

She Stoops to Conquer Oliver Goldsmith	Albert Harris	Robert Cothran	Bill Black	L.J. DeCuir

The Questions of Hamlet
    adapt: Peter Garvie, from William Shakespeare
	Wandalie
	    Henshaw
		Marianne Custer	Bill Black	Marianne Custer

The Cleveland Play House

WILLIAM RHYS
Acting Artistic Director

AL MILANO
Managing Director

ROBERT F. FRANKEL
Board President

Box 1989
Cleveland, OH 44106
(216) 795-7010 (business)
(216) 795-7000 (box office)

FOUNDED 1915
Raymond O'Neil

SEASON
October-June

FACILITIES
8500 Euclid Ave.
Kenyon C. Bolton Theatre
Seating capacity: 612
Stage: proscenium

Francis E. Drury Theatre
Seating capacity: 501
Stage: proscenium

Charles S. Brooks Theatre
Seating capacity: 160
Stage: proscenium

FINANCES
July 1, 1984-June 30, 1985
Operating expenses: $3,200,000

AUDIENCE
Annual attendance: 150,000
Subscribers: 11,225

BOOKED-IN EVENTS
Theatre

AEA LORT (C) contract

Note: During the 1983-84 and 1984-85 seasons, Richard Oberlin served as artistic director.

Productions	Directors	Sets	Costumes	Lights

The Dining Room
    A.R. Gurney, Jr.
	William
	    Roudebush
		Richard Gould	Jeffrey M. Smart	Richard Gould

Billy Bishop Goes to War John Gray and Eric Peterson	M. Seth Reines	James Irwin	Kim A. Trotter	James Irwin
The Tempest William Shakespeare	Toby Robertson	Richard Gould	Estelle Painter	Dennis Parichy
A Day in Hollywood/A Night in the Ukraine book and lyrics: Dick Vosburgh; music: Frank Lazarus	Jim Corti	Richard Gould	Estelle Painter	Richard Gould
A Christmas Carol adapt: Doris Baizley, from Charles Dickens	William Rhys	Charles Berliner	Charles Berliner	James Irwin

Chevaliere
    David Trainer
	William
	    Roudebush
		Richard Gould	Frances Blau	Richard Gould

Children of a Lesser God Mark Medoff	Paul Lee	James Irwin	Kim A. Trotter	James Irwin
The Three Musketeers adapt: Eberle Thomas, from Alexander Dumas	Philip Kerr	Richard Gould	Estelle Painter	Richard Gould

Mass Appeal
    Bill C. Davis
	William
	    Roudebush
		Richard Gould	Jeffrey M. Smart	Richard Gould

Amadeus Peter Shaffer	Philip Kerr	Paul Rodgers	Estelle Painter	Paul Rodgers
Home Samm-Art Williams	Woodie King, Jr.	Richard Gould	Frances Blau	Richard Gould

PRODUCTIONS 1983–84

Productions	Directors	Sets	Costumes	Lights
Canterbury Tales book: Martin Starkie and Nevil Coghill; lyrics: Nevil Coghill; music: Richard Hill and John Hawkins	Jim Corti	Gary C. Eckhart	Colleen Muscha	James Irwin
Peter Pan J.M. Barrie	Paul Lee	Richard Gould	Estelle Painter	Kerro Knox 3

PRODUCTIONS 1984–85

Productions	Directors	Sets	Costumes	Lights
The Archbishop's Ceiling Arthur Miller	Jonathan Bolt	Gary C. Eckhart	Frances Blau	Richard Gould
The Waiting Room Catherine Muschamp	William Rhys	James Irwin	Kirk A. Dow	James Irwin
The Royal Family George S. Kaufman and Edna Ferber	Paul Lee	Richard Gould	Estelle Painter	Richard Gould
A Luv Musical book adapt: Jeffrey Sweet from Murray Schisgal; music: Howard Marren; lyrics: Susan Birkenhead	Michael Maggio	Richard Gould	Frances Blau	Richard Gould
A Christmas Carol adapt: Doris Baizley, from Charles Dickens	William Rhys	Charles Berliner	Charles Berliner	James Irwin
Angels Fall Lanford Wilson	Thomas S. Oleniacz	Richard Gould	Kirk A. Dow	Richard Gould
Dramatic License Kenneth Ludwig	Dennis Zacek	Richard Gould	Frances Blau	Richard Gould
Billy Budd adapt: Louis O. Coxe and Robert Chapman, from Herman Melville	Philip Kerr	Gary C. Eckhart	Estelle Painter	Dennis Parichy
Painting Churches Tina Howe	J.J. Garry, Jr.	Richard Gould	Kirk A. Dow	Richard Gould
The Guardsman Ferenc Molnar; trans: Frank Marcus	William Rhys	Paul Rodgers	Estelle Painter	Paul Rodgers
End of the World Arthur Kopit	T. Riccio	Richard Gould	Frances Blau	Richard Gould
Fool for Love Sam Shepard	Evie McElroy	James Irwin	Frances Blau	James Irwin
High Spirits Noel Coward; book adapt, music and lyrics: Timothy Gray and Hugh Martin	William Rhys	Richard Gould	Estelle Painter	Richard Gould

Coconut Grove Playhouse

ARNOLD MITTELMAN
Producing Artistic Director

JORDAN BOCK
Managing Director

MARSHALL TAYLOR
Board Chairman

Box 616
Miami, FL 33133
(305) 442-2662 (business)
(305) 442-4000 (box office)

FOUNDED 1977
Thomas Spencer, Gerald Pulver

SEASON
July-May

FACILITIES
3500 Main Hwy., Coconut Grove
Seating capacity: 796
Stage: proscenium

FINANCES
July 1, 1984-June 30, 1985
Operating expenses: $2,673,634

AUDIENCE
Annual attendance: 115,000
Subscribers: 8,400

TOURING CONTACT
Judith Delgado

BOOKED-IN EVENTS
Theatre, dance, opera, film

AEA LORT (B) contract

Note: During the 1983-84 and 1984-85
seasons, Jose Ferrer served as
artistic director.

PRODUCTIONS 1983–84

Productions	Directors	Sets	Costumes	Lights
Light Up the Sky Moss Hart	Jose Ferrer	David Trimble	Barbara A. Bell	David Goodman
A Funny Thing Happened on the Way to the Forum book: Burt Shevelove and Larry Gelbart; music and lyrics: Stephen Sondheim	Peter P. Fuchs	William Schroder	Ellis Tillman	Pat Simmons
Cat on a Hot Tin Roof Tennessee Williams	Jose Ferrer	David Trimble	Barbara A. Bell	David Goodman
Life with Father Howard Lindsay and Russel Crouse	Jeremiah Morris	Kenneth N. Kurtz	Maria Marrero	Toni Goldin
Dancing in the End Zone Bill C. Davis	Jose Ferrer	David Trimble	Debbie Ann Thompson	James Riley
A Soldier's Play (Negro Ensemble Company production) Charles Fuller	Douglas Turner Ward	Felix E. Cochren	Judy Dearing	Allen Lee Hughes
When Hell Freezes Over, I'll Skate Paul Laurence Dunbar and lindamichellebaron	Vinnette Carroll	William Schroder	William Schroder	Pat Simmons

---

PRODUCTIONS 1984–85

Productions	Directors	Sets	Costumes	Lights
When You Comin' Back Red Ryder? Mark Medoff	Miguel Ferrer	David Trimble	Barbara A. Bell	Michael Newton-Brown
The Glass Menagerie Tennessee Williams	Jose Ferrer	David Trimble	Barbara A. Bell	David Goodman
Sleuth Anthony Shaffer	Jose Ferrer	David Trimble	Ellis Tillman	Marsha Hardy
Pump Boys and Dinettes John Foley, Mark Hardwick, Debra Monk, Cass Morgan, John Schimmel and Jim Wann	B.J. Allen	Doug Johnson and Christopher Nowak	Patricia McGourty	B.J. Allen
'night, Mother Marsha Norman	Bryna Wortman	David Trimble	Barbara A. Bell	David Goodman
Home Samm-Art Williams	Woodie King, Jr.	David Trimble	Barbara A. Bell	Marsha Hardy
America's Sweetheart book: John Weidman and Alfred Uhry; music: Robert Waldman; lyrics: Alfred Uhry	Gerald Freedman	Kevin Rupnik	Jeanne Button	Pat Collins
Last of the Red Hot Lovers Neil Simon	Barry J.W. Steinman	David Trimble	Ellis Tillman	Mitch Acker

Cocteau Repertory

EVE ADAMSON
Artistic Director

ROBERT M. HUPP
Managing Director

CHAUNCE SKILLING
Board President

330 Bowery
New York, NY 10012
(212) 677-0060

FOUNDED 1971
Eve Adamson

SEASON
September-May

FACILITIES
Bouwerie Lane Theatre
Seating capacity: 140
Stage: modified thrust

FINANCES
July 1, 1984-June 30, 1985
Operating expenses: $200,000

AUDIENCE
Annual attendance: 20,000
Subscribers: 1,200

PRODUCTIONS 1983–84

Productions	Directors	Sets	Costumes	Lights
Judas Robert Patrick	Eve Adamson	Douglas McKeown		Giles Hogya
The Beaux' Stratagem George Farquhar	Giles Hogya	Giles Hogya	Richard von Ernst	Giles Hogya
King John William Shakespeare	Eve Adamson	Giles Hogya	Jeffrey Wallach	Giles Hogya
Epicoene Ben Jonson	Gerald Chapman	Jose Lengson	Jose Lengson	Gregory Laird
The Oresteia Aeschylus; adapt: Robert Lowell	Douglas McKeown	Robert Joel Schwartz	Melina Root	Gregory Laird
Antiquities John Arndt	Eve Adamson	Gregory Laird	Gregory Laird	Gregory Laird

PRODUCTIONS 1984–85

Productions	Directors	Sets	Costumes	Lights
Theatre in the Time of Nero and Seneca Edvard Radzinsky; trans: Alma H. Law	Eve Adamson	Christopher Martin	Christopher Martin	Giles Hogya
Cymbeline William Shakespeare	Douglas McKeown	Mina Albergo	Richard von Ernst	Edward R.F. Matthews
Goat Song Franz Werfel	Eve Adamson	Robert Joel Schwartz	Wade Battley	Craig Smith
The Importance of Being Earnest Oscar Wilde	Giles Hogya	Giles Hogya	Richard von Ernst	Giles Hogya
L'Aiglon Edmond Rostand; trans: Louis N. Parker	Eve Adamson	Jeffrey Wallach	Jeffrey Wallach	Craig Smith
The Maids Jean Genet; trans: Bernard Frechtman	Barbara Schofield	Barbara Schofield and Craig Smith	Barbara Schofield and Craig Smith	Barbara Schofield and Craig Smith

Court Theatre

D. NICHOLAS RUDALL
Artistic Director

MARK TIARKS
Managing Director

5706 South University
Chicago, IL 60637
(312) 962-7005 (business)
(312) 753-4472 (box office)

FOUNDED 1954
University of Chicago

SEASON
September-May

FACILITIES
Abelson Auditorium
5535 South Ellis Ave.
Seating capacity: 251
Stage: modified thrust

FINANCES
July 1, 1983-June 30, 1984
Operating expenses: $682,786

AUDIENCE
Annual attendance: 37,806
Subscribers: 4,855

AEA Chicago Area Theatre contract

PRODUCTIONS 1983-84

Productions	Directors	Sets	Costumes	Lights
Hay Fever Noel Coward	Susan Dafoe	Linda Buchanan	Jessica Hahn	Rita Pietraszek
A Midsummer Night's Dream William Shakespeare	Nicholas Rudall	Linda Buchanan	Nan Zabriskie	Rita Pietraszek
Hedda Gabler Henrik Ibsen adapt: Nicholas Rudall	Susan Dafoe	Linda Buchanan	Nancy Missimi	Roma A. Flowers
Misalliance George Bernard Shaw	Nicholas Rudall	Joseph Nieminski	Nancy Missimi	Rita Pietraszek
Long Day's Journey into Night Eugene O'Neill	Nicholas Rudall	Linda Buchanan	Linda Buchanan	Ron Greene

PRODUCTIONS 1984-85

Productions	Directors	Sets	Costumes	Lights
Much Ado About Nothing William Shakespeare	Nicholas Rudall	Joseph Nieminski	Julie Jackson	Robert Shook
The Misanthrope Molière; trans: Richard Wilbur	Munson Hicks	Michael Merritt	Jessica Hahn	Rita Pietraszek
The Philanthropist Christopher Hampton	Nicholas Rudall	Michael Merritt	Jessica Hahn	Rita Pietraszek
Arms and the Man George Bernard Shaw	Nicholas Rudall	Joseph Nieminski	Nancy Missimi	Robert Shook
The Birthday Party Harold Pinter	Susan Dafoe	Ron Greene	Nan Zabriskie	Ron Greene
Every Good Boy Deserves Favour Tom Stoppard and Andre Previn	Michael Maggio	Ron Greene	Juli Hrovat-Walker	Ron Greene

Crossroads Theatre Company

LEE RICHARDSON
Artistic Director

RICK KHAN
Executive Director

PENELOPE LATTIMER
Board President

320 Memorial Pkwy.
New Brunswick, NJ 08901
(201) 249-5625 (business)
(201) 249-5560 (box office)

FOUNDED 1978
Lee Richardson, Rick Khan

SEASON
September-May

FACILITIES
Seating capacity: 150
Stage: arena

FINANCES
July 1, 1984-June 30, 1985
Operating expenses: $487,187

AUDIENCE
Annual attendance: 35,000
Subscribers: 1,300

TOURING CONTACT
Rick Khan

AEA letter of agreement

PRODUCTIONS 1983–84

Productions	Directors	Sets	Costumes	Lights
It's Showdown Time Bill Evans	Lee Richardson	Bill Motyka	Alvin Perry	Gary W. Fassler
Zooman and the Sign Charles Fuller	Lee Richardson	Bill Motyka	Alvin Perry	Bob Scheeler
Ain't Misbehavin' music and lyrics: Fats Waller, et al.; adapt: Richard Maltby, Jr.	Rick Khan	Felix E. Cochren	Judy Dearing	Shirley Prendergast
Langston adapt: Rick Khan, from Langston Hughes	Rick Khan	Gary W. Fassler	Alvin Perry	Gary W. Fassler
Pantomime Derek Walcott	Lee Richardson	Daniel Proett	Alvin Perry	Susan A. White
Don't Bother Me, I Can't Cope Micki Grant	Rick Khan	Daniel Proett	Nancy Konrady	Shirley Prendergast

---

PRODUCTIONS 1984–85

Productions	Directors	Sets	Costumes	Lights
Steal Away Ramona King	Lee Richardson	Daniel Proett	Judy Dearing	Susan A. White
American Buffalo David Mamet	Lee Richardson	Daniel Proett	Judy Dearing	Susan A. White
Bubbling Brown Sugar Loften Mitchell	Rick Khan	Felix E. Cochren	Judy Dearing	Dan Stratman
When the Chickens Came Home to Roost and *Zora* Laurence Holder	Israel Hicks	Wynn P. Thomas	Anita D. Ellis	Shirley Prendergast
Slow Dance on the Killing Ground William Hanley	Lee Richardson and Rick Khan	Bill Motyka	Vicki Esposito- McLaughlin	William Grant, III
Sweet Daddy Love Don Evans	Lee Richardson	Daniel Proett	Alvin Perry	Bernadette Englert

---

CSC: City Stage Co.

CRAIG D. KINZER
Artistic Director

WILL MAITLAND WEISS
Managing Director

FRAN SMYTH
Board President

136 East 13th St.
New York, NY 10003
(212) 674-4205 (business)
(212) 674-4210 (box office)

FOUNDED 1967
Christopher Martin

SEASON
October-May

FACILITIES
Seating capacity: 199
Stage: flexible thrust

FINANCES
July 1, 1984-June 30, 1985
Operating expenses: $296,000

AUDIENCE
Annual attendance: 15,000
Subscribers: 1,250

AEA Off Broadway contract

Note: During the 1983-84 season, Christopher Martin served as artistic director; during the 1984-85 season Will Maitland Weiss, Craig D. Kinzer and Christopher Martin served as co-directors.

PRODUCTIONS 1983-84

Productions	Directors	Sets	Costumes	Lights
Big and Little Botho Strauss; trans: Christopher Martin and Daniel Woker	Christopher Martin	Christopher Martin	Miriam Nieves	Rick Butler
Faust, Parts I and II Johann Wolfgang Von Goethe	Christopher Martin	Christopher Martin	Miriam Nieves	Rick Butler
Hamlet William Shakespeare; adapt: Christopher Martin and Karen Sunde	Christopher Martin	Christopher Martin	Miriam Nieves	Christopher Martin
Dance of Death August Strindberg; adapt: Christopher Martin	Christopher Martin	Terry A. Bennett	Terry A. Bennett	Christopher Martin

PRODUCTIONS 1984-85

Productions	Directors	Sets	Costumes	Lights
Agamemnon Aeschylus; trans: Robert Fagles	Christopher Martin	Christopher Martin	Kalina Ivanov	Christopher Martin
Elektra/Orestes Aeschylus; trans: Robert Fagles	Christopher Martin	Christopher Martin	Blanche Blakeny	Christopher Martin
Georges Dandin Molière; trans: Alex Szogyi	Laurence Maslon	Laurence Maslon	Miriam Nieves	Rick Butler
The Underpants Carl Sternheim; trans: Eric Bentley	Craig D. Kinzer	Rick Butler	Miriam Nieves	Rick Butler
Frankenstein adapt: Laurence Maslon and company, from Mary Shelley	Craig D. Kinzer	Laurence Maslon and George D. Xenos	Blanche Blakeny	Whitney Quesenbery

Cumberland County Playhouse

JIM CRABTREE
Producing/Administrative Director

MARY CRABTREE
Consulting Producer

BRUCE EVANS
Board Chairman

Box 484
Crossville, TN 38555
(615) 484-2300 (business)
(615) 484-5000 (box office)

FOUNDED 1965
Paul Crabtree, Margaret Keyes
  Harrison, Moses Dorton

SEASON
March-November

FACILITIES
Cumberland County Playhouse
Seating capacity: 485
Stage: flexible

Fairfield Dinner Theater
Seating capacity: 165
Stage: proscenium

Theater-in-the-Woods
Seating capacity: 199
Stage: outdoor arena

FINANCES
January 1, 1984-December 31, 1984
Operating expenses: $372,072

AUDIENCE
Annual attendance: 54,500
Subscribers: 1,200

TOURING CONTACT
Scot Copeland

BOOKED-IN EVENTS
Theatre, music, dance

AEA Guest Artist contract

PRODUCTIONS 1983–84

Productions	Directors	Sets	Costumes	Lights
Temperance: A Very Dry Musical book and lyrics: Jim Crabtree; music: Ann Crabtree	Jim Crabtree	Nathan K. Braun	Amelie Crabtree	John Partyka
The Crucible Arthur Miller	Jim Crabtree	Nathan K. Braun	Amelie Crabtree	John Partyka
Pippin book: Roger O. Hirson; music and lyrics: Stephen Schwartz	Jim Crabtree	Carolyn Ott	Laura Brookhart	Steve Woods
Bye, Bye, Birdie book: Michael Stewart; music: Charles Strouse; lyrics: Lee Adams	Mary Crabtree	Carolyn Ott	Mary Crabtree	Steve Woods
A Midsummer Night's Dream William Shakespeare; book and lyrics adapt: Jim Crabtree; music: Dennis Davenport	Jim Crabtree	Jim Crabtree	Don Bolinger	Steve Woods
Blithe Spirit Noel Coward	Mary Crabtree	Martha Hill	Amelie Crabtree	Scott Leathers
Dames at Sea book and lyrics: George Haimsohn and Robin Miller; music: Jim Wise	Mary Crabtree	Jim Crabtree	Amelie Crabtree	Scott Leathers
The Teahouse of the August Moon John Patrick	Mary Crabtree	Deborah Raymond	Amelie Crabtree and Don Bolinger	Scott Leathers
A Homestead Album book and lyrics: Jim Crabtree; music: Dennis Davenport	Jim Crabtree	Doyle Vaden and Paul Nail	Amelie Crabtree	Scott Leathers

PRODUCTIONS 1984–85

Productions	Directors	Sets	Costumes	Lights
My Fair Lady book and lyrics: Alan Jay Lerner; music: Frederick Loewe	Mary Crabtree	Leonard Harman	Mary Crabtree and Amelie Crabtree	Scott Leathers
Dark of the Moon Howard Richardson and William Berney	Jim Crabtree	Jim Crabtree	Amelie Crabtree and Don Bolinger	Scott Leathers
Foxfire Susan Cooper and Hume Cronyn; music: Jonathan Holtzman	Jim Crabtree	Xavier Ironside and Jim Crabtree	Don Bolinger	Steve Woods

Productions	Directors	Sets	Costumes	Lights
Coast to Coast book: Jim Crabtree and Dennis Davenport; music: Dennis Davenport; lyrics: Jim Crabtree	Jim Crabtree	Jim Crabtree	Amelie Crabtree	Scott Leathers
Reynard the Fox Arthur Fauquez	Scot Copeland	Renee Dunshee and Paul Nail	Paul Nail	Greg Madera
The Silver Whistle Robert McEnroe	Mary Crabtree	Martha Hill	Amelie Crabtree	Jim Crabtree
Second Sons: A Story of Rugby, Tennessee book and lyrics: Jim Crabtree; music: Dennis Davenport	Jim Crabtree	Leonard Harman	Amelie Crabtree	Ron Fry and Jim Crabtree
Quilters book: Molly Newman and Barbara Damashek; music and lyrics: Barbara Damashek	Jim Crabtree	Ron Fry	Amelie Crabtree	Ron Fry
Tennessee, USA! book, music and lyrics: Paul Crabtree	Jim Crabtree	Jim Crabtree and Nathan K. Braun	Mary Crabtree	Ron Fry
Annie book: Thomas Meehan; music: Charles Strouse; lyrics: Martin Charnin	Jim Crabtree	Ron Fry	Amelie Crabtree	Jim Crabtree

Dallas Theater Center

ADRIAN HALL
Artistic Director

PETER DONNELLY
Executive Managing Director

WILLIAM A. CUSTARD
Board President

3636 Turtle Creek Blvd.
Dallas, TX 75219-5598
(214) 526-8210 (business)
(214) 526-8857 (box office)

FOUNDED 1959
Robert D. Stecker, Sr., Beatrice Handel,
Paul Baker, Dallas citizens

SEASON
September-June

FACILITIES
Frank Lloyd Wright Theater
Seating capacity: 466
Stage: modified thrust

"In the Basement"
Seating capacity: 200
Stage: flexible

Arts District Theater
2401 Flora St.
Seating capacity: 400
Stage: flexible

FINANCES
September 1, 1984-August 31, 1985
Operating expenses: $3,381,000

AUDIENCE
Annual attendance: 100,000
Subscribers: 8,783

AEA LORT (C) contract

Productions	Directors	Sets	Costumes	Lights
Billy Bishop Goes to War John Gray and Eric Peterson	Richard Jenkins	Eugene Lee	Donna M. Kress	Eugene Lee
Galileo Bertolt Brecht; trans: James Schevill	Adrian Hall	Eugene Lee	Donna M. Kress	Eugene Lee
The Wild Duck Henrik Ibsen; trans: Michael Meyer	Adrian Hall	Eugene Lee	Donna M. Kress	Roger Morgan
Fool for Love Sam Shepard	David Wheeler	Eugene Lee	Donna M. Kress	Eugene Lee
Seven Keys to Baldpate George M. Cohan	Peter Gerety	Eugene Lee	Donna M. Kress	Zack Herring
Lady Audley's Secret Douglas Seale, George Goehring and John Kuntz	Word Baker	Word Baker	Donna M. Kress	Robert Shook

PRODUCTIONS 1983–84

Productions	Directors	Sets	Costumes	Lights
Cloud 9 Caryl Churchill	Word Baker	James Maronek	Donna M. Kress	Robert Shook
Tom Jones adapt: Larry Arrick, from Henry Fielding; music: Barbara Damashek; lyrics: Barbara Damashek and Larry Arrick	Larry Arrick	Eugene Lee	Donna M. Kress	Eugene Lee

PRODUCTIONS 1984–85

Productions	Directors	Sets	Costumes	Lights
Misalliance George Bernard Shaw	Philip Minor	Eugene Lee	Donna M. Kress	Natasha Katz
Amadeus Peter Shaffer	Patrick Hines	Robert D. Soule	Donna M. Kress	Natasha Katz
A Christmas Carol adapt: Adrian Hall and Richard Cummings, from Charles Dickens	Adrian Hall	Eugene Lee	Donna M. Kress	Marcus Abbott
Passion Play Peter Nichols	Adrian Hall	Eugene Lee	Donna M. Kress	Marcus Abbott
Good C.P. Taylor	Adrian Hall	Eugene Lee	Donna M. Kress	Marcus Abbott
The Three Sisters Anton Chekhov; trans: Randall Jarrell	Suzanne Shephard	Leo Yashimura	Donna M. Kress	Linda Blase
You Can't Take It with You George S. Kaufman and Moss Hart	Peter Gerety	Keith Raywood	Donna M. Kress	Eugene Lee

Delaware Theatre Company

CLEVELAND MORRIS
Artistic Director

DENNIS LUZAK
Managing Director

CHARLES F. RICHARDS, JR.
Board Chairman

Box 516
Wilmington, DE
(302) 594-1100

FOUNDED 1979
Peter DeLaurier, Cleveland Morris,
Ceal Phelan

SEASON
October–March

FACILITIES
Water St.
Seating capacity: 300
Stage: flexible

FINANCES
September 1, 1984-August 31, 1985
Operating expenses: $385,076

AUDIENCE
Annual attendance: 42,000
Subscribers: 3,535

TOURING CONTACT
Dennis Luzak

BOOKED-IN EVENTS
Music

AEA letter of agreement

PRODUCTIONS 1983–84

Productions	Directors	Sets	Costumes	Lights
Triple Play Joseph Hart	Peter DeLaurier	Howard P. Beals, Jr.	Teri Beals	Benjamin F. Levenberg
Man with a Load of Mischief John Clifton and Ben Tarver	Dorothy Danner	Lewis Folden	Teri Beals and E. Lee Florance	Benjamin F. Levenberg

Productions	Directors	Sets	Costumes	Lights
Dial M for Murder Frederick Knott	Gavin Cameron-Webb	Gavin Cameron-Webb	Eric Schaeffer	Benjamin F. Levenberg
Aim for the Heart Kenneth Rich	Cleveland Morris	Howard P. Beals, Jr.	E. Lee Florance	Benjamin F. Levenberg
The Prime of Miss Jean Brodie Jay Presson Allen	Cleveland Morris	Eric Schaeffer	E. Lee Florance	Benjamin F. Levenberg

PRODUCTIONS 1984-85

Productions	Directors	Sets	Costumes	Lights
The Rivals Richard Brinsley Sheridan	Cleveland Morris	Lewis Folden	E. Lee Florance	Benjamin F. Levenberg
You Never Know book: Rowland Leigh; music: Cole Porter and Robert Katcher; lyrics: Cole Porter, Rowland Leigh and Edwin Gilbert	Derek Wolshonak	Lewis Folden	E. Lee Florance	Bruce K. Morriss
Medal of Honor Rag Tom Cole	Paul Hastings	Timothy M. Durham	E. Lee Florance	Bruce K. Morriss
Stage Struck Simon Gray	Gavin Cameron-Webb	Eric Schaeffer	E. Lee Florance	Bruce K. Morriss
A Streetcar Named Desire Tennessee Williams	Cleveland Morris	Eric Schaeffer	E. Lee Florance	Bruce K. Morriss

Dell'Arte Players Company

MICHAEL FIELDS
JOAN SCHIRLE
DONALD FORREST
Co-Artistic Directors

MICHAEL FIELDS
Managing Director

FRED CRANSTON
Board President

Box 816
Blue Lake, CA 95525
(707) 668-5411 (business)
(707) 668-5782 (box office)

FOUNDED 1971
Alain Schons, Joan Schirle, Michael Fields, Jael Weisman, Jon Paul Cook, Jane Hill, Carlo Mazzone-Clementi

SEASON
Year-round

FACILITIES
Dell'Arte Bldg.
1st and H Sts.
Seating capacity: 100
Stage: studio

FINANCES
October 1, 1983-September 30, 1984
Operating expenses: $193,098

AUDIENCE
Annual attendance: 30,500

TOURING CONTACT
Michael Fields

BOOKED-IN EVENTS
Theatre, music, dance, performance art

AEA letter of agreement

PRODUCTIONS 1983-84

Productions	Directors	Sets	Costumes	Lights
Malpractice, or Love's the Best Doctor book adapt: Michael Fields, Donald Forrest and Michele Linfante, from Molière; music and lyrics: Bonnie Lockhart	Jael Weisman	Andy Stacklin	Mimi Mace and Donald Forrest	Ted Vukovich

PRODUCTIONS 1983–84

Productions	Directors	Sets	Costumes	Lights
The Road Not Taken: A Scar Tissue Mystery book: Michael Fields, Donald Forrest, Joan Schirle and Jael Weisman; music: Tony Heimer; lyrics: Tony Heimer and Joan Schirle	Jael Weisman	Ivan Hess	Nancy Betts	Ted Vukovich
Whiteman Meets Bigfoot adapt: Michael Fields, Joan Schirle, Jael Weisman, Alain Schons, Steve Most, Mara Sabinson and Donald Forrest, from R. Crumb; music and lyrics: Joan Schirle	Jael Weisman	Alain Schons	Laura Hussey	Alain Schons
The Great Claus Caper Paoli Lacey and company	Paoli Lacey	Randy Jewell	Donna Knight	Michael Foster

PRODUCTIONS 1984–85

Productions	Directors	Sets	Costumes	Lights
The Road Not Taken: A Scar Tissue Mystery book: Michael Fields, Donald Forrest, Joan Schirle and Jael Weisman; music: Tony Heimer; lyrics: Tony Heimer and Joan Schirle	Jael Weisman	Ivan Hess	Nancy Betts	Ted Vukovich
Malpractice, or Love's the Best Doctor book adapt: Michael Fields, Donald Forrest and Michele Linfante, from Molière; music and lyrics: Bonnie Lockhart	Jael Weisman	Andy Stacklin	Mimi Mace	Ted Vukovich
The Great Claus Caper Paoli Lacey and company	Paoli Lacey	Randy Jewell	Donna Knight	Michael Foster

Denver Center Theatre Company

DONOVAN MARLEY
Artistic Director

SARAH LAWLESS
Executive Director

DONALD R. SEAWELL
Board Chairman

1050 13th St.
Denver, CO 80204
(303) 893-4200 (business)
(303) 893-4100 (box office)

FOUNDED 1980
Denver Center for the Performing Arts

SEASON
October-June

FACILITIES
The Stage
Seating capacity: 550
Stage: thrust

The Space
Seating capacity: 450
Stage: arena

The Source
Seating capacity: 156
Stage: thrust

FINANCES
July 1, 1984-June 30, 1985
Operating expenses: $4,500,000

AUDIENCE
Annual attendance: 240,000
Subscribers: 13,245

TOURING CONTACT
Jacquie Kitzelman

AEA LORT (B) and Theatre for Young Audiences contracts

PRODUCTIONS 1983–84

Productions	Directors	Sets	Costumes	Lights
Spokesong Stewart Parker	Peter Hackett	Robert Blackman	Robert Blackman	Kent Dorsey
Cyrano de Bergerac Edmond Rostand; trans: Brian Hooker	Wallace Chappell	Mark Donnelly	Deborah Trout	Allen Lee Hughes

PRODUCTIONS 1983–84

Productions	Directors	Sets	Costumes	Lights
The Front Page Ben Hecht and Charles MacArthur	Jerry Zaks	Kent Dorsey	Deb Dryden	Kent Dorsey
The Night of the Iguana Tennessee Williams	Walter Schoen	Christopher M. Idoine	Christina Haatainen	Danny Ionazzi
Romeo and Juliet William Shakespeare	Carolyn Eves	Kent Dorsey	Elizabeth Covey	Kent Dorsey
The Importance of Being Earnest Oscar Wilde	John Broome	Susan Benson	Susan Benson	James Sale
Trumpets and Drums Bertolt Brecht	Barbara Damashek	Michael Stauffer	Deb Dryden	Allen Lee Hughes
Crossfire Theodore Faro Gross	Bruce K. Sevy	Tom Buderwitz	Tom Buderwitz	Tom Buderwitz
Darwin's Sleepless Nights Merle Kessler	Bill Allard	Van Hansen	Hilary Waters	Van Hansen
Doorplay Sally Laurie	Dan Hiester	Kent Conrad	Judy Pederson	Kent Conrad
On the Verge or The Geography of Yearning Eric Overmyer	Roberta Levitow	Clay Snider	Clay Snider	Clay Snider

PRODUCTIONS 1984–85

Productions	Directors	Sets	Costumes	Lights
They Knew What They Wanted Sidney Howard	James Moll	Guido Tondino	Andrew V. Yelusich	James Sale
Ringers Frank X. Hogan	Donovan Marley	Richard L. Hay	Andrew V. Yelusich	James Sale
Hamlet William Shakespeare	Allen Fletcher	Warren Travis	Warren Travis	James Sale
The Time of Your Life William Saroyan	Donovan Marley	Guido Tondino	Andrew V. Yelusich	James Sale
Lahr and Mercedes James McLure	Peter Hackett	Pavel M. Dobrusky	Pavel M. Dobrusky	Pavel M. Dobrusky
Design for Living Noel Coward	Allen Fletcher	Richard L. Hay	Andrew V. Yelusich	James Sale
Pericles William Shakespeare	Laird Williamson	Laird Williamson and Andrew V. Yelusich	Andrew V. Yelusich	James Sale
The Immigrant Mark Harelik	Mark Harelik and Randal Myler	Catherine Poppe	Anne Thaxter Watson	Marty Contente
Painting Churches Tina Howe	Peter Hackett	Robert Franklin	Anne Thaxter Watson	James Sale
Accidental Death of an Anarchist Dario Fo; adapt: Richard Nelson	Caroline Eves	Richard L. Hay	Andrew V. Yelusich	James Sale
The Female Entertainer Elizabeth Levin	Edward Payson Call	Eric Fielding	Andrew V. Yelusich	Eric Fielding
Don Juan Molière	Garland Wright	Douglas Stein	Ann Hould-Ward	Scott Pinkney
Quilters book: Molly Newman and Barbara Damashek; music and lyrics: Barbara Damashek	Randal Myler	John Dexter	Deborah Trout	Rodney J. Smith

Detroit Repertory Theatre

BRUCE E. MILLAN
Artistic Director

ROBERT WILLIAMS
Executive Director

DOROTHY J. BROWN
Advisory Board Chairperson

13103 Woodrow Wilson Ave.
Detroit, MI 48238
(313) 868-1347

FOUNDED 1957
Bruce E. Millan, Barbara Busby, T.O.
  Andrus

SEASON
September-June

FACILITIES
Detroit Repertory Theatre
Seating capacity: 196
Stage: proscenium

FINANCES
January 1, 1984-December 31, 1984
Operating expenses: $219,204

AUDIENCE
Annual attendance: 18,189
Subscribers: 585

AEA letter of agreement

PRODUCTIONS 1983–84

Productions	Directors	Sets	Costumes	Lights
The Man Who Killed the Buddha Martin Epstein	Dee Andrus	Bruce Millan	Anne Saunders	Marylynn Kacir
Valesa, A Nightmare Jerzy Tymicki; trans: Jeffrey and Maya Haddow	Bruce Millan	Burce Millan	Anne Saunders	Kenneth R. Hewitt, Jr.
Ceremonies in Dark Old Men Lonne Elder, III	Dee Andrus	Bruce Millan	Pamela Brown	Kenneth R. Hewitt, Jr.
Keysearchers Istvan Orkeny; adapt: Clara Gyorgyey	Bruce Millan	Bruce Millan	Anne Saunders	Kenneth R. Hewitt, Jr.
A Day out of Time Alan Foster Friedman	Bruce Millan	Bruce Millan	Anne Saunders	Kenneth R. Hewitt, Jr.

PRODUCTIONS 1984–85

Productions	Directors	Sets	Costumes	Lights
Master Harold . . . and the boys Athol Fugard	Bruce Millan	Bruce Millan	Anne Saunders	Kenneth R. Hewitt, Jr.
Goodnight, Grandpa Walter Landau	Dee Andrus	Bruce Millan	Anne Saunders	Kenneth R. Hewitt, Jr.
J.B. Archibald MacLeish	Barbara Busby	Al Flood	Anne Saunders	Kenneth R. Hewitt, Jr. and Marylynn Kacir
In the Sweet Bye and Bye Donald Driver	Bruce Millan	Bruce Millan	Anne Saunders	Kenneth R. Hewitt, Jr.

Dorset Theatre Festival

JILL CHARLES
Artistic Director

JOHN NASSIVERA
Producing Director

PAUL E. WHEELER
Board President

Box 519
Dorset, VT 05251
(802) 867-2223 (business)
(802) 867-5777 (box office)

FOUNDED 1976
Jill Charles, John Nassivera

SEASON
June-September

FACILITIES
Cheney Road
Seating capacity: 218
Stage: proscenium

FINANCES
January 1, 1984-December 31, 1984
Operating expenses: $201,977

AUDIENCE
Annual attendance: 14,000
Subscribers: 350

AEA letter of agreement

PRODUCTIONS 1984

Productions	Directors	Sets	Costumes	Lights
George Washington Slept Here Moss Hart and George S. Kaufman	John Morrison	William John Aupperlee	Janet Bobcean	William John Aupperlee
The Matchmaker Thornton Wilder	Jill Charles	William John Aupperlee	Janet Bobcean	William John Aupperlee
Making a Killing John Nassivera	Anthony McKay	William John Aupperlee	Janet Bobcean	Janet Bobcean
Greater Tuna Joe Sears, Jaston Williams and Ed Howard	Jill Charles	William John Aupperlee	Janet Bobcean	Jeff Bernstein

---

PRODUCTIONS 1985

Productions	Directors	Sets	Costumes	Lights
The Golden Age A.R. Gurney, Jr.	Edgar Lansbury	William John Aupperlee	David Pearson	Jeff Bernstein
The Lusty and Comical History of Tom Jones adapt: John Morrison, from Henry Fielding	John Morrison	William John Aupperlee	David Pearson	Jeff Bernstein
The 1940s Radio Hour Walton Jones	Jill Charles	William John Aupperlee	David Pearson	Jeff Bernstein
Family Affairs Lynne Kadish	Anthony McKay	William John Aupperlee	David Pearson	Jeff Bernstein
Fifth of July Lanford Wilson	Jill Charles	William John Aupperlee	David Pearson	Jeff Bernstein
A Hard Look at Old Times adapt: John Nassivera, from Walter Hard	Jill Charles	William John Aupperlee	David Pearson	Jeff Bernstein

East West Players

MAKO
Artistic Director

JANET MITSUI
Administrator

ANDREW WONG
Board President

4424 Santa Monica Blvd.
Los Angeles, CA 90029
(213) 660-0366 (business)
(213) 660-0366, 0867 (box office)

FOUNDED 1965
Mako, James Hong, June Kim, Guy
    Lee, Pat Li, Yet Lock, Beulah Quo

SEASON
October-June

FACILITIES
Seating capacity: 99
Stage: flexible

FINANCES
July 1, 1984-June 30, 1985
Operating expenses: $175,000

AUDIENCE
Annual attendance: 60,000
Subscribers: 700

TOURING CONTACT
Janet Mitsui

*AEA Theatre for Young Audiences
    contract*

PRODUCTIONS 1983-84

Productions	Directors	Sets	Costumes	Lights
Live Oak Store Hiroshi Kashiwagi	Shizuko Hoshi	Fred Chuang	Terence Tam Soon	Rae Creevey
You're on the Tee and *Ripples in the Pond* Jon Shirota	Dana Lee	Rae Creevey	Susan Gee	Rae Creevey
Asaga Kimashita Velina Houston	Shizuko Hoshi	Fred Chuang		Rae Creevey
The Grunt Childe Lawrence O'Sullivan	Dana Lee	Rae Creevey	Susan Gee	Rae Creevey
Paint Your Face on a Drowning in the River Craig Kee Strete	Mako	Will Guest, Terry Isumi and Virginia Galko	Susan Gee and Desi Griffin	Rae Creevey
Visitors from Nagasaki Perry Miyake, Jr.	Betty Muramota	Rae Creevey	Rodney Kageyama	Rae Creevey

---

PRODUCTIONS 1984-85

Productions	Directors	Sets	Costumes	Lights
A Song for a Nisei Fisherman Philip Kan Gotanda; music: Philip Kan Gotanda and Kazu Matsui	Shizuko Hoshi	Fred Chuang	Susan Gee	Rae Creevey
The Music Lessons Wakako Yamauchi	Mako	Mako	Terrence Tam Soon	Rae Creevey
The Threepenny Opera book and lyrics: Bertolt Brecht; music: Kurt Weill; adapt: Mark Blitzstein	Mako	Rae Creevey	Shigeru Yaji	Rae Creevey

---

The Emmy Gifford Children's Theater

BILL KIRK
Artistic Director

NANCY DUNCAN
Executive Director

GAIL ERWIN
Board President

3504 Center St.
Omaha, NE 68105
(402) 344-2431 (business)
(402) 345-4849 (box office)

FOUNDED 1949
Emmy Gifford, 19 child-advocacy
  agencies

SEASON
September-May

FACILITIES
Seating capacity: 525
Stage: proscenium

FINANCES
June 1, 1984-May 31, 1985
Operating expenses: $472,223

AUDIENCE
Annual attendance: 72,000
Subscribers: 5,616

TOURING CONTACT
Eve Felder

PRODUCTIONS 1983-84

Productions	Directors	Sets	Costumes	Lights
Charlotte's Web adapt: Joseph Robinette, from E.B. White	Bill Kirk	Steve Wheeldon	Sherri Geerdes	Steve Wheeldon
Cinderella Now Gail Erwin	Bill Kirk	Steve Wheeldon	Sherri Geerdes	Steve Wheeldon
The Adventures of Huckleberry Finn adapt: Linda Johnson, from Mark Twain	Nancy Duncan	Steve Wheeldon	Sherri Geerdes	Steve Wheeldon

A Wrinkle in Time
    adapt: Susan Dieckman, from Madeleine
    L'Engle
	Bill Kirk	Steve Wheeldon	Sherri Geerdes	Steve Wheeldon

James and the Giant Peach adapt: Bill Kirk, from Roald Dahl	Bill Kirk	Steve Wheeldon	Sherri Geerdes	Steve Wheeldon

Cinderella Now
    Gail Erwin
	Mark Hoeger	Carol Kimball	Sherri Geerdes	Dennis Sterns
				  and Mary
				  Ellen Rozmajzl

PRODUCTIONS 1984-85

Productions	Directors	Sets	Costumes	Lights

Little House on the Prairie
    adapt: Gail Erwin, from Laura Ingalls Wilder
	Bill Kirk	Heartland
		  Studios
			Sherri Geerdes	John Wolf

Peter Pan
    book: J. M. Barrie; music: Mark Charlap and
    Jule Styne; lyrics: Carolyn Leigh, Betty
    Comden and Adolph Green
	Bill Kirk	Steve Wheeldon	Sherri Geerdes	Steve Wheeldon

Wind in the Willows
    adapt: Moses Goldberg, from Kenneth
    Grahame
	Bill Kirk	Steve Wheeldon	Sherri Geerdes	Steve Wheeldon

Helen and Annie Nancy Duncan	Bill Kirk	Steve Wheeldon	Tanya Lee	Steve Wheeldon

The Hobbit
    adapt: Patricia Gray, from J.R.R. Tolkien
	Bill Kirk and
	  Nancy Duncan
		Steve Wheeldon	Sherri Geerdes	Steve Wheeldon

The Revenge of Baba Yaga company-developed	Mark Hoeger	Steve Wheeldon	Sherri Geerdes	John Wolf

Empire State Institute for the Performing Arts

PATRICIA B. SNYDER
Producing Director

CLIFTON R. WHARTON, JR.
Chancellor, State University of New
York

ROBERT J. MORGADO
Board Chairman

Empire State Plaza
Albany, NY 12223
(518) 474-1199 (business)
(518) 473-3750 (box office)

FOUNDED 1976
Empire State Youth Theatre Institute
(State University of New York),
Governor Nelson A. Rockefeller
Empire State Plaza Performing Arts
Center Corporation

SEASON
September-June

FACILITIES
Mainstage
Seating capacity: 886
Stage: flexible

Studio Theatre
Seating capacity: 450
Stage: thrust

FINANCES
April 1984-March 31, 1985
Operating expenses: $2,501,512

AUDIENCE
Annual attendance: 80,000
Subscribers: 1,215

TOURING CONTACT
Gwynne Smith

BOOKED-IN EVENTS
Theatre, music, dance

*AEA Theatre for Young Audiences
contract*

PRODUCTIONS 1983–84

Productions	Directors	Sets	Costumes	Lights
The All-Time, Good-Time Knickerbocker Follies book: Hugh Wheeler; music and lyrics: various	Patricia Birch	Richard Finkelstein	Robert Anton, Karen Kammer, Fred Voelpel, Patrizia von Brandenstein and Sally Whitmore	Edward Effron
Our Town Thornton Wilder	W.A. Frankonis	Wynn Thomas	Karen Kammer	Walter Uhrman
Hizzoner--the Mayor! Paul Shyre	Paul Shyre	Elton Elder	Elton Elder	Steven T. Howell
Raggedy Ann and Andy book: Timothy Mason; music and lyrics: Joe Raposo	Patricia Birch	Marsha Louis Eck	Marsha Louis Eck	Richard Winkler
The Crucible Arthur Miller	Edward Lange	Gerry Hariton and Vicki Baral	Brent Griffin	Gerry Hariton and Vicki Baral
The Threepenny Opera book and lyrics: Bertolt Brecht; music: Kurt Weill	W.A. Frankonis	Klaus Holm	Patton Campbell	Edward Effron
Sleeping Beauty adapt: Richard Shaw and company	Joseph Balfior and Adrienne Posner	Marsha Louis Eck	Patrizia von Brandenstein	Lloyd S. Riford, III
Ten Little Indians Agatha Christie	Terence Lamude	Duke Durfee	Sandra A. Dianetti	Ann G. Wrightson

PRODUCTIONS 1984–85

Productions	Directors	Sets	Costumes	Lights
The Wind in the Willows book and lyrics: John Jakes; music: Claire Strauch	Edmund Waterstreet	Marsha Louis Eck	Marsha Louis Eck	Lary Opitz
A Doll's House Henrik Ibsen; trans: Eva LeGalliene	Ed Lange	Richard Finkelstein	Brent Griffin	Richard Finkelstein
Raggedy Ann book: William Gibson; music and lyrics: Joe Raposo	Patricia Birch	Gerry Hariton and Vicki Baral	Carrie Robbins	Richard Nelson
On the Home Front Gail Kriegel	W.A. Frankonis	Duke Durfee	Judy E. Dearing	Victor En Yu Tan

Productions	Directors	Sets	Costumes	Lights
The Taming of the Shrew William Shakespeare	Terence Lamude	Klaus Holm	Barbara Forbes	Ann G. Wrightson
The Prince and the Pauper adapt: John Vreeke; music: Diane Leslie; lyrics: Ronald Alexander	W.A. Frankonis	Wynn Thomas	Barbara Forbes	Lloyd S. Riford, III
Handy Dandy William Gibson	Arthur Storch	Victor A. Becker	Maria Marrero	Judy Rasmuson
I Remember Mama John van Druten	Joseph Balfior	Klaus Holm	Karen Kammer	Klaus Holm and Richard Finkelstein

The Empty Space

M. BURKE WALKER
Artistic Director

RICHARD ALLAN EDWARDS
Acting Artistic Director, 1985-86

KEVIN M. HUGHES
Managing Director

DIANA C. BROZE
Board President

95 South Jackson St.
Seattle, WA 98104
(206) 587-3737 (business)
(206) 467-6000 (box office)

FOUNDED 1970
M. Burke Walker, Charles Younger,
Julian Schembri, James Royce

SEASON
October-June

FACILITIES
Seating capacity: 225
Stage: flexible

FINANCES
July 1, 1984-June 30, 1985
Operating expenses: $770,000

AUDIENCE
Annual attendance: 35,000
Subscribers: 3,100

BOOKED-IN EVENTS
Theatre, music, dance

AEA letter of agreement

PRODUCTIONS 1983–84

Productions	Directors	Sets	Costumes	Lights
Oktoberfest Odon von Horvath; trans: Roger Downey	M. Burke Walker	Scott Weldin	Frances Kenney	Rick Paulsen
The Fabulous Sateens: Spill the Beans The Fabulous Sateens	Linda Hartzell	William Bloodgood	Candice Cain	Michael Davidson
The Vampires Harry Kondoleon	John Kazanjian	Jennifer Lupton	Nina Moser	Jeff Robbins
Broadway Philip Dunning and George Abbott	Robert Moss	Karen Gjelsteen	Ron Erickson	Michael Davidson
Kitchen, Church and Kids Franca Rame and Dario Fo; adapt: Roger Downey	Linda Hartzell	Jennifer Lupton	Michael Murphy	Rick Paulsen
K2 Patrick Meyers	M. Burke Walker	Scott Weldin	Michael Murphy	Michael Davidson

PRODUCTIONS 1984–85

Productions	Directors	Sets	Costumes	Lights
The Day They Came from Way Out There book and lyrics: John Engerman, Rex McDowell, Phil Shallat and Bob Wright; music: John Engerman	Jeff Steitzer	Bill Forester	Celeste Cleveland and Sally Richardson	Jim Royce
Careless Love John Olive	M. Burke Walker	Jennifer Lupton	Frances Kenney	Michael Davidson
Husbandry Patrick Tovatt	Rita Giomi	Karen Gjelsteen	G. Auguste Beuttler	Rick Paulsen
Bunk Klauniada, John Kazanjian and Todd Moore	John Kazanjian	Nina Moser	Nina Moser	Jeff Robbins
Execution of Justice Emily Mann	M. Burke Walker	Scott Weldin	Michael Murphy	Rick Paulsen
Beyond Therapy Christopher Durang	Warner Shook	Scott Weldin	Sally Richardson	Jeff Robbins

The Ensemble Studio Theatre

CURT DEMPSTER
Artistic Director

ERIK MURKOFF
Managing Director

G. H. DENNISTON, JR.
Board Chairman

549 West 52nd St.
New York, NY 10019
(212) 247-4982 (business)
(212) 247-3405 (box office)

FOUNDED 1971
Curt Dempster

SEASON
October-June

FACILITIES
Mainstage
Seating capacity: 99
Stage: flexible

Workshop
Seating capacity: 50
Stage: flexible

Workshop
12 West End Ave.
Seating capacity: 40
Stage: flexible

FINANCES
July 1, 1984-June 30, 1985
Operating expenses: $650,000

AUDIENCE
Annual attendance: 30,000
Subscribers: 400

AEA letter of agreement

PRODUCTIONS 1983–84

Productions	Directors	Sets	Costumes	Lights
To Gillian on Her 37th Birthday Michael Brady	Pamela Berlin	Robert Thayer	Deborah Shaw	Allen Lee Hughes
Broken Eggs Eduardo Machado	James Hammerstein	Keith Gonzales	Deborah Shaw	Cheryl Thacker
Marathon '84:				
House, Danny Cahill	Bruce Ornstein	Mark Fitzgibbons	Deborah Shaw	Karl E. Haas
Bite the Blind, Ara Watson	David Margulies	Mark Fitzgibbons	Deborah Shaw	Karl E. Haas
Remember Crazy Zelda?, Shel Silverstein	Art Wolff	Mark Fitzgibbons	Deborah Shaw	Karl E. Haas
Blood Bond, Gina Barnett	Melodie Somers	Mark Fitzgibbons	Isis C. Mussenden	Karl E. Haas
At Home, Richard Dresser	Jerry Zaks	Mark Fitzgibbons	Isis C. Mussenden	Karl E. Haas

PRODUCTIONS 1983–84

Productions	Directors	Sets	Costumes	Lights
Fine Line, Janice Van Horne	Harris Yulin	Mark Fitzgibbons	Isis C. Mussenden	Karl E. Haas
Slam!, Jane Willis	Shirley Kaplan	Mark Fitzgibbons	Isis C. Mussenden	Karl E. Haas
Been Taken, Roger Hedden	Billy Hopkins	Jane Musky	Hilary Rosenfeld	Karl E. Haas
Jazz, Elizabeth Albrecht	Elaine Petricoff	Jane Musky	Hilary Rosenfeld	Karl E. Haas
Vermont Sketches, David Mamet	Gregory Mosher	Jane Musky	Hilary Rosenfeld	Karl E. Haas
A Sense of Loss, Mark Malone	Robin Saex	Jane Musky	Hilary Rosenfeld	Karl E. Haas
Saxophone Music, Bill Bozzone	Risa Bramon	Jane Musky	Linda Vigdor	Karl E. Haas
Ariel Bright, Katherine Long	John Schwab	Jane Musky	Linda Vigdor	Karl E. Haas
Raving, Paul Rudnick	Peter Mark Schifter	Jane Musky	Linda Vigdor	Karl E. Haas

PRODUCTIONS 1984–85

Productions	Directors	Sets	Costumes	Lights
The Bloodletters Richard Greenberg	Shirley Kaplan	Edward T. Gianfrancesco	Bruce Harrow	Richard Lund
Once on a Summer's Day book and lyrics: Arthur Perlman; music: Jeffrey Lunden	John Henry Davis	Phillipp Jung	Donna Zakowska	Michael Orris Watson
The Crate Shel Silverstein	Art Wolff	Sally de Valenzuela	Isis C. Mussenden	Karl E. Haas
Marathon '85:				
The Frog Prince, David Mamet	Peter Maloney	Dana Hasson	Martha Hally	Greg MacPherson
Mariens Kammer, Roger Hedden	Billy Hopkins	Dana Hasson	Martha Hally	Greg MacPherson
Men Without Dates, *Jane Willis*	Shirley Kaplan	Dana Hasson	Martha Hally	Greg MacPherson
Life Under Water, Richard Greenberg	Don Scardino	Dana Hasson	Martha Hally	Greg MacPherson
Aggressive Behavior, Stuart Spencer	Jane Hoffman	Marlene Marta	Deborah Shaw	Greg MacPherson
Desperadoes, Keith Reddin	Mary B. Robinson	Marlene Marta	Deborah Shaw	Greg MacPherson
Between Cars, Alan Zweibel	Risa Bramon	Marlene Marta	Deborah Shaw	Greg MacPherson
Road to the Graveyard, Horton Foote	Curt Dempster	Marlene Marta	Deborah Shaw	Greg MacPherson
The Semi-Formal, Louisa Jerauld	Billy Hopkins	Brian Martin	Colleen Muscha	Greg MacPherson
North of Providence, Edward Allan Baker	Risa Bramon	Brian Martin	Colleen Muscha	Greg MacPherson
One Tennis Shoe, Shel Silverstein	Art Wolff	Brian Martin	Colleen Muscha	Greg MacPherson
Painting a Wall, David Lan	Joe Gilford	Brian Martin	Colleen Muscha	Greg MacPherson

Eureka Theatre Company

ANTHONY TACCONE
Artistic Director

MARY MASON
General Manager

CHRISTINA ORTH
Board President

2730 16th St.
San Francisco, CA 94103
(415) 558-9811 (business)
(415) 558-9898 (box office)

FOUNDED 1972
Robert Woodruff, Chris Silva

SEASON
October-August

FACILITIES
Seating capacity: 200
Stage: flexible

FINANCES
October 1, 1984-September 30, 1985
Operating expenses: $481,000

AUDIENCE
Annual attendance: 25,000
Subscribers: 1,500

AEA letter of agreement

PRODUCTIONS 1983-84

Productions	Directors	Sets	Costumes	Lights
Cloud 9 Caryl Churchill	Richard Seyd	Jeffrey Beecroft	William Eddelman	Jackie Manassee
Still Life Emily Mann	Anthony Taccone and Susan Marsden	Randy Richards	Barbara Bush	James Brentano

PRODUCTIONS 1984-85

Productions	Directors	Sets	Costumes	Lights
Accidental Death of an Anarchist Dario Fo; adapt: Joan Holden and Suzanne Cowan	Anthone Taccone	Peggy Snider	Eliza Chugg	Kurt Landisman
Top Girls Caryl Churchill	Susan Marsden	Ferdinand Penker	Roberta Yuen	Kurt Landisman
Husbandry Patrick Tovatt	Oskar Eustis	Gene Angell and Ron Pratt	Eliza Chugg	Novella T. Smith
The Danube Maria Irene Fornes	Susan Marsden	Tatiana de Stempel	Patricia Polen	James Brentano
The Threepenny Opera book and lyrics: Bertolt Brecht; music: Kurt Weill; adapt: Marc Blitzstein	Oskar Eustis and Richard Seyd	Andy Stacklin	Beaver Bauer	Kurt Landisman
Execution of Justice Emily Mann	Oskar Eustis and Anthony Taccone	Victoria Smith	Eliza Chugg	Derek Duarte

Fairmount Theatre of the Deaf

MICHAEL G. REGNIER
Artistic Director

PEGGY SHUMATE
Executive Director

JONATHAN WISE
Board President

11206 Euclid Ave.
Cleveland, OH 44106
(216) 231-8787

FOUNDED 1975
Brian Kilpatrick, Charles St. Clair

SEASON
September-June

FACILITIES
Cleveland Play House/Brooks Theatre
8600 Euclid Ave.
Seating capacity: 160
Stage: proscenium

FINANCES
July 1, 1983-June 30, 1984
Operating expenses: $108,000

AUDIENCE
Annual attendance: 45,000

TOURING CONTACT
Michael G. Regnier

PRODUCTIONS 1983–84

Productions	Directors	Sets	Costumes	Lights
Smircus! A Sign and Mime Circus Adrian Blue and Deborah Taylor	Deborah Taylor	Bruce Keller and Don McBride	Harriet Cone, Robert Tolaro, Debbie Anne Rennie and Juliette Johnson-Webb	Dennis Fyffe
Total Communication company-developed	Michael G. Regnier			
A Phoenix Too Frequent Christopher Fry; sign-language trans: Juliette Johnson-Webb and company	Michael G. Regnier	John J. Ashby	Thomas Swales	John J. Ashby

PRODUCTIONS 1984–85

Productions	Directors	Sets	Costumes	Lights
Smircus! A Sign and Mime Circus Adrian Blue and Deborah Taylor	Michael G. Regnier and Lane Stewart	Bruce Keller and Don McBride	Harriet Cone, Robert Tolaro, Debbie Anne Rennie and Juliette Johnson-Webb	Dennis Fyffe
Total Communication company-developed	Michael G. Regnier			

Florida Studio Theatre

RICHARD HOPKINS
Artistic Director

ANN GRAHAM
Administrative Director

ROBERT DRABIK
Board President

1241 North Palm Ave.
Sarasota, FL 33577
(813) 366-9017 (business)
(813) 366-9796 (box office)

FOUNDED 1973
Jon Spelman

SEASON
January-June

FACILITIES
Seating capacity: 165
Stage: modified thrust

FINANCES
July 1, 1984-June 30, 1985
Operating expenses: $320,000

AUDIENCE
Annual attendance: 19,000
Subscribers: 2,500

TOURING CONTACT
Ann Graham

BOOKED-IN EVENT
Theatre, music, film

AEA letter of agreement

PRODUCTIONS 1983–84

Productions	Directors	Sets	Costumes	Lights
The World of Carl Sandburg Norman Corwin	Susann Brinkley	David S.S. Davis	Vicki Holden	Paul D. Romance
What I Did Last Summer A.R. Gurney, Jr.	Susann Brinkley	David S.S. Davis	Jeffrey Wolz	Paul D. Romance
Beyond Therapy Christopher Durang	Richard Hopkins	David S.S. Davis	Jeffrey Wolz	Paul D. Romance
True West Sam Shepard	Richard Hopkins	David S.S. Davis	Jeffrey Wolz	Paul D. Romance
Absurd Person Singular Alan Ayckbourn	Richard Hopkins	David S.S. Davis	Jeffrey Wolz	Paul D. Romance
Do You Turn Somersaults? Aleksei Arbuzov; trans: Ariadne Nicolaeff	Susann Brinkley	David S.S. Davis	Jeffrey Wolz	Paul D. Romance

PRODUCTIONS 1984–85

Productions	Directors	Sets	Costumes	Lights
Crimes of the Heart Beth Henley	Carolyn Michel	Paul Bannan	Robert A. Horek	Paul D. Romance
Absent Friends Alan Ayckbourn	Richard Hopkins	Paul Bannan	Robert A. Horek	Paul D. Romance
Agnes of God John Pielmeier	Richard Hopkins	Paul Bannan	Robert A. Horek	Paul D. Romance
American Buffalo David Mamet	Jeff Mousseau	Paul Bannan	Robert A. Horek	Paul D. Romance
El Grande de Coca-Cola Ron House, Diz White, Alan Shearman, John Neville-Andrews and Sally Willis; music: Alan Shearman and John Neville-Andrews	Alkis Papoutsis	Paul Bannan	Robert A. Horek	Paul D. Romance

Folger Theatre

JOHN NEVILLE-ANDREWS
Artistic Producer

MARY ANN DE BARBIERI
Managing Director

R. ROBERT LINOWES
Board Chairman

201 East Capitol St., SE
Washington, DC 20003
(202) 547-3230 (business)
(202) 546-4000 (box office)

FOUNDED 1969
Folger Shakespeare Library, O.B.
 Hardison, Richmond Crinkley

SEASON
October-June

FACILITIES
Seating capacity: 253
Stage: thrust

FINANCES
July 1, 1984-June 30, 1985
Operating expenses: $1,723,459

AUDIENCE
Annual attendance: 60,000
Subscribers: 4,487

AEA LORT (C) contract

PRODUCTIONS 1983–84

Productions	Directors	Sets	Costumes	Lights
The School for Scandal Richard Brinsley Sheridan	Allen R. Belknap	Charles Vaughan, III	Bary Allen Odom	Richard Winkler
The Mayor of Zalamea Pedro Calderon de la Barca; adapt: Adrian Mitchell	Michael Bogdanov	John A. Rush	Lee Anne Dorsey	Allen Lee Hughes and Michael Bogdanov
Henry V William Shakespeare	Philip Kerr	Russell Metheny	Bary Allen Odom	Stuart Duke
Troilus and Cressida William Shakespeare	John Neville-Andrews	Lewis Folden	Bary Allen Odom	Allen Lee Hughes

PRODUCTIONS 1984–85

Productions	Directors	Sets	Costumes	Lights
King Lear William Shakespeare	John Neville-Andrews	Russell Metheny	Ann Hould-Ward	Stuart Duke
Crossed Words Hugh Atkins and Mike Laflin	Davey Marlin-Jones	Lewis Folden	Paige Southard	Lewis Folden
Much Ado About Nothing William Shakespeare	John Neville-Andrews	William Barclay	John Carver Sullivan	Daniel M. Wagner
Hamlet William Shakespeare	Lindsay Anderson	John Lee Beatty	Judianna Makovsky	Jeffrey Beecroft
A Midsummer Night's Dream William Shakespeare	John Neville-Andrews	Lewis Folden	Elizabeth Covey	Richard Winkler

Ford's Theatre

DAVID H. BELL
Artistic Director

FRANKIE HEWITT
Executive Producer

A.J. PIETRANTONE
Business Manager

511 Tenth St., NW
Washington, DC 20004
(202) 638-2941 (business)
(202) 347-4833 (box office)

FOUNDED 1968
Frankie Hewitt

SEASON
September-June

FACILITIES
Seating capacity: 741
Stage: modified proscenium

FINANCES
October 1, 1983-September 30, 1984
Operating expenses: $2,900,000

AUDIENCE
Annual attendance: 135,000

TOURING CONTACT
David H. Bell

BOOKED-IN EVENTS
Theatre, music, dance

AEA Special Production contract

PRODUCTIONS 1983–84

Productions	Directors	Sets	Costumes	Lights
A Christmas Carol adapt: Rae Allen and Timothy Near, from Charles Dickens	Timothy Near	Christina Weppner	Christina Weppner	John Gisondi
On Shiloh Hill Bill Schustik and Suzanne Benham	Byron F. Ringland	James Noone	Dona Granata	David Segal

PRODUCTIONS 1984–85

Productions	Directors	Sets	Costumes	Lights
A Christmas Carol adapt: Rae Allen and Timothy Near, from Charles Dickens	Ted Weiant	Christina Weppner	Christina Weppner	John Gisondi
Godspell book: John-Michael Tabelak; music and lyrics: Stephen Schwartz	David H. Bell	James Fouchard	Doug Marmee	Jeff Davis

Free Street Theater

PATRICK HENRY
Producer/Artistic Director

CARROL McCARREN
General Manager

NANCY MEYERSON
Board President

441 West North Ave.
Chicago, IL 60610
(312) 642-1234

FOUNDED 1969
Patrick Henry

SEASON
variable

FINANCES
April 1, 1984-March 31, 1985
Operating expenses: $223,577

AUDIENCE
Annual attendance: 90,000

TOURING CONTACT
Irene-Aimee Depke

*AEA Chicago Area Theatre contract and
letter of agreement*

PRODUCTIONS 1984

Productions	Directors	Sets	Costumes	Lights
The Last Flower adapt: Patrick Henry, from James Thurber	Patrick Henry			
A Different Drummer Patrick Henry	Patrick Henry			
Stupid Charlie and the Airplane adapt: Patrick Henry, from Ed Rawson	Patrick Henry			
Dance, Dance, Dance Patrick Henry	Patrick Henry			
Musicmini Patrick Henry	Patrick Henry			

PRODUCTIONS 1985

Productions	Directors	Sets	Costumes	Lights
To Life! Patrick Henry	Patrick Henry			John Aldridge
What Do You Want to Be When You Grow Old? Patrick Henry	Patrick Henry			John Aldridge
Take the Chance book adapt: Patrick Henry, from Ira Rogers; music and lyrics: Tricia Alexander, Patrick Henry and Doug Lofstrom	Patrick Henry			
Chicago book: Patrick Henry; music and lyrics: Tricia Alexander, Patrick Henry and Doug Lofstrom	Patrick Henry			Rob Hamilton

Fulton Opera House

KATHLEEN A. COLLINS
Artistic Director

STEVEN B. LIBMAN
Managing Director

W. JEFFREY SIDEBOTTOM
Board President

Box 1865
Lancaster, PA 17603
(717) 394-7133 (business)
(717) 397-7425 (box office)

FOUNDED 1963
Fulton Opera House Foundation

SEASON
October-August

FACILITIES
12 North Prince St.
Seating capacity: 909
Stage: proscenium

FINANCES
October 1, 1983-September 30, 1984
Operating expenses: $669,717

AUDIENCE
Annual attendance: 110,000
Subscribers: 5,047

TOURING CONTACT
Barry Kornhauser

BOOKED-IN EVENTS
Theatre, music, dance

AEA letter of agreement

PRODUCTIONS 1983-84

Productions	Directors	Sets	Costumes	Lights
The Wind in the Willows adapt: Moses Goldberg, from Kenneth Grahame	Kathleen Collins	William F. Teske	Beth Dunkelberger	Jim Jackson
Step on a Crack Suzan Zeder	Kathleen Collins	Clifford Clayton	Beth Dunkelberger	Jim Jackson
Robinson and Friday Hansjorg Schneider	Carol Tanzman	William F. Teske	Beth Dunkelberger	
Beauty and the Beast Barry Kornhauser	Kathleen Collins	William F. Teske	Beth Dunkelberger	
Tintypes Mary Kyte, Mel Marvin and Gary Pearle	Kathleen Collins	William F. Teske	Virginia M. West	William Simmons
Talley's Folly Lanford Wilson	Kathleen Collins	Joseph Dodd	Beth Dunkelberger	William Simmons
They're Playing Our Song book: Neil Simon; music: Marvin Hamlisch; lyrics: Carole Bayer Sager	Ken Gargaro	Mary E. Lewis	Virginia M. West	William Simmons

PRODUCTIONS 1984-85

Productions	Directors	Sets	Costumes	Lights
The Best Christmas Pageant Ever Barbara Robinson	Kathleen Collins	Norman B. Dodge, Jr.	Virginia M. West	Jim Jackson
Mother Hicks Suzan Zeder	Kathleen Collins	Norman B. Dodge, Jr.	Beth Dunkelberger	Jim Jackson
Ama and the White Crane Maureen O'Toole	Ron Nakahara	Herbert H. O'Dell	Virginia M. West	Jim Jackson
The 'Write' Stuff Kathleen Collins and Barry Kornhauser	Kathleen Collins		Beth Dunkelberger	Jim Jackson
Quilters book: Molly Newman and Barbara Damashek; music and lyrics: Barbara Damashek	Kathleen Collins	Norman B. Dodge, Jr.	Virginia M. West	William Simmons
The Dining Room A.R. Gurney, Jr.	Kathleen Collins	Norman B. Dodge, Jr.	Beth Dunkelberger	William Simmons
Crimes of the Heart Beth Henley	Michael Nash	Norman B. Dodge, Jr.	Virginia M. West	William Simmons

George Street Playhouse

ERIC KREBS
Artistic Director

GEOFFREY COHEN
General Manager

LORA TREMAYNE
Board President

9 Livingston Ave.
New Brunswick, NJ 08901
(201) 846-2895 (business)
(201) 246-7717 (box office)

FOUNDED 1974
Eric Krebs, John Herochik

SEASON
October-May

FACILITIES
Stage I
Seating capacity: 367
Stage: thrust

Stage II
Seating capacity: 90
Stage: flexible

Stage III
Seating capacity: 75
Stage: cabaret

FINANCES
July 1, 1983-June 30, 1984
Operating expenses: $988,000

AUDIENCE
Annual attendance: 75,000
Subscribers: 4,200

TOURING CONTACT
Sharon Rothe

BOOKED-IN EVENTS
Theatre, music, dance

AEA LORT (C) contract

PRODUCTIONS 1983-84

Productions	Directors	Sets	Costumes	Lights
Children of a Lesser God Mark Medoff	Sue Lawless	Daniel Proett	Linda Reynolds	Gary W. Fassler
The Old Flag Vincent Canby	John Schwab	David Mitchell	Hilary Rosenfeld	Daniel Stratman
Beyond Therapy Christopher Durang	Maureen Heffernan	Rob Hamilton	Linda Reynolds	Phil Monat
Master Harold . . . and the boys Athol Fugard	Bob Hall	Daniel Proett	Linda Reynolds	Reid Bartlett
A Streetcar Named Desire Tennessee Williams	Eric Krebs	Daniel Proett	Vicki McLaughlin	Daniel Stratman

PRODUCTIONS 1984-85

Productions	Directors	Sets	Costumes	Lights
The Taming of the Shrew William Shakespeare	Edward Stern	Michael Miller	Lewis D. Rampino	Daniel Stratman
A Little Night Music book: Hugh Wheeler; music and lyrics: Stephen Sondheim	Maureen Heffernan	Daniel Proett	Michael Cesario	Phil Monat
'night, Mother Marsha Norman	Maureen Heffernan	Reid Bartlett	Crystal K. Craft	Daniel Stratman
Productions of The Acting Company:				
As You Like It, William Shakespeare	Mervyn Willis	Stephen McCabe	Stephen McCabe	Dennis Parichy
Pieces of 8, Beckett, Pinter, Ionesco, Lardner, Albee, Anderson, Feiffer and Stoppard	Alan Schneider	Mark Fitzgibbons	Carla Kramer	Richard Riddell
A New Way to Pay Old Debts, Philip Massinger	Michael Kahn	John Kasarda	Judith Dolan	Dennis Parichy
The Skin of Our Teeth, Thornton Wilder	Gerald Freedman	Joel Fontaine	Jeanne Button	Dennis Parichy
The Importance of Being Earnest Oscar Wilde	Bob Hall	Dan Stratman	Patricia Adshead	Phil Monat
True West Sam Shepard	John Pynchon Holms	Reid Bartlett	Judith K. Hart	Daniel Stratman

Germinal Stage Denver

ED BAIERLEIN
Director/Manager

1820 Market St.
Denver, CO 80202
(303) 296-1192

FOUNDED 1974
Ed Baierlein, Sallie Diamond, Ginger
   Valone, Jack McKnight

SEASON
October-August

FACILITIES
Seating capacity: 132
Stage: thrust

FINANCES
September 1, 1984-August 31, 1985
Operating expenses: $75,000

AUDIENCE
Annual attendance: 10,000
Subscribers: 550

PRODUCTIONS 1983–84

Productions	Directors	Sets	Costumes	Lights
Waiting for Godot Samuel Beckett	Ed Baierlein	Ed Baierlein	Gisela Boderite	Ed Baierlein
Winter Madness: *A Separate Peace*, Tom Stoppard; *Action* and *Camera Obscura*, Robert Patrick; *Jack, Or the Submission*, Eugene Ionesco	Ed Baierlein	Ed Baierlein	Brenda Johnson	Ed Baierlein
The Lover Harold Pinter	Ed Baierlein	Ed Baierlein	Ed Baierlein	Ed Baierlein
The Loves of Cass McGuire Brian Friel	Laura Cuetara	Peg Bruck	Gisela Boderite	Ed Baierlein
The Typists Murray Schisgal	Ed Baierlein	Ed Baierlein	Ed Baierlein	Ed Baierlein
King Ubu Alfred Jarry; trans: George Wellwarth and Michael Benedikt	Ed Baierlein	Ed Baierlein	Brenda Johnson	Ed Baierlein
Counting the Ways Edward Albee	Ed Baierlein	Ed Baierlein	Ed Baierlein	Ed Baierlein
High Spirits Hugh Martin and Timothy Gray	Ed Baierlein	Ed Baierlein	Gisela Boderite	Ed Baierlein
Overruled George Bernard Shaw	Laura Cuetara	Laura Cuetara	Laura Cuetara	Laura Cuetara

PRODUCTIONS 1984–85

Productions	Directors	Sets	Costumes	Lights
The Unvarnished Truth Royce Ryton	Ed Baierlein	Ed Baierlein	Ed Baierlein	Ed Baierlein
The Vise Luigi Pirandello; trans: William Murray	Laura Cuetara	Laura Cuetara	Laura Cuetara	Laura Cuetara
Nightpiece Wolfgang Hildesheimer	Laura Cuetara	Laura Cuetara	Laura Cuetara	Laura Cuetara
All Over Edward Albee	Ed Baierlein	Ed Baierlein	Ed Baierlein	Ed Baierlein
A Kind of Alaska Harold Pinter	Ed Baierlein	Ed Baierlein	Ed Baierlein	Ed Baierlein
The Philanderer George Bernard Shaw	Laura Cuetara	Laura Cuetara	Laura Cuetara	Laura Cuetara
Venus Observed Christopher Fry	Ed Baierlein	Ed Baierlein	Ed Baierlein	Ed Baierlein

GeVa Theatre

HOWARD J. MILLMAN
Producing Director

HERBERT L. REES
Board Chairman

75 Woodbury Blvd.
Rochester, NY 14607
(716) 232-1366 (business)
(716) 232-1363 (box office)

FOUNDED 1972
William and Cynthia Selden

SEASON
October-July

FACILITIES
Seating capacity: 500
Stage: thrust

FINANCES
July 1, 1984-June 30, 1985
Operating expenses: $1,300,000

AUDIENCE
Annual attendance: 75,000
Subscribers: 9,000

BOOKED-IN EVENTS
Dance

AEA LORT (C) contract

PRODUCTIONS 1983-84

Productions	Directors	Sets	Costumes	Lights
I'm Getting My Act Together and Taking It on the Road book and lyrics: Gretchen Cryer; music: Nancy Ford	Judith Haskell	Patricia Woodbridge	Betsey Sherman Norland	Phil Monat
Uncle Vanya Anton Chekhov	Thomas Gruenewald	William Barclay	Pamela Scofield	Phil Monat
The Dining Room A.R. Gurney, Jr.	Beth Dixon	Richard Hoover	Martha Kelly	Walter R. Uhrman
A Hell of a Town Monte Merrick	Allan Carlsen	Ray Recht	Pamela Scofield	F. Mitchell Dana
Quilters book: Molly Newman and Barbara Damashek; music and lyrics: Barbara Damashek	Howard J. Millman	Ursula Belden and Cathrine Poppe	Pamela Scofield	Phil Monat
Born Yesterday Garson Kanin	Edward Stern	Richard Hoover and Cynthia Sweetland	Pamela Scofield	Phil Monat and Nic Minetor

PRODUCTIONS 1984-85

Productions	Directors	Sets	Costumes	Lights
Billy Bishop Goes to War John Gray and Eric Peterson	John Henry Davis	Ray Recht	Sylvia Sheret Newman	F. Mitchell Dana
All My Sons Arthur Miller	Howard J. Millman	William Barclay	Holly Cole	Phil Monat
Planet Fires Thomas Babe	John Henry Davis	Ray Recht	Pamela Scofield	F. Mitchell Dana
The Foreigner Larry Shue	Walton Jones	Kevin Rupnik	Connie Singer	Walter Uhrman
And a Nightingale Sang... C.P. Taylor	Gideon Y. Schein	Richard Hoover	Pamela Scofield	Victor En Yu Tan
The Royal Family George S. Kaufman and Edna Ferber	Howard J. Millman	Holmes Easley	Pamela Scofield	Phil Monat
Black Coffee Agatha Christie	Barbara Redmond	Bob Barnett	Martha Kelly	Nic Minetor

Goodman Theatre

ROCHE SCHULFER
Producer

KATHRINE MURPHY
General Manager

DAVID OFNER
Board Chairman

200 South Columbus Dr.
Chicago, IL 60603
(312) 443-3811 (business)
(312) 443-3800 (box office)

FOUNDED 1925
Art Institute of Chicago

SEASON
October-July

FACILITIES
Goodman Series Stage
Seating capacity: 683
Stage: proscenium

Goodman Theatre Studio
Seating capacity: 135
Stage: proscenium

Briar Street Theatre
3133 North Halsted
Seating capacity: 280
Stage: flexible

FINANCES
July 1, 1984-June 30, 1985
Operating expenses: $4,519,000

AUDIENCE
Annual attendance: 229,100
Subscribers: 20,050

BOOKED-IN EVENTS
Theatre, dance

AEA LORT (B) and (D) contracts

Note: During the 1983-84 and 1984-85 seasons, Gregory Mosher served as artistic director.

PRODUCTIONS 1983–84

Productions	Directors	Sets	Costumes	Lights
A Raisin in the Sun Lorraine Hansberry	Thomas Bullard	Karen Schulz	Judy Dearing	Dennis Parichy
Candida George Bernard Shaw	Munson Hicks	Joseph Nieminski	Nan Cibula	Robert Christen
The Time of Your Life William Saroyan	D.W. Moffett	Tom Lynch	Nan Cibula	Robert Christen
The Road Wole Soyinka	Wole Soyinka	Patricia Woodbridge	Judy Dearing	Steven Strawbridge
The Three Moscowteers adapt: Paul Magid, from Alexander Dumas	Robert Woodruff	Kate Edmunds	Susan Hilferty	James F. Ingalls
Glengarry Glen Ross David Mamet	Gregory Mosher	Michael Merritt	Nan Cibula	Kevin Rigdon
Hey, Stay a While book and lyrics: John Guare; music: Galt MacDermot, Jan Warner and John Guare	Larry Sloan	Phillip Eickhoff	Nan Cibula	Kevin Rigdon
Hurlyburly David Rabe	Mike Nichols	Tony Walton	Ann Roth	Jennifer Tipton
A Christmas Carol adapt: Barbara Field, from Charles Dickens	Tony Mockus	Joseph Nieminski	James Edmund Brady	Robert Christen

PRODUCTIONS 1984–85

Productions	Directors	Sets	Costumes	Lights
Candide book adapt: Hugh Wheeler, from Voltaire; music: Leonard Bernstein; lyrics: Richard Wilbur, Stephen Sondheim and James Latouche	Munson Hicks	John Lee Beatty,	Christa Scholtz	Judy Rasmusson
The Adventures of Huckleberry Finn adapt: Organic Theater Company, from Mark Twain (An Organic Theater Company production)	Stuart Gordon	John Paoletti and Mary Griswold	John Paoletti and Mary Griswold	Geoffrey Bushor
The Water Engine David Mamet	Steven Schachter	John Lee Beatty	Jessica Hahn	Dennis Parichy
The Cherry Orchard Anton Chekhov; adapt: David Mamet	Gregory Mosher	Michael Merritt	Nan Cibula	Kevin Rigdon
The Spanish Prisoner and *The Shawl* David Mamet	Gregory Mosher	Michael Merritt	Nan Cibula	Kevin Rigdon
A Christmas Carol adapt: Gregory Mosher and Larry Sloan, from Charles Dickens	Gregory Mosher	Kate Edmunds	Christa Scholtz	Duane Schuler

Goodspeed Opera House

MICHAEL PRICE
Executive Director

RICHARD SCHNELLER
Foundation President

NORWICK R.G. GOODSPEED
Board Chairman

Box A
East Haddam, CT 06423
(203) 873-8664 (business)
(203) 873-8668 (box office)

FOUNDED 1963
Goodspeed Opera House Foundation

SEASON
April-December

FACILITIES
Goodspeed Opera House
Goodspeed Landing
Seating capacity: 400
Stage: proscenium

Goodspeed-at-Chester
The Norma Terris Theatre
North Main St., Chester
Seating capacity: 200
Stage: proscenium

AUDIENCE
Annual attendance: 142,000
Subscribers: 7,000

AEA LORT (A) and (D) contracts

PRODUCTIONS 1983-84

Productions	Directors	Sets	Costumes	Lights
Gay Divorce book: Dwight Taylor, Kenneth Webb and Samuel Hoffenstein; music and lyrics: Cole Porter	Robert Brink	James Leonard Joy	David Toser	Craig Miller
Miss Liberty book: Robert E. Sherwood; music and lyrics: Irving Berlin	Bill Gile	Vittorio Capecce	David Toser	Jeff Davis
Oh, Boy! book and lyrics: Guy Bolton and P.G. Wodehouse; music: Jerome Kern	Thomas Gruenewald	James Leonard Joy	David Toser	Richard Winkler

---

PRODUCTIONS 1984-85

Productions	Directors	Sets	Costumes	Lights
The Boys from Syracuse book: George Abbott; music: Richard Rodgers; lyrics: Lorenz Hart	Dennis Rosa	James Leonard Joy	David Toser	Craig Miller
Follow Thru book: Laurence Schwab and B.G. DeSylva; music and lyrics: B.G. DeSylva, Lew Brown and Ray Henderson	Robert Nigro	James Leonard Joy	David Toser	Pat Collins
Take Me Along book adapt: Joseph Stein and Robert Russell, from Eugene O'Neill; music and lyrics: Bob Merrill	Thomas Gruenewald	James Leonard Joy	David Toser	Craig Miller
Harrigan 'n Hart book: Michael Stewart; music: Max Showalter; lyrics: Peter Walker	Edward Stone	James Leonard Joy	Ann Hould-Ward	Marilyn Rennagel
Mrs. McThing book and lyrics adapt: Michael Colby, from Mary Chase; music: Jacques Urbont	Edward Stone	Mark Morton	Susan Hirschfeld	Jason Kantrowitz
A Broadway Baby book: Carl Kleinschmitt; music: Nacio Herb Brown; lyrics: Arthur Freed	Thommie Walsh	Nicky Nadeau	William Ivey Long	Marilyn Rennagel
The Dream Team book: Richard Wesley; music: Thomas Tierney; lyrics: John Forster	Dan Siretta	James Leonard Joy	Judy Dearing	Beverly Emmons

The Great-American Theatre Company

TERI SOLOMON MITZE
Producer

JUDY INSTENES
Business Manager

JOYCE TIBER
Board President

Box 92123
Milwaukee, WI 53202
(414) 276-4230

FOUNDED 1976
Teri Solomon Mitze, Thomas Mitze

SEASON
October–May

FACILITIES
Pabst Theater
144 East Wells St.
Seating capacity: 1,432
Stage: proscenium

Madison Civic Center
211 State St.
Seating capacity: 2,215
Stage: proscenium

West Hi Auditorium
Green Bay
Seating capacity: 1,500
Stage: proscenium

FINANCES
July 1, 1984-June 30, 1985
Operating expenses: $403,949

AUDIENCE
Annual attendance: 112,000

TOURING CONTACT
Teri Solomon Mitze

BOOKED-IN EVENTS
Children's theatre

PRODUCTIONS 1983–84

Productions	Directors	Sets	Costumes	Lights
Welcome to the Zoo book: Bill Solly and Donald Ward; music and lyrics: Bill Solly	Montgomery Davis		Rose-Marie Seck Costello	Curt Crain, Jr.
The Miracle Worker William Gibson	Leslie Reidel	Allen H. Jones	Ted Boerner	Daniel Bouvarney

PRODUCTIONS 1984–85

Productions	Directors	Sets	Costumes	Lights
Turn on the Lights book: Bill Solly and Donald Ward; music and lyrics: Bill Solly	Montgomery Davis		Ellen Kozak	Curt Crain, Jr.
Tom Sawyer adapt: Hugh Corcoran and Stefanie Warren, from Mark Twain	Leslie Reidel	Allen H. Jones	Ted Boerner	Daniel Bovarney

Great Lakes Theater Festival

GERALD FREEDMAN
Artistic Director

MARY BILL
Managing Director

THOMAS G. STAFFORD
Board President

1501 Euclid Ave., Suite 250
Cleveland, OH 44115
(216) 241-5490 (business)
(216) 241-6000 (box office)

FOUNDED 1962
Community members

SEASON
July-October, December

FACILITIES
Ohio Theatre
1511 Euclid Ave.
Seating capacity: 815
Stage: proscenium

FINANCES
February 1, 1984-January 31, 1985
Operating expenses: $1,630,511

AUDIENCE
Annual attendance: 51,855
Subscribers: 5,252

BOOKED-IN EVENTS
Theatre

AEA LORT (B) contract

Note: During the 1984 season, Vincent
Dowling served as artistic director.
The theatre was formerly known as
Great Lakes Shakespeare Festival.

PRODUCTIONS 1984

Productions	Directors	Sets	Costumes	Lights
The Taming of the Shrew William Shakespeare	Larry Arrick	John Ezell	Lewis D. Rampino	Robert Jared
She Stoops to Conquer Oliver Goldsmith	David Trainer	John Ezell	Lewis D. Rampino	Robert Jared
Our Town Thornton Wilder	Kenneth Albers	John Ezell	Estelle Painter	Robert Jared
Alcestis and Apollo, or The Alcestiad Thornton Wilder	Vincent Dowling and Jeffrey Bihr	John Ezell	Hollis Jenkins-Evans	Robert Jared
Peg O' My Heart J. Hartley Manners	Vincent Dowling and John Q. Bruce	John Ezell	John Glaser	Robert Jared
A Midsummer Night's Dream William Shakespeare	Vincent Dowling and John Love	John Ezell	John Glaser	Robert Jared

PRODUCTIONS 1985

Productions	Directors	Sets	Costumes	Lights
Twelfth Night William Shakespeare	Gerald Freedman	John Ezell	Jeanne Button	Tom Skelton
The Skin of Our Teeth Thornton Wilder	Gerald Freedman and Richard Hamburger	John Ezell	Jeanne Button	Tom Skelton
The Game of Love book and lyrics adapt: Tom Jones, from Arthur Schnitzler; music: Jacques Offenbach; additional music: Nancy Ford	Gerald Freedman	John Ezell	Lew Rampino	Spencer Mosse
Tartuffe Molière; trans: Richard Wilbur	Kenneth Frankel	John Ezell	Lew Rampino	Spencer Mosse
Take One Step book: Gerald Freedman; music: John Morris; lyrics: Gerald Freedman and John Morris	Gerald Freedman	John Ezell	Lew Rampino	Tom Skelton

The Group Theatre Company

RUBEN SIERRA
Artistic Director

SCOTT CALDWELL
Managing Director

JANICE M. MONTI
Board Chairman

3940 Brooklyn Ave. NE
Seattle, WA 98105
(206) 545-4969 (business)
(206) 543-4327 (box office)

FOUNDED 1978
Ruben Sierra, Scott Caldwell, Gilbert
Wong

SEASON
September-June

FACILITIES
Ethnic Theatre
Seating capacity: 197
Stage: modified thrust

FINANCES
July 1, 1984-June 30, 1985
Operating expenses: $290,000

AUDIENCE
Annual attendance: 23,000
Subscribers: 1,500

TOURING CONTACT
Scott Caldwell

BOOKED-IN EVENTS
Theatre

AEA letter of agreement

PRODUCTIONS 1983–84

Productions	Directors	Sets	Costumes	Lights
Desert Fire Roger Holzberg and Martin Casella	Ruben Sierra	Gilbert Wong	Martha E. Mattus	Rex Carleton
Strange Snow Stephen Metcalfe	Rita Giomi	Alex Hutton	Mary Ellen Walter	Carmine Simone
Voices of Christmas Ruben Sierra	Tim Bond	Alex Hutton		Rex Carleton
Nuts Tom Topor	Linda Hartzell	Gilbert Wong	Mary Ellen Walter	Rex Carleton
Talking With Jane Martin	Ruben Sierra	Gilbert Wong	Michael Murphy	Rex Carleton
Articus and the Angel Ruben Sierra; music: Chad Henry	Ruben Sierra	Gilbert Wong	Nina Moser	Geoffrey Sedgwick

PRODUCTIONS 1984–85

Productions	Directors	Sets	Costumes	Lights
Reagan's Women Peggy Shannon	Chris Sumption	Matthew Rawdon	Gay Howard	Frank Butler
Lemons Kent Broadhurst	Linda Hartzell	Gilbert Wong	Rose Pederson	Carmine Simone
Voices of Christmas Ruben Sierra	Ruben Sierra	Alex Hutton	Gilbert Wong	Rex Carleton
Sizwe Bansi Is Dead Athol Fugard	Tim Bond	Alex Hutton	Mary Ellen Walter	Rex Carleton
Split Second Dennis McIntyre	John Kazanjian	Alex Hutton	Rose Pederson	Rex Carleton
Orinoco! Emilio Carballido	Ruben Sierra	Gilbert Wong	Mary Ellen Walter	Rex Carleton
I Am Celso adapt: Ruben Sierra and Jorge Huerta, from Leo Romero	Jorge Huerta	Gilbert Wong	Gilbert Wong	Rex Carleton

The Guthrie Theater

DONALD SCHOENBAUM
Managing Director

MARTHA ATWATER
Board President

725 Vineland Place
Minneapolis, MN 55403
(612) 347-1100 (business)
(612) 377-2224 (box office)

FOUNDED 1963
Tyrone Guthrie, Oliver Rea, Peter
  Zeisler

SEASON
June-March

FACILITIES
Seating capacity: 1,441
Stage: thrust

FINANCES
April 1, 1984-March 31, 1985
Operating expenses: $7,566,544

AUDIENCE
Annual attendance: 410,594
Subscribers: 19,600

TOURING CONTACT
Chris Tschida

BOOKED-IN EVENTS
Theatre, dance, music, comedy

AEA LORT (A) contract

Note: During the 1983-84 and 1984-85
seasons, Liviu Ciulei served as
artistic director.

PRODUCTIONS 1983-84

Productions	Directors	Sets	Costumes	Lights
The Threepenny Opera book and lyrics: Bertolt Brecht; music: Kurt Weill; adapt: Marc Blitzstein	Liviu Ciulei	Liviu Ciulei	Carrie Robbins	Richard Riddell
Guys and Dolls book adapt: Jo Swerling and Abe Burrows, from Damon Runyon; music and lyrics: Frank Loesser	Garland Wright	Paul Zalon	Kurt Wilhelm	Frances Aronson
The Entertainer John Osborne	Edward Payson Call	Ming Cho Lee	Ann Wallace	Dawn Chiang
The Seagull Anton Chekhov; trans; Jean-Claude van Itallie	Lucian Pintilie	Radu Boruzescu	Miruna Boruzescu	Paul Scharfenberger
A Christmas Carol adapt: Barbara Field, from Charles Dickens	Christopher Markle	Jack Edwards	Jack Edwards	Paul Scharfenberger
The Importance of Being Earnest Oscar Wilde	Garland Wright	Michael Miller and Garland Wright	Jack Edwards	Craig Miller
Hedda Gabler Henrik Ibsen; trans: Siri Senje and Tom Creamer	Christopher Markle	Douglas Stein	Gene Lakin	William Armstrong
Master Harold . . . and the boys Athol Fugard	Athol Fugard	Jane Clark	Sheila McLamb	David Noling

---

PRODUCTIONS 1984-85

Productions	Directors	Sets	Costumes	Lights
A Soldier's Play Charles Fuller (A Negro Ensemble Company production)	Douglas Turner Ward	Felix H. Cochren	Judy Dearing	Allen Lee Hughes
Hang on to Me book: Maxim Gorky; music and lyrics: George and Ira Gershwin; trans: Maria M. Markof-Belaeff; adapt: Peter Sellars	Peter Sellars	Adrianne Lobel	Dunya Ramicova	James Ingalls
The Three Sisters Anton Chekhov	Liviu Ciulei	Liviu Ciulei	Jack Edwards	Dawn Chiang
Tartuffe Molière	Lucian Pintilie	Radu Boruzescu	Miruna Boruzescu	Beverly Emmons
'night, Mother Marsha Norman	Christopher Markle	Jack Edwards	Jack Edwards	Bill Armstrong
Twelfth Night William Shakespeare	Liviu Ciulei	Radu Boruzescu	Miruna Boruzescu	Dawn Chiang

PRODUCTIONS 1984–85

Productions	Directors	Sets	Costumes	Lights
A Christmas Carol adapt: Barbara Field, from Charles Dickens	Christopher Markle	Jack Barkla	Jack Edwards	Paul Scharfenberger
Anything Goes book: Howard Lindsay, Russel Crouse, Guy Bolton and P. G. Wodehouse; music and lyrics: Cole Porter	Garland Wright	Thomas Lynch	Patricia McGourty	Craig Miller

The Harold Clurman Theatre

JACK GARFEIN
Artistic Director

CRAIG S. DORFMAN
General Manager

RITA E. HAUSER
Board Chairman

412 West 42nd St.
New York, NY 10036
(212) 594-2828 (business)
(212) 594-2370 (box office)

FOUNDED 1978
Jack Garfein, Harold Clurman

SEASON
July–June

FACILITIES
Harold Clurman Theatre
Seating capacity: 99
Stage: proscenium

Samuel Beckett Theatre
Seating capacity: 99
Stage: proscenium

FINANCES
July 1, 1984-June 30, 1985
Operating expenses: $700,000

AUDIENCE
Annual attendance: 100,000

BOOKED-IN EVENTS
Theatre, music, dance

AEA Off Broadway contract

PRODUCTIONS 1983–84

Productions	Directors	Sets	Costumes	Lights
Rockaby Samuel Beckett	Alan Schneider	Rocky Greenberg	Carla Kramer	Rocky Greenberg
Ohio Impromptu, Catastrophe and *What Where* Samuel Beckett	Alan Schneider	Marc D. Malamud	Carla Kramer	Marc D. Malamud
Endgame Samuel Beckett	Alvin Epstein	Avigdor Arikha	Avigdor Arikha	Jennifer Tipton

PRODUCTIONS 1984–85

Productions	Directors	Sets	Costumes	Lights
All Strange Away Samuel Beckett	Gerald Thomas			
A Kurt Weill Cabaret music: Kurt Weill; adapt: Alvin Epstein and Martha Schlamme	Alvin Epstein			Kevin Rigdon
Rommel's Garden Harvey Gabor	Jack Garfein	Charles Henry McLennahan	Ruth Morley	Jackie Manassee
Childhood and *For No Good Reason* Nathalie Sarraute	Simone Benmussa	Simone Benmussa and Antoni Taule	Gail Brassard	Simone Benmussa

Hartford Stage Company

MARK LAMOS
Artistic Director

DAVID HAWKANSON
Managing Director

DEANNA SUE SUCSY
Board President

50 Church St.
Hartford, CT 06103
(203) 525-5601 (business)
(203) 527-5151 (box office)

FOUNDED 1964
Jacques Cartier

SEASON
October-June

FACILITIES
John W. Huntington Theatre
Seating capacity: 489
Stage: thrust

FINANCES
July 1, 1984-June 30, 1985
Operating expenses: $2,100,000

AUDIENCE
Annual attendance: 90,500
Subscribers: 9,500

AEA LORT (C) contract

PRODUCTIONS 1983–84

Productions	Directors	Sets	Costumes	Lights
And a Nightingale Sang... C. P. Taylor	Terry Kinney	David Jenkins	Jess Goldstein	David K. H. Elliot
As You Like It William Shakespeare	Mark Lamos	Michael H. Yeargan	Dunya Ramicova	Craig Miller
Of Mice and Men John Steinbeck	Mary B. Robinson	Lowell Detweiler	Lowell Detweiler	Paul Gallo
The Value of Names Jeffrey Sweet	Emily Mann	Marjorie Bradley Kellogg	Jennifer von Mayrhauser	Pat Collins
The Three Sisters Anton Chekhov; adapt: Lanford Wilson	Mark Lamos	John Conklin	Dunya Ramicova	Pat Collins
Home Samm-Art Williams	Clay Stevenson	G.W. Mercier	G.W. Mercier	Mimi Jordan Sherin

PRODUCTIONS 1984–85

Productions	Directors	Sets	Costumes	Lights
Anatol Arthur Schnitzler; trans: Frank Marcus	Mark Lamos	John Conklin	John Conklin	Pat Collins
The Mystery Plays adapt: John Russell Brown	Mary B. Robinson	John Conklin	John Conklin	Robert Wierzel
Passion Play Peter Nichols	Mark Lamos	Marjorie Bradley Kellogg	Jess Goldstein	Pat Collins
America's Sweetheart book: John Weidman and Alfred Uhry; music: Robert Waldman; lyrics: Alfred Uhry	Gerald Freedman	Kevin Rupnik	Jeanne Button	Pat Collins
Desire Under the Elms Eugene O'Neill	Mary B. Robinson	Hugh Landwehr	Jess Goldstein	Paulie Jenkins
The Tempest William Shakespeare	Mark Lamos	Michael H. Yeargan	Dunya Ramicova	Pat Collins

The Hartman Theatre

MARGARET BOOKER
Artistic Director

H. RIDGELY BULLOCK
Board Chairman

Box 521
Stamford, CT 06904
(203) 324-6781 (business)
(203) 323-2131 (box office)

FOUNDED 1975
Del and Margot Tenney

SEASON
September-May

FACILITIES
Stamford Center for the Arts
307 Atlantic St.
Seating capacity: 654
Stage: proscenium

FINANCES
July 1, 1984-June 30, 1985
Operating expenses: $1,094,000

AUDIENCE
Annual attendance: 80,000
Subscribers: 7,349

AEA LORT (B) contract

PRODUCTIONS 1983–84

Productions	Directors	Sets	Costumes	Lights
Rocket to the Moon Clifford Odets	Edwin Sherin	John Falabella	David Murin	Jeff Davis
The Chain Elia Kazan	Elia Kazan	Tony Straiges	Jane Greenwood	Allen Lee Hughes
Bedrock David Epstein	Melvin Bernhardt	Steven Rubin	Steven Rubin	Craig Miller
Cantorial Ira Levin	Edwin Sherin	Marjorie Bradley Kellogg	Ann Roth	Jeff Davis
Stem of a Briar Beddow Hatch	Leonard Peters	Hugh Landwehr	Carol Oditz	Richard Winkler
The Me Nobody Knows book adapt: Robert H. Livingston and Herb Schapiro, from Stephen M. Joseph; music: Gary William Friedman; lyrics: Will Holt	Edwin Sherin	John Falabella	John Falabella	Jeff Davis

PRODUCTIONS 1984–85

Productions	Directors	Sets	Costumes	Lights
The Torch-Bearers George Kelly	Elinor Renfield	Victor Capecce	Mariann Verheyen	Jeff Davis
Over My Dead Body adapt: Anthony J. Fingleton and Michael Sutton, from Robert L. Fish	Edwin Sherin	Victor Capecce	Judianna Makovsky	Jeff Davis
Beloved Friend Nancy Pahl Gilsenan	David Chambers	Oliver Smith	Marie Anne Chiment	Arden Fingerhut
Black Comedy and The Public Eye Peter Shaffer	Peter Pope	Douglas W. Schmidt and David N. Feight	Carol Oditz	Jeff Davis
The Team adapt: Terence Feely, from Terence Feely and Brian Clemens	Edwin Sherin	Guido Tondino	Mariann Verheyen	Jeff Davis
Greater Tuna Jaston Williams, Joe Sears and Ed Howard	Darwin Knight	David Crank	Lana Fritz	Jeff Davis

The Hippodrome State Theatre

GREGORY HAUSCH
MARY HAUSCH
Producing Directors

DIANA SARDO
Business Manager

CHARLES I. HOLDEN, JR.
Board Chairman

25 Southeast 2nd Pl.
Gainesville, FL 32601
(904) 373-5968 (business)
(904) 375-4477 (box office)

FOUNDED 1973
Gregory Hausch, Mary Hausch, Kerry
McKenney, Orin Wechsberg

SEASON
July-June

FACILITIES
Mainstage
Seating capacity: 266
Stage: modified thrust

Second Stage
Seating capacity: 86
Stage: flexible

FINANCES
June 1, 1984-May 31, 1985
Operating expenses: $750,000

AUDIENCE
Annual attendance: 130,000
Subscribers: 3,000

TOURING CONTACT
Gregory Hausch, Toni Gwaltney

BOOKED-IN EVENTS
Music, dance, art shows, comedy, film

AEA LORT (D) contract

PRODUCTIONS 1983–84

Productions	Directors	Sets	Costumes	Lights
Mass Appeal Bill C. Davis	Marshall New	Tony and Hope White	Leslie Klein	Sheldon Warshaw
I'm Getting My Act Together and Taking It on the Road Gretchen Cryer and Nancy Ford	Mary Hausch	Hope White	Vicki Pennington	Sheldon Warshaw
Amadeus Peter Shaffer	Marshall New	Carlos Francisco Asse	Marilyn Wall-Asse	Sheldon Warshaw
A Christmas Carol adapt: Gregory Hausch, from Charles Dickens	Gregory Hausch	Carlos Francisco Asse	Marilyn Wall-Asse	Sheldon Warshaw
The Servant of Two Masters Carlo Goldoni	Gregory Hausch	Carlos Francisco Asse	Marilyn Wall-Asse	Jerome Gardner
Cloud 9 Caryl Churchill	Mary Hausch	Carlos Francisco Asse	Marilyn Wall-Asse	Jerome Gardner
Crimes of the Heart Beth Henley	Gregory Hausch	Carlos Francisco Asse	Marilyn Wall-Asse	Jerome Gardner
True West Sam Shepard	Mary Hausch	Carlos Francisco Asse	Marilyn Wall-Asse	Jerome Gardner

PRODUCTIONS 1984–85

Productions	Directors	Sets	Costumes	Lights
The Middle Ages A.R. Gurney, Jr.	Gregory Hausch	Carlos Francisco Asse	Marilyn Wall-Asse	Jerome Gardner
Isn't It Romantic Wendy Wasserstein	Gregory Hausch	Carlos Francisco Asse	Marilyn Wall-Asse	Todd Bedell
The Dresser Ronald Harwood	Mary Hausch	Carlos Francisco Asse	Marilyn Wall-Asse	Todd Bedell
A Christmas Carol adapt: Gregory Hausch, from Charles Dickens	James Wren	Carlos Francisco Asse	Marilyn Wall-Asse	Todd Bedell
Turning Over Brian Thompson	Kerry McKenney	Carlos Francisco Asse	Marilyn Wall-Asse	Todd Bedell
The Comedy of Errors William Shakespeare	Sid Homan and Kerry McKenney	Carlos Francisco Asse	Marilyn Wall-Asse	Carlos Francisco Asse
Rhinoceros Eugene Ionesco	Mary Hausch	Carlos Francisco Asse	Marilyn Wall-Asse	Kerry McKenney and Bob Robins
Sweet Tango of Lies Mario Vargas Llosa; trans: Kerry McKenney and Anthony Oliver Smith	Kerry McKenney	Carlos Francisco Asse	Marilyn Wall-Asse	Carlos Francisco Asse

Honolulu Theatre for Youth

JOHN KAUFFMAN
Artistic Director

JANE CAMPBELL
Managing Director

SUZANNE CASE
Board President

Box 3257
Honolulu, HI 96801
(808) 521-3487

FOUNDED 1955
Nancy Corbett

SEASON
July-May

FINANCES
June 1, 1984-May 31, 1985
Operating expenses: $520,230

AUDIENCE
Annual attendance: 140,000

TOURING CONTACT
Jane Campbell

BOOKED-IN EVENTS
Theatre, puppetry, mime

PRODUCTIONS 1983–84

Productions	Directors	Sets	Costumes	Lights
Frankenstein adapt: Nick Di Martino, from Mary Shelley	John Kauffman	Charles Walsh	Eddy Barrows	Lloyd S. Riford, III
Newcomer Janet Thomas	John Kauffman	Mary Lewis	Eddy Barrows	Lloyd S. Riford, III
Pinocchio adapt: John Kauffman; music: Bert Moon; lyrics: Tremaine Tamayose	John Kauffman	Charles Walsh	Eddy Barrows	Mary Lewis
Sparks Tremaine Tamayose	John Kauffman	Gerald Kawaoka	Eddy Barrows and Lindy Fisher	
The Original Absurd Musical Review for Children Arne Zaslove	John Kauffman		Eddy Barrows	

PRODUCTIONS 1984–85

Productions	Directors	Sets	Costumes	Lights
Mime to the Max company-developed	John Kauffman			Gerald Kawaoka
Flash Gordon Conquers the Planet of Evil Lewis L. Stout; music: Don Nahaku	Karen Brilliande-White	Patrick Kelly	Eddy Barrows	Lloyd S. Riford, III
To Kill a Mockingbird adapt from Harper Lee	John Kauffman	Robert E. Campbell	Eddy Barrows	Lloyd S. Riford, III
East of the Sun and West of the Moon Brian Kral; music: Don Nahaku	John Kauffman	Mary Lewis	Eddy Barrows	Lloyd S. Riford, III
Island Slices Karen Yamamoto Hackler; music: Bert Moon	Karen Yamamoto Hackler	Sarah Moon	Lindy Fisher	Sarah Moon
The Best Christmas Pageant Ever Barbara Robinson	Dando Kluever	Mary Lewis	Eddy Barrows	Don Ranney
Raven the Hungry Nick DiMartino	John Kauffman	Charles Walsh	Eddy Barrows	
Sparks Tremaine Tamayose	John Kauffman	Gerald Kawaoka	Eddy Barrows and Lindy Fisher	
The Codebreaker Pauline C. Conley	Jay Broad	William Forrester	Eddy Barrows	Mary Lewis
The Belle of Amherst William Luce	John Kauffman		Kathe James	

Horse Cave Theatre

WARREN HAMMACK
Director

PAMELA WHITE
Administrative Director

SUSANNE WINTSCH
Board President

Box 215
Horse Cave, KY 42749
(502) 786-1200 (business)
(502) 786-2177 (box office)

FOUNDED 1977
Horse Cave citizens

SEASON
June-September

FACILITIES
107-109 Main St.
Seating capacity: 355
Stage: thrust

FINANCES
October 1, 1983-September 30, 1984
Operating expenses: $237,989

AUDIENCE
Annual attendance: 12,000
Subscribers: 600

AEA letter of agreement

PRODUCTIONS 1984

Productions	Directors	Sets	Costumes	Lights
A Doll's House Henrik Ibsen	Warren Hammack	Linda Blase	Galen Logsdon	Linda Blase
Hay Fever Noel Coward	Christopher Schario	Linda Blase	Galen Logsdon	Linda Blase
Paducah Sallie Bingham	Warren Hammack	Linda Blase	Galen Logsdon	Martha Parks
Murder at the Howard Johnson's Ron Clark and Sam Bobrick	Breton Frazier	Sam Hunt	Galen Logsdon	Martha Parks
Twelfth Night William Shakespeare	Warren Hammack	John Partyka	Galen Logsdon	Martha Parks

PRODUCTIONS 1985

Productions	Directors	Sets	Costumes	Lights
Vanities Jack Heifner	Breton Frazier	Sam Hunt	Rebecca Shouse	Greg Etter
Desire Under the Elms Eugene O'Neill	Warren Hammack	John Partyka	Rebecca Shouse	John Partyka
East of Nineveh Jim Peyton	Michael Hankins	John Partyka	Rebecca Shouse	John Partyka
Henry IV, Part 1 William Shakespeare	Warren Hammack	John Partyka	Rebecca Shouse	John Partyka

Hudson Guild Theatre

DAVID KERRY HEEFNER
Producing Director

JAMES ABAR
Associate Director

SUSAN E. SCHUUR
Board President

441 West 26th St.
New York, NY 10001
(212) 760-9836 (business)
(212) 760-9810 (box office)

FOUNDED 1896
John Lovejoy Elliott

SEASON
October-June

FACILITIES
Arthur Strasser Auditorium
Seating capacity: 135
Stage: proscenium

FINANCES
July 1, 1984-June 30, 1985
Operating expenses: $234,000

AUDIENCE
Annual attendance: 20,000
Subscribers: 2,000

AEA letter of agreement

PRODUCTIONS 1983–84

Productions	Directors	Sets	Costumes	Lights
Sand Dancing Kenneth Pressmen	Robert Moss	Paul Wonsek	Jeanne Button	Paul Wonsek
Wednesday Julia Kearsley	Geraldine Fitzgerald	Ron Placzek	Mariann Verheyen	Phil Monat
Getting Along Famously Michael Jacobs	Joan Darling	James Leonard Joy	Mariann Verheyen	Phil Monat
Love Letters on Blue Paper Arnold Wesker	Kenneth Frankel	Paul Wonsek	Mariann Verheyen	Jeff Davis
Brownstone book: Andrew Cadiff; music: Peter Larson and Josh Rubins; lyrics: Josh Rubins	Andrew Cadiff	Paul Wonsek	Thomas McKinley	Paul Wonsek

---

PRODUCTIONS 1984–85

Productions	Directors	Sets	Costumes	Lights
Burkie Bruce Graham	Lynn M. Thompson	William Barclay	Anne Morrell	Phil Monat
The Accrington Pals Peter Whelan	Daniel Gerroll	Robert Thayer	Pamela Scofield	Phil Monat
Outside Waco Patricia Griffith	June Rovenger	Daniel Proett	Patricia Adshead	Phil Monat
September in the Rain John Godber	David Kerry Heefner		Mary L. Hayes	Phil Monat
Submariners Tom McClenaghan	David Kerry Heefner	Daniel Proett	Pamela Scofield	Phil Monat

The Huntington Theatre Company

PETER ALTMAN
Producing Director

MICHAEL MASO
Managing Director

GERALD GROSS
Board President

264 Huntington Ave.
Boston, MA 02115
(617) 353-3320 (business)
(617) 266-3913 (box office)

FOUNDED 1982
Boston University

SEASON
September-June

FACILITIES
Boston University Theatre
Seating capacity: 850
Stage: proscenium

FINANCES
July 1, 1984-June 30, 1985
Operating expenses: $1,561,251

AUDIENCE
Annual attendance: 100,000
Subscribers: 9,000

AEA LORT (B) contract

PRODUCTIONS 1983–84

Productions	Directors	Sets	Costumes	Lights
Design for Living Noel Coward	Ken Ruta	Richard Isackes	Mariann Verheyen	Marcus Dillard
Uncommon Women and Others Wendy Wasserstein	Larry Carpenter	James Leonard Joy	Ann Wallace	Frances Aronson
Cyrano de Bergerac Edmond Rostand	Jacques Cartier	Richard Isackes	James B. Harris	Roger Meeker
Plenty David Hare	Edward Gilbert	David Jenkins	Ann Wallace	Pat Collins
On the Razzle Johann Nestroy; adapt: Tom Stoppard	Thomas Gruenewald	James Leonard Joy	Mariann Verheyen	Jeff Davis

---

PRODUCTIONS 1984–85

Productions	Directors	Sets	Costumes	Lights
You Never Know book: Rowland Leigh and Paul Lazarus; music and lyrics: Cole Porter	James Leonard Joy	James Leonard Joy	John Falabella	Craig Miller
Twelfth Night William Shakespeare	Thomas Gruenewald	Franco Colavecchia and David Sumner	Mariann Verheyen	William Mintzer
Uncle Vanya Anton Chekhov	Jacques Cartier	Richard Isackes	Ann Wallace	Roger Meeker
Terra Nova Ted Tally	Michael Murray	Karl Eigsti	Mariann Verheyen	Spencer Mosse
The Plough and the Stars Sean O'Casey	Pamela Berlin	John Falabella	Susan Tsu	James F. Ingalls

Illinois Theatre Center

STEVE S. BILLIG
Artistic Director

ETEL BILLIG
Managing Director

TERRANCE MITCHELL
Board President

400A Lakewood Blvd.
Park Forest, IL 60466
(312) 481-3510

FOUNDED 1976
Steve and Etel Billig

SEASON
September-May

FACILITIES
Seating capacity: 189
Stage: modified thrust

FINANCES
September 1, 1984-August 31, 1985
Operating expenses: $208,000

AUDIENCE
Annual attendance: 56,000
Subscribers: 3,087

TOURING CONTACT
Etel Billig

BOOKED-IN EVENTS
Theatre

AEA Chicago Area Theatre contract

PRODUCTIONS 1983–84

Productions	Directors	Sets	Costumes	Lights
Happily Ever After Steve S. Billig	Steve S. Billig	Jonathan Roark	Cathy Bieber	Richard Peterson
Teibele and Her Demon Isaac Bashevis Singer and Eve Friedman	Etel Billig	Jonathan Roark	Henriette Swearingen	Richard Peterson
The Most Happy Fella Frank Loesser	Steve S. Billig	Jonathan Roark	Henriette Swearingen	Richard Peterson
Do Lord Remember Me James DeJongh	Steve S. Billig	Jonathan Roark	Cathy Bieber	Richard Peterson
Harry and Thelma in the Woods Stan Lachow	Dan Le Monnier	Jonathan Roark	Vera Wright	Richard Peterson
A Life Hugh Leonard	Etel Billig	Jonathan Roark	Vera Wright	Richard E. Poshard

---

PRODUCTIONS 1984–85

Productions	Directors	Sets	Costumes	Lights
The Show-Off George Kelly	Steve S. Billig	Jonathan Roark	Henriette Swearingen	Millicent Gordon
Foxfire Susan Cooper and Hume Cronyn	Richard Pickren	Jonathan Roark	Henriette Swearingen	Richard Peterson
Charlotte Sweet Michael Colby and Gerald Markoe; music: Gerald Markoe; lyrics: Michael Colby	Steve S. Billig	Jonathan Roark	Henriette Swearingen	Richard Peterson
My Sister in This House Wendy Kesselman	Steve S. Billig	Jonathan Roark	Henriette Swearingen	Richard Peterson
Relatively Speaking Alan Ayckbourn	Etel Billig	Jonathan Roark	Henriette Swearingen	Jonathan Roark
Blithe Spirit Noel Coward	Steve S. Billig	Jonathan Roark	Henriette Swearingen	Jonathan Roark
Pack Up Your Troubles Steve S. Billig	Steve S. Billig	Jonathan Roark	Henriette Swearingen	Jonathan Roark

Illusion Theater

MICHAEL ROBINS
BONNIE MORRIS
Producing Directors

JOHN MONTILINO
Managing Director

PETER HAMES
Board President

304 North Washington Ave.
Minneapolis, MN 55401
(612) 339-4944

FOUNDED 1974
Michael Robins, Carole Harris
   Lipschultz

SEASON
October-June

FACILITIES
Studio
Seating capacity: 50-100
Stage: thrust

Southern Theatre
1420 Washington Ave.
Seating capacity: 150
Stage: flexible

FINANCES
July 1, 1984-June 30, 1985
Operating expenses: $426,500

AUDIENCE
Annual attendance: 55,000

TOURING CONTACT
Nancy Riestenberg

AEA letter of agreement

PRODUCTIONS 1983–84

Productions	Directors	Sets	Costumes	Lights
Touch Cordelia Anderson, Michael Robins, Bonnie Morris and company	Michael Robins			
No Easy Answers Cordelia Anderson and company	D. Scott Glaser			
The Coconuts book and lyrics: George S. Kaufman; music; Irving Berlin and Michael Koerner	David Feldshuh	David Krchelich	Barrie Smeeth	David Krchelich
Eavesdrop David Michael Erickson and company; music: Mark Bloom	Michael Robins	David Krchelich	Robb Gordon	Edward Bevan
Push-ups Lee Blessing, Michael Robins and Alfred Harrison	D. Scott Glasser	David Krchelich	Barrie Smeeth	David Krchelich
For Adults Only Cordelia Anderson, Bonnie Morris, Michael Robins and company	D. Scott Glasser	Edward Bevan	Robb Gordon	Edward Bevan
The Illusion Show company-developed	Steven Dietz and Michael Robins	Edward Bevan	Robb Gordon	Edward Bevan

PRODUCTIONS 1984–85

Productions	Directors	Sets	Costumes	Lights
Some Other Time Frank Pike and company; music: Michael Koerner	Michael Robins and Scott Rubsam	Kirby Moore	Leisa Luis	Hugh Graham
Restoration Edward Bond; music: Nick Bicat and Mark Bloom	Michael Robins	Michael Sommers	Robb Gordon	Hugh Graham
Unexpected Company: Illusion Show '85 company-developed	Steven Dietz, Laurie Grossman, Chris Cinque and Kevin Kling	Hugh Graham	Kristian Kraai	David Johnson
For Adults Only Cordelia Anderson, Bonnie Morris, Michael Robins and company; music: Mark Bloom	Michael Robins	Hugh Graham		Hugh Graham

PRODUCTIONS 1984–85

Productions	Directors	Sets	Costumes	Lights
The Angels of Swedenborg Ping Chong	Ping Chong	Ping Chong	Mel Carpenter	Hugh Graham
Wanderlust Steven Dietz and company	Steven Dietz	Hugh Graham	Robb Gordon and Kristian Kraai	David Johnson
The Einstein Project Paul D'Andrea, Jon Klein and company; music: Kim D. Sherman	David Feldshuh	Paul Krajniak	Janet Groenert	Hugh Graham
Touch and *No Easy Answers* Cordelia Anderson, Bonnie Morris, Michael Robins and company	Michael Robins			

The Independent Eye

CONRAD BISHOP
Producing Director

LINDA BISHOP
Administrative Director

STEPHEN PATTERSON
Board Chairman

208 East King St.
Lancaster, PA 17602
(717) 393-9088

FOUNDED 1974
Conrad and Linda Bishop

SEASON
September-May

FACILITIES
Eye Theatre Works
Seating capacity: 100
Stage: flexible

FINANCES
July 1, 1984-June 30, 1985
Operating expenses: $118,552

AUDIENCE
Annual attendance: 14,000
Subscribers: 200

TOURING CONTACT
Kim Conlin-Hockney

BOOKED-IN EVENTS
Theatre, music, poetry, mime

PRODUCTIONS 1984–85

Productions	Directors	Sets	Costumes	Lights
Moves Camilla Schade	Camilla Schade	Mark E. McCall		Joanne Bender
Waiting for Godot Samuel Beckett	Conrad Bishop	Roman Tatarowicz		Roman Tatarowicz
Summer Sisters Conrad Bishop and Elizabeth Fuller	Conrad Bishop	Mark E. McCall		Conrad Bishop
The Want Ads Conrad Bishop and Elizabeth Fuller	Conrad Bishop	Conrad Bishop		Conrad Bishop

PRODUCTIONS 1984–85

Productions	Directors	Sets	Costumes	Lights
Restaurant Camilla Schade	Camilla Schade	Scott Spangler		Conrad Bishop
Dark of the Moon H. Richardson and W. Berney; music: Linda Bishop	Conrad Bishop	Richard S. Shandler	Beth Dunkelberger	Brian Toland
Macbeth William Shakespeare	Conrad Bishop	Conrad Bishop		Conrad Bishop

Productions	Directors	Sets	Costumes	Lights
Under Milkwood Dylan Thomas	Conrad Bishop	Herbert H. O'Dell		Conrad Bishop
Dreamers Conrad Bishop	Conrad Bishop	Herbert H. O'Dell		Conrad Bishop and James Jackson

Indiana Repertory Theatre

TOM HAAS
Artistic Director

JESSICA L. ANDREWS
Managing Director

EDGAR G. DAVIS
Board Chairman

140 West Washington St.
Indianapolis, IN 46204
(317) 635-5277 (business)
(317) 635-5252 (box office)

FOUNDED 1972
Benjamin Mordecai, Gregory Poggi,
Edward Stern

SEASON
October–May

FACILITIES
Mainstage
Seating capacity: 583
Stage: proscenium

Upperstage
Seating capacity: 245
Stage: proscenium

Cabaret
Seating capacity: 150
Stage: modified thrust

FINANCES
July 1, 1984-June 30, 1985
Operating expenses: $2,108,078

AUDIENCE
Annual attendance: 188,000
Subscribers: 9,584

BOOKED-IN EVENTS
Theatre, music, dance, nightclub acts

AEA LORT (B) contract

Productions	Directors	Sets	Costumes	Lights
Henry IV, Parts 1 and 2 William Shakespeare	Tom Haas	Steven Rubin	Leon Brauner and Nancy Pope	Craig Miller
Mass Appeal Bill C. Davis	Martin Platt	Leslie Taylor	Nancy Pope	Robert Shook
A Christmas Carol adapt: Tom Haas, from Charles Dickens	David Adamson	Karen Schulz	Susan Hilferty	Rachel Budin
Pump Boys and Dinettes John Foley, Mark Hardwick, Debra Monk, Cass Morgan, John Schimmel and Jim Wann	Marnie Carmichael	Leslie Taylor	Nancy Pope	Robert Shook
Heartbreak House George Bernard Shaw	Ben Cameron	Leslie Taylor	Lawrence Casey	Rachel Budin
Joan and Charles with Angels Robert Montgomery	Tom Haas	Karen Schulz	Jeanne Button	Rachel Budin
The Island Athol Fugard, John Kani and Winston Ntshona	Jim O'Connor	Leslie Taylor		Robert Shook
Whodunnit Anthony Shaffer	Ben Cameron	Russell Metheny	Gail Brassard	Stuart Duke
South Pacific book and lyrics: Oscar Hammerstein, II; music: Richard Rodgers	Tom Haas	Steven Rubin	Bobbi Owen	Craig Miller

PRODUCTIONS 1984–85

Productions	Directors	Sets	Costumes	Lights
The Man Who Came to Dinner George S. Kaufman and Moss Hart	Tom Haas	Michael H. Yeargan	Gail Brassard	Michael Lincoln
Fool for Love Sam Shepard	Amy Saltz	Richard F. Mays	Nancy Pope	Michael Lincoln
A Christmas Carol adapt: Tom Haas, from Charles Dickens	Tom Haas	Karen Schulz	Susan Hilferty	Rachel Budin
Tintypes Mary Kyte, Mel Marvin and Gary Pearle	Frederick Farrar	James Burbeck	Nancy Pope	Stuart Duke
Painting Churches Tina Howe	Paul Moser	Russell Metheny	Gail Brassard	Stuart Duke
The Three Sisters Anton Chekhov	Tom Haas	Karen Schulz	Susan Hilferty	Mary Jo Dondlinger
'night, Mother Marsha Norman	Paul Moser	Russell Metheny	Nancy Pope	Stuart Duke
The Diary of Anne Frank Frances Goodrich and Albert Hackett	David Rotenberg	Russell Metheny	Nancy Pope	Rachel Budin
The School for Wives Molière	Tom Haas	Kate Edmunds	Bill Walker	Rachel Budin

INTAR

MAX FERRA
Artistic Director

DENNIS FERGUSON-ACOSTA
Managing Director

STANLEY STAIRS
Board President

Box 788
New York, NY 10108
(212) 695-6134 (business)
(212) 279-4200 (box office)

FOUNDED 1966
Max Ferra, Frank Robles, Elsa Ortiz
  Robles, Antonio Gonzales-Jaen,
  Oscar Garcia, Benjamin Lopez,
  Gladys Ortiz

SEASON
September-June

FACILITES
Mainstage
420 West 42nd St.
Seating capacity: 99
Stage: proscenium

Stage Two
508 West 53rd St.
Seating capacity: 99
Stage: proscenium

FINANCES
July 1, 1983-June 30, 1984
Operating expenses: $447,021

AUDIENCE
Annual attendance: 13,300

BOOKED-IN EVENTS
Theatre, music, dance, lectures

*AEA Mini contract and letter of
  agreement*

PRODUCTIONS 1984

Productions	Directors	Sets	Costumes	Lights
Sarita book and lyrics: Maria Irene Fornes; music: Leon Odenz	Maria Irene Fornes	Donald Eastman	Gabriel Berry	Anne E. Militello
Equinox Mario Diament; trans: Simone Z. Karlin and Evelyn Strouse	Moni Yakim	Don Coleman	K.L. Fredericks	Lisa Grossman
The Cuban Swimmer and *Dog Lady* Milcha Sanchez-Scott	Max Ferra	Ming Cho Lee	Connie Singer	Anne E. Militello

Productions	Directors	Sets	Costumes	Lights
Impact Juan Shamsul Alam	George Ferencz	Jun Maeda	Sally J. Lesser	Blu
Cold Air Virgilio Pinera; trans and adapt: Maria Irene Fornes	Maria Irene Fornes	Ricardo Morin	Gabriel Berry	Anne E. Militello
Savings book and lyrics: Dolores Prida; music: Leon Odenz	Max Ferra	Robert McBroom	Karen Barbano	Robert McBroom

Interart Theatre

MARGOT LEWITIN
Artistic Director

MELODY BROOKS
Acting Managing Director

BILL PERLMAN
Board Chairman

549 West 52nd St.
New York, NY 10019
(212) 246-1050

FOUNDED 1971
Marjorie De Fazio, Margot Lewitin,
Alice Rubenstein, Jane Chambers

SEASON
September-June

FACILITIES
Interart Theatre
Seating capacity: 74
Stage: flexible

Interart Theatre Annex
552 West 53rd St.
Seating capacity: 60
Stage: flexible

FINANCES
July 1, 1984-June 30, 1985
Operating expenses: $106,500

AUDIENCE
Annual attendance: 9,000

AEA Mini contract

Productions	Directors	Sets	Costumes	Lights
Through the Leaves Franz Xaver Kroetz; trans: Roger Downey	JoAnne Akalaitis	Douglas Stein	Kurt Wilhelm	Frances Aronson
Feast or Famine Sondra Segal *Notes from the Moroccan Journals* Nancy du Plessis	Roberta Sklar	Seth Price	Beth Kuhn	Jackie Manassee
New Women Directors Festival: *A Perfect Analysis by a Parrot*, Tennessee Williams	Carol Morley	Doris Mezler Andelberg	Doris Mezler Andelberg	Bill Hanauer
The Berry-Picker, James Purdy	Waltrudis Mathes	Doris Mezler Andelberg	Doris Mezler Andelberg	Bill Hanauer
Trifles, Susan Glaspell	Anne West	Doris Mezler Andelberg	Doris Mezler Andelberg	Bill Hanauer
Joe: A Dramatic Idiocy and *Stops*, Robert Auletta	Gaylen Ross	Doris Mezler Andelberg	Doris Mezler Andelberg	Bill Hanauer

Productions	Directors	Sets	Costumes	Lights
About Anne Anne Sexton	Salome Jens	Seth Price		Jackie Manassee

PRODUCTIONS 1984-85

Productions	Directors	Sets	Costumes	Lights
Beatrice Roth's Trilogy Beatrice Roth	Valeria Wasilewski	Seth Price		Rocky Greenberg
Walking Through Bernett Belgreier	Melody Brooks	Daniel Kenney		Paula Gordon

Intiman Theatre Company

ELIZABETH HUDDLE
Artistic Director

PETER DAVIS
Managing Director

PAMELA SCHELL
Board President

Box 2763
Seattle, WA 98111
(206) 624-4541 (business)
(206) 624-2992 (box office)

FOUNDED 1972
Margaret Booker

SEASON
June-October

FACILITIES
Broadway Performance Hall
1625 Broadway
Seating capacity: 295
Stage: proscenium

FINANCES
January 1, 1984-December 31, 1984
Operating expenses: $1,021,873

AUDIENCE
Annual attendance: 50,000
Subscribers: 4,400

TOURING CONTACT
Peter Davis

AEA LORT (C) contract

Note: During the 1983-84 and 1984-85 seasons, Margaret Booker served as artistic director.

PRODUCTIONS 1984

Productions	Directors	Sets	Costumes	Lights
Hobson's Choice Harold Brighouse	James Moll	Scott Weldin	Liz Covey	James Sale
Long Day's Journey into Night Eugene O'Neill	Margaret Booker	David Potts	Ron Erickson	Greg Sullivan
The Country Wife William Wycherly	Anthony Cornish	Robert Dahlstrom	Michael Olich	Jim Verdery
Blood Wedding Federico Garcia Lorca	Margaret Booker	Michael Miller	Deb Dryden	James Sale
Myth Weavers Arturo Uslar-Pietri	Gustavo Tambascio	Martin Lopez	Martin Lopez	Robert Peterson
The Dance and the Railroad David Henry Hwang	Tzi Ma	Karen Gjelsteen	Karen Gjelsteen	Michael Davidson

PRODUCTIONS 1985

Productions	Directors	Sets	Costumes	Lights
You Never Can Tell George Bernard Shaw	James Moll	Gilbert Wong	Liz Covey	Michael Davidson
Hedda Gabler Henrik Ibsen	Margaret Booker	David Potts	John Sullivan	James Sale
Duet for One Tom Kempinski	Robert Loper	Michael Miller	Sarah Nash Gates	Peter W. Allen

The Julian Theatre

RICHARD REINECCIUS
Artistic/General Director

GEORGE CROWE
Board Chairman

953 De Haro St.
San Francisco, CA 94107
(415) 647-5525 (business)
(415) 647-8098 (box office)

FOUNDED 1965
Richard Reineccius, Douglas Giebel,
  Brenda Berlin

SEASON
September–June

FACILITIES
Potrero Hill Neighborhood House
Seating capacity: 175
Stage: flexible

FINANCES
July 1, 1984–June 30, 1985
Operating expenses: $156,000

AUDIENCE
Annual attendance: 20,050
Subscribers: 305

TOURING CONTACT
Staff

BOOKED-IN EVENTS
Theatre, music, dance

AEA letter of agreement

PRODUCTIONS 1983–84

Productions	Directors	Sets	Costumes	Lights
'34 book and lyrics: Robert Carson; music: William Young	Richard Reineccius	Michael Dingle	Pamela Minor	Scott DeStefano
Igugu-Lethu U-Zulu Dance Theatre	company	company	company	Michael Dingle
For Better, Not for Worse Selaelo Maredi	Selaelo Maredi	Michael Dingle	Selaelo Maredi	Michael Dingle
Oh, Danny Boy A.K. Bierman	Richard Rekow and David Parr	Dale Altvater	Pamela Minor	Dale Altvater
My Sister in This House Wendy Kesselman	Brenda Berlin	Ken Holamon	Pamela Mason-Brune	Susan Paigen
More Than Comedy—Less Than Tragedy Darryl Henriques	Darryl Henriques	Design Stage		Design Stage

PRODUCTIONS 1984–85

Productions	Directors	Sets	Costumes	Lights
Feel the Spirit—A Tribute to Paul Robeson Joe Carter	Richard Reineccius		Joe Carter	David Holcomb
The American adapt: George Crowe, from Howard Fast	David Parr	Design Stage	Sharon Slowley	David Holcomb
Homeland Selaelo Maredi and Steve Friedman	John Doyle	Laura Settlemier	Kam Devereaux	Bob Cardana
S'Kotiphola Selaelo Maredi	Selaelo Maredi	Alan Curreri	Kam Devereaux	Richard Reineccius

La Jolla Playhouse

DES McANUFF
Artistic Director

ALAN LEVEY
Managing Director

WILLARD P. VANDERLAAN
Board President

Box 12039
La Jolla, CA 92037
(619) 452-6760 (business)
(619) 452-3960 (box office)

FOUNDED 1947
Gregory Peck, Dorothy McGuire, Mel
Ferrer

SEASON
June-September

FACILITIES
*Mandell Weiss Center for the
Performing Arts*
La Jolla Village Dr. and Torrey Pines
Road
Seating capacity: 492
Stage: proscenium

Warren Theatre
Gilman Dr. and Rupertus Way
Seating capacity: 248
Stage: thrust

FINANCES
November 1, 1983-October 31, 1984
Operating expenses: $1,364,309

AUDIENCE
Annual attendance: 45,000
Subscribers: 7,000

AEA LORT (B) contract

PRODUCTIONS 1984

Productions	Directors	Sets	Costumes	Lights
Big River: The Adventures of Huckleberry Finn book adapt: William Hauptman, from Mark Twain; music and lyrics: Roger Miller	Des McAnuff	Heidi Landesman	Patricia McGourty	Richard Riddell
Maybe I'm Doing It Wrong music and lyrics: Randy Newman	Susan Cox	Jill Moon	Paki Wolfe	Michael Chybowski
War Babies Robert Coe	James Simpson	Michael H. Yeargan	Patricia McGourty	Richard Riddell
As You Like It William Shakespeare	Des McAnuff	John Arnone	Patricia McGourty	Richard Riddell

PRODUCTIONS 1985

Productions	Directors	Sets	Costumes	Lights
Merrily We Roll Along book: George Furth; music and lyrics: Stephen Sondheim	James Lapine	Loren Sherman	Ann Hould-Ward	Beverly Emmons
A Man's a Man Bertolt Brecht; trans: Gerhard Nelhaus	Robert Woodruff	Douglas Stein	Susan Dennison	Richard Riddell
Ghost on Fire Michael Weller	Timothy Near	Tom Lynch	Jennifer von Mayrhauser	Kent Dorsey
The Seagull Anton Chekhov; trans: Jean-Claude van Itallie	Des McAnuff	John Arnone	Patricia McGourty	Richard Riddell

Lamb's Theatre Company

CAROLYN ROSSI COPELAND
Executive Director

KENDYL MONROE
Board Chairman

130 West 44th St.
New York, NY 10036
(212) 575-0300, 221-1031 (business)
(212) 997-1780 (box office)

FOUNDED 1984
Carolyn Rossi Copeland

SEASON
September-June

FACILITIES
Lamb's Theatre
Seating capacity: 285-377
Stage: proscenium

Little Theatre at the Lamb's
Seating capacity: 85
Stage: flexible

FINANCES
July 1, 1984-June 30, 1985
Operating expenses: $158,000

AUDIENCE
Annual attendance: 9,000

TOURING CONTACT
Carolyn Rossi Copeland

AEA letter of agreement

PRODUCTIONS 1984

Productions	Directors	Sets	Costumes	Lights
Courage John Pielmeier	Susan Gregg	Pat Woodbridge	Karen Gerson	Karl E. Haas

PRODUCTIONS 1985–86

Productions	Directors	Sets	Costumes	Lights
Porch Jeffrey Sweet	Nan Harris	Michael C. Smith	Neal Bishop	Marc D. Malamud
Gifts of the Magi book adapt and lyrics: Randy Courts and Mark St. Germain, from O. Henry	Christopher Catt	Michael C. Smith	Hope Hanafin	Heather Carson
Pippin book: Roger O. Hirson; music and lyrics: Stephen Schwartz	Christopher Catt	Tom Barnes	Hope Hanafin	Marc D. Malamud
Episode 26 Howard Korder	Christopher Catt	Michael C. Smith	Andrea N. Carini	Heather Carson

L.A. Public Theatre

PEG YORKIN
Artistic Director/Board President

SUZAN MILLER
General Manager

8105 West Third St.
Los Angeles, CA 90048
(213) 651-0491 (business)
(213) 659-6415 (box office)

FOUNDED 1973
Community members

SEASON
Year-round

FACILITIES
Coronet Theatre
366 North LaCienega Blvd.
Seating capacity: 272
Stage: proscenium

FINANCES
August 1, 1984-July 31, 1985
Operating expenses: $919,009

AUDIENCE
Annual attendance: 69,050
Subscribers: 3,138

AEA LORT (C) contract

PRODUCTIONS 1983-84

Productions	Directors	Sets	Costumes	Lights

Extremities
    William Mastrosimone
	Robert Allen
	    Ackerman
		Marjorie Bradley
		    Kellogg
			Marianna Elliott	Barbara Ling

Beyond Therapy Christopher Durang	Paul Benedict	John Kavelin	Carol Brolaski	Barbara Ling

The Dining Room
    A.R. Gurney, Jr.
	John Frank Levy	D. Martyn
		    Bookwalter
			Carol Brolaski	Barbara Ling

PRODUCTIONS 1984-85

Productions	Directors	Sets	Costumes	Lights

The Dining Room
    A.R. Gurney, Jr.
	John Frank Levy	D. Martyn
		    Bookwalter
			Carol Brolaski	Barbara Ling

Melody Sisters Anne Commire	Anne Commire	John Kavelin	Garland Riddle	Barbara Ling
Geniuses Jonathan Reynolds	Paul Benedict	John Kavelin	Carol Brolaski	Barbara Ling

Baby with the Bathwater
    Christopher Durang
	Matt Casella	Gerry Hariton
		    and Vicki
		    Baral
			Charles Berliner	Gerry Hariton
				    and Vicki
				    Baral

L.A. Stage Company

SUSAN DIETZ
Artistic Director

LENNY BEER
Board President

205 North Canon Dr.
Beverly Hills, CA 90210
(213) 859-2646 (business)
(213) 859-2643 (box office)

FOUNDED 1980
Susan Dietz, Lenny Beer, Jason
    Wallach

SEASON
Year-round

FACILITIES
L.A. Stage Co.
Seating capacity: 377
Stage: proscenium

L.A. Stage Co. West
Seating capacity: 348
Stage: proscenium

FINANCES
July 1, 1984-June 30, 1985
Operating expenses: $1,253,000

AUDIENCE
Annual attendance: 100,000

BOOKED-IN EVENTS
Comedy, music

AEA LORT (B) and Theatre for Young
    Audiences contracts

PRODUCTIONS 1983–84

Productions	Directors	Sets	Costumes	Lights
Sister Mary Ignatius Explains It All for You Christopher Durang	Warner Shook	Gerry Hariton and Vicki Baral	Elaine Saussotte	Gerry Hariton and Vicki Baral Karen Katz
Penn and Teller Penn Jillette and Teller				
Cloud 9 Caryl Churchill	Don Amendolia	Gerry Hariton and Vicki Baral	Sylvia Moss	Gerry Hariton and Vicki Baral

PRODUCTIONS 1984–85

Productions	Directors	Sets	Costumes	Lights
Translations Brian Friel	Warner Shook	Gerry Hariton and Vicki Baral	Robert Blackman	Gerry Hariton and Vicki Baral
Dreamhouse Stuart Duckworth	Tony Richardson	Richard Hernandez	Richard Hernandez	Tony Richardson
Greater Tuna Joe Sears, Jaston Williams and Ed Howard	Ed Howard	Kevin Rupnik	Linda Fisher	Judy Rasmuson
True West Sam Shepard	Gary Sinise	Kevin Rigdon		Kevin Rigdon
Penn and Teller Penn Jillette and Teller				Karen Katz
Isn't It Romantic Wendy Wasserstein	Gerald Gutierrez	Andrew Jackness	Ann Emonts	James Ingalls

L.A. Theatre Works

SUSAN ALBERT LOEWENBERG
Producing Director

SARA MAULTSBY
Associate Producing Director

SUSAN A. GRODE
Board President

681 Venice Blvd.
Venice, CA 90291
(213) 827-0808

FOUNDED 1974
Jeremy Blahnik, Robert Greenwald,
  Susan Albert Loewenberg

SEASON
October–August

FINANCES
October 1, 1983–September 30, 1984
Operating expenses: $465,324

AUDIENCE
Annual attendance: 20,000
Subscribers: 500

TOURING CONTACT
Sara Maultsby

BOOKED-IN EVENTS
Theatre, music, dance

AEA LORT (D) contract

PRODUCTIONS 1983–84

Productions	Directors	Sets	Costumes	Lights
Through the Leaves Franz Xaver Kroetz; trans: Roger Downey	Jan Eliasberg	Wing Lee	Susan Nininger	Russell Pyle
Decadence Steven Berkoff	Steven Berkoff	Brian Bailey		Brian Bailey
Wazo Wazo Mimi Seton	Tony Abatemarco	Leslie McDonald	Susan Nininger	
Greek Steven Berkoff	Steven Berkoff	Gerry Hariton and Vicki Baral	Peter Mitchell	Brian Bailey
The Long White Dress of Love Rob Sullivan	Darrell Larson		Kate Lindsay	Barbara Ling
Vampire Guts Susan LaTempa	Russ Petranto	Leslie McDonald	Mary Malin	Stephen Bennett
A Midsummer Night's Dream William Shakespeare	Tim Robbins	Tim Robbins	Susan Nininger	Paul Cutone
Agamemnon Aeschylus; adapt: Steven Berkoff	Steven Berkoff	Leslie McDonald	Susan Nininger and Peter Mitchell	Stephen Bennett
Fran and *Johnny Dakota Writes It Down* Nancy Barr	Robert Spera and Noreen Hennessy	Mark Stock		Barbara Ling
The Happiest Girl in the Whole Wide World Christina Banks	David Schweizer	Susan Nininger		Barbara Ling

---

PRODUCTIONS 1984–85

Productions	Directors	Sets	Costumes	Lights
Kaspar Peter Handke; trans: Michael Roloff	Joseph Di Mattia	Joseph Di Mattia		
The Shaper John Steppling	John Steppling			Karen Musser
Mizlansky/Zilinsky Jon Robin Baitz	Tony Abatemarco	Nina Ruscio	Elizabeth Zarzyka	Karen Musser
The Circus of Dr. Lao adapt: David Kaplan, from Charles G. Finney	David Kaplan	David Kaplan	David Kaplan	David Kaplan
The Coyote Cycle	Murray Mednick	Robert Behling	Dona Granata, Michele Jo Blanche and Louise Hayter	Matthew Goulish

---

Living Stage Theatre Company

ROBERT A. ALEXANDER
Director

CATHERINE IRWIN
Managing Director

RICHARD W. SNOWDON
Board Chairman

Arena Stage
6th and Maine Aves., SW
Washington, DC 20024
(202) 554-9066

FOUNDED 1966
Robert A. Alexander

SEASON
September-July

FACILITIES
Living Stage Theatre
1901 14th St., NW
Seating capacity: 125
Stage: flexible

FINANCES
July 1, 1984-June 30, 1985
Operating expenses: $390,528

AUDIENCE
Annual attendance: 10,000

TOURING CONTACT
Laura Penn, Robert Alexander

BOOKED-IN EVENTS
Theatre, music, dance, poetry

AEA LORT (B) contract

PRODUCTIONS 1983–85

Productions	Directors	Sets	Costumes	Lights
All performances company-developed from improvisations	Robert A. Alexander			

Long Island Stage Company

CLINTON J. ATKINSON
Producing Artistic Director

ANDREW COHN
Managing Director

GEORGE GIMPEL
Board Chairman

Box 190
Hempstead, NY 11550
(516) 546-4600 (business)
(516) 766-2455 (box office)

FOUNDED 1975
Susan E. Barclay

SEASON
October-June

FACILITIES
Hays Theatre
Molloy College
Seating capacity: 298
Stage: proscenium

FINANCES
August 1, 1984-July 31, 1985
Operating expenses: $530,000

AUDIENCE
Annual attendance: 29,000
Subscribers: 3,700

AEA letter of agreement

PRODUCTIONS 1983–84

Productions	Directors	Sets	Costumes	Lights
The Marquise Noel Coward	Clinton J. Atkinson	Dan Conway	Jose Lengson	John Hickey
Roadside Lynn Riggs	Clinton J. Atkinson	Ron Placzek	Felicia Hittner	John Hickey
Journey's End R.C. Sherriff	Clinton J. Atkinson	Dan Conway	Fran Rosenthal	John Hickey
The Middle Ages A.R. Gurney, Jr.	Charles Karchmer	David Weller	Fran Rosenthal	Bob Bessoir
The Little Foxes Lillian Hellman	Clinton J. Atkinson	Jack Bell Stewart	Joan Vick	John Hickey

PRODUCTIONS 1984–85

Productions	Directors	Sets	Costumes	Lights
Volpone Ben Jonson; adapt: Stefan Zweig; trans: Ruth Langer	Clinton J. Atkinson	Jack Bell Stewart	David Navarro Velasquez	John Hickey
Dial M for Murder Frederick Knott	Clinton J. Atkinson	Dan Conway	Jose Lengon	John Hickey
The Caretaker Harold Pinter	Clinton J. Atkinson	Dan Conway	Fran Rosenthal	John Hickey
Candida George Bernard Shaw	Clinton J. Atkinson	Steve Perry	David Navarro Velasquez	John Hickey
Baby Grand P.J. Barry	Clinton J. Atkinson	Dan Conway	Fran Rosenthal	John Hickey
The Country Girl Clifford Odets	Norman Hall	John Iacovelli	David Navarro Velasquez	John Hickey

Long Wharf Theatre

ARVIN BROWN
Artistic Director

M. EDGAR ROSENBLUM
Executive Director

C. NEWTON SCHENCK
Board Chairman

222 Sargent Dr.
New Haven, CT 06511
(203) 787-4284 (business)
(203) 787-4282 (box office)

FOUNDED 1965
Jon Jory, Harlan Kleiman

SEASON
October-June

FACILITIES
Mainstage
Seating capacity: 484
Stage: thrust

Stage II
Seating capacity: 199
Stage: flexible

FINANCES
July 1, 1984-June 30, 1985
Operating expenses: $3,072,000

AUDIENCE
Annual attendance: 142,500
Subscribers: 16,686

AEA LORT (B) and (D) contracts

PRODUCTIONS 1983–84

Productions	Directors	Sets	Costumes	Lights
The Hostage Brendan Behan	Joseph Maher	Hugh Landwehr	Bill Walker	Ronald Wallace
Not Quite Jerusalem Paul Kember	John Tillinger	Andrew Jackness	William Ivey Long	Judy Rasmuson
Accent on Youth Samson Raphaelson	Kenneth Frankel	David Jenkins	David Murin	Pat Collins
Requiem for a Heavyweight Rod Serling	Arvin Brown	Marjorie Bradley Kellogg	Bill Walker	Ronald Wallace
Shivaree William Mastrosimone	Daniel Sullivan	Robert Dahlstrom	Sally Richardson	Ronald Wallace
The Homesteaders Nina Shengold	John Pasquin	Michael Yeargan	Linda Fisher	Judy Rasmuson
The Bathers Victor Steinbach	Steven Robman	Marjorie Bradley Kellogg	Natashia Landau	Pat Collins
Under the Ilex Clyde Talmadge	Charles Nelson Reilly	Marjorie Bradley Kellogg	Noel Taylor	Ronald Wallace

Productions	Directors	Sets	Costumes	Lights
Tobacco Road adapt: Jack Kirkland, from Erskine Caldwell	Arvin Brown	Michael Yeargan	Bill Walker	Ronald Wallace
Rainsnakes Per Olov Enquist; trans: Harry G. Carlson	Jose Quintero	John Lee Beatty	Jane Greenwood	Judy Rasmuson
Oliver, Oliver Paul Osborn	Vivian Matalon	Tom Schwinn	Linda Fisher	John Hastings
The Common Pursuit Simon Gray	Kenneth Frankel	David Jenkins	David Murin	Pat Collins
Blue Window Craig Lucas	Norman Rene	Loy Arcenas	Walker Hicklin	Debra Kletter
Cat on a Hot Tin Roof Tennessee Williams	Edward Gilbert	Hugh Landwehr	Bill Walker	Judy Rasmuson
Albert Herring adapt: Benjamin Britten, from Guy de Maupassant; libretto: Eric Crozier; music: Benjamin Britten	Arvin Brown	Michael Yeargan	David Murin	Ronald Wallace
Bullie's House Thomas Keneally and Irvin S. Bauer	Kenneth Frankel	Marjorie Bradley Kellogg	Jennifer von Mayrhauser	Judy Rasmuson

Looking Glass Theatre

JEANNIE WALKER
Producing Director

JOHN J. BROUGH, JR.
Board President

175 Mathewson St.
Providence, RI 02903
(401) 331-9080

FOUNDED 1965
Elaine Ostroff, Arthur Torg

SEASON
October–June

FINANCES
July 1, 1984–June 30, 1985
Operating expenses: $75,000

AUDIENCE
Annual attendance: 55,000

TOURING CONTACT
Linda D'Ambra

Note: During the 1983-84 and 1984-85 seasons, Pamela Messore served as artistic director.

PRODUCTIONS 1983–84

Productions	Directors	Sets	Costumes	Lights
Writers of the Northeast adapt: Michael Ducharme and Eileen Boarman, from Emily Dickinson and Edith Wharton; and Bradford Greer and Pamela Messore, from Henry David Thoreau and Walt Whitman	Michael Ducharme and Pamela Messore		Jeffrey Burrows	
Pandora! Maureen Ryan-Estes	Maureen Ryan-Estes	Butch Bennett	Roger Lemelin	
Asabranca, the White Dove Jewel Beth Davis	Pamela Messore	Kyle Kelley	Linda McNeilly	

PRODUCTIONS 1984–85

Productions	Directors	Sets	Costumes	Lights
Antigone Sophocles; adapt: Taki Votoras	Pamela Messore	Michael McGarty	Michael Koch	
A Child's Christmas in Wales adapt from Dylan Thomas	Raymond Picozzi	Barbara Rosencrantz		

PRODUCTIONS 1984–85

Productions	Directors	Sets	Costumes	Lights
The Velveteen Rabbit book adapt: Margery Williams; music and lyrics: Stephan Snyder	Pamela Messore	Michael McGarty	David Cabral	
And Then What Happened, Paul Revere? adapt: Pamela Messore, from Jean Fritz	Pamela Messore		David Cabral	

Los Angeles Theatre Center

BILL BUSHNELL
Artistic Producing Director

DIANE WHITE
Producer

STEPHEN RICHARD
Managing Director

DOUGLAS R. RING
President

514 South Spring St.
Los Angeles, CA 90013
(213) 627-6500 (business)
(213) 488-1122 (box office)

FOUNDED 1985
Bill Bushnell

SEASON
Year-round

FACILITIES
Tom Bradley Theatre
Seating capacity: 499
Stage: Open stage

Theatre #2
Seating capacity: 295
Stage: proscenium or end stage

Theatre #3
Seating capacity: 326
Stage: thrust

Theatre #4
Seating capacity: 99
Stage: flexible

FINANCES
May 1, 1984-April 30, 1985
Operating expenses: $1,744,895

AUDIENCE
Annual attendance: 76,000
Subscribers: 14,450

TOURING CONTACT
Cornell Coley

BOOKED-IN EVENTS
Theatre, music, dance, intermedia art, poetry

AEA LORT (C) and (D) contracts and letter of agreement

Note: The theatre was formerly known as Los Angeles Actors' Theatre, founded in 1975 by Ralph Waite.

PRODUCTIONS 1983–84

Productions	Directors	Sets	Costumes	Lights
Sure Feels Good book, music and lyrics: Fredric Myrow	Bill Bushnell	A. Clark Duncan	Garland W. Riddle	Barbara Ling
Sade-Sack adapt: Robert M. Hammond, from Pascal Vrebos	Adam Leipzig	Leonard Degen	Karen Miller	Ilya Mindlin
An Enemy of the People Henrik Ibsen; adapt: Charles Marowitz	Charles Marowitz	Timian	Marianna Elliot	Barbara Ling
Sus Barrie Keeffe	Edmund J. Cambridge	Timian	Timian and Jill A. Brousard	Timian and Todd Jared
Walking to Waldham and Happiness Mayo Simon	Alan Mandell	Mary Angelyn Brown	Jill A. Brousard	Barbara Ling
The Cage Rick Cluchey	R.S. Bailey	San Quentin Drama Workshop	San Quentin Drama Workshop	Todd Jared
Secret Honor Donald Freed and Arnold M. Stone	Robert Harders	Russell Pyle		Russell Pyle

Productions	Directors	Sets	Costumes	Lights

Venus and Adonis
  adapt: Benjamin Stewart, from William
  Shakespeare
	Benjamin
	  Stewart
				Russell Pyle

Bill and Eddie
  Robert Harders
	Bill Bushnell	Arpad Petrass		Dawn
				  Hollingsworth

Sherlock's Last Case
  Charles Marowitz
	Charles
	  Marowitz
		Timian	Timian	Russell Pyle

The White Crow: Eichmann in Jerusalem
  Donald Freed
	Charles
	  Marowitz
		Timian	Timian	Timian

Productions	Directors	Sets	Costumes	Lights
A Taste for the Forbidden Tim Kelly	R.S. Bailey	A. Clark Duncan	Armand Coutu	Jose Lopez

Women and Water and *Gardenia*
  John Guare
	Bill Bushnell	Mary Angelyn
		  Brown and
		  Timian
			Marianna Elliot	Martin Aronstein

Topokana Martyrs' Day
  Jonathan Falla
	John Hancock	A. Clark Duncan	Karen Miller
			  Kennedy
				Martin Aronstein

Company Samuel Beckett	S.E. Gontarski	Timian	Timian	Timian

Hamlet
  William Shakespeare; adapt: Charles Marowitz
	Charles
	  Marowitz
		Timian	Timian and
			  Armand Coutu
				Timian and
				  Todd Jared

Mabou Mines

JOANNE AKALAITIS, LEE BREUER,
  L.B. DALLAS, ELLEN McELDUFF,
  RUTH MALECZECH, GREG
  MEHRTEN, TERRY O'REILLY,
  FREDERICK NEUMANN, BILL
  RAYMOND
Company Members

CYNTHIA HEDSTROM
Manager

TERRY O'REILLY
Board Chairman

150 First Ave.
New York, NY 10009
(212) 473-0559

FOUNDED 1970
JoAnne Akalaitis, Lee Breuer, Philip
  Glass, Ruth Maleczech, David
  Warrilow

SEASON
Year-round

FINANCES
July 1, 1984-June 30, 1985
Operating expenses: $495,650

AUDIENCE
Annual attendance: 9,000

TOURING CONTACT
Rena Shagan Associates; Jeff Jones,
  Performing Artservices

Productions	Directors	Sets	Costumes	Lights

Dead End Kids
  JoAnne Akalaitis
	JoAnne Akalaitis	Robert Israel
		  and JoAnne
		  Akalaitis
			Sally Rosen	Beverly Emmons

Pretty Boy Greg Mehrten	Greg Mehrten	L.B. Dallas	Linda Muir	Julie Archer

PRODUCTIONS 1983–84

Productions	Directors	Sets	Costumes	Lights
Imagination Dead/Imagine Samuel Beckett	Ruth Maleczech	Linda Hartinian and L.B. Dallas		Toby Scott, Anne E. Militello and L.B. Dallas
Company Samuel Beckett	Honora Fergusson and Frederick Neumann	Gerald Marks		Craig Miller
Through the Leaves Franz Xaver Kroetz; trans: Roger Downey	JoAnne Akalaitis	Douglas Stein	Kurt Wilhelm	Frances Aronson
Cold Harbor Dale Worsley	Bill Raymond and Dale Worsley	Linda Hartinian	Greg Mehrten	Sabrina Hamilton

PRODUCTIONS 1984–85

Productions	Directors	Sets	Costumes	Lights
Hajj Lee Breuer	Lee Breuer	Julie Archer		Julie Archer
A Prelude to Death in Venice Lee Breuer	Lee Breuer	Alison Yerxa and L.B. Dallas		Julie Archer
Cold Harbor Dale Worsley	Bill Raymond and Dale Worsley	Linda Hartinian	Greg Mehrten	Sabrina Hamilton
Through the Leaves Franz Xaver Kroetz; trans: Roger Downey	JoAnne Akalaitis	Douglas Stein	Kurt Wilhelm	Frances Aronson
Company Samuel Beckett	Honora Fergusson and Frederick Neumann	Gerald Marks		Craig Miller
Flow My Tears, the Policeman Said adapt: Linda Hartinian, from Philip K. Dick	Bill Raymond	Linda Hartinian	Gabriel Berry	Anne E. Militello

Magic Theatre

JOHN LION
General Director

MARCIA A. O'DEA
General Manager

PHILIP D. ARMOUR, III
Board President

Fort Mason Center, Bldg. D
San Francisco, CA 94123
(415) 441-8001 (business)
(415) 441-8822 (box office)

FOUNDED 1967
John Lion

SEASON
October-June

FACILITIES
Magic Theatre Northside
Seating capacity: 130
Stage: thrust

Magic Theatre Southside
Seating capacity: 130
Stage: proscenium

FINANCES
September 1, 1983-August 31, 1984
Operating expenses: $570,000

AUDIENCE
Annual attendance: 40,000
Subscribers: 2,000

BOOKED-IN EVENTS
Theatre, performance art

AEA letter of agreement

PRODUCTIONS 1983–84

Productions	Directors	Sets	Costumes	Lights
The Grass House Adele Edling Shank	Theodore Shank	John Ammirati	Deborah Capen D'Orazi	Joe Dignan
Private Scenes Joel Homer	Maggie Harrer	Andy Stacklin	Margaret Anne Dunn	Barbara DuBois
City Preacher Ed Bullins	John Doyle	Peter Maslin	Gael Russell	Margaret Anne Dunn
These Men Mayo Simon	Albert Takazauckas	Andy Stacklin	Roberta Yuen	Barbara DuBois
The Sister Joseph Memorial Gymnasium Lucy Lewis	Simon L. Levy	John Rathman	Ardyss Golden	Patty Ann Farrell
Superstitions and *The Sad Lament of Pecos Bill on the Eve of Killing His Wife* Sam Shepard	Julie Hebert	Karen Schulz	Rita Yovino	Jack Carpenter
Skaters Stephen Wylie	Andrew Doe	Ferdinand Penker	Lorraine Forman	Margaret Anne Dunn
Cutting Canvas James Keller and Albert Takazauckas	Albert Takazauckas	Andy Stacklin	Beaver Bauer	Mal Sturchio

PRODUCTIONS 1984–85

Productions	Directors	Sets	Costumes	Lights
Geniuses Jonathan Reynolds	Albert Takazauckas	Andy Stacklin and Ferdinand Penker	Dora Leitner	Barbara DuBois
Outcalls/Riptides Alan Finneran	Alan Finneran	Alan Finneran	Karin Epperlein	Brian Mulhern
War Horses Adele Edling Shank	Theodore Shank	Barbara J. Mesney	Rondi Hilstrom Davis	Joe Dignan
The Couch Lynne Kaufman	Simon Levy	Ferdinand Penker	Walter Watson	Margaret Anne Dunn
Angel City Sam Shepard	John Lion	Andy Stacklin	Margaret Anne Dunn	Kurt Landisman
Neon Psalms Thomas Strelich	Andrew Doe	Peggy McDonald	Catherine Verdier	Joe Dignan
Love in the 3rd Degree O-Lan Jones and Kathleen Cramer	Julie Hebert	Joel Eis	Beaver Bauer	Margaret Anne Dunn

Manhattan Theatre Club

LYNNE MEADOW
Artistic Director

BARRY GROVE
Managing Director

EDWIN C. COHEN
Board Chairman

453 West 16th St., 2nd Fl.
New York, NY 10011
(212) 645-5590 (business)
(212) 246-8989 (box office)

FOUNDED 1970
A.E. Jeffcoat, Margaret Kennedy, Philip
  Barber, Gene Frankel, William
  Gibson, Barbara Hirschl, Gerard L.
  Spencer, George Tabori, A. Joseph
  Tandet and Peregrine Whittlesey

SEASON
October-May

FACILITIES
Downstage
Seating capacity: 174
Stage: proscenium

Upstage
Seating capacity: 100
Stage: modified thrust

The Space at City Center
131 West 55th St.
Seating capacity: 299
Stage: modified thrust

FINANCES
July 1, 1984-June 30, 1985
Operating expenses: $2,132,060

AUDIENCE
Annual attendance: 54,865
Subscribers: 6,751

AEA Off Broadway contract

PRODUCTIONS 1983–84

Productions	Directors	Sets	Costumes	Lights
The Philanthropist Christopher Hampton	Andre Ernotte	Kate Edmunds	Linda Fisher	F. Mitchell Dana
Friends Lee Kalcheim	Barnet Kellman	David Jenkins	Patricia McGourty	Ian Calderon
Mensch Meier Franz Xaver Kroetz; trans: Roger Downey	Jacques Levy	Ray Recht	Susan Hilferty	Robert Jared
Other Places Harold Pinter	Alan Schneider	John Lee Beatty	Jess Goldstein	Rocky Greenberg
Blue Plate Special book: Tom Edwards; music: Harris Wheeler; lyrics: Mary L. Fisher	Art Wolff	David Jenkins	David Murin	Arden Fingerhut
A Backers' Audition book, music and lyrics: Douglas Bernstein and Denis Markell	Martin Charnin	Ray Recht	Linda Fisher	Marc B. Weiss
Park Your Car in Harvard Yard Israel Horovitz	Lynne Meadow	John Lee Beatty	Jennifer von Mayrhauser	Marc B. Weiss
The Miss Firecracker Contest Beth Henley	Stephen Tobolowsky	John Lee Beatty	Jennifer von Mayrhauser	Dennis Parichy

PRODUCTIONS 1984–85

Productions	Directors	Sets	Costumes	Lights
In Celebration David Storey	Lindsay Anderson	John Lee Beatty	Linda Fisher	Dennis Parichy
Messiah Martin Sherman	David Leveaux	Tony Straiges	Linda Fisher	James F. Ingalls
Hang on to the Good Times book and lyrics: Richard Maltby, Jr., Gretchen Cryer and Nancy Ford; music and lyrics: Gretchen Cryer and Nancy Ford	Richard Maltby, Jr.	James Morgan	Karen Gerson	Mary Jo Dondlinger
Digby Joseph Dougherty	Ron Lagomarsino	James Leonard Joy	Rita Ryack	Curt Ostermann
California Dog Fight Mark Lee	Bill Bryden	Santo Loquasto	Rita Ryack	Andy Phillips
Husbandry Patrick Tovatt	Jon Jory	David Jenkins	Marcia Dixcy	F. Mitchell Dana

Productions	Directors	Sets	Costumes	Lights
What's Wrong with This Picture? Donald Margulies	Claudia Weill	Adrianne Lobel	Rita Ryack	Beverly Emmons
Secrets of the Lava Lamp adapt: Adriana Trigiani, from Camille Saviola	Stuart Ross		Jackie Manassee	

Mark Taper Forum

GORDON DAVIDSON
Artistic Director

WILLIAM P. WINGATE
Executive Managing Director

J. DAVID HAFT
Board President

135 North Grand Ave.
Los Angeles, CA 90012
(213) 972-7353 (business)
(213) 410-1062 (box office)

FOUNDED 1967
Gordon Davidson

SEASON
Year-round

FACILITIES
Mainstage
205 North Grand Ave.
Seating capacity: 767
Stage: thrust

Taper, Too
2580 Cahuenga Blvd. East
Seating capacity: 99
Stage: flexible

Itchey Foot
801 West Temple St.
Seating capacity: 99
Stage: cabaret

James A. Doolittle Theatre
1615 North Vine St.
Seating capacity: 1,049
Stage: proscenium

FINANCES
July 1, 1984-June 30, 1985
Operating expenses: $8,370,000

AUDIENCE
Annual attendance: 293,629
Subscribers: 30,000

TOURING CONTACT
Stephen J. Albert

BOOKED-IN EVENTS
Theatre

*AEA LORT (A) and (B) contracts and
99-seat waiver*

PRODUCTIONS 1983–84

Productions	Directors	Sets	Costumes	Lights
Cat on a Hot Tin Roof Tennessee Williams	Jose Quintero	John Lee Beatty	Noel Taylor	Marilyn Rennagel
An American Comedy Richard Nelson	John Madden	Andrew Jackness	Julie Weiss	James F. Ingalls, Jr.
Quilters book: Molly Newman and Barbara Damashek; music and lyrics: Barbara Damashek	Barbara Damashek	Ursula Belden	Marianna Elliott	Allen Lee Hughes
The Genius Howard Brenton	Ben Levit	Douglas W. Schmidt	Csilla Marki	Tharon Musser
The American Clock: A Mural for the Theatre Arthur Miller	Gordon Davidson	Ralph Funicello	Marianna Elliott	Martin Aronstein
Wild Oats: A Romance of the Old West James McLure	Tom Moore	Ralph Funicello	Robert Blackman	Martin Aronstein
Moby Dick—Rehearsed Orson Welles	Edward Payson Call	Ralph Funicello	Robert Blackman	Martin Aronstein
New Theatre for Now: *Dead End Kids: A History of Nuclear Power,* JoAnne Akalaitis (A Mabou Mines production)	JoAnne Akalaitis	Robert Israel and JoAnne Akalaitis	Sally Rosen	B.-St. John Schofield
Made in America, Alvin Boretz	Steven Robman	D. Martyn Bookwalter	Molly Harris Campbell	Paulie Jenkins

PRODUCTIONS 1983–84

Productions	Directors	Sets	Costumes	Lights
Pass/Fail, Peter Noah	Robert Berlinger	D. Martyn Bookwalter	Garland Riddle	Paulie Jenkins
Cakewalk, Michael Genelin and Joseph Charney	John Frank Levey	D. Martyn Bookwalter	Carol Brolaski	Paulie Jenkins
Beckett, Beckett, Beckett! (Ohio Impromptu, Catastrophe, Rockaby, Enough, Footfalls), Samuel Beckett	Alan Schneider	Marc D. Malamud and Rocky Greenberg	Carla Kramer	Marc D. Malamud and Rocky Greenberg
Wire book, music and lyrics: Hayden Wayne	Ben Levit	Larry Fulton	Karen Miller	Brian Gale
The Regard of Flight Bill Irwin, M.C. O'Connor and Doug Skinner		John Ivo Gilles		Joan Arhelger
In the Belly of the Beast adapt: Adrian Hall and Robert Woodruff, from Jack Henry Abbott	Robert Woodruff	John Ivo Gilles	Carol Brolaski	Paulie Jenkins
A Private View Vaclav Havel; trans: Vera Blackwell	Elizabeth Huddle	Michael Devine	Martha Burke	Greg Sullivan
A Family Album Peter C. Brosius, Rosanna Staffa and the ITP company; music: Gregg Johnson and Victoria Ann-Lewis; lyrics: Victoria Ann-Lewis	Peter C. Brosius	Susan Nininger	Susan Nininger	

PRODUCTIONS 1984–85

Productions	Directors	Sets	Costumes	Lights
Viva Vittorio! adapt: Vittorio Gassman, from Jean Paul Sarte, Luigi Pirandello, Luciano Codignola and Franz Kafka	Vittorio Gassman	John De Santis		John De Santis
The Hands of Its Enemy Mark Medoff	Gordon Davidson	Michael Devine	Carol Brolaski	Paulie Jenkins
Passion Play Peter Nichols	Gwen Arner	D. Martyn Bookwalter	Robert Blackman	Martin Aronstein
Traveler in the Dark Marsha Norman	Gordon Davidson	Ming Cho Lee	Susan Denison	Marilyn Rennagel
In the Belly of the Beast adapt: Adrian Hall and Robert Woodruff, from Jack Henry Abbott	Robert Woodruff	John Ivo Gilles	Carol Brolaski	Paulie Jenkins
Undiscovered Country Arthur Schnitzler; adapt: Tom Stoppard	Ken Ruta	Ralph Funicello	Sam Kirkpatrick	Martin Aronstein
Measure for Measure William Shakespeare	Robert Egan	Ralph Funicello	Robert Blackman	Martin Aronstein
Talking With Jane Martin	Michael Peretzian	Cliff Faulkner	Susan Denison	Brian Gale
Mansamente Marcos Caetano Ribas and Rachel Ribas				
Swimming to Cambodia, Parts One and Two Spalding Gray				
Five of Us Len Jenkin	Tony Abatemarco	Tony Abatemarco	Susan Denison	Greg Sullivan
A Family Album Peter C. Brosius, Rosana Staffa and company; music: Jeff Hull and Tollak Ollestad; lyrics: Jeff Hull, Tollak Ollestad and Peter C. Brosius	Peter C. Brosius	John Ivo Gilles	Perri Kimono	
School Talk Peter C. Brosius and company; music: Jeff Hull, Tollak Ollestad and Mimi Seton; lyrics: Jeff Hull, Tollak Ollestad and Peter C. Brosius	Peter C. Brosius	John Ivo Gilles	Perri Kimono	

McCarter Theatre Company

NAGLE JACKSON
Artistic Director

ALISON HARRIS
Managing Director

EDWARD E. MATTHEWS
Board President

91 University Pl.
Princeton, NJ 08540
(609) 452-3616 (business)
(609) 452-5200 (box office)

FOUNDED 1972
Daniel Seltzer

SEASON
October-April

FACILITIES
Mainstage
Princeton University
Seating capacity: 1,077
Stage: proscenium

Murray-Dodge Theatre
Seating capacity: 198
Stage: proscenium

Princeton Inn College Theatre
Seating capacity: 100
Stage: flexible

Forbes College Theatre
Seating Capacity: 200
Stage: flexible

FINANCES
July 1, 1984-June 30, 1985
Operating expenses: $3,025,979

AUDIENCE
Annual attendance: 200,000
Subscribers: 15,000

TOURING CONTACT
James Olson

BOOKED-IN EVENTS
Theatre, music, dance

AEA LORT (B) contract

PRODUCTIONS 1983-84

Productions	Directors	Sets	Costumes	Lights
Play Memory Joanna McClelland Glass; music: Larry Grossman	Harold Prince	Clarke Dunham	William Ivey Long	Ken Billington
St. Joan George Bernard Shaw	Nagle Jackson	Daniel Boylen	Elizabeth Covey	Richard Moore
Ah, Wilderness! Eugene O'Neill	Margaret Booker	David Potts	Susan Rheaume	Richard Moore
The Dining Room A.R. Gurney, Jr.	Nagle Jackson	James Wolk	Susan Rheaume	Richard Moore
At This Evening's Performance Nagle Jackson	Nagle Jackson	Elizabeth K. Fischer	Emelle Holmes	Richard Moore
A Christmas Carol adapt: Nagle Jackson, from Charles Dickens; music: Larry Delinger	Francis X. Kuhn	Brian Martin	Elizabeth Covey	Richard Moore
Judevine: A Vermont Anthology David Budbill	Robert Lanchester	Lisa Martin Cameron	Barb Taylorr	Richard Moore

PRODUCTIONS 1984-85

Productions	Directors	Sets	Costumes	Lights
The School for Wives Molière; trans: Richard Wilbur	Nagle Jackson	Robert Perdziola	Elizabeth Covey	Richard Moore
The Dawns Are Quiet Here Boris Vassiliev; trans: Alex Miller; music: Gregory Piatigorsky	Alex Dmitriev	James Morgan	Susan Rheaume	Richard Moore
Faustus in Hell adapt: Nagle Jackson, from Goethe and various authors; and *The Show of the Deadly Sins*, various authors	Nagle Jackson	Elizabeth K. Fischer	Kathleen Blake	Richard Moore
Under Milk Wood Dylan Thomas; music: Lee Hoiby	Robert Lanchester	Elizabeth K. Fischer	Susan Rheaume	Richard Moore
A Raisin in the Sun Lorraine Hansberry	Terry Burgler	Charles Caldwell	Julie Keen	Lynne M. Hartman
A Christmas Carol adapt: Nagle Jackson, from Charles Dickens; music: Larry Delinger	Francis X. Kuhn	Brian Martin	Elizabeth Covey	Richard Moore
Act Without Words I and *Happy Days* Samuel Beckett	Robert Lanchester	Joseph C. Anderson	Barb Taylorr	Richard Moore

Merrimack Repertory Theatre

DANIEL L. SCHAY
Producing Director

RICHARD E. DOBROTH
Board President

Box 228
Lowell, MA 01853
(617) 454-6324 (business)
(617) 454-3926 (box office)

FOUNDED 1979
John R. Briggs, Mark Kaufman

SEASON
November-April

FACILITIES
Liberty Hall
50 East Merrimack St.
Seating capacity: 374
Stage: thrust

FINANCES
July 1, 1984-June 30, 1985
Operating expenses: $437,200

AUDIENCE
Annual attendance: 23,000
Subscribers: 2,800

AEA LORT (D) contract

PRODUCTIONS 1983–84

Productions	Directors	Sets	Costumes	Lights
Arms and the Man George Bernard Shaw	Daniel L. Schay	Edward Cesaitis	Barbara Forbes	David Lockner
A Christmas Carol adapt: Larry Carpenter, from Charles Dickens	Larry Carpenter	Edward Cesaitis	Amanda Aldridge	David Lockner
Mass Appeal Bill C. Davis	Terence Lamude	David Lockner	Amanda Aldridge	Ted Bohlin and David Lockner
Of Mice and Men John Steinbeck	Brian Smiar	Gary English	Amanda Aldridge	David Lockner
Chapter Two Neil Simon	Gavin Cameron-Webb	Alison Ford	Amanda Aldridge	David Lockner
Working book adapt: Stephen Schwartz, from Studs Terkel; music and lyrics: Stephen Schwartz, et al.	Richard Rose	Duke Durfee and David Lockner	Amanda Aldridge	David Lockner

---

PRODUCTIONS 1984–85

Productions	Directors	Sets	Costumes	Lights
A Christmas Carol adapt: Larry Carpenter, from Charles Dickens	Larry Carpenter	Edward Cesaitis	Amanda Aldridge	David Lockner
Monday After the Miracle William Gibson	Ted Davis	Alison Ford	Barbara Forbes	David Lockner
Stage Struck Simon Gray	Nora Hussey	Leslie Taylor	Amanda Aldridge	David Lockner
A Raisin in the Sun Lorraine Hansberry	Daniel L. Schay	David Lockner	Virginia V. Aldous	Ted Bohlin
Strange Snow Stephen Metcalfe	Grey Cattell Johnson	Leslie Taylor	Amanda Aldridge	David Lockner
A Little Night Music book: Hugh Wheeler; music and lyrics: Stephen Sondheim	Richard Rose	Gary English	Amanda Aldridge	David Lockner

---

Milwaukee Repertory Theater

JOHN DILLON
Artistic Director

SARA O'CONNOR
Managing Director

T. MICHAEL BOLGER
Board President

929 North Water St.
Milwaukee, WI 53202
(414) 273-7121 (business)
(414) 273-7206 (box office)

FOUNDED 1954
Mary John

SEASON
September-May

FACILITIES
Mainstage
Seating capacity: 504
Stage: thrust

Pabst Theater
144 East Wells St.
Seating capacity: 1,398
Stage: proscenium

Court Street Theater
315 West Court St.
Seating capacity: 99
Stage: flexible

FINANCES
July 1, 1984-June 30, 1985
Operating expenses: $2,326,055

AUDIENCE
Annual attendance: 176,499
Subscribers: 18,613

TOURING CONTACT
Fran Serlin-Cobb

AEA LORT (A), (C) and (D) contracts

PRODUCTIONS 1983–84

Productions	Directors	Sets	Costumes	Lights
Much Ado About Nothing William Shakespeare	William Ludel	Laura Maurer and Tim Thomas	Sam Fleming	Spencer Mosse
American Buffalo David Mamet	John Dillon	Ralph Funicello	Kurt Wilhelm	Dan J. Kotlowitz
The Splintered Wood William Stancil	Sharon Ott	Laura Maurer and Tim Thomas	Patricia M. Risser	Dennis Parichy
The Forest Alexander Ostrovsky	John Dillon	Laura Maurer and Tim Thomas	Carol Oditz	Spencer Mosse
The Rules of the Game Luigi Pirandello	Stephen Katz	Richard Hoover	Kurt Wilhelm	John Gisondi
Translations Brian Friel	Nick Faust	Laura Maurer and Tim Thomas	Sam Fleming	Dan J. Kotlowitz
A Christmas Carol adapt: Nagle Jackson, from Charles Dickens	Nick Faust	Christopher M. Idoine	Elizabeth Covey	Dan J. Kotlowitz
Antony and Me Andrew Johns	Rob Goodman	Laura Maurer and Tim Thomas	Mary Piering	Miriam Hack
The Revenge of the Space Pandas David Mamet	Kristine Thatcher	Laura Maurer and Tim Thomas	Cecelia Mason	Mark Nash
The Frog Prince David Mamet	John Dillon	Laura Maurer and Tim Thomas	Sam Fleming	Mark Nash
Kingdom Come Amlin Gray	Sharon Ott	Laura Maurer and Tim Thomas	Colleen Muscha	Dan J. Kotlowitz
Inclined to Agree Daniel Stein	Daniel Stein and Christopher Gibson	Paule and Daniel Stein	Paule Stein	Daniel Brovarney
Wormwood and *Outlanders* Amlin Gray	Eric Hill	Joseph M. Sankey	Gayle M. Strege	Russell Swift

---

PRODUCTIONS 1984–85

Productions	Directors	Sets	Costumes	Lights
The Revenger's Tragedy Cyril Tourneur	Sharon Ott	Kate Edmunds	Kurt Wilhelm	Rachel Budin

PRODUCTIONS 1984–85

Productions	Directors	Sets	Costumes	Lights
Wenceslas Square Larry Shue	John Dillon	Laura Maurer and Tim Thomas	Sam Fleming	Victor En Yu Tan
Master Harold . . . and the boys Athol Fugard	Israel Hicks	Michael Olich	Sam Fleming	Dawn Chiang
A Christmas Carol adapt: Amlin Gray, from Charles Dickens	Nick Faust	Stuart Wurtzel	Carol Oditz	John McLain
The Devil's Disciple George Bernard Shaw	Gregory Boyd	Hugh Landwehr	Sam Fleming	Robert Jared
Top Girls Caryl Churchill	John Dillon	John Ezell	Michael Olich	Spencer Mosse
A Woman Without Means William Stancil	Kenneth Albers	Bil Mikulewicz	Sam Fleming	Dan J. Kotlowitz
Miss Lulu Bett Zona Gale	Nick Faust	Laura Maurer and Tim Thomas	Kurt Wilhelm	Dan J. Kotlowitz
Macbeth "Rehearsed" William Shakespeare	Tom Blair	Kenneth Kloth	Sam Fleming	Robert Zenoni
Rhumba for 8 in 12 E-Z Lessons George Freek	Jonathan Smoots	John Story, II	Cecelia Mason	Valerie Goldston
On Vacation Jean-Claude Grumberg, trans: Sara O'Connor	Eric Hill	Joseph M. Sankey	Gayle M. Strege	Miriam Hack
The Brawl Jean-Claude Grumberg, trans: Sara O'Connor	Eric Hill	Joseph M. Sankey	Gregory Brown	Miriam Hack
The Elocution of Benjamin Franklin Steve J. Spears	William Rhys	Joseph M. Sankey		Robert Zenoni

Mirror Repertory Company

SABRA JONES
Artistic Director

WEILER/MILLER ASSOCIATES
Producing General Managers

ANNE AUCHINCLOSS
Board Chairperson

% Weiler/Miller Associates
1540 Broadway, Suite 704
New York, NY 10036
(212) 997-1139, 888-6087 (business)
(212) 223-6440, 223-6441 (box office)

FOUNDED 1983
Sabra Jones

SEASON
January-May

FACILITIES
Theatre at Saint Peter's Church
619 Lexington Ave.
Seating capacity: 199
Stage: modified proscenium

FINANCES
July 1, 1984-June 30, 1985
Operating expenses: $791,000

AUDIENCE
Annual attendance: 18,584
Subscribers: 622

TOURING CONTACT
Weiler/Miller Associates

BOOKED-IN EVENTS
Music, dance

AEA letter of agreement

PRODUCTIONS 1983–84

Productions	Directors	Sets	Costumes	Lights
Paradise Lost Clifford Odets	John Strasberg	Ron Placzek	Heidi Hollmann	Mal Sturchio
Inheritors Susan Glaspell	John Strasberg	Ron Placzek	Heidi Hollmann	Mal Sturchio

PRODUCTIONS 1983–84

Productions	Directors	Sets	Costumes	Lights
Rain John Colton	John Strasberg	Ron Placzek	Heidi Hollmann	Mal Sturchio
Ghosts Henrik Ibsen; trans: Eve Le Gallienne	John Strasberg	Ron Placzek	Heidi Hollmann	Mal Sturchio
The Hasty Heart John Patrick	Porter Van Zandt	Ron Placzek	Heidi Hollmann	Mal Sturchio

PRODUCTIONS 1984–85

Productions	Directors	Sets	Costumes	Lights
Madwoman of Chaillot Jean Giraudoux	Stephen Porter	James Tilton	Gail Cooper Hecht	James Tilton
Clarence Booth Tarkington	Arthur Storch	James Tilton	Arnold S. Levine	James Tilton
Vivat! Vivat Regina! Robert Bolt	John Strasberg	James Tilton	Gail Cooper Hecht	James Tilton

Missouri Repertory Theatre

GEORGE KEATHLEY
Artistic Director

JAMES D. COSTIN
Executive Director

JAMES B. JUDD
Board Chairman/President

Performing Arts Center
4949 Cherry St.
Kansas City, MO 64110
(816) 932-4466 (business)
(816) 276-2700 (box office)

FOUNDED 1964
Patricia McIlrath, James Costin

SEASON
July-September; December-March

FACILITIES
Helen F. Spencer Theatre
Seating capacity: 595-730
Stage: flexible

Studio Theatre 116
Seating capacity: 75-100
Stage: flexible

FINANCES
May 1, 1984-April 30, 1985
Operating expenses: $2,218,835

AUDIENCE
Annual attendance: 110,000
Subscribers: 5,160

TOURING CONTACT
Bob Thatch

AEA LORT (B) contract

Note: During the 1983-84 and 1984-85
seasons, Patricia McIlrath served as
artistic director.

PRODUCTIONS 1983–84

Productions	Directors	Sets	Costumes	Lights
Sea Marks Gardner McKay	Patricia McIlrath	James F. Gohl	Vincent Scassellati	Richard Moore
The Importance of Being Earnest Oscar Wilde	Francis J. Cullinan	Wray Steven Graham	Baker S. Smith	Richard Moore
The Dresser Ronald Harwood	George Keathley	Harry Feiner	Nigel Boyd	Richard Moore
The Speckled Band: An Adventure of Sherlock Holmes Arthur Conan Doyle	Albert Pertalion	Howard Bay	Victoria Marshall	Howard Bay

PRODUCTIONS 1983–84

Productions	Directors	Sets	Costumes	Lights
Life with Father Howard Lindsay and Russel Crouse	John Reich	Carolyn L. Ross	John Carver Sullivan	William D. Anderson
Retro Aleksandr Galin	Albert Pertalion	John Ezell	Vincent Scassellati	William D. Anderson
Trio Kado Kostzer and Alfredo Arias; adapt and trans; Felicia Hardison Londre	James Assad	John Ezell	Vincent Scassellati	William D. Anderson
The Taming of the Shrew William Shakespeare	Pamela Hawthorne	Harry Feiner	John Carver Sullivan	Harry Feiner

PRODUCTIONS 1984–85

Productions	Directors	Sets	Costumes	Lights
Strider book: Mark Rozovsky; lyrics: Uri Riashentsev and Steve Brown; adapt: Robert Kalfin and Steve Brown, from Tolstoy; music: Mark Rozovsky, S. Vetkin and Norman Berman	James Assad	Herbert L. Camburn	Vincent Scassellati	William D. Anderson
True West Sam Shepard	Albert Pertalion	Harry Feiner	Vincent Scassellati	Joseph Appelt
Come Back, Little Sheba William Inge	Patricia McIlrath	Robert Moody	Baker S. Smith	William D. Anderson
Fifteen Strings of Cash Chu Su-chen	Ying Ruocheng	John Ezell	Karen Gerson	Joseph Appelt
Romeo and Juliet William Shakespeare	Leon Rubin	Herbert L. Camburn	Steven B. Feldman	Joseph Appelt
Crimes of the Heart Beth Henley	Pamela Hawthorne	Roger LaVoie	Vincent Scassellati	Jon Terry
Masters of the Sea Gardner McKay	Albert Pertalion	Jack Ballance	Vincent Scassellati	Robert R. Scales
Peter Pan J.M. Barrie	Jerome Kilty	John Ezell	Baker S. Smith	Joseph Appelt

Music-Theatre Group/Lenox Arts Center

LYN AUSTIN
Producing Director

DIANE WONDISFORD
Managing Director

JOHN G. HOLMES
Board Chairman

735 Washington St.
New York, NY 10014
(212) 924-3108 (business)
(212) 265-4375 (box office)

Citizens Hall
Stockbridge, MA 01262
(413) 298-3460 (business)
(413) 298-9463 (box office)

FOUNDED 1971
Lyn Austin

SEASON
New York
September-May

Stockbridge
June-August

FACILITIES
St. Clement's Church
423 West 46th St., NY
Seating capacity: 99
Stage: flexible

Citizens Hall
Stockbridge, MA
Seating capacity: 75
Stage: flexible

FINANCES
July 1, 1984-June 30, 1985
Operating expenses: $640,500

AUDIENCE
Annual attendance: 34,850
Subscribers: 250

TOURING CONTACT
Diane Wondisford

AEA letter of agreement

PRODUCTIONS 1983-84

Productions	Directors	Sets	Costumes	Lights
The Mother of Us All Gertrude Stein; music: Virgil Thomson	Stanley Silverman	Power Boothe	Lawrence Casey	William Armstrong
Gogol's Wife adapt: Jeff Wanshel, from Tomasso Landolfi	Martha Clarke		Edi Giguere	Penny Stagenga
Dr. Selavy's Magic Theatre book and lyrics: Richard Foreman; music: Stanley Silverman	Richard Foreman	Richard Foreman and Nancy Winters	Lindsay W. Davis	Pat Collins
The Garden of Earthly Delights Martha Clarke; music: Richard Peaslee	Martha Clarke	Peter Foy	Jane Greenwood	Paul Gallo
Street Dreams book: Jack Curtis; music: William Eaton	Peter Gennaro	Nancy Winters	Joan V. Evans	Marilyn Rennagel

---

PRODUCTIONS 1984-85

Productions	Directors	Sets	Costumes	Lights
Dr. Selavy's Magic Theatre book and lyrics: Richard Foreman; music: Stanley Silverman	Richard Foreman	Richard Foreman and Nancy Winters	Lindsay W. Davis and Joan V. Evans	Pat Collins and Whitney Quesenbery
Africanis Instructus book and lyrics: Richard Foreman; music: Stanley Silverman	Roy Brocksmith	Cabot McMullen	Jim Buff	Whitney Quesenbery
The Garden of Earthly Delights Martha Clarke; music: Richard Peaslee	Martha Clarke	Peter Foy	Jane Greenwood	Paul Gallo
The Making of Americans book and lyrics adapt: Leon Katz; music: Al Carmines	Anne Bogart	Nancy Winters and Jim Buff	Jim Buff and Nancy Winters	Carol Mullins
The Courtroom Bill Irwin; music: Doug Skinner	Bill Irwin	Loren Sherman	Ann Emonts	Jan Kroeze

---

Nebraska Theatre Caravan

CHARLES JONES
Founding Director

CAROLYN RUTHERFORD
Managing Director

BARBARA FORD
Board President

6915 Cass St.
Omaha, NE 68132
(402) 553-4890

FOUNDED 1976
Charles Jones, Omaha Community
  Playhouse

SEASON
September–May

FACILITIES
Omaha Playhouse
Seating capacity: 600
Stage: proscenium

FINANCES
June 30, 1984–July 1, 1985
Operating expenses: $607,675

AUDIENCE
Annual attendance: 224,000

TOURING CONTACT
Debra Fox

PRODUCTIONS 1983–84

Productions	Directors	Sets	Costumes	Lights
Tintypes Mary Kyte, Mel Marvin and Gary Pearle	Carl Beck	James Othuse	Denise Ervin	James Othuse
The Greenwood Tales of Robin Hood Eleanor Brodie Jones	Carl Beck	Steven Wheeldon	Denise Ervin	Steven Wheeldon
Hamlet William Shakespeare; adapt: Charles Jones	Charles Jones	Steven Wheeldon	Denise Ervin	Steven Wheeldon
Cole book adapt: Benny Green and Alan Strachen; music and lyrics: Cole Porter	Carl Beck	Steven Wheeldon	Denise Ervin	Steven Wheeldon
A Christmas Carol adapt: Charles Jones, from Charles Dickens	Charles Jones, Eleanor Brodie Jones, John Bennett and Joanne Cady	James Othuse	Denise Ervin	James Othuse

PRODUCTIONS 1984–85

Productions	Directors	Sets	Costumes	Lights
Cyrano! Edmond Rostand; adapt: John Foley	Carl Beck	James Othuse	Denise Ervin	James Othuse
The Dragon and St. George Charles Jones	Charles Jones	James Othuse	Denise Ervin	James Othuse
Candide book adapt: Hugh Wheeler, from Voltaire; lyrics: Richard Wilbur, Stephen Sondheim and John Latouche; music: Leonard Bernstein	Carl Beck	James Othuse	Denise Ervin	Matt McDonnell
A Christmas Carol adapt: Charles Jones, from Charles Dickens	Charles Jones, Carl Beck, John Bennett and Joanne Cady	James Othuse	Denise Ervin	James Othuse

New American Theater

J.R. SULLIVAN
Producing Director

DAVID BYRD
Board President

118 North Main St.
Rockford, IL 61101
(815) 963-9454 (business)
(815) 964-8023 (box office)

FOUNDED 1972
J.R. Sullivan

SEASON
September–July

FACILITIES
Mainstage
Seating capacity: 300
Stage: thrust

Charlotte's Web
Seating capacity: 200
Stage: cabaret

FINANCES
July 1, 1984–June 30, 1985
Operating expenses: $467,250

AUDIENCE
Annual attendance: 44,000
Subscribers: 3,650

TOURING CONTACT
Dan Shephard

*AEA Small Professional Theatre
contract*

PRODUCTIONS 1983–84

Productions	Directors	Sets	Costumes	Lights
Mass Appeal Bill C. Davis	J.R. Sullivan	Michael S. Philippi	Jon R. Accardo	Dan Kasten
Have You Anything to Declare? Maurice Henequin and Pierre Veber	Alan Carlsen	Michael S. Philippi	Jon R. Accardo	Michael S. Philippi
Ludlow Ladd and *Charlotte Sweet* Michael Colby and Gerald Jay Markoe	J.R. Sullivan	James Wolk	Jon R. Accardo	James Wolk
Amadeus Peter Shaffer	J.R. Sullivan	Michael S. Philippi	Jon R. Accardo	Michael S. Philippi
The New Spoon River adapt: J.R. Sullivan, from Edgar Lee Masters	J.R. Sullivan	Michael S. Philippi	Jon R. Accardo	Michael S. Philippi
Careless Love John Olive	J.R. Sullivan	Michael S. Philippi	Jon R. Accardo	Michael S. Philippi
Blithe Spirit Noel Coward	J.R. Sullivan	Michael S. Philippi	Jon R. Accardo	Michael S. Philippi
Simply Heavenly Langston Hughes	George Davis	Jack Pine	Deborah Atkins Archer	Jack Pine

---

PRODUCTIONS 1984–85

Productions	Directors	Sets	Costumes	Lights
The Taming of the Shrew William Shakespeare	J.R. Sullivan	Michael S. Philippi	Jon R. Accardo	Michael S. Philippi
Foxfire Susan Cooper and Hume Cronyn	J.R. Sullivan	Michael S. Philippi	Jon R. Accardo	Michael S. Philippi
The Adventures of Huckleberry Finn adapt: Timothy Mason, from Mark Twain	J.R. Sullivan	Bill Gleave	Jon R. Accardo	Bill Gleave
Translations Brian Friel	J.R. Sullivan	Michael S. Philippi	Jon R. Accardo	Michael S. Philippi
Master Harold . . . and the boys Athol Fugard	J.R. Sullivan	Michael S. Philippi	Jon R. Accardo	Michael S. Philippi
Crimes of the Heart Beth Henley	Tim Olds	Bill Gleave	Jon R. Accardo	Anthony Cywinski
Black Coffee Agatha Christie	Alan Carlsen	Bill Gleave	Jon R. Accardo	Anthony Cywinski
The Boys in Autumn Bernard Sabath	J.R. Sullivan	Anthony Cywinski	Jon R. Accardo	Shawn Gracyalny Carey
Bullshot Crummond Ron House, Diz White, Alan Shearman, Derek Cunningham and John Neville-Andrews	J.R. Sullivan	Keith Grace	Lynn A. Fox	Andrea C. Stufflebeem
Villainous Company Amlin Gray	J.R. Sullivan	Arnie Pocs	Lynn A. Fox	
Talking With Jane Martin	Tim Olds and J.R. Sullivan		Lynn A. Fox	

New Arts Theatre

STEPHEN HOLLIS
Artistic Director

CHRISTOPHER OWENS
Producing Director

DAVID YODER
Managing Director

GEORGE W. COLLINS, III
Board Chairman

702 Ross Ave.
Dallas, TX 75202
(214) 761-9064

FOUNDED 1975
Christopher Nichols

SEASON
September–June

FACILITIES
Seating capacity: 225
Stage: modified proscenium

FINANCES
January 1, 1984–December 31, 1984
Operating expenses: $336,878

AUDIENCE
Annual attendance: 29,000
Subscribers: 1,750

BOOKED-IN EVENTS
Theatre, dance

*AEA Small Professional Theatre
contract*

PRODUCTIONS 1983–84

Productions	Directors	Sets	Costumes	Lights
Goodnight, Mr. Sherlock Holmes Charles Dee Mitchell	David Yoder	George Sampedro	Cheryl Denson	Mark Widener
Cat on a Hot Tin Roof Tennessee Williams	Christopher Nichols	Cheryl Denson	Cheryl Denson	Mark Widener
Christmas in Old Vic Christopher Owens	Christopher Owens	Roger Farkash	Marybeth Sorrell	David Yoder
Sorrows of Stephen Peter Parnell	Christopher Nichols	Philip Baldwin	Camille Crawley	George Sampedro
Who's Afraid of Virginia Woolf? Edward Albee	Christopher Owens	George Sampedro	Mary Therese D'Avignon	Ken Hudson
Wild Oats John O'Keeffe	Christopher Owens	Roger Farkash	Sarajane Milligan	Chuck Sheffield
Beyond Therapy Christopher Durang	David Yoder	Christopher Owens	Susan Bier	David Yoder

---

PRODUCTIONS 1984–85

Productions	Directors	Sets	Costumes	Lights
On the Razzle Tom Stoppard	Jeff Steitzer	Roger Farkash	Sarajane Milligan	Ken Hudson
Betrayal Harold Pinter	Christopher Owens	Chris Rusch	Sarajane Milligan	Chris Rusch
Spokesong Stewart Parker	Cynthia White	Chris Rusch	Sarajane Milligan	Tony Tucci
Last Gas Till Turnpike Lanie Robertson	Jerry Felix	Henry Smith	Sarajane Milligan	Stephen Cowles
Possessed for Romance Sharon Ratcliffe	Patricia Hammarstrom	Stephen Cowles	Sarajane Milligan	Stephen Cowles
Batteries Not Included book and lyrics: James Hammerstein, David Curtis and Alice Whitfield; music: Ralph Affoumado	James Hammerstein	Randell Wright	Sarajane Milligan	Stephen Cowles
Eminent Domain Percy Granger	Patricia Hammarstrom	Roger Farkash	Sarajane Milligan	David Opper
What I Did Last Summer A.R. Gurney, Jr.	Christopher Owens	Christopher Owens	Jim Covault	Sandra Turney

---

New Dramatists

THOMAS G. DUNN
Executive Director

CHRIS SILVA
Program Director

MILTON GOLDMAN
Board Chairman

424 West 44th St.
New York, NY 10036
(212) 757-6960

FOUNDED 1949
Michaela O'Harra, John Golden, Moss
  Hart, Oscar Hammerstein, II, Richard
  Rodgers, John Wharton, Howard
  Lindsay

SEASON
September–June

FACILITIES
Mainstage
Seating capacity: 90
Stage: flexible

Lindsay/Crouse Studio
Seating capacity: 60
Stage: flexible

FINANCES
July 1, 1984–June 30, 1985
Operating expenses: $410,000

AUDIENCE
Annual attendance: 2,050

PRODUCTIONS 1983–84

Productions	Directors	Sets	Costumes	Lights
Knife Edge Bryan Oliver	Rhea Gaisner			
Bombs on the Halfshell Stephen Levi	Peter Phillips			
Nights and Days Emily Mann	Susan Gregg			
Bodacious Flapdoodle Mac Wellman	Page Burkholder			
Panic in Longueuil Rene Daniel Dubois; trans: Gideon Y. Schein	Gideon Y. Schein			
Cop Shop Robert Lord				
Hidden Parts Lynne Alvarez				
Tomorrowland Jeffrey Jones				
'round Midnight Laura Harrington	Alma Becker			
Lucian's Woods David J. Hill				

PRODUCTIONS 1984–85

Productions	Directors	Sets	Costumes	Lights
Bert & Maisey Robert Lord				
The Able Bodied Seaman Alan Bowne	Susan Gregg			
For Her Own Good Tom Dunn	Cheryl Faraone			
State of the Union company-developed	Director's Unit			
The Wonderful Tower of Humbert Lavoignet Lynne Alvarez	Page Burkholder			
Between the Acts Joan Schenkar	Rhea Gaisner			
His Master's Voice Dick D. Zigun	John Pynchon Holms			
Sally's Gone, She Left Her Name Russell Davis	Tony Giordano			
Eleven Zulu Sean Clark	John Pynchon Holms			
The Memory Theatre of Giulio Camillo Matthew Maguire				

PRODUCTIONS 1984–85

Productions	Directors	Sets	Costumes	Lights
Pavan for the Princess of Cleves Romulus Linney				
Energumen Mac Wellman	Becky Harrison			
Fried Chicken and Invisibility OyamO	Peter Wallace			
Eat Rocks Pedro Pietri	Alma Becker			
End of Radio Sherry Kramer	Page Burkholder			
Cruising Close to Crazy Laura Cunningham				
Women of Manhattan John Patrick Shanley				
Free Fall Laura Harrington	Alma Becker			
The Boys of Winter John Pielmeier	Susan Gregg			
Cherry Soda Water Stephen Levi	Scott Rubsam			
Bang Laura Cunningham	Casey Childs			
Mr. and Mrs. Coffee William Sibley	Scott Rubsam			
The Tattler Terri Wagener	Peter Wallace			
Holy Ghosts Romulus Linney				
Souvenirs Sheldon Rosen	Page Burkholder			
The Mole Shirley Hillard	Becky Harrison			
El Hermano Romulus Linney	Gideon Y. Schein			
Harvest Sun John Olive	Bob Hall			
It Isn't Cricket Robert Lord	Ethan Silverman			
The White Death Daniel Therriault	Alma Becker			
Beautiful Bodies Laura Cunningham				
Hope Comes at Night book: Pam Winfrey; music: Brenda Hutchinson	Gideon Y. Schein			
Sand Mountain Matchmaking Romulus Linney				
Frugal Repast Sheldon Rosen	Susan Gregg			
China Wars Robert Lord	Ethan Silverman			
Union Boys James Yoshimura	John Pasquin			
Tomorrowland Jeffrey Jones				
The White Death Daniel Therriault	Alma Becker			
American Ladies Tom Dunn				

New Federal Theatre

WOODIE KING, JR.
Producer

ANTHONY WINSLOW JONES
Board Chairman

466 Grand St.
New York, NY 10002
(212) 598-0400

FOUNDED 1970
Woodie King, Jr.

SEASON
September–June

FACILITIES
Playhouse
Seating capacity: 350
Stage: proscenium

Experimental Theatre
Seating capacity: 150
Stage: thrust

Recital Hall
Seating capacity: 100
Stage: thrust

FINANCES
July 1, 1984–June 30, 1985
Operating expenses: $300,000

AUDIENCE
Annual attendance: 8,000

TOURING CONTACT
Woodie King, Jr.

BOOKED-IN EVENTS
Theatre, music, dance

AEA letter of agreement

PRODUCTIONS 1983–84

Productions	Directors	Sets	Costumes	Lights
Searock Children Is Strong Children Paul Webster	Paul Webster	Terry Chandler	Jane Milligan	Pam Demont
Trial of Adam Clayton Powell, Jr. Billy Graham	Dianne Kerksey	Billy Graham	Karen Perry	Zebedee Collins
Shades of Brown Michael Picardie	Joan Kemp-Welch	Loren Sherman		
Basin Street Michael Hulett and G. William Oakley	G. William Oakley	Robert Edmonds	Judy Dearing	Jeremy Johnson
Hospice Pearl Cleage	Frances Foster	Lew Harrison	Vicki Jones	Lynne Reed
Incandescent Tones Rise Collins	Marjorie Moon	Lew Harrison	Rise Collins	Lew Harrison
Games Joyce Walker-Joseph	Elizabeth Van Dyke	Bob Edmonds	Karen Perry	Shirley Prendergast
Parting Nubia Kai	Bette Howard	May Callas	Vicki Jones	Lew Harrison
Waltz of the Stork Boogie Melvin Van Peebles	Melvin Van Peebles	Kurt Lundell	Jeffrey N. Mazor	William H. Grant
Welcome to the Black River Samm-Art Williams	Walter Dallas	Richard Harmon	Judy Dearing	William H. Grant
Oh! Oh! Obesity Gerald W. Deas	Bette Howard	May Callas	Vicki Jones	Zebedee Collins

---

PRODUCTIONS 1984–85

Productions	Directors	Sets	Costumes	Lights
Hooch Charles Michael Moore	Chuck Smith	Llewellyn Harrison	Karen Perry	William Grant, III
The Last Danceman Alan Foster Friedman	John Pynchon Holms	Richard Harmon	Sheila Kehoe	Richard Harmon
Fraternity Jordan Budde	Gideon Y. Schein	Jane Clark	Judy Dearing	Victor En Yu Tan
Twenty Year Friends J.E. Gaines	Andre Mtumi	Terry Chandler	Celia Bryant	Jeffrey Richar
Selma Tommy Butler	Cliff Roquemore		Judy Dearing	Bill Grant
Becoming Garcia Tato Laviera	Esteban Vega	Pete Cauldwell	Karlos	Bill Grant
Thrombo Albert Bermel	Leonardo Shapiro	Jane Clark	Gene Lakin	William Armstrong

PRODUCTIONS 1984–85

Productions	Directors	Sets	Costumes	Lights
Long Time Since P.J. Gibson	Bette Howard	Charles H. McClennahan	Judy Dearing	William H. Grant, III
Ameri/Cain Gothic Paul Carter Harrison	Woodie King, Jr.	Richard Harmon	Judy Dearing	William H. Grant, III

New Jersey Shakespeare Festival

PAUL BARRY
Artistic Director

ELLEN BARRY
Producing Director

DOUGLAS S. EAKELEY
Board President

Drew University
Route 24
Madison, NJ 07940
(201) 377-5330 (business)
(201) 377-4487 (box office)

FOUNDED 1963
Paul Barry

SEASON
June–December

FACILITIES
Bowne Theatre
Seating capacity: 238
Stage: thrust

FINANCES
January 1, 1984–December 31, 1984
Operating expenses: $525,885

AUDIENCE
Annual attendance: 40,000
Subscribers: 3,200

BOOKED-IN EVENTS
Theatre, music, dance, mime,
children's theatre

AEA LORT (D) contract

PRODUCTIONS 1984

Productions	Directors	Sets	Costumes	Lights
Othello William Shakespeare	Paul Barry	Timothy Scalet	Jim Buff	Richard Dorfman
The Merchant of Venice William Shakespeare	Paul Barry	Timothy Scalet	Jim Buff	Richard Dorfman
The School for Scandal Richard Brinsley Sheridan	Paul Barry	Timothy Scalet	Heidi Hollmann	Richard Dorfman
All the Way Home adapt: Tad Mosel, from James Agee	Paul Barry	N.B. Dodge, Jr.	Jim Buff	Terry Kaye
The Sunshine Boys Neil Simon	Paul Barry	N.B. Dodge, Jr.	Mitchell S. Bloom	Terry Kaye
The Crucible Arthur Miller	Paul Barry	N.B. Dodge, Jr.	Heidi Hollmann	Terry Kaye

PRODUCTIONS 1985

Productions	Directors	Sets	Costumes	Lights
Henry VIII William Shakespeare	Paul Barry	Paul Barry	Robin Borts	Richard Dorfman
A Man for All Seasons Robert Bolt	Paul Barry	Paul Barry	Robin Borts	Richard Dorfman
The Merry Wives of Windsor William Shakespeare	Paul Barry	Paul Barry	Heidi Hollmann	Richard Dorfman
The Plough and the Stars Sean O'Casey	Paul Barry	Mark Evancho	Jim Buff	Terry Kaye

PRODUCTIONS 1985

Productions	Directors	Sets	Costumes	Lights
Light up the Sky Moss Hart	Paul Barry	Mark Evancho	Mitchell S. Bloom	Terry Kaye
A Lesson from Aloes Athol Fugard	Paul Barry	Mark Evancho	Mitchell S. Bloom	Terry Kaye

New Playwrights' Theatre

ARTHUR BARTOW
Artistic Director

B. THOMAS MASBACH
Board Chairman

1742 Church St., NW
Washington, DC 20036
(202) 232-4527 (business)
(202) 232-1122 (box office)

FOUNDED 1972
Harry M. Bagdasian

SEASON
September–June

FACILITIES
Seating capacity: 125
Stage: modified proscenium

FINANCES
July 1, 1984–June 30, 1985
Operating expenses: $300,000

AUDIENCE
Annual attendance: 14,706
Subscribers: 880

BOOKED-IN EVENTS
Music

*AEA Small Professional Theatre
contract*

PRODUCTIONS 1983–84

Productions	Directors	Sets	Costumes	Lights
Beyond Your Command Ralph Pape	Ron Canada	Douglas A. Cumming	Jane Schloss Phelan	Lewis Folden
Flesh Eaters Ernest Joselovitz	James C. Nicola	Russell Metheny	Jane Schloss Phelan	Daniel M. Wagner
The Library of Congress Talent Show Mark Stein	Steven Albrezzi	Lewis Folden	Jane Schloss Phelan	Lewis Folden
The Groves of Academe Mark Stein	Steven Albrezzi	Lewis Folden	Jane Schloss Phelan	Lewis Folden
Gardenia and *Lydie Breeze* John Guare	James C. Nicola and Lloyd Rose	Lewis Folden	Mary Ann Powell	Nancy Schertler

PRODUCTIONS 1984–85

Productions	Directors	Sets	Costumes	Lights
Burial Customs Phoef Sutton	Arthur Bartow	Lewis Folden	Georgia O. Baker	Daniel M. Wagner
The Beautiful Lady book: Elizabeth Swados and Paul Schmidt; music and lyrics: Elizabeth Swados	Elizabeth Swados	Lewis Folden	Jane Schloss Phelan	Lewis Folden
Four Monologues Spalding Gray				Steven Summers
After My Own Heart Paul J. Donnelly, Jr.	Arthur Bartow	Lewis Folden	Jane Schloss Phelan	Steven Summers

New Stage Theatre

JANE REID-PETTY
Producing Director

PETER DE LAURIER
Resident Artistic Director

GEORGE P. HEWES, III
Board President

1100 Carlisle St.
Jackson, MS 39202
(601) 948-3533 (business)
(601) 948-3531 (box office)

FOUNDED 1966
Jane Reid-Petty

SEASON
September–June

FACILITIES
Meyer Crystal Auditorium
Seating capacity: 364
Stage: proscenium

Jimmy Hewes Room
Seating capacity: 100
Stage: flexible

FINANCES
July 1, 1984–June 30, 1985
Operating expenses: $410,000

AUDIENCE
Annual attendance: 40,000
Subscribers: 3,000

AEA letter of agreement

PRODUCTIONS 1983–84

Productions	Directors	Sets	Costumes	Lights
Gershwin! book: Ben Bagley; music: George Gershwin; lyrics: Ira Gershwin	Ivan Rider	Sandy McNeal and Jimmy Robertson	Martha Wood	Bryan Leather
Private Lives Noel Coward	Ivan Rider	Sandy McNeal and Jimmy Robertson	Nana True	Bryan Leather
A Streetcar Named Desire Tennessee Williams	John R. Briggs	Sandy McNeal and Jimmy Robertson	Martha Wood	Bryan Leather
The Dining Room A.R. Gurney, Jr.	Peter De Laurier	Sandy McNeal and Jimmy Robertson	Martha Wood	Bryan Leather
The Wake of Jamey Foster Beth Henley	Lynn Polan	Sandy McNeal and Jimmy Robertson	Martha Wood	Bryan Leather
Oh, Mr. Faulkner, Do You Write? John Maxwell	William Partlan	Jimmy Robertson	Martha Wood	Bryan Leather
Village Wooing George Bernard Shaw	Peter De Laurier	Bryan Leather	Martha Wood	Bill McCarty, III
The Jewish Wife Bertolt Brecht	Peter De Laurier	John R. Briggs	Martha Wood	Bryan Leather

PRODUCTIONS 1984–85

Productions	Directors	Sets	Costumes	Lights
The Taming of the Shrew William Shakespeare	John R. Briggs	Sandy McNeal and Jimmy Robertson	Shari Cochran	Bryan Leather
Agnes of God John Pielmeier	Peter De Laurier	Sandy McNeal and Jimmy Robertson	Shari Cochran	Paul Jefferson
A Christmas Carol adapt: Peter De Laurier, from Charles Dickens	John R. Briggs	Sandy McNeal and Jimmy Robertson	Shari Cochran	Bryan Leather
True West Sam Shepard	John R. Briggs	Bryan Leather	Shari Cochran	Paul Jefferson
Private Contentment Reynolds Price	Ivan Rider	Sandy McNeal and Jimmy Robertson	Shari Cochran	Paul Jefferson
A Season of Dreams adapt: Jane Reid-Petty and Patti Carr Black, from Eudora Welty	Jane Reid-Petty	Sandy McNeal and Jimmy Robertson	Shari Cochran	Paul Jefferson

Productions	Directors	Sets	Costumes	Lights
27 Wagons Full of Cotton Tennessee Williams	Paul Jefferson	Bryan Leather	Shari Cochran	Chikahide Komura
Talk to Me Like the Rain . . . Tennessee Williams	John R. Briggs	Bryan Leather	Shari Cochran	Chikahide Komura

New York Shakespeare Festival

JOSEPH PAPP
Producer

JASON STEVEN COHEN
Associate Producer

LAUREL ANN WILSON
General Manager

LuESTHER T. MERTZ
Board Chairman

Public Theater
425 Lafayette St.
New York, NY 10003
(212) 598-7100 (business)
(212) 598-7150 (box office)
(212) 861-7277 (Delacorte box office)

FOUNDED 1954
Joseph Papp

SEASON
Year-round

FACILITIES
Newman Theater
Seating capacity: 299
Stage: proscenium

Martinson Hall
Seating capacity: 190
Stage: flexible

LuEsther Hall
Seating capacity: 150
Stage: flexible

Susan Stein Shiva Theater
Seating capacity: 100
Stage: flexible

Anspacher Theater
Seating capacity: 275
Stage: ¾ arena

Delacorte Theater
Central Park
Seating capacity: 1,932
Stage: thrust

FINANCES
July 1, 1984–June 30, 1985
Operating expenses: $10,613,575

AUDIENCE
Annual attendance: 1.5 million
Subscribers: 8,005

BOOKED-IN EVENTS
Film, Festival Latino en Nueva York, music

AEA LORT (B) and Off Broadway contracts

Productions	Directors	Sets	Costumes	Lights
A Chorus Line book: James Kirkwood and Nicholas Dante; music: Marvin Hamlisch; lyrics: Edward Kleban	Michael Bennett	Robin Wagner	Theoni V. Aldredge	Tharon Musser
The Human Comedy book and lyrics adapt: William Dumaresq, from William Saroyan; music: Galt McDermot	Wilford Leach	Bob Shaw	Rita Ryack	James F. Ingalls
A Midsummer Night's Dream William Shakespeare; adapt: Amy Saltz	Amy Saltz	Patricia Woodbridge	Julie Taymor	Ann Wrightson
Found a Peanut Donald Margulies	Claudia Weill	Thomas Lynch	Jane Greenwood	Beverly Emmons
Serenading Louie Lanford Wilson (NYSF/Second Stage production)	John Tillinger	Loren Sherman	Clifford Capone	Richard Nelson
Ice Bridge John F. Forster (NYSF/Veterans' Ensemble Theatre Company production)	Edward Cornell	Salvatore Tagliarino	Lee Entwisle	Marcia Madeira and Terry Wuthrich
A Private View Vaclav Havel; trans: Vera Blackwell	Lee Grant	Marjorie Bradley Kellogg	Carol Oditz	Arden Fingerhut

PRODUCTIONS 1983-84

Productions	Directors	Sets	Costumes	Lights
The Third Annual Young Playwrights Festival: (NYSF/Dramatists Guild production) *Romance*, Catherine Castellani	Elinor Renfield	Mark Fitzgibbons	Carla Kramer and John David Ridge	Richard Riddell
Meeting the Winter Bike Rider, Juan Nunez	Elinor Renfield			
Fixed Up, Patricia Durkin	Shelly Raffle			
In the Garden, Anne Harris	James Milton			
Tender Places, Jason Brown	Shelly Raffle	Loren Sherman	Patricia McGourty	Mal Sturchio
Orgasmo Adulto Escapes from the Zoo Franca Rame and Dario Fo; adapt: Estelle Parsons		Santo Loquasto	Ruth Morley	Jennifer Tipton
Lenny and the Heartbreakers book: Kenneth Robins; music: Scott Killian and Kim D. Sherman; lyrics: Kenneth Robins, Scott Killian and Kim D. Sherman	Murray Louis and Alwin Nikolais	Alwin Nikolais and Nancy Winters	Lindsay W. Davis	Alwin Nikolais and Peter Koletzke
Fen Caryl Churchill	Les Waters	Annie Smart	Annie Smart	Tom Donnellan
The Nest of the Woodgrouse Victor Rozov; trans: Susan Layton	Joseph Papp	Loren Sherman	Theoni V. Aldredge	Arden Fingerhut
My Uncle Sam Len Jenkin	Len Jenkin	John Arnone	Kurt Wilhelm	Frances Aronson
Emmett: A One Mormon Show Emmett Foster	Emmett Foster			Gerard P. Bourcier
Sound and Beauty David Henry Hwang	John Lone	Andrew Jackness	Lydia Tanji	John Gisondi
Cinders Janusz Glowacki; trans: Christina Paul	John Madden	Andrew Jackness	Jane Greenwood	Paul Gallo
Henry V William Shakespeare	Wilford Leach	Bob Shaw	Lindsay W. Davis	Paul Gallo
The Golem H. Leivick; trans: J.C. Augenlicht	Richard Foreman	Richard Foreman and Nancy Winters	Natasha Landau	Pat Collins

PRODUCTIONS 1984-85

Productions	Directors	Sets	Costumes	Lights
A Chorus Line book: James Kirkwood and Nicholas Dante; music: Marvin Hamlisch; lyrics: Edward Kleban	Michael Bennett	Robin Wagner	Theoni V. Aldredge	Tharon Musser
La Bohème libretto: Henry Murger; adapt: Giuseppe Giacosa and Luigi Illica; new lyrics: David Spencer; music: Giacomo Puccini	Wilford Leach	Bob Shaw	Jane Greenwood	Paul Gallo
Salonika Louise Page	John Madden	Andrew Jackness	Dunya Ramicova	Paul Gallo
The Ballad of Soapy Smith Michael Weller	Robert Egan	Eugene Lee	Robert Blackman	Jennifer Tipton
Virginia Edna O'Brien	David Leveaux	Santo Loquasto	Santo Loquasto	Arden Fingerhut
Tracers company-developed (NYSF/Veteran's Ensemble Theatre Company production)	John DiFusco	John Falabella	David Navarro Velasquez	Terry Wuthrich
Coming of Age in Soho Albert Innaurato	Albert Innaurato	Loren Sherman	Ann Emonts	James F. Ingalls
Tom and Viv Michael Hastings	Max Stafford-Clark	Antony McDonald and Jock Scott	Antony McDonald and Jock Scott	Robin Myerscough-Walker
The Marriage of Bette and Boo Christopher Durang	Jerry Zaks	Loren Sherman	William Ivey Long	Paul Gallo
Rat in the Skull Ron Hutchinson	Max Stafford-Clark	Peter Hartwell	Peter Hartwell	Andy Phillips
The Normal Heart Larry Kramer	Michael Lindsay-Hogg	Eugene Lee and Keith Raywood	Bill Walker	Natasha Katz

Productions	Directors	Sets	Costumes	Lights

Measure for Measure
    William Shakespeare
	Joseph Papp	Robin Wagner	Lindsay W.
			    Davis
				Richard Nelson

The Mystery of Edwin Drood
    book adapt, music and lyrics: Rupert Holmes,
    from Charles Dickens
	Wilford Leach	Bob Shaw	Lindsay W.
			    Davis
				Paul Gallo

New York Theatre Workshop

JEAN PASSANANTE
Artistic Director

NANCY KASSAK DIEKMANN
Managing Director

STEPHEN GRAHAM
Board Chairman/Executive Director

220 West 42nd St.
New York, NY 10036
(212) 302-7737 (business)
(212) 279-4200 (box office)

FOUNDED 1979
Stephen Graham

SEASON
November–May

FACILITIES
Perry Street Theatre
31 Perry St.
Seating capacity: 95
Stage: proscenium

FINANCES
December 1, 1983–November 30, 1984
Operating expenses: $213,932

AUDIENCE
Annual attendance: 6,680

AEA letter of agreement

PRODUCTIONS 1983–84

Productions	Directors	Sets	Costumes	Lights

Great Divide
    Robert Litz
	David Rotenberg	Peter David
		    Gould
			V. Jane Suttell	John Hickey

Souvenirs Sheldon Rosen	Stephen Katz	Loy Arcenas	Deborah Shaw	John Gisondi

PRODUCTIONS 1984–85

Productions	Directors	Sets	Costumes	Lights

War on the Third Floor
    Pavel Kohout; trans: Elizabeth Diamond
	Elizabeth
	    Diamond
		Sally de
		    Valenzuela
			Muriel Stockdale	Susan Chute

The Grand Hysteric and *The Box*
    Sheldon Rosen
	T. Riccio	Sally de
		    Valenzuela
			Gene Lakin	Susan Chute

My Life in Art
    Victor Steinbach
	Rebecca
	    Harrison
		Sally de
		    Valenzuela
			Muriel Stockdale	Susan Chute

A Fool's Errand
    Chris Ceraso
	Jim Peskin	Sally de
		    Valenzuela
			Gene Lakin	Susan Chute

The Fantod
    Amlin Gray; music: Norman L. Berman
	Stephen Katz	Richard Hoover	Andrew B.
			    Marlay
				John Gisondi

Sally's Gone, She Left Her Name Russell Davis	Tony Giordano	Jane Clark	Linda Fisher	John Gisondi

Northlight Theatre

MICHAEL MAGGIO
Artistic Director

SUSAN MEDAK
Managing Director

LLOYD MORGAN
Board Chairman

2300 Green Bay Road
Evanston, IL 60201
(312) 869-7732 (business)
(312) 869-7278 (box office)

FOUNDED 1974
Gregory Kandel

SEASON
September–July

FACILITIES
Kingsley Theatre
Seating capacity: 298
Stage: proscenium

FINANCES
July 1, 1984–June 30, 1985
Operating expenses: $820,000

AUDIENCE
Annual attendance: 63,000
Subscribers: 6,869

AEA LORT (D) contract

PRODUCTIONS 1983–84

Productions	Directors	Sets	Costumes	Lights
Sondheim Suite music and lyrics: Stephen Sondheim	Michael Maggio	John Paoletti and Mary Griswald	Kaye Nottbusch	Robert Shook
What I Did Last Summer A.R. Gurney, Jr.	Michael Maggio	Joseph Nieminski	Kaye Nottbusch	Robert Shook
Meetings Mustapha Matura	James O'Connor	Jeffrey Bauer	Jessica Hahn	Rita Petraszek
Ballerina Arne Skouen	Michael Maggio	Linda Buchanan	Kerry Fleming	Robert Shook
The Price Arthur Miller	Sheldon Patinkin	Michael Merritt	Julie Jackson	Geoffrey Bushor
What the Butler Saw Joe Orton	Michael Maggio	Joseph Nieminski	Kerry Fleming	Robert Shook

PRODUCTIONS 1984–85

Productions	Directors	Sets	Costumes	Lights
City on the Make book adapt: Jeff Berkson, Denise DeClue and John Karraker, from Nelson Algren; music: Jeff Berkson and John Karraker	Michael Maggio	Michael Merritt	Kaye Nottbusch	Robert Shook
Quartermaine's Terms Simon Gray	B.J. Jones	Joseph Nieminski	Kaye Nottbusch	Rita Pietraszek
Teibele and Her Demon Isaac Bashevis Singer and Eve Friedman	Kyle Donnelly	Michael S. Philippi	Jordan Ross	Michael S. Philippi
Heart of a Dog adapt: Frank Galati, from Mikhail Bulgakov; trans: Xenia Youhn	Michael Maggio	Linda Buchanan	Julie Jackson	Robert Shook
Bing and Walker James Farrell	Jimmy A. Bickerstaff	Gary Baugh	Kaye Nottbusch	Rita Pietraszek

Odyssey Theatre Ensemble

RON SOSSI
Artistic Director

FRANK GRUBER
Board Chairman

12111 Ohio Ave.
Los Angeles, CA 90025
(213) 879-5221 (business)
(213) 826-1626 (box office)

FOUNDED 1969
Ron Sossi

SEASON
January–December

FACILITIES
Odyssey I
Seating capacity: 99
Stage: proscenium

Odyssey II
Seating capacity: 95
Stage: thrust

Odyssey III
Seating capacity: 92
Stage: thrust

FINANCES
July 1, 1984–June 30, 1985
Operating expenses: $347,000

AUDIENCE
Annual attendance: 32,000
Subscribers: 1,500

TOURING CONTACT
Lucy Pollak

BOOKED-IN EVENTS
Experimental theatre

AEA 99-seat waiver

PRODUCTIONS 1983–84

Productions	Directors	Sets	Costumes	Lights
Chucky's Hunch Rochelle Owens	Elinor Renfield	Abe Lubelski	Carla Kramer	Peter Kaczorowski
The Frogs Aristophanes; book adapt: Burt Shevelove; music and lyrics: Stephen Sondheim	Ron Sossi	Donald Cate	Camille Argus	Christine Lomaka
In the Matter of J. Robert Oppenheimer Heinar Kipphardt	Frank Condon	Nancy Eisenman	Brenda Waugh	Ilya Mindlin
Marie and Bruce Wallace Shawn	Ron Sossi	Phil Dagort	Susan Denison	Steve Cuden
Lullabye and Goodnight Elizabeth Swados	Bill Castellino	Joanne McMaster	Diana Eden	Christine Lomaka

PRODUCTIONS 1984–85

Productions	Directors	Sets	Costumes	Lights
The Whale Concerts Liebe Gray	Liebe Gray	Lance Parker and Phil Grisier	Sue Talbot and Catherine Stifter	Gayle Marks
Mother Courage Bertolt Brecht; music: Paul Dessau	Ron Sossi	Jim Newton	Esther Kashkin	Dawn Hollingsworth
Creatures Gar Campbell	Gar Campbell	Mary Angelyn Brown	Karen Keech Beasley	Russell Pyle
Edmond David Mamet	Ron Sossi	Russell Pyle	Susan Denison	Russell Pyle
Hess Michael Burrell	Frank Condon	Liz Thomas	Barbara Cox	Steve Cuden
The Portage to San Cristobal of A.H. adapt: Christopher Hampton, from George Steiner	Ron Sossi	John Hieronymus Stone	Lisa Lovaas	Dawn Hollingsworth
Summit Conference Robert David MacDonald	Danny Goldman	Liz Thomas	Barbara Cox	Steve Cuden
The Miser Molière	Frank Condon	W. Lansing Barbour	Barbara Cox	David A. Taylor
Rap Master Ronnie book and lyrics: Garry Trudeau; music: Elizabeth Swados	Frank Condon and Bill Castellino	Don Llewellyn	Lisa Lovaas	Christine Lomaka

The Old Creamery Theatre Company

THOMAS PETER JOHNSON
Artistic Director

MICHAEL McLAUGHLIN
Board President

Box 160
Garrison, IA 52229
(319) 477-3925 (business)
(319) 477-3165 (box office)

FOUNDED 1971
Ann Olson, Erica Zaffarano, Merritt
Olsen, Steve Kock, Judy Johnson,
Thomas Peter Johnson, David Olson,
Rita Berendes, David Berendes, Mick
Denniston

SEASON
June–September; October–May touring

FACILITIES
Mainstage
Seating capacity: 250
Stage: thrust

Brenton Stage
Seating capacity: 110
Stage: thrust

FINANCES
January 1, 1984–December 31, 1984
Operating expenses: $450,304

AUDIENCE
Annual attendance: 100,000

TOURING CONTACT
C. Thomas Cunliffe

*AEA Small Professional Theatre
contract*

PRODUCTIONS 1984

Productions	Directors	Sets	Costumes	Lights
Wally's Cafe Ron Clark and Sam Bobrick	Thomas Peter Johnson	Rod McCulley	Cara McCulley	Rod McCulley
Here Lies Jeremy Troy Jack Sharkey	Thomas Peter Johnson	Rod McCulley	Jean Jordan	Rod McCulley
A Coupla White Chicks Sitting Around Talking John Ford Noonan	Richard D. Burk	Rod McCulley	Jean Jordan	Beth Johns
Ten Nights in a Bar-Room William W. Pratt	Thomas Peter Johnson	Jan Czechowski	Jean Jordan	Beth Johns
Mass Appeal Bill C. Davis	Mick Denniston	Thomas Peter Johnson	Jean Jordan	Beth Johns
The Fantasticks book and lyrics: Tom Jones; music: Harvey Schmidt	Steve Abolt	Thomas Peter Johnson	Jean Jordan	Beth Johns
Playing Doctor Mick Denniston and Thomas Peter Johnson	Thomas Peter Johnson	Thomas Peter Johnson	Marquetta Senters	Beth Johns
Deathtrap Ira Levin	Steve Shaffer	Thomas Peter Johnson	Meg Merckens	Beth Johns

---

PRODUCTIONS 1985

Productions	Directors	Sets	Costumes	Lights
Playing Doctor Mick Denniston and Thomas Peter Johnson	Thomas Peter Johnson	Thomas Peter Johnson	Marquetta Senters	Thomas Peter Johnson
Ladyhouse Blues Kevin O'Morrison	Anne Oberbroeckling	Jan Czechowski	Anne Oberbroeckling	Jan Czechowski
The Diary of Anne Frank Francis Goodrich and Albert Hackett	Thomas Peter Johnson	Jan Czechowski	Mary Woolever	Jan Czechowski
Not Now, Darling Ray Cooney and John Chapman	Thomas Peter Johnson and Terry Dyrland	Jan Czechowski	Marquetta Senters	Jan Czechowski
You're a Good Man, Charlie Brown book, music and lyrics: Clark Gesner	Richard O. Burk	Thomas Peter Johnson	Marquetta Senters	Richard D. Burk
Greater Tuna Jaston Williams, Joe Sears and Ed Howard	Thomas Peter Johnson	Thomas Peter Johnson	Marquetta Senters	Thomas Peter Johnson

Old Globe Theatre

JACK O'BRIEN
Artistic Director

THOMAS HALL
Managing Director

DIXIE UNRUH
Board Chairman

Box 2171
San Diego, CA 92112
(619) 231-1941 (business)
(619) 239-2255 (box office)

FOUNDED 1937
Community members

SEASON
December–October

FACILITIES
Old Globe Theatre
El Prado, Balboa Park
Seating capacity: 581
Stage: proscenium

Lowell Davies Festival Stage
Seating capacity: 612
Stage: thrust

Cassius Carter Centre Stage
Seating capacity: 225
Stage: arena

FINANCES
November 1, 1983–October 31, 1984
Operating expenses: $6,123,805

AUDIENCE
Annual attendance: 275,000
Subscribers: 50,000

TOURING CONTACT
Thomas Hall

BOOKED-IN EVENTS
Theatre, music, dance, film, lectures

AEA LORT (B) contract

PRODUCTIONS 1984

Productions	Directors	Sets	Costumes	Lights
Kiss Me, Kate book: Bella and Sam Spewack; music and lyrics: Cole Porter	Jack O'Brien	Richard Seger	Robert Morgan	Robert Peterson
Taking Steps Alan Ayckbourn	Craig Noel	Nick Reid	Dianne Holly	John B. Forbes
Catsplay Istvan Orkeny; trans: Clara Gyorgyey	Jack O'Brien	Kent Dorsey	Noel Taylor	Robert Peterson
Angels Fall Lanford Wilson	Andrew J. Traister	Alan K. Okazaki	Dianne Holly	John B. Forbes
Quartermaine's Terms Simon Gray	David McClendon	Fred M. Duer	Deborah M. Dryden	Steven B. Peterson
Strange Snow Stephen Metcalfe	Warner Shook	Fred M. Duer	Sally Cleveland	Steven B. Peterson
Elektra Sophocles	Diana Maddox	Kent Dorsey	Lewis Brown	John B. Forbes
Rashomon adapt: Fay and Michael Kanin, from Ryunosike Akutagawa	Craig Noel	Richard Seger	Lewis Brown	Kent Dorsey
The Merry Wives of Windsor William Shakespeare	Daniel Sullivan	Steven Rubin	Robert Morgan	Robert Peterson
Breakfast with Les and Bess Lee Kalcheim	David McClendon	Kent Dorsey	Robert Morgan	John B. Forbes
Scapino! Frank Dunlop and Jim Dale	David Ogden Stiers	Douglas W. Schmidt	Robert Morgan	Robert Peterson
Othello William Shakespeare	Jack O'Brien	Diana Maddox	Richard Seger	Lewis Brown

PRODUCTIONS 1985

Productions	Directors	Sets	Costumes	Lights

Foxfire
    adapt: Susan Cooper and Hume Cronyn, from
    Eliot Wigginton
	Andrew J.
	    Traister
		Alan K. Okazaki	Sally Cleveland	John B. Forbes

Vikings Stephen Metcalfe	Warner Shook	Fred M. Duer	Sally Cleveland	Kent Dorsey
Stage Struck Simon Gray	David Hay	Alan K. Okazaki	Dianne Holly	John B. Forbes

Season's Greetings
    Alan Ayckbourn
	Jack O'Brien	Kent Dorsey	Robert
			    Blackman
				Robert Peterson

Of Mice and Men John Steinbeck	Craig Noel	Steven Rubin	Steven Rubin	Kent Dorsey

The Torch-Bearers
    George Kelly
	Jack O'Brien	Richard Seger	Robert
			    Blackman
				John B. Forbes

Greater Tuna
    Jaston Williams, Joe Sears and Ed Howard
	David
	    McClendon
		Fred Duer	Lewis Brown	John B. Forbes

Fallen Angels
    Noel Coward
	Tom Moore	Douglas W.
		    Schmidt
			Lewis Brown	Greg Sullivan

A Midsummer Night's Dream William Shakespeare	Jack O'Brien	Bob Morgan	Bob Morgan	Kent Dorsey
Painting Churches Tina Howe	Bob Berlinger	Alan K. Okazaki	Sally Cleveland	John B. Forbes

Richard III
    William Shakespeare
	John Houseman	Douglas W.
		    Schmidt
			Lewis Brown	Greg Sullivan

London Assurance Dion Boucicault	Craig Noel	Richard Seger	Deb Dryden	Kent Dorsey

Omaha Magic Theatre

JO ANN SCHMIDMAN
Producing Artistic Director/Board
    President

2309 Hanscom Blvd.
Omaha, NE 68105
(402) 346-1227

FOUNDED 1968
Jo Ann Schmidman

SEASON
June–May

FACILITIES
1417 Farnam St.
Seating capacity: 93
Stage: flexible

FINANCES
June 1, 1984–May 31, 1985
Operating expenses: $216,331

AUDIENCE
Annual attendance: 165,000

TOURING CONTACT
Rose Marie Whiteley

BOOKED-IN EVENTS
Theatre, music, film, performance art

PRODUCTIONS 1983–84

Productions	Directors	Sets	Costumes	Lights

Dingaling
    James Larson
	Jo Ann
	    Schmidman
		Sora Kim	Jo Ann
			    Schmidman
				Marg Heaney

Fifteen Million Fifteen-Year-Olds
    Megan Terry; music: Joe Budenholzer
	Jo Ann
	    Schmidman
		Sora Kim	Megan Terry	Marg Heaney

Room 17C
    Rosalyn Drexler
	Jo Ann
	    Schmidman
		Sora Kim	Greg Gibson,
			    Diane Degan,
			    Meg Flamer
			    and Dorothy
			    Oleson
				Marg Heaney

Productions	Directors	Sets	Costumes	Lights
X-Rayed-Iate: E-Motion in Action book and lyrics: Megan Terry and Jo Ann Schmidman; music: John J. Sheehan	Jo Ann Schmidman	Sora Kim	Jo Ann Schmidman	James Larson
Kegger book and lyrics: Megan Terry; music: Marianne de Pury and Joe Budenholzer	Jo Ann Schmidman	company and South Omaha Boys' Club	Megan Terry and company	Jo Ann Schmidman
Quakes Megan Terry; music: John J. Sheehan	Jo Ann Schmidman	Sora Kim	Ralph Lee and company	Marg Heaney
Watch Where We Walk Jo Ann Schmidman; music: John J. Sheehan	Jo Ann Schmidman	Sora Kim	Greg Gibson, Diane Degan, Meg Flamer and Dorothy Oleson	Marg Heaney
Giant Creature Parade Ralph Lee; music: company-developed	Ralph Lee		Ralph Lee and company	Fluorescent
Comings and Goings Megan Terry	Roberta Larson	James Larson	Roberta Larson	James Larson
Pariah Tim Thompson	Tim Thompson	Jo Ann Schmidman	Tim Thompson	Jo Ann Schmidman
Dinner with Andre the Giant book, music and lyrics: Bill Frenzer	Bill Frenzer	Jo Ann Schmidman and Bill Frenzer	Bill Frenzer	Jo Ann Schmidman and Bill Frenzer
Rodeo book and lyrics: Joe Budenholzer; music: Joe Budenholzer and Jerry Kazakevicius	Joe Budenholzer	Joe Budenholzer and Jo Ann Schmidman	Joe Budenholzer	Joe Budenholzer and Jo Ann Schmidman
Digital Sex book, music and lyrics: Steve Sheehan	Steve Sheehan	Steve Sheehan and Jo Ann Schmidman	company	Jo Ann Schmidman
Initiation Jo Ann Schmidman; music: John J. Sheehan	Jo Ann Schmidman	Sora Kim	Jo Ann Schmidman	Marg Heaney
No Heroes book, music and lyrics: Mark Blackman	Mark Blackman	company	company	Jo Ann Schmidman
Cellophane Ceiling book, music and lyrics: John Wolf	John Wolf	company	company	Jo Ann Schmidman

Productions	Directors	Sets	Costumes	Lights
An Unexpected Evening with June Havoc, or Baby June Remembers June Havoc	June Havoc	June Havoc	June Havoc	June Havoc and Jo Ann Schmidman
Astro*Bride book and lyrics: Jo Ann Schmidman; music: John J. Sheehan, Joe Budenholzer and Jerry Kazakevicius: additional lyrics: Megan Terry and Sora Kim	Jo Ann Schmidman	Sora Kim	Dorothy Oleson	Linda Erhard
Kegger book and lyrics: Megan Terry; music: Marianne de Pury and Joe Budenholzer	Sharon Ross	company and South Omaha Boys' Club	Megan Terry and company	Jo Ann Schmidman
Road from Morocco Rebekah Presson	Roberta Larson	Sora Kim	Dorothy Oleson	Jo Ann Schmidman
Battery Daniel Therriault	Jo Ann Schmidman	Sora Kim	Janet Lipsey	Jo Ann Schmidman
Cablevisions James Larson; music: John J. Sheehan	Jo Ann Schmidman	Sora Kim	Dorothy Oleson	Colbert McClellan
Mummer's Parade Megan Terry	Jo Ann Schmidman	company	company	company
Katmandu Megan Terry	Jo Ann Schmidman	Megan Terry	Megan Terry	Jo Ann Schmidman
X-tras book, music and lyrics: John Desek and Brian Babier	John Desek	John Desek and Brian Babier	company	Jo Ann Schmidman
Vaudeville June Havoc	June Havoc	June Havoc	Megan Terry	Jo Ann Schmidman

One Act Theatre Company of San Francisco

SIMON L. LEVY
Artistic Director

STEVE SIGEL
General Manager

MIKE BRADFORD
Board President

430 Mason St.
San Francisco, CA 94102
(415) 421-5355 (business)
(415) 421-6162 (box office)

FOUNDED 1976
Peter Tripp, Jean Schiffman, Laurellee
 Westaway

SEASON
October–August

FACILITIES
Mainstage
Seating capacity: 140
Stage: thrust

Lunchtime Theatre
Seating capacity: 140
Stage: thrust

FINANCES
August 1, 1984–July 31, 1985
Operating expenses: $280,000

AUDIENCE
Annual attendance: 24,000
Subscribers: 1,650

TOURING CONTACT
Steve Sigel

BOOKED-IN EVENTS
Theatre, music

AEA Policy Statement

PRODUCTIONS 1983–84

Productions	Directors	Sets	Costumes	Lights
Out of Our Father's House Paula Wagner, Jack Hofsiss and Eve Merriam	Ric Prindle	Peggy McDonald	Suzanne Raftery	Derek Duarte
Chocolate Cake Mary Gallagher	Ken Grantham	Peggy McDonald	Suzanne Raftery	Derek Duarte

The Dead End Kid
    book: Michael Lynch; music: Steve Sigel and
    Andy Kulberg; lyrics: Steve Sigel
	Simon L. Levy	Jeffer Whitman	Gael Russell	Rhonda
				 Birnbaum

Noonday Demons Peter Barnes	Ric Prindle	Everett Chase	Judy Boraas	William R. Simonds
A Slight Ache Harold Pinter	Stefani Priest	Everett Chase	Judy Boraas	William R. Simonds
Once Around the Block William Saroyan	Richard Howes	Stephen Elspas	Gael Russell	Graham Gilbert
Hughie Eugene O'Neill	Tom McDermott	Stephen Elspas	Gael Russell	Graham Gilbert
Three More Sleepless Nights Caryl Churchill	Susan Marsden	Bruce Brisson	Judy Boraas	James McCracken
Last Call at Paradise Tavern Terry Mack Murphy	Larry Russell	Bruce Brisson	Judy Boraas	James McCracken
The Real Inspector Hound Tom Stoppard	William I. Oliver	James McCracken	Tamara Teague	Ann McDowell
Gosforth's Fete Alan Ayckbourn	Darrell Zink	Michael Allen	Tamara Teague	Ann McDowell

Lunchtime Theatre:

Productions	Directors	Sets	Costumes	Lights
Snowangel, Lewis John Carlino	Tom McDermott	Stephen Elspas		
Third and Oak: The Laundromat, Marsha Norman	Larry Russell	Stephen Elspas		
Duck Variations, David Mamet	Ric Prindle			
Out of the Can into the Ring, Michael Hennessey	Ric Prindle	Ofra Confino		Michael Allen
The Tiger, Murray Schisgal	David DeRose			Michael Allen
The Plumber's Apprentice, Mark Stein	Tammis Doyle			Michael Allen
An Hour with John Malloy, John Malloy				Michael Allen
Doreen, Alun Owen	Ric Prindle	David Case		
Vivien, Percy Granger	Wanda McCaddon	James McCracken		Michael Allen
The 75th, Israel Horovitz	Bill Oliver	James McCracken		Michael Allen
Visitors from Hollywood, Neil Simon		James McCracken		
Overruled, George Bernard Shaw	Andrea Gordon	James McCracken	Eva Schegulla	James McCracken

Productions	Directors	Sets	Costumes	Lights
Cabin 12 John Bishop	Richard Howes	Stephen Elspas	Ofra Confino	James McCracken
Thymus Vulgaris Lanford Wilson	Andrea Gordon	Stephen Elspas	Ofra Confino	James McCracken
Taco Jesus Michael Lynch	Simon L. Levy	Peggy McDonald	Judy Boraas	Rhonda Birnbaum
Open Admissions Shirley Lauro	Carla Sarvis	James McCracken	Eva Schegulla	Ellen Shireman
Statements After an Arrest Under the Immorality Act Athol Fugard	Simon L. Levy	James McCracken	Eva Schegulla	Ellen Shireman
Nice People Dancing to Good Country Music and *Toys for Men* Lee Blessing	Susan Marsden	Andy Stacklin	Judy Boraas	Ellen Shiremen
Margaret Carol Braverman	Simon L. Levy and Carol Braverman	Andrew Deshong	Diane Harrell	Joe Dignan
The Elephant Man Bernard Pomerance	Simon L. Levy	Andrew Deshong	Diane Harrell	Joe Dignan
Villainous Company Amlin Gray	Ric Prindle	Ric Tringali	Gael Russell	Rhonda Birnbaum
All's Well That Ends as You Like It Michael Green	David Case	Ric Tringali	Gael Russell	Rhonda Birnbaum
The (15-Minute) Dogg's Troupe Hamlet Tom Stoppard	David Case	Ric Tringali	Gael Russell	Rhonda Birnbaum
Lunchtime Theatre: *Actors*, Conrad Bromberg	Anita Merzell	James McCracken	Eva Schegulla	James McCracken
Overruled, George Bernard Shaw	Andrea Gordon	James McCracken	Eva Schegulla	James McCracken
The Two of Us, Michael Frayn	Ken Grantham	James McCracken	Gary Walker	James McCracken
Visitors from London, Neil Simon	Andrea Gordon	James McCracken	Eva Schegulla	James McCracken
The Public Eye, Peter Shaffer	Ellery Edwards	James McCracken	Ofra Confino	James McCracken
End of the Beginning, Sean O'Casey	Eli Simon	James McCracken	Judy Boraas	James McCracken
The Frog Prince, David Mamet	Sandi Langsner	Ric Tringali	Eva Schegulla	Rhonda Birnbaum

O'Neill Theater Center

GEORGE C. WHITE
President

LLOYD RICHARDS
Artistic Director, National Playwrights
   Conference

234 West 44th St., Suite 901
New York, NY 10036
(212) 382-2790

305 Great Neck Road
Waterford, CT 06385
(203) 443-5378 (business)
(203) 443-1238 (box office)

FOUNDED 1964
George C. White

SEASON
July–August

FACILITIES
Barn Theater
Seating capacity: 200
Stage: flexible

Amphitheater
Seating capacity: 300
Stage: thrust

Instant Theater
Seating capacity: 200
Stage: arena

FINANCES
July 1, 1984–June 30, 1985
Operating expenses: $2,261,000

AUDIENCE
Annual attendance: 5,000

BOOKED-IN EVENTS
Theatre, music

AEA LORT (C) contract

PRODUCTIONS 1984

Productions	Directors	Sets	Costumes	Lights
Raw Youth Neal Bell	Amy Saltz	Kate Edmunds and G.W. Mercier		Ann Wrightson
War of the Roses Lee Blessing	Dennis Scott	Kate Edmunds and G.W. Mercier		Ann Wrightson
Mitzi's Glory Carl Capotorto	William Partlan	Kate Edmunds and G.W. Mercier		Ann Wrightson
Tough Girls Paula Cizmar and Douglas Gower	Andrew Weyman	Kate Edmunds and G.W. Mercier		Ann Wrightson
American Music Bennett Cohen	Claudia Weill	Kate Edmunds and G.W. Mercier		Ann Wrightson
The Square Root of Three Michael Golder	Steven Robman	Kate Edmunds and G.W. Mercier		Ann Wrightson
Family Face Richard Hamburger	Steven Robman	Kate Edmunds and G.W. Mercier		Ann Wrightson
Gallup John Haskell	Dennis Scott	Kate Edmunds and G.W. Mercier		Ann Wrightson
Moonya Cindy Lou Johnson	Dennis Scott	Kate Edmunds and G.W. Mercier		Ann Wrightson
The Quiet in the Land Jerry McGlown	Claudia Weill	Kate Edmunds and G.W. Mercier		Ann Wrightson
National Anthems Dennis McIntyre	Ron Lagomarsino	Kate Edmunds and G.W. Mercier		Ann Wrightson
Saute Stephen Davis Parks	Amy Saltz	Kate Edmunds and G.W. Mercier		Ann Wrightson
Savage in Limbo John Patrick Shanley	William Partlan	Kate Edmunds and G.W. Mercier		Ann Wrightson
Joe Turner's Come and Gone August Wilson	Amy Saltz	Kate Edmunds and G.W. Mercier		Ann Wrightson
Oak and Ivy Kathleen McGhee-Anderson	Ron Lagomarsino	Kate Edmunds and G.W. Mercier		Ann Wrightson

Productions	Directors	Sets	Costumes	Lights
Jass John Pielmeier	Steven Robman	Kate Edmunds and Fred Voelpel		Ann Wrightson
Butterfly Richard Wesley	Ron Lagomarsino	Kate Edmunds and Fred Voelpel		Ann Wrightson
Union Boys James Yoshimura	Susan Gregg	Kate Edmunds and Fred Voelpel		Ann Wrightson
the dreamer examines his pillow John Patrick Shanley	Barnet Kellman	Kate Edmunds and Fred Voelpel		Ann Wrightson
A Child's Tale Carl Capotorto	Dennis Scott	Kate Edmunds and Fred Voelpel		Ann Wrightson
All Good Men George Rubino	Andrew Weyman	Kate Edmunds and Fred Voelpel		Ann Wrightson
Josh White—An American Folktale OyamO	Gordon Rigsby	Kate Edmunds and Fred Voelpel		Ann Wrightson
Fun James Bosley	Dennis Scott	Kate Edmunds and Fred Voelpel		Ann Wrightson
Jazz Wives Jazz Lives Laura Maria Censabella	Amy Saltz	Kate Edmunds and Fred Voelpel		Ann Wrightson
In This Fallen City Brian Williams	Steven Robman	Kate Edmunds and Fred Voelpel		Ann Wrightson
Trinity Site Janeice Scarbrough	William Partlan	Kate Edmunds and Fred Voelpel		Ann Wrightson
Thaw: A Russian Melodrama Roger Cornish	William Partlan	Kate Edmunds and Fred Voelpel		Ann Wrightson
Fun in the Physical World James D'Entremont	Roger Hendricks Simon	Kate Edmunds and Fred Voelpel		Ann Wrightson
Deutschland Robert Kinerk	Dennis Scott	Kate Edmunds and Fred Voelpel		Ann Wrightson

Ontological-Hysteric Theatre

RICHARD FOREMAN
Artistic Director/Board President

GEORGE ASHLEY
Administrative Director

% Performing Artservices
325 Spring St., Suite 347
New York, NY 10013
(212) 243-6153

FOUNDED 1968
Richard Foreman

FINANCES
July 1, 1980–June 30, 1981
Operating expenses: $90,000

PRODUCTIONS 1983–84

Productions	Directors	Sets	Costumes	Lights
La Robe de Chambre de Georges Bataille Richard Foreman	Richard Foreman	Richard Foreman	Richard Foreman	Richard Foreman
Dr. Selavy's Magic Theater book and lyrics: Richard Foreman; music: Stanley Silverman	Richard Foreman	Richard Foreman	Richard Foreman	Richard Foreman

---

PRODUCTIONS 1984–85

Productions	Directors	Sets	Costumes	Lights
The Birth of the Poet book and lyrics: Kathy Acker; music: Peter Gordon	Richard Foreman	David Salle	David Salle	David Salle
The Golem H. Leivick; adapt: Richard Foreman	Richard Foreman	Richard Foreman	Richard Foreman	Richard Foreman
Miss Universal Happiness Richard Foreman	Richard Foreman	Richard Foreman	Richard Foreman	Richard Foreman

---

Oregon Shakespearean Festival

JERRY TURNER
Artistic Director

WILLIAM PATTON
Executive Director

GORDON MEDARIS
Board President

Box 158
Ashland, OR 97520
(503) 482-2111 (business)
(503) 482-4331 (box office)

FOUNDED 1935
Angus Bowmer

SEASON
February–October

FACILITIES
15 South Pioneer St.
Angus Bowmer Theater
Seating capacity: 601
Stage: thrust

Elizabethan Theatre
Seating capacity: 1,194
Stage: outdoor

Black Swan Theatre
Seating capacity: 138
Stage: arena

FINANCES
November 1, 1983–October 31, 1984
Operating expenses: $4,394,012

AUDIENCE
Annual attendance: 459,681

TOURING CONTACT
Paul Nicholson

AEA Special Production contract

Productions	Directors	Sets	Costumes	Lights
Troilus and Cressida William Shakespeare	Richard E.T. White	William Bloodgood	Michael Olich	Robert Peterson
London Assurance Dion Boucicault	Hugh Evans	Richard L. Hay	Jeannie Davidson	Greg Sullivan
Dracula Richard Sharp	Richard Greer	Richard L. Hay	Jeannie Davidson	Robert Peterson
Hay Fever Noel Coward	James Moll	Richard L. Hay	Michael Olich	Greg Sullivan
Cat on a Hot Tin Roof Tennessee Williams	Pat Patton	William Bloodgood	Claudia Everett	James Sale
The Revenger's Tragedy Cyril Tourneur	Jerry Turner	William Bloodgood	Jeannie Davidson	James Sale
The Taming of the Shrew William Shakespeare	Pat Patton	William Bloodgood	Michael Olich	James Sale
Henry VIII William Shakespeare	James Edmondson	Richard L. Hay	Jeannie Davidson	James Sale
The Winter's Tale William Shakespeare	Hugh Evans	Richard L. Hay	Barbara Bush	James Sale
Translations Brian Friel	Jerry Turner	William Bloodgood	Jeannie Davidson	Robert Peterson
Seascape with Sharks and Dancer Don Nigro	Dennis Bigelow	William Bloodgood	Jeannie Davidson	Robert Peterson

Productions	Directors	Sets	Costumes	Lights
King Lear William Shakespeare	Jerry Turner	Richard L. Hay	Jeannie Davidson	Robert Peterson
Light up the Sky Moss Hart	Pat Patton	William Bloodgood	Claudia Everett	Greg Sullivan
Trelawny of the "Wells" Arthur Wing Pinero	James Edmondson	William Bloodgood	Deborah M. Dryden	Robert Peterson
Crimes of the Heart Beth Henley	James Moll	Jesse Hollis	Jeannie Davidson	Robert Peterson
An Enemy of the People Henrik Ibsen; trans and adapt: Jerry Turner	Jerry Turner	Richard L. Hay	Claudia Everett	James Sale
The Merchant of Venice William Shakespeare	Albert Takazauckas	William Bloodgood	Jeannie Davidson	James Sale
King John William Shakespeare	Pat Patton	Richard L. Hay	Sarah Nash Gates	James Sale
All's Well That Ends Well William Shakespeare	Tony Amendola	William Bloodgood	Merrily Murray-Walsh	James Sale
Strange Snow Stephen Metcalfe	Andrew Traister	William Bloodgood	Frances Kenny	Robert Peterson
The Majestic Kid Mark Medoff	Edward Hastings	Jesse Hollis	Jeannie Davidson	Robert Peterson
Lizzie Borden in the Late Afternoon Cather MacCallum	Lou Salerni	Jeannie Davidson	Jeannie Davidson	James Sale

Pan Asian Repertory Theatre

TISA CHANG
Artistic/Producing Director

ELIZABETH A. HYSLOP
Managing Director

ROBERT B. RADIN
Board Chairman

47 Great Jones St.
New York, NY 10012
(212) 505-5655

FOUNDED 1977
Tisa Chang

SEASON
October–June

FACILITIES
Playhouse 46
423 West 46th St.
Seating capacity: 99
Stage: proscenium

FINANCES
September 1, 1984–August 31, 1985
Operating expenses: $240,000

AUDIENCE
Annual attendance: 11,000
Subscribers: 183

TOURING CONTACT
Elizabeth A. Hyslop

*AEA Theatre for Young Audiences
contract and letter of agreement*

PRODUCTIONS 1983–84

Productions	Directors	Sets	Costumes	Lights
Yellow Fever R.A. Shiomi	Raul Aranas	Christopher Stapleton	Eiko Yamaguchi	Dawn Chiang
A Song for a Nisei Fisherman Philip Kan Gotanda	Raul Aranas	Atsushi Moriyasu	Eiko Yamaguchi	Victor En Yu Tan
The Face Box Wakako Yamauchi	Ron Nakahara	Ron Kajiwara	Eiko Yamaguchi	Toshiro Ogawa
Empress of China Ruth Wolff	Tisa Chang	Bob Phillips	Eiko Yamaguchi	Victor En Yu Tan

PRODUCTIONS 1984–85

Productions	Directors	Sets	Costumes	Lights
Chipshot Donald G. McNeil, Jr.	Raul Aranas	Bob Phillips	Eiko Yamaguchi	Victor En Yu Tan
State Without Grace Linda Kalayaan Faigao	Aida Limjoco	Robert Bullock	Linda Taoka	Victor En Yu Tan
Manoa Valley Edward Sakamoto	Kati Kuroda	Bob Phillips	Eiko Yamaguchi	Richard Dorfman
Eat a Bowl of Tea Ernest Abuba	Tisa Chang	Alex Polner	Eiko Yamaguchi	Richard Dorfman

Paper Mill Playhouse

ANGELO DEL ROSSI
Executive Producer

JIM THESING
Administrative Director

ROBERT SMITH
Board President

Brookside Dr.
Millburn, NJ 07041
(201) 379-3636 (business)
(201) 376-4343 (box office)

FOUNDED 1934
Frank Carrington, Antoinette Scudder

SEASON
September–July

FACILITIES
Playhouse
Seating capacity: 1,192
Stage: proscenium

FINANCES
July 1, 1984–June 30, 1985
Operating expenses: $6,097,500

AUDIENCE
Annual attendance: 395,000
Subscribers: 31,819

BOOKED-IN EVENTS
Children's theatre, music, dance

AEA Council on Stock Theatre contract

PRODUCTIONS 1983–84

Productions	Directors	Sets	Costumes	Lights
Annie book: Thomas Meehan; music: Charles Strouse; lyrics: Martin Charnin	Jerry Adler	Michael Hotopp	Gail Cooper-Hecht	David Kissel
Fiddler on the Roof book: Joseph Stein; music: Jerry Bock; lyrics: Sheldon Harnick	Frank Coppola	Philip Rodzen	Guy Geoly	Patricia Donovan
The Guardsman Ferenc Molnar; trans: Grace I. Colbron and Hans Bartsch	David Rothkopf	Robert Barnes	Julie Weiss	Frances Aronson
The Show-Off George Kelly	William H. Putch	James M. Fouchard	Arnold S. Levin	David Kissel
Joseph and the Amazing Technicolor Dreamcoat book and lyrics: Tim Rice: music: Andrew Lloyd Webber	Tony Tanner	Karl Eigsti	Guy Geoly	Barry Arnold
The Desert Song book and lyrics: Oscar Hammerstein, II and Frank Mandel; music: Sigmund Romberg	Robert Johanson	Michael Anania	Guy Geoly	David Kissel

---

PRODUCTIONS 1984–85

Productions	Directors	Sets	Costumes	Lights
Amadeus Peter Shaffer	Robert Johanson	John Bury	Guy Geoly	Frances Aronson
Guys and Dolls book: Abe Burrows and Jo Swerling; music and lyrics: Frank Loesser	Robert Johanson	Michael Anania	Guy Geoly	Frances Aronson
Side by Side by Sondheim music and lyrics: Stephen Sondheim, et al.	Robert Johanson	David Kissel	Alice S. Hughes	David Kissel
Inherit the Wind Jerome Lawrence and Robert E. Lee	John Going	Michael Anania	Guy Geoly	Mimi Jordan Sherin
Show Boat book and lyrics: Oscar Hammerstein, II; music: Jerome Kern	Robert Johanson	Michael Anania	Guy Geoly	Brian MacDevitt
Evita book and lyrics: Tim Rice; music: Andrew Lloyd Webber	Frank Marino	Tim O'Brian	Guy Geoly	Jackie Manassee

---

PCPA Theaterfest

VINCENT DOWLING
Producing/Artistic Director

BEN COOPER
General Manager of Conservatory

SUE POHLS
Board Chairman

Box 1700
Santa Maria, CA 93456
(805) 928-7731 (business)
(805) 922-8313 (box office)

FOUNDED 1964

SEASON
November–September

FACILITIES
Marian Performing Arts Center
Seating capacity: 508
Stage: thrust

Solvang Festival Stage
Seating capacity: 787
Stage: thrust

FINANCES
October 1, 1983–September 30, 1984
Operating expenses: $2,400,000

AUDIENCE
Annual attendance: 97,545
Subscribers: 3,291

TOURING CONTACT
Olwen O'Herlihy

AEA letter of agreement and Guest Artist contract

Note: During the 1983-84 season, Laird Williamson served as artistic director.

PRODUCTIONS 1983–84

Productions	Directors	Sets	Costumes	Lights
Bus Stop William Inge	Lawrence Hecht	Bernard Vyzga	Janet S. Morris	Greg Sullivan
Medea Euripides; adapt: Robinson Jeffers	Caroline Eves	Jack Shouse	Mary Fleming	Greg Sullivan
Working book adapt: Stephen Schwartz, from Studs Terkel; music and lyrics: Stephen Schwartz, et al.	Randal Myler	Jack Shouse	Janet S. Morris	Wendy Heffner
Misalliance George Bernard Shaw	James Moll	Jack Shouse	Andrew V. Yelusich	Wendy Heffner
The Suicide Nikolai Erdman; trans: Peter Tegel	John C. Fletcher	Warren Travis	Mary Fleming	Greg Sullivan
Camelot book and lyrics: Alan J. Lerner; music: Frederick Loewe	Michael Winters	Mark Donnelly	Warren Travis	Greg Sullivan
Annie book: Thomas Meehan; music: Charles Strouse; lyrics: Martin Charnin	Robert Blackman	Robert Blackman	Robert Blackman	Wendy Heffner
Foxfire Susan Cooper and Hume Cronyn	Laird Williamson	Andrew V. Yelusich	Andrew V. Yelusich	Wendy Heffner

PRODUCTIONS 1984–85

Productions	Directors	Sets	Costumes	Lights
My Lady Luck adapt: James A. Brown, from Robert Service	Vincent Dowling	Jack Shouse	Jack Shouse	Jack Shouse
A Child's Christmas in Wales adapt: Jeremy Brooks and Adrian Mitchell, from Dylan Thomas	Vincent Dowling	Jack Shouse	Lewis D. Rampino	Wendy Heffner
Long Day's Journey into Night Eugene O'Neill	Bernard Kates	John Dexter	Jack Shouse	John Dexter
Peg O' My Heart J. Hartley Manners	John Love	John Ezell	Janet S. Morris	Tenna Matthews
The Sound of Music book and lyrics: Oscar Hammerstein, II; music: Richard Rodgers	Cash Baxter	Jack Shouse	Lewis D. Rampino	Robert Jared
And a Nightingale Sang . . . C.P. Taylor	Bernard Kates	John Dexter	Clare Marie Verheyen	D. Martyn Bookwalter
Painting Churches Tina Howe	Jonathan Gillard	John Wilson	Patti Whitelock	Robert Jared
Amadeus Peter Shaffer	Cash Baxter	D. Martyn Bookwalter	Lewis D. Rampino	D. Martyn Bookwalter

Productions	Directors	Sets	Costumes	Lights
Hamlet William Shakespeare	Vincent Dowling	D. Martyn Bookwalter	Lewis D. Rampino	D. Martyn Bookwalter
Gypsy book: Arthur Laurents; music: Jule Styne; lyrics: Stephen Sondheim	Jack Shouse	John Wilson	Clare Marie Verheyen	Robert Jared
Floodgate James Buchanan	Ben Cooper	Greg Timm	April Guttierrez	Michael Peterson
I Do, I Do book and lyrics: Tom Jones; music: Harvey Schmidt	John C. Fletcher	Everett Chase	Janet S. Morris	Robert Jared

Pennsylvania Stage Company

GREGORY S. HURST
Producing Director

DANIEL FALLON
General Manager

DAVID H. KELLY
Board President

837 Linden St.
Allentown, PA 18101
(215) 434-6110 (business)
(215) 433-3394 (box office)

FOUNDED 1977
Anna Rodale

SEASON
October–July

FACILITIES
J.I. Rodale Theatre
Seating capacity: 274
Stage: proscenium

FINANCES
July 1, 1984–June 30, 1985
Operating expenses: $1,100,500

AUDIENCE
Annual attendance: 75,000
Subscribers: 6,000

BOOKED-IN EVENTS
Solo artists, theatre, dance, music

AEA LORT (C) contract

Productions	Directors	Sets	Costumes	Lights
Sleuth Anthony Shaffer	Stephen Rothman	Quentin Thomas	Johanna Forte	Quentin Thomas
All My Sons Arthur Miller	Gregory S. Hurst	Richard Hoover	Karen Gerson	Richard Hoover
A Christmas Carol adapt: Pam Pepper, from Charles Dickens	Pam Pepper	William Barclay	Colleen Muscha	Phil Monat
Copperhead Erik Brogger	Gregory S. Hurst	Curtis Dretsch	Martha Kelly	Curtis Dretsch
Children of a Lesser God Mark Medoff	Robert H. Livingston	Russell C. Smith	Johanna Forte	William M. Frein
The Further Adventures of Sally Russell Davis	Tony Giordano	Karen Schulz	Stephen Strawbridge	Karen Schulz
I Do, I Do book and lyrics: Tom Jones; music: Harvey Schmidt	Julianne Boyd	Robert Thayer	Ann Hould-Ward	Robert Thayer
The Fourposter Jan De Hartog	Yvonne Adriane			

PRODUCTIONS 1984-85

Productions	Directors	Sets	Costumes	Lights
Just So book adapt: Mark St. Germain, from Rudyard Kipling; music: Doug Katsaros; lyrics: David Zippel	Julianne Boyd	Atkin Pace	Ann Hould-Ward	Craig Miller
Harvey Mary Chase	Kevin Kelly	Richard Hoover	David Loveless	Rick Gray
A Christmas Carol adapt: Pam Pepper, from Charles Dickens	Pam Pepper	William Barclay	Collen Muscha	Curtis Dretsch
A Walk Out of Water Donald Driver	Gregory S. Hurst	Atkin Pace	Martha Kelly	Curtis Dretsch
True West Sam Shepard	Pam Pepper	Richard Hoover	Gail Cooper-Hecht	Mark Hendren
Equus Peter Shaffer	Jamie Brown	Quentin Thomas	Martha Kelly	Curtis Dretsch
Stage Struck Simon Gray	Gregory S. Hurst	Gary C. Eckhart	Karen Gerson	Mark Hendren

The People's Light and Theatre Company

DANNY S. FRUCHTER
Producing Director

GREGORY T. ROWE
General Manager

WILLIAM D. RAVDIN
Board President

39 Conestoga Road
Malvern, PA 19355
(215) 647-1900 (business)
(215) 644-3500 (box office)

FOUNDED 1974
Danny S. Fruchter, Margaret E.
  Fruchter, Richard L. Keeler, Ken
  Marini

SEASON
April–January

FACILITIES
Mainstage
Seating capacity: 400
Stage: flexible

Second Stage
Seating capacity: 80
Stage: modified thrust

FINANCES
February 1, 1984–January 31, 1985
Operating expenses: $1,174,719

AUDIENCE
Annual attendance: 60,598
Subscribers: 7,050

TOURING CONTACT
Gregory T. Rowe

BOOKED-IN EVENTS
Storytelling

AEA LORT (D) contract

PRODUCTIONS 1983-84

Productions	Directors	Sets	Costumes	Lights
Antigone Jean Anouilh; adapt: Lewis Galantiere	Israel Hicks	James F. Pyne, Jr.	Megan Fruchter	James F. Pyne, Jr.
At Fifty, She Discovered the Sea Denise Chalem; trans: Sara O'Connor	June Fortunato	Norman B. Dodge, Jr.	Megan Fruchter	Arden Fingerhut
The Bird of Ill Omen Joseph Pintauro	Margaret Denithorne	Norman B. Dodge, Jr.	Megan Fruchter	Arden Fingerhut
City Lights—An Urban Sprawl J. Rufus Caleb	Murphy Guyer	Joe Ragey	Megan Fruchter	Arden Fingerhut
Lover's Leap Dick D. Zigun	Louis Lippa	Joe Ragey	Megan Fruchter	Arden Fingerhut

PRODUCTIONS 1983-84

Productions	Directors	Sets	Costumes	Lights
Malek's Dependents Gary Slezak	Steven D. Albrezzi	Norman B. Dodge, Jr.	Megan Fruchter	Arden Fingerhut
Valentines and Killer Chili Kent R. Brown	Israel Hicks	Joe Ragey	Megan Fruchter	Arden Fingerhut
The War Brides Terri Wagener	Abigail Adams	Joe Ragey	Colleen Muscha	Arden Fingerhut
The American Century Murphy Guyer	Steven D. Albrezzi	Norman B. Dodge, Jr.	Megan Fruchter	Arden Fingerhut
The Workroom Jean-Claude Grumberg; trans: Daniel A. Stein and Sara O'Connor	Michael Nash	Patricia Woodbridge	Barbara Forbes	James F. Pyne, Jr.
The Misanthrope Molière; trans: Richard Wilbur	Steven D. Albrezzi	Eric Schaeffer	Megan Fruchter	Joe Ragey
Under Milk Wood Dylan Thomas	Louis Lippa	James F. Pyne, Jr.	Megan Fruchter	James F. Pyne, Jr.

PRODUCTIONS 1984-85

Productions	Directors	Sets	Costumes	Lights
Awake and Sing! Clifford Odets	Michael Nash	Joe Ragey	Barbara Forbes	Joe Ragey
Taken in Marriage Thomas Babe	Abigail Adams	James F. Pyne, Jr.	Megan Fruchter	James F. Pyne, Jr.
The Defector Louis Lippa	Ken Marini		Megan Fruchter	
Love Suicide at Schofield Barracks Romulus Linney	Danny S. Fruchter	Joe Ragey	Megan Fruchter	Joe Ragey
Sleeping Beauty Laurence Klavan	Steve Kaplan	Joe Ragey	Megan Fruchter	Joe Ragey
The Tattler: The Story and Stories of a Pathological Liar Terri Wagener	Abigail Adams	Joe Ragey	Megan Fruchter	Joe Ragey
What Leona Figured Out David Hill	Tom Teti		Susan Dinsmore- Smythe	
Boesman and Lena Athol Fugard	Murphy Guyer	Joe Ragey	Megan Fruchter	Joe Ragey
Our Town Thornton Wilder	Abigail Adams	Joe Ragey	Barbara Forbes	Joe Ragey

Periwinkle Productions

SUNNA RASCH
Artistic Director/Board President

CATHY FARRIS
Business Manager

J. LAWRENCE COULTER
Board Chairman

19 Clinton Ave.
Monticello, NY 12701
(914) 794-1666

205 West End Ave., 19W
New York, NY 10023 (studio)
(212) 877-7027

FOUNDED 1963
Sunna Rasch

SEASON
Year-round

FINANCES
August 1, 1984–July 31, 1985
Operating expenses: $121,000

AUDIENCE
Annual attendance: 100,000

TOURING CONTACT
Cathy Ferris, Sunna Rasch

PRODUCTIONS 1983–84

Productions	Directors	Sets	Costumes	Lights
Once Upon a Time Bob Shea	Bob Shea	Bob Shea		
America, Yes! Sunna Rasch	Jerry Whiddon	Scott Laughead	Susan Scherer	
Mad Poet Strikes Again! Sunna Rasch	Scott Laughead	Everett Hoag	Susan Scherer	
Halfway There Lynnette Serrano, Sunna Rasch, Peter Ciani, Cathy Farris and Everett Hoag; music: Kenneth Laufer	Jack Sims	Lynnette Serrano and Everett Hoag	Marcie Miller	David Oberon

PRODUCTIONS 1984–85

Productions	Directors	Sets	Costumes	Lights
The Magic Word Sunna Rasch	Scott Laughead	Sunna Rasch	Susan Scherer	
America, Yes! Sunna Rasch	Scott Laughead	Scott Laughead	Susan Scherer	
Mad Poet Strikes Again! Sunna Rasch	Scott Laughead	Everett Hoag	Susan Scherer	
Halfway There Lynnette Serrano, Sunna Rasch, Peter Ciani, Cathy Farris, Everett Hoag; music: Kenneth Laufer	Jack Sims	Lynnette Serrano and Everett Hoag	Marcie Miller	Ronald Selke and Bill Kadra

Perseverance Theatre

MOLLY D. SMITH
Artistic Director

DEBORAH BALEY
Producing Director/Board President

914 Third St.
Douglas, AK 99824
(907) 364-2151, -2152 (business)
(907) 364-2421 (box office)

FOUNDED 1979
Molly D. Smith

SEASON
September–May

FACILITIES
Mainstage
Seating capacity: 150
Stage: thrust

Original Stage
Seating capacity: 82
Stage: flexible

FINANCES
July 1, 1984–June 30, 1985
Operating expenses: $600,000

AUDIENCE
Annual attendance: 11,661
Subscribers: 1,100

TOURING CONTACT
Tom Linklater

PRODUCTIONS 1983–84

Productions	Directors	Sets	Costumes	Lights
K2 Patrick Meyer	Molly D. Smith	Bill C. Ray	Susan Kaufman	James Sale
As You Like It William Shakespeare	John Broome	Jonathan Douglas	Barbara Casement	Joe Ross
Cat on a Hot Tin Roof Tennessee Williams	Joe Ross	James Sale	Barbara Casement	James Sale
The Greeks adapt: John Barton and Kenneth Cavander	Molly D. Smith	Maurice McClelland and Lou Zeldis	Maurice McClelland and Lou Zeldis	Joe Ross
Lifelines Jennifer Wilke	Kate Bowns	Jack Cannon	Bev Finley	James Sale
Rites of Passage (Selections from *Key Exchange*, Kevin Wade; *Whose Life Is It Anyway*, Brian Clark; *Insignificance*, Terry Johnson)	Rita Giomi	Mary Ellen Frank	Barbara Casement	Joe Ross
Yup 'ik Antigone adapt: Dave Hunsaker, from Sophocles	Dave Hunsaker	Bill C. Ray		Jim Simard

PRODUCTIONS 1984–85

Productions	Directors	Sets	Costumes	Lights
Top Girls Caryl Churchill	Molly D. Smith	Jennifer Lupton	Lou Zeldis	Spencer Mosse
True West Sam Shepard	Jamieson McLean	Jim Coates	Barbara Casement	Spencer Mosse
Candide book adapt: Hugh Wheeler, from Voltaire; music: Leonard Bernstein; lyrics: Richard Wilbur and Stephen Sondheim	Roberta Levitow	Bill C. Ray	Deborah Trout	James Sale
Fifth of July Lanford Wilson	Joe Ross and Kate Bowns	Daniel Cockrell	Corine Geldhof	Terry Tavel
Island of Tears Jack Cannon	Molly D. Smith	Bill C. Ray	Barbara Casement	Lee Riggs
Dreams and Ambitions Kayla Epstein	Kayla Epstein	Mary Ellen Frank	Suzanne Gaffney	Kay Dickson
Walker in the Snow Dave Hunsaker	Molly D. Smith	Jennifer Lupton	Lou Zeldis	Spencer Mosse

The Philadelphia Company

SARA GARONZIK
Artistic Director

CHRISTINA L. STERNER
General Manager

LEWIS C. ROSS
Board President

The Bourse Bldg., Suite 735
21 South 5th St.
Philadelphia, PA 19106
(215) 592-8333

FOUNDED 1974
Robert Hedley, Jean Harrison

SEASON
November–June

FACILITIES
Plays and Players Theatre
1714 Delancey St.
Seating capacity: 324
Stage: proscenium

FINANCES
September 1, 1984–August 31, 1985
Operating expenses: $370,000

AUDIENCE
Annual attendance: 16,600

BOOKED-IN EVENTS
One-man shows, music

AEA letter of agreement

PRODUCTIONS 1983–84

Productions	Directors	Sets	Costumes	Lights
Wings Arthur Kopit	Dugald MacArthur	Michael Wright Stockton	Frankie Fehr	Curt Senie
Lone Star and *Laundry and Bourbon* James McLure	Lynn M. Thomson	Ken Becker	Frankie Fehr	George Black
Final Passages Robert Schenkkan	Sara Garonzik	Daniel Boylen	Frankie Fehr	Daniel Boylen
Getting Out Marsha Norman	Sara Garonzik	Ken Becker	Janus Stefanowicz	George Black
True West Sam Shepard	Dugald MacArthur	Michael Wright Stockton	Frankie Fehr	Curt Senie
Strange Snow Stephen Metcalfe	Lynn M. Thomson	M. R. Daniels	Frankie Fehr	Don Ehman
Fifth of July Lanford Wilson	Sara Garonzik	Keith Gonzales	Janus Stefanowicz	James L. Leitner

PRODUCTIONS 1984–85

Productions	Directors	Sets	Costumes	Lights
Terra Nova Ted Tally	Dugald MacArthur	Ellen Cooper	Pamela Scofield	Curt Senie
Geniuses Jonathan Reynolds	Sara Garonzik	Robert Little	Janus Stefanowicz	James L. Leitner
To Gillian on Her 37th Birthday Michael Brady	Lynn M. Thomson	M. R. Daniels	Frankie Fehr	James L. Leitner
Fool for Love Sam Shepard	Anita Khanzadian	M. R. Daniels and Scott Roper	Susan Trimble	Don Ehman

Philadelphia Drama Guild

GREGORY POGGI
Producing Director

MARK D. BERNSTEIN
Business Manager

DANIEL PROMISLO
Board Chairman

112 South 16th St., Suite 802
Philadelphia, PA 19102
(215) 563-7530 (business)
(215) 898-6791 (box office)

FOUNDED 1956
Sidney S. Bloom

SEASON
October–May

FACILITIES
Zellerbach Theatre
3680 Walnut St.
Seating capacity: 944
Stage: thrust

FINANCES
June 1, 1984–May 31, 1985
Operating expenses: $1,725,000

AUDIENCE
Annual attendance: 102,476
Subscribers: 18,092

AEA LORT (B) contract

PRODUCTIONS 1983–84

Productions	Directors	Sets	Costumes	Lights
Teibele and Her Demons Isaac Bashevis Singer and Eve Friedman	Steven Schachter	Barry Robison	James E. Brady	William Armstrong
The Member of the Wedding Carson McCullers	William Woodman	John Jensen	Constance R. Wexler	William Armstrong
The Dining Room A. R. Gurney, Jr.	Charles Karchmer	John Falabella	Frances Fehr	Jeff Davis
Black Comedy Peter Shaffer	Jerry Zaks	John Falabella	Jess Goldstein	Ann Wrightson
The Father August Strindberg; adapt: Oliver Hailey	William Woodman	Dan Boylan	Jess Goldstein	F. Mitchell Dana

PRODUCTIONS 1984–85

Productions	Directors	Sets	Costumes	Lights
Oliver, Oliver Paul Osborn	Vivian Matalon	Tom Schwinn	Linda Fisher	Richard Nelson
The Power and the Glory adapt: Denis Cannan, from Graham Greene	William Woodman	George Tsypin	Kurt Wilhelm	Frances Aronson
Love Gifts Charles Traeger	Steven Schachter	Kevin Rupnik	Cynthia O'Neal	Craig Miller
The Price Arthur Miller	Eugene Lesser	Roger Mooney	Frances Fehr	Brian MacDevitt
Arsenic and Old Lace Joseph Kesselring	Charles Karchmer	John Falabella	Jess Goldstein	Jeff Davis

Philadelphia Festival Theatre for New Plays

CAROL ROCAMORA
Artistic/Producing Director

GREGORY G. ALEXANDER
Board Chairman

3700 Chestnut St.
Philadelphia, PA 19104
(215) 222-5000 (business)
(215) 898-6791 (box office)

FOUNDED 1982

SEASON
April–June

FACILITIES
Harold Prince Theatre, Annenberg Center
3680 Walnut St.
Seating capacity: 200
Stage: thrust

FINANCES
July 1, 1984–June 30, 1985
Operating expenses: $267,400

AUDIENCE
Annual attendance: 12,000
Subscribers: 1,906

AEA letter of agreement

PRODUCTIONS 1984

Productions	Directors	Sets	Costumes	Lights
Tandem: An Evening of Six One-Acts:				
Pros, Granvilette Williams	Lynn Thompson	Phil Graneto	Vickie McLaughlin	Curt Senie
Hattie's Dress, Walt Vail	Jan Silverman	Phil Graneto	Vickie McLaughlin	Curt Senie
Turbulence, Barbara Schneider	Walt Jones	Phil Graneto	Vickie McLaughlin	Curt Senie
Breakfast at the Track, Lanford Wilson	Walt Jones	Phil Graneto	Vickie McLaughlin	Curt Senie
6:15 on the 104, Elinor Jones	Walt Jones	Phil Graneto	Vickie McLaughlin	Curt Senie
Tandem, Fred Sirasky	Walt Jones	Phil Graneto	Vickie McLaughlin	Curt Senie
Douglas Robert Litz	David Rotenberg	Phil Graneto	Vickie McLaulin	Curt Senie
Burkie Bruce Graham	Lynn Thomson	Phil Graneto	Vickie McLaulin	Curt Senie
Why the Lord Came to Sand Mountain and *Soul of a Tree* Romulus Linney	Romulus Linney	Phil Graneto	Vickie McLaulin	Curt Senie

PRODUCTIONS 1985

Productions	Directors	Sets	Costumes	Lights
Side Effects Bayldone Coakley	Lynn Thomson	Eric Schaeffer	Vickie McLaughlin	Curt Senie
Split Decision Kevin Heelan	Michael Bloom	Eric Schaeffer	Vickie McLaughlin	Curt Senie
God's Attic John Erlanger	Charles Conwell	Eric Schaeffer	Vickie McLaughlin	Curt Senie
Sky Readers: An Evening of 5 One-Act Plays:				
Sky Readers, William Wise	Steve Kaplan	Eric Schaeffer	Vickie McLaughlin	Curt Senie
Smoke, Laurence Klavan	Steve Kaplan	Eric Schaeffer	Vickie McLaughlin	Curt Senie
Buck Fever, Bill Bozzone	Steve Kaplan	Eric Schaeffer	Vickie McLaughlin	Curt Senie
Strikes, Mark St. Germain	Jan Silverman	Eric Schaeffer	Vickie McLaughlin	Curt Senie
The Agreement, Janet Neipris	Julianne Boyd	Eric Schaeffer	Vickie McLaughlin	Curt Senie

Pioneer Memorial Theatre

CHARLES MOREY
Artistic Director

KEITH ENGAR
Executive Producer

DALE A. KIMBALL
Board Chairman

The University of Utah
Salt Lake City, UT 84112
(801) 581-7118 (business)
(801) 581-6961 (box office)

FOUNDED 1962
C. Lowell Lees, University of Utah,
   local citizens

SEASON
September–June

FACILITIES
Lees Main Stage
3rd South and University Sts.
Seating capacity: 1,000
Stage: proscenium

FINANCES
July 1, 1984–June 30, 1985
Operating expenses: $1,788,000

AUDIENCE
Annual attendance: 91,180
Subscribers: 10,111

TOURING CONTACT
Shirley Kilgore

*AEA University/Resident Theatre
   Association contract*

PRODUCTIONS 1983–84

Productions	Directors	Sets	Costumes	Lights
Barnum book: Mark Bramble; music: Cy Coleman; lyrics: Michael Stewart	Mary Porter Hall	George Maxwell	Elizabeth Novak	Peter L. Willardson
A Man for All Seasons Robert Bolt	William Glover	Ariel Ballif	Ariel Ballif	Richard J. Harris
Life with Father Howard Lindsay and Russel Crouse	Charles Morley	Richard J. Harris	Elizabeth Novak	Ingra Draper
Man of La Mancha book: Dale Wasserman; music: Mitch Leigh; lyrics: Joe Darion	Travis DeCastro	Ronald Crosby	George Maxwell	Peter J. Willardson
On Golden Pond Ernest Thompson	Jim Jansen	Steven Rubin	Callie Floor	Roger Marmaro
Peter Pan book: James M. Barrie; music: Mark Charlap and Jule Styne; lyrics: Carolyn Leigh, Betty Comden and Adolph Green	Peter Foy	Ronald Crosby	Claudia Boddy	Megan McCormick

---

PRODUCTIONS 1984–85

Productions	Directors	Sets	Costumes	Lights
The Music Man book, music and lyrics: Meredith Wilson	Jerry Grayson	Ronald Crosby	Elizabeth Novak	Peter L. Willardson
Amadeus Peter Shaffer	Charles Morey	Ariel Ballif	Elizabeth Novak	Peter L. Willardson
Harvey Mary Chase	Charles Morey	George Maxwell	David C. Paulin	Spencer Brown
Candide book adapt: Hugh Wheeler, from Voltaire; music: Leonard Bernstein; lyrics: Stephen Sondheim, Richard Wilbur and John LaTouche	Charles Karchmer	Ariel Ballif	Elizabeth Novak	Peter L. Willardson
A Raisin in the Sun Lorraine Hansberry	Marilyn Holt	George Maxwell	Kevin L. Alberts	Roger Marmaro
The Sound of Music book: Howard Lindsay and Russel Crouse; music: Richard Rodgers; lyrics: Oscar Hammerstein, II	John Fearnley	Ronald Crosby	David C. Paulin	Ingra Draper

---

Pittsburgh Public Theater

WILLIAM T. GARDNER
Producing Director

DAVID W. HUNTER
Board President

One Allegheny Sq.
Pittsburgh, PA 15212
(412) 323-8200 (business)
(412) 321-9800 (box office)

FOUNDED 1975
Joan Apt, Margaret Rieck, Ben
Shaktman

SEASON
September–June

FACILITIES
Seating capacity: 474
Stage: arena

FINANCES
September 1, 1984–August 31, 1985
Operating expenses: $2,175,000

AUDIENCE
Annual attendance: 102,300
Subscribers: 12,642

AEA LORT (C) contract

Note: During the 1983–84 season,
Larry Arrick served as artistic
director.

PRODUCTIONS 1983–84

Productions	Directors	Sets	Costumes	Lights
Hay Fever Noel Coward	Mel Shapiro	Cletus Anderson	Cletus Anderson	Kristine Bick
A History of the American Film Christopher Durang	Larry Arrick	Thomas A. Walsh	Merrily Murray-Walsh	Gary Mintz
K2 Patrick Meyers	Larry Arrick	Ursula Belden	Flozanne A. John	Robert Jared
Nora-Julie adapt: Ingmar Bergman, from Henrik Ibsen and August Strindberg	Larry Arrick	Sam Kirkpatrick	Elizabeth P. Palmer	Dennis Parichy
Waiting for Godot Samuel Beckett	Larry Arrick	Robert D. Soule	Flozanne A. John	Gary Mintz
The Dining Room A. R. Gurney, Jr.	Susan Einhorn	Bob Davidson	Maria Marrero	Victor En Yu Tan

---

PRODUCTIONS 1984–85

Productions	Directors	Sets	Costumes	Lights
'night, Mother Marsha Norman	Peter Bennett	Gary English	Flozanne A. John	Kirk Bookman
Misalliance George Bernard Shaw	Philip Minor	John Wright Stevens	Jeffrey Ullman	John Wright Stevens
Strange Snow Stephen Metcalfe	Susan Einhorn	Harry Feiner	Flozanne A. John	Ann Wrightson
Room Service John Murray and Allen Boretz	Larry Arrick	Ursula Belden	Susan Tsu	Kristine Bick
Becoming Memories Arthur Giron	Lee Sankowich	Harry Feiner	Flozanne A. John	Kirk Bookman
Private Lives Noel Coward	Philip Minor	Allen Cornell	Jeffrey Ullman	Ann Wrightson

Playhouse on the Square

JACKIE NICHOLS
Executive Director

PAUL LORMAND
Managing Director

NINO SHIPP
Board President

51 South Cooper St.
Memphis, TN 38104
(901) 725-0776 (business)
(901) 726-4656 (box office)

FOUNDED 1968
Jackie Nichols

SEASON
Year-round

FACILITIES
Playhouse on the Square
Seating capacity: 200
Stage: thrust

Circuit Playhouse
1705 Poplar Ave.
Seating capacity: 150
Stage: proscenium

FINANCES
July 1, 1984–June 30, 1985
Operating expenses: $335,000

AUDIENCE
Annual attendance: 45,000
Subscribers: 1,200

PRODUCTIONS 1983–84

Productions	Directors	Sets	Costumes	Lights
The Pirates of Penzance book: W. S. Gilbert; music: Arthur Sullivan	Cathey Crowell Sawyer	Craig Spain	John L. Board	Steve Forsyth
The Miracle Worker William Gibson	Cathey Crowell Sawyer	Jackie Nichols	John L. Board	Richard Crowell
The 1940's Radio Hour Walton Jones	Kimberly Dobbs	Susan Christensen	John L. Board	Betsy Cooprider
Black Coffee Agatha Christie	Michael McDonnell	Russell Smith	John L. Board	Steve Forsyth
Julius Caesar William Shakespeare	Cathey Crowell Sawyer	Mark Holder	David Jilg	Richard Crowell
Ain't Misbehavin' music and lyrics: Fats Waller, et al.; adapt: Richard Maltby, Jr.	Cathey Crowell Sawyer	Jackie Nichols	John L. Board	Tim Osteen

PRODUCTIONS 1984–85

Productions	Directors	Sets	Costumes	Lights
The Mikado book and lyrics: W.S. Gilbert; music: Arthur Sullivan	Robert Robinson	Jackie Nichols	Kris Hanley	Steve Forsyth
Hedda Gabler Henrik Ibsen	David Ostwald	Susan Christensen	Andrea Ames	Betsy Cooprider
Two by Two book: Peter Stone; music: Richard Rodgers; lyrics: Martin Charnin	Jamie Brown	Susan Christensen	Andrea Ames	Steve Forsyth
Coup/Clucks Jane Martin	Gene Wilkins	Jackie Nichols	Andrea Ames	Steve Forsyth
The Diary of Anne Frank Frances Goodrich and Albert Hackett	Anthony Isbell	Jackie Nichols	Andrea Ames	Steve Forsyth
A Day in Hollywood/A Night in the Ukraine book and lyrics: Dick Vosburgh; music: Frank Lazarus	Ken Zimmerman	Jackie Nichols	Andrea Ames	Steve Forsyth
The Dining Room A.R. Gurney, Jr.	Cathey Crowell Sawyer	James Owens	Catherine Coscarelly	Steve Forsyth

PlayMakers Repertory Company

DAVID HAMMOND
Artistic Director

JONATHAN L. GILES
Managing Director

MILLY S. BARRANGER
Executive Producer

203 Graham Memorial 052-A
University of North Carolina
Chapel Hill, NC 27514
(919) 962-1122 (business)
(919) 962-1121 (box office)

FOUNDED 1976
Arthur L. Houseman

SEASON
September–May

FACILITIES
Paul Green Theatre
Seating capacity: 503
Stage: thrust

PlayMakers Theatre
Seating capacity: 285
Stage: proscenium

FINANCES
July 1, 1984–June 30, 1985
Operating expenses: $421,615

AUDIENCE
Annual attendance: 52,011
Subscribers: 3,542

AEA LORT (D) contract

Note: During the 1983–84 and 1984–85 seasons, Gregory Boyd served as artistic director.

PRODUCTIONS 1983–84

Productions	Directors	Sets	Costumes	Lights
As You Like It William Shakespeare	Gregory Boyd	Linwood Taylor	Marianne Custer	Robert Jared
The Importance of Being Earnest Oscar Wilde	Douglas Johnson	Linwood Taylor	Bobbi Owen	Robert Jared
Travesties Tom Stoppard	Gregory Boyd	Linwood Taylor	Bobbi Owen	Robert Jared
Dracula: A Musical Nightmare book and lyrics: Douglas Johnson; music: John Aschenbrenner	Douglas Johnson	Nancy Thun	Bobbi Owen	Robert Jared

PRODUCTIONS 1984–85

Productions	Directors	Sets	Costumes	Lights
Three Guys Naked from the Waist Down book and lyrics: Jerry Colker; music: Michael Rupert	Andrew Cadiff	Clarke Dunham	Thomas McKinley	Ken Billington
Ring Round the Moon Jean Anouilh	Douglas Johnson	Linwood Taylor	Bobbi Owen	Bill Andrews
Our Town Thornton Wilder	Gregory Boyd	Linwood Taylor	Bobbi Owen	Charles Catotti
Measure for Measure William Shakespeare	Gregory Boyd	Linwood Taylor	Bobbi Owen	Robert Jared
Cloud 9 Caryl Churchill	Ben Cameron	Linwood Taylor	Deborah Newhall	Robert Jared
Curse of the Starving Class Sam Shepard	Gregory Boyd	Linwood Taylor	Laurel Clayson	Robert Jared
Cyrano de Bergerac Edmond Rostand	Gregory Boyd	Linwood Taylor	Bobbi Owen	Robert Jared

The Playwrights' Center

JOAN PATCHEN
Executive Director

SUSAN M. JACOB
Finance Manager

JEANNE KELLER
Board President

2301 Franklin Ave. East
Minneapolis, MN 55406
(612) 332-7481

FOUNDED 1971
Gregg Almquist, Erik Brogger, Barbara
Field, Charles Nolte

SEASON
Year-round

FACILITIES
Seating capacity: 150
Stage: flexible

FINANCES
July 1, 1984–June 30, 1985
Operating expenses: $283,000

AUDIENCE
Annual attendance: 80,000

TOURING CONTACT
Arthur J. Schwartz

AEA letter of agreement

Note: During the 1983–84 and 1984–85
seasons, Carolyn Bye served as
executive director.

PRODUCTIONS 1983–85

Productions	Directors	Sets	Costumes	Lights
Seasons strictly devoted to staged readings, workshops and touring.				

Playwrights Horizons

ANDRE BISHOP
Artistic Director

PAUL S. DANIELS
Executive Director

ANNE WILDER
Board Chairman

416 West 42nd St.
New York, NY 10036
(212) 564-1235 (business)
(212) 279-4200 (box office)

FOUNDED 1971
Robert Moss

SEASON
Year-round

FACILITIES
Mainstage
Seating capacity: 150
Stage: proscenium

Studio
Seating capacity: 74
Stage: flexible

FINANCES
September 1, 1983–August 31, 1984
Operating expenses: $3,500,000

AUDIENCE
Annual attendance: 170,000
Subscribers: 3,400

AEA Off Broadway contract

PRODUCTIONS 1983–84

Productions	Directors	Sets	Costumes	Lights
Baby with the Bathwater Christopher Durang	Jerry Zaks	Loren Sherman	Rita Ryack	Jennifer Tipton
Isn't It Romantic Wendy Wasserstein	Gerald Gutierrez	Andrew Jackness	Ann Emonts	James F. Ingalls
Fables for Friends Mark O'Donnell	Douglas Hughes	Christopher Nowak	Linda Fisher	David Noling

PRODUCTIONS 1983–84

Productions	Directors	Sets	Costumes	Lights
Terra Nova Ted Tally	Gerald Gutierrez	Douglas Stein	Ann Emonts	Paul Gallo
Elm Circle Mick Casale	Pamela Berlin	Bennet Averyt	Sheila McLamb	Bennet Averyt

PRODUCTIONS 1984–85

Productions	Directors	Sets	Costumes	Lights
Romance Language Peter Parnell	Sheldon Larry	Loren Sherman	Sheila McLamb	Jeff Davis

Life and Limb
  Keith Reddin
	Thomas Babe	John Arnone	David C.
			  Woolar
				Stephen
				  Strawbridge

4th Annual Young Playwrights Festival:
Field Day, Leslie Kaufman
	Don Scardino	Loren Sherman	Jennifer von
			  Mayrhauser
				Stephen
				  Strawbridge

Sonata, Elizabeth Hirschorn	Shelley Rattle	Loren Sherman	Jennifer von
			  Mayrhauser
				Stephen
				  Strawbridge

True to Life, Marc Ratcliff	Ben Levit	Loren Sherman	Jennifer von
			  Mayrhauser
				Stephen
				  Strawbridge

The Ground Zero Club, Charlie Schulman	John Ferraro	Loren Sherman	Jennifer von
			  Mayrhauser
				Stephen
				  Strawbridge

Fighting International Fat Jonathan Reynolds	David Trainer	Tony Straiges	Rita Ryack	Frances Aronson
Raw Youth Neal Bell	Amy Saltz	Tom Lynch	Kurt Wilhelm	Anne Wrightson

Portland Stage Company

BARBARA ROSOFF
Artistic Director

PATRICIA EGAN
Managing Director

PHILIP H. GRANTHAM
Board President

Box 1458
Portland, ME 04104
(207) 774-1043 (business)
(207) 774-0465 (box office)

FOUNDED 1974
Ted Davis

SEASON
November–April

FACILITIES
Portland Performing Arts Center
24A Forest Ave.
Seating capacity: 290
Stage: proscenium

FINANCES
June 1, 1984–May 31, 1985
Operating expenses: $523,700

AUDIENCE
Annual attendance: 37,800
Subscribers: 3,080

TOURING CONTACT
Matthew Bliss, Patricia Egan

BOOKED-IN EVENTS
Theatre

AEA letter of agreement

PRODUCTIONS 1983–84

Productions	Directors	Sets	Costumes	Lights
The Threepenny Opera book and lyrics: Bertolt Brecht; music: Kurt Weill; adapt: Marc Blitzstein	Barbara Rosoff	Maxine W. Klein	Martha Hally	Arden Fingerhut

Productions	Directors	Sets	Costumes	Lights
Crimes of the Heart Beth Henley	Lynn Polan	Leslie Taylor	Barbara Forbes	Jackie Manassee
Native American Constance Congdon	Barbara Rosoff	John Doepp	Martha Hally	Jackie Manassee
Fallen Angels Noel Coward	Ron Lagomarsino	Patricia Woodbridge	Hope Hanafin	Kevin Gallagher
Terra Nova Ted Tally	Barbara Rosoff and Arden Fingerhut	John Conklin	Martha Hally	Jackie Manassee
Madonna of the Powder Room Paul Cizmar	Barbara Rosoff	Patricia Woodbridge	Amanda Aldridge	Arden Fingerhut

PRODUCTIONS 1984-85

Productions	Directors	Sets	Costumes	Lights
The Portable Pioneer and Prairie Show book: David Chambers; music: Mel Marvin; lyrics: David Chambers and Mel Marvin	Stephen Zuckerman	James Bakkom	Martha Hally	Curt Osterman
Goodbye Freddy Elizabeth Diggs	Barbara Rosoff	Johniene Papandreas	Martha Hally	Jackie Manassee
Misalliance George Bernard Shaw	Art Wolff	Patricia Woodbridge	Kiki Smith	Arden Fingerhut
'night, Mother Marsha Norman	Arden Fingerhut	Laura Maurer	Deborah Shippee-O'Brien	Arden Fingerhut
Cloud 9 Caryl Churchill	Barbara Rosoff	George Tsypin	David Murin	Jeff Davis
The Member of the Wedding Carson McCullers	Wendy Chapin	John Doepp	Martha Hally	Jackie Manassee

Repertorio Español

RENE BUCH
Artistic Director

GILBERTO ZALDIVAR
Producer/Board President

138 East 27th St.
New York, NY 10016
(212) 889-2850

FOUNDED 1968
Gilberto Zaldivar, Rene Buch

SEASON
Year-round

FACILITIES
Gramercy Arts Theatre
Seating capacity: 140
Stage: proscenium

FINANCES
September 1, 1983–August 31, 1984
Operating expenses: $623,000

AUDIENCE
Annual attendance: 60,000

TOURING CONTACT
Gilberto Zaldivar

PRODUCTIONS 1983-84

Productions	Directors	Sets	Costumes	Lights
La Valija Julio Mauricio	Rene Buch	Robert Weber Federico	Robert Weber Federico	Robert Weber Federico
Cafe con Leche Gloria Gonzalez; trans: Rene Buch	Rene Buch	Robert Weber Federico	Robert Weber Federico	Robert Weber Federico

PRODUCTIONS 1983–84

Productions	Directors	Sets	Costumes	Lights
Habana Rene Buch and Pablo Zinger	Rene Buch	Robert Weber Federico	Robert Weber Federico	Robert Weber Federico
Dona Francisquita/La Discreta Enamorada book: Lope de Vega; music: Amadeo Vives; lyrics: Fernandez Shaw	Rene Buch	Robert Weber Federico	Robert Weber Federico	Robert Weber Federico
Bodas de Sangre Federico Garcia Lorca	Rene Buch	Robert Weber Federico	Robert Weber Federico	Robert Weber Federico
La Zapatera Prodigiosa Federico Garcia Lorca	Peter Wallace	Robert Weber Federico	Robert Weber Federico	Robert Weber Federico
El Dia Que Me Quieras Jose Ignacio Cabrujas	Rene Buch	Robert Weber Federico	Robert Weber Federico	Robert Weber Federico
Los Japoneses No Esperan Ricardo Talesnik	Ricardo Talesnik	Robert Weber Federico	Robert Weber Federico	Robert Weber Federico
A Secret Agravio Secreta Venganza Pedro Calderon de La Barca	Rene Buch	Robert Weber Federico	Robert Weber Federico	Robert Weber Federico

PRODUCTIONS 1984–85

Productions	Directors	Sets	Costumes	Lights
Habana Rene Buch and Pablo Zinger	Rene Buch	Robert Weber Federico	Robert Weber Federico	Robert Weber Federico
Puerto Rico: Encanto y Cancion Rene Buch and Pablo Zinger	Rene Buch	Robert Weber Federico	Robert Weber Federico	Robert Weber Federico
Dona Francisquita/La Discreta Enamorada book: Lope de Vega; music: Amadeo Vives; lyrics: Fernandez Shaw	Rene Buch	Robert Weber Federico	Robert Weber Federico	Robert Weber Federico
La Valija Julio Mauricio	Rene Buch	Robert Weber Federico	Robert Weber Federico	Robert Weber Federico
Bodas de Sangre Federico Garcia Lorca	Rene Buch	Robert Weber Federico	Robert Weber Federico	Robert Weber Federico
Cafe con Leche Gloria Gonzalez; trans: Rene Buch	Rene Buch	Robert Weber Federico	Robert Weber Federico	Robert Weber Federico
Luisa Fernanda book and lyrics: Fernandez Shaw and F. Romero; music: Moreno Torroba	Rene Buch	Robert Weber Federico	Robert Weber Federico	Robert Weber Federico
Acto Cultural Jose Ignacio Cabrujas	Rene Buch	Robert Weber Federico	Robert Weber Federico	Robert Weber Federico

The Repertory Theatre of St. Louis

DAVID CHAMBERS
Producing Director

STEVEN WOOLF
Managing Director

RUSSELL VANDENBROUCKE
Associate Producing Director

PETER H. BUNCE
Board Chairman

BOX 28030
St. Louis, MO 63119
(314) 968-7340 (business)
(314) 968-4925 (box office)

FOUNDED 1966
Webster College

SEASON
September–April

FACILITIES
130 Edgar Road
Mainstage
Seating capacity: 733
Stage: thrust

Studio Theatre
Seating capacity: 125
Stage: flexible

FINANCES
June 1, 1984–May 31, 1985
Operating expenses: $2,376,346

AUDIENCE
Annual attendance: 120,278
Subscribers: 12,630

TOURING CONTACT
Stuart M. Manewith

BOOKED-IN EVENTS
Theatre

*AEA LORT (B) and Theatre for Young
Audiences contracts*

PRODUCTIONS 1983–84

Productions	Directors	Sets	Costumes	Lights
The Glass Menagerie Tennessee Williams	Timothy Near	Carolyn Ross	Carolyn Ross	Max De Volder
The Dining Room A.R. Gurney, Jr.	Marita Woodruff	Dorothy Marshall	Dorothy Marshall	Peter E. Sargent
Tintypes Mary Kyte, Mel Marvin and Gary Pearle	Pamela Hunt	John Roslevich, Jr.	Dorothy Marshall	Peter E. Sargent
Sleuth Anthony Shaffer	Edward Stern	Carolyn Ross	Carolyn Ross	Max De Volder
Medea Euripides; adapt: Robinson Jeffers	Gregory Boyd	Tim Jozwick	Dorothy Marshall	Glenn Dunn
The Importance of Being Earnest Oscar Wilde	Ian Trigger	Carolyn Ross	Carolyn Ross	Peter E. Sargent
True West Sam Shepard	Timothy Near	Bill Schmiel	Michael Ganio	Max De Volder
The Unseen Hand and *Killer's Head* Sam Shepard	Milton R. Zoth	John Roslevich, Jr.	Bonnie J. Cutter	Glenn Dunn
Tongues/Savage Love Sam Shepard and Joseph Chaikin; music: William Uttley and Robert Debellis	Larry Lillo	Michael Ganio	Steven Epstein	Max De Volder
The Tortoise Wins by a Hare adapt: Kim A. Bozark	Wayne Salomon	Michael Ganio	Steve Epstein	
All the World's a Stage adapt: Kim A. Bozark	Wayne Salomon	Michael Ganio	Steve Epstein	

PRODUCTIONS 1984–85

Productions	Directors	Sets	Costumes	Lights
A Raisin in the Sun Lorraine Hansberry	Hal Scott	Bill Schmiel	Dorothy L. Marshall	Max De Volder
Master Harold . . . and the boys Athol Fugard	Jim O'Connor	Arthur Ridley	Arthur Ridley	Peter E. Sargent
The 1940's Radio Hour Walton Jones	John Going	John Roslevich, Jr.	Dorothy L. Marshall	Peter E. Sargent
Dial M for Murder Frederick Knott	Geoffrey Sherman	Tim Jozwick	Arthur Ridley	Max De Volder
The Price Arthur Miller	Edward Stern	John Ezell	Dorothy L. Marshall	Peter E. Sargent
The Comedy of Errors William Shakespeare	Geoffrey Sherman	Carolyn L. Ross	Dorothy L. Marshall	Glenn Dunn

PRODUCTIONS 1984–85

Productions	Directors	Sets	Costumes	Lights
Waiting for Godot Samuel Beckett	Milton R. Zoth	Tim Jozwick	Elizabeth Eisloffel	Max De Volder
Still Life Emily Mann	Fontaine Syer	Peggy Dupuy	Laura Hanson	Glenn Dunn
Annulla, An Autobiography Emily Mann	Timothy Near	Arthur Ridley	Arthur Ridley	Max De Volder
The Gift of the Magi and Other Holiday Tales adapt: Kim A. Bozark	Wayne Salomon	Larry Biedenstein	Gail Lamoreaux	
It's Greek to Me adapt: Kim A. Bozark	Wayne Salomon	Larry Biedenstein	Elizabeth Eisloffel	
Things That Go Bump in the Night adapt: Kim A. Bozark	Wayne Salomon	Larry Biedenstein	Elizabeth Eisloffel	

River Arts Repertory

LAWRENCE SACHAROW
Artistic Director

BRUCE ALLARDICE
General Manager

IRA JANOW
Board Chairman

361 West 36th St.
New York, NY 10018
(212) 736-2012

Byrdcliffe Theatre
Woodstock, NY 12498
(914) 679-2493 (business)
(914) 679-2100 (box office)

FOUNDED 1978
Lawrence Sacharow

SEASON
July–September

FACILITIES
Seating capacity: 150
Stage: flexible

FINANCES
April 1, 1984–March 31, 1985
Operating expenses: $85,937

AUDIENCE
Annual attendance: 5,000
Subscribers: 150

BOOKED-IN EVENTS
Theatre, music

AEA letter of agreement

PRODUCTIONS 1984

Productions	Directors	Sets	Costumes	Lights
Long Day's Journey into Night Eugene O'Neill	Lawrence Sacharow	Marek Dobrowolski	Marianne Powell-Parker	Joanna Schielke
Oh Dad, Poor Dad Mamma's Hung You in the Closet and I'm Feeling Sad Arthur Kopit	Rob Thirkield	Marek Dobrowolski	Marianne Powell-Parker	Joanna Schielke
A Country Doctor Len Jenkin	Lawrence Sacharow	Marek Dobrowolski	Marianne Powell-Parker	Joanna Schielke

PRODUCTIONS 1985

Productions	Directors	Sets	Costumes	Lights
The Seagull Anton Chekhov; trans: Jean-Claude van Itallie	Lawrence Sacharow	Marek Dobrowolski	Marianne Powell-Parker	Joanna Schielke
Saint's Day John Whiting	Rob Thirkield	Warren Jorgensen	Marianne Powell-Parker	Frances Aronson
Breaking Up Is Hard to Do Michael Cristofer	Michael Cristofer	Marek Dobrowolski	Marianne Powell-Parker	Frances Aronson

The Road Company

ROBERT H. LEONARD
Producing Director

NANCY FISCHMAN
Board President

Box 5278 EKS
Johnson City, TN 37603
(615) 926-7726

FOUNDED 1975
Robert H. Leonard

SEASON
December, April–May (resident);
  September–November, February–
  March (touring)

FACILITIES
Mountain Home Memorial Theater
Seating capacity: 672
Stage: proscenium

The Down Home
301 West Main St.
Seating capacity: 175
Stage: cabaret

FINANCES
July 1, 1984–June 30, 1985
Operating expenses: $59,922

AUDIENCE
Annual attendance: 27,000

TOURING CONTACT
Barbara McNeese

BOOKED-IN EVENTS
Theatre

PRODUCTIONS 1983–84

Productions	Directors	Sets	Costumes	Lights
One Potato, Two Rebecca Ranson	Bob Leonard	Parris Zirkenbach	company	Parris Zirkenbach
Gold Dust music: Jon Jory; lyrics: Jim Wann	Bob Leonard	Mike Russell	company	Bob Leonard

PRODUCTIONS 1984–85

Productions	Directors	Sets	Costumes	Lights
The Happy Ever After Margaret Baker	Bob Leonard	Don Evans	company	Bob Leonard
Blind Desire company-developed	Bob Leonard	Bob Leonard	Kelly R. Hill, Jr.	Bob Leonard
My Sister in This House Wendy Kesselman	Bob Leonard	George McAtee	Theresa D'Avignon	Bob Leonard
Edward David Torbett	Randy Buck	Bob Leonard	Christine Murdock	Bob Leonard
Adjoining Trances Randy Buck	Bob Leonard	Parris Zirkenbach	Debbie McClintock	Bob Leonard
Jacques Brel Is Alive and Well and Living in Paris adapt: Eric Blau and Mort Shuman; music and lyrics: Jacques Brel	Bob Leonard			

Roadside Theater

DUDLEY COCKE
Director

DONNA PORTERFIELD
Managing Director

PAT MARTIN
Board Chairman

Box 743
Whitesburg, KY 41858
(606) 633-0108

FOUNDED 1974
Don Baker

SEASON
Year-round

FACILITIES
Appalshop Theater
306 Madison St.
Seating capacity: 165
Stage: thrust

FINANCES
January 1, 1984–December 31, 1984
Operating expenses: $166,690

AUDIENCE
Annual attendance: 38,000

TOURING CONTACT
Jeff Hawkins

BOOKED-IN EVENTS
Theatre, music

PRODUCTIONS 1983–84

Productions	Directors	Sets	Costumes	Lights
Mountain Tales and Music company-adapt	company			Don Baker
Red Fox/Second Hangin' Don Baker and Dudley Cocke	Don Baker, Dudley Cocke and Michael Posnick			Don Baker
Brother Jack book: Don Baker and Ron Short; music: Ron Short	Don Baker and Dudley Cocke			Ron Short
South of the Mountain book and music: Ron Short	Dudley Cocke and Ron Short			Jeff Sergeant
In Ya Blood book and music: Jeff Hawkins	Jeff Hawkins			Jeff Sergeant and Melissa Reedy
Temptations Jeff Hawkins	Jeff Hawkins			

PRODUCTIONS 1984–85

Productions	Directors	Sets	Costumes	Lights
Mountain Tales and Music company-adapt	company			Don Baker
Red Fox/Second Hangin' Don Baker and Dudley Cocke	Don Baker, Dudley Cocke and Michael Posnick			Don Baker
Brother Jack book: Don Baker and Ron Short; music: Ron Short	Don Baker and Dudley Cocke			Ron Short
South of the Mountain book and music: Ron Short	Dudley Cocke and Ron Short			Jeff Sergeant

Round House Theatre

JERRY WHIDDON
Artistic Director

LINDA YOST
Arts Coordinator

12210 Bushey Dr.
Silver Spring, MD 20902
(301) 468-4172 (business)
(301) 468-4234 (box office)

FOUNDED 1978
June Allen, Montgomery County
  Department of Recreation

SEASON
October–June

FACILITIES
Seating capacity: 218
Stage: thrust

FINANCES
July 1, 1984–June 30, 1985
Operating expenses: $498,730

AUDIENCE
Annual attendance: 70,000
Subscribers: 2,300

TOURING CONTACT
Vicki Arnold

BOOKED-IN EVENTS
Theatre, children's theatre

AEA Guest Artist contract

Note: During the 1983-84 season,
  Jeffrey B. Davis served as artistic
  director.

PRODUCTIONS 1983–84

Productions	Directors	Sets	Costumes	Lights

The Petrified Forest
  Robert E. Sherwood
	Jeffrey B. Davis	Douglas A.
		  Cumming
			John K. Gabbert	Rosemary
				  Pardee-Holz

Loot
  Joe Orton; music: Roy Barber
	Kenneth M. Fox	Richard H.
		  Young
			Kate Cowart	Michael Kritzer

Antigone
  Sophocles; adapt: Dudley Fitts and Robert
  Fitzgerald
	Mark Jaster	Douglas A.
		  Cumming
			Kevin Reid	Richard H.
				  Young

When the Wind Blows
  Raymond Briggs
	Gillian Drake	Russell Metheny	Rosemary
			  Pardee-Holz
				Richard H.
				  Young

The Madwoman of Chaillot
  Jean Giraudoux
	Jeffrey B. Davis	Richard H.
		  Young
			Catherine Adair	Robert Graham
				  Small

PRODUCTIONS 1984–85

Productions	Directors	Sets	Costumes	Lights

Custer
  Robert Ingham; adapt: David Cromwell
	David Cromwell	Richard H.
		  Young
			Rosemary
			  Pardee-Holz
				Jane Williams

The Good Doctor
  Neil Simon
	Douglas A.
	  Cumming
		Ronald J. Olsen	Rosemary
			  Pardee-Holz
				Scott Bethke

Waiting for Godot
  Samuel Beckett; music: Roy Barber
	Douglas A.
	  Cumming
		Jane Williams	Cheryl Brand	Susan Munson

Rashomon
  adapt: Fay and Michael Kanin, from
  Ryunosuke Akutagawa
	Richard H.
	  Young
		Richard H.
		  Young
			Rosemary
			  Pardee-Holz
				Scott Bethke

The 1940's Radio Hour
  Walton Jones
	Jim Humphrey	Richard H.
		  Young
			Rosemary
			  Pardee-Holz
				Scott Bethke

The Salt Lake Acting Company

EDWARD J. GRYSKA
Artistic Director

DAVID KIRK CHAMBERS
Producing Director

LINDA KRUSE
Board President

168 West 500 North
Salt Lake City, UT 84103
(801) 363-0526 (business)
(801) 363-0525 (box office)

FOUNDED 1970
Edward J. Gryska

SEASON
September–June

FACILITIES
Seating capacity: 160
Stage: flexible

FINANCES
June 30, 1984–July 1, 1985
Operating expenses: $285,000

AUDIENCE
Annual attendance: 18,000
Subscribers: 756

PRODUCTIONS 1983–84

Productions	Directors	Sets	Costumes	Lights
Saturday's Voyeur: Roadshow '83 Nancy Borgenicht and Michael Buttars	Edward J. Gryska	Ladd Lambert	Jackie Cintura	Ladd Lambert
Women Behind Bars Tom Eyen	Edward J. Gryska	Ladd Lambert	T.L. Finn	Ladd Lambert
The Salmon Run David Kranes	David Kirk Chambers	Ladd Lambert	Gail McCulloch	Megan McCormick
Still Life Emily Mann	Molly Fowler	Steve Jolley	company	Steve Jolley
Cloud 9 Caryl Churchill	Edward J. Gryska	Ladd Lambert	Creative Costumes	Megan McCormick

PRODUCTIONS 1984–85

Productions	Directors	Sets	Costumes	Lights
Saturday's Voyeur: Roadshow '84 Nancy Borgenicht and Michael Buttars	Edward J. Gryska	Ladd Lambert	#1 Rags	Ladd Lambert
Pacific Overtures book: John Weidman; music and lyrics: Stephen Sondheim; additional material: Hugh Wheeler	Edward J. Gryska	Bill Beilke	T.L. Finn	Megan McCormick
Sister Mary Ignatius Explains It All for You Christopher Durang	Max Robinson	Ladd Lambert		Megan McCormick
Wave's Home for Hurtin' Tammies Gail Wronsky	David Kirk Chambers	Cory Dangerfield	Claudia Hellstrom	Megan McCormick
In a Coal Burning House Jeffrey Kinghorn	Edward J. Gryska	Ladd Lambert	Alice Reynolds	Peter Willardson
Fool for Love Sam Shepard	David Kirk Chambers	Cory Dangerfield		Gary Justesen

San Diego Repertory Theatre

SAM WOODHOUSE
Producing Director

DOUGLAS JACOBS
Artistic Director

JOHN M. McCANN
Managing Director

JENNIFER S. HANKINS
Board President

1620 Sixth Ave.
San Diego, CA 92101
(619) 231-3586 (business)
(619) 235-8025 (box office)

FOUNDED 1976
Sam Woodhouse, Douglas Jacobs

SEASON
April–December

FACILITIES
Lyceum Theatre
Broadway Place
Seating capacity: 570
Stage: thrust

Arena Space
Broadway Place
Seating capacity: 200
Stage: flexible

6th Avenue Playhouse
Seating capacity: 213
Stage: proscenium

FINANCES
July 1, 1984–June 30, 1985
Operating expenses: $825,000

AUDIENCE
Annual attendance: 74,000
Subscribers: 6,000

TOURING CONTACT
John M. McCann

BOOKED-IN EVENTS
Theatre, music, dance, performance
art

AEA letter of agreement

PRODUCTIONS 1984

Productions	Directors	Sets	Costumes	Lights
K2 Patrick Meyers	Andrew J. Traister	Dan Dryden	Mary Gibson	Steven B. Peterson
Beyond Therapy Christopher Durang	Walter Schoen	Dan Dryden	Mary Gibson	Nels Martin
The Tooth of Crime Sam Shepard	Sam Woodhouse	Roger L. Costello	Mary Gibson	Steven B. Peterson
Crimes of the Heart Beth Henley	Tavis Ross	Steven B. Peterson	Gordon J. Lusk	Steven B. Peterson
Ah, Wilderness! Eugene O'Neill	Douglas Jacobs	Dan Dryden	Mary Gibson	Steven B. Peterson
Long Day's Journey into Night Eugene O'Neill	Sam Woodhouse	Dan Dryden	Mary Gibson	Steven B. Peterson
A Christmas Carol adapt: Douglas Jacobs, from Charles Dickens; music: Jonathan Sacks and Linda Vickerman	Douglas Jacobs	Steven B. Peterson	Mary Gibson	Steven B. Peterson

PRODUCTIONS 1985

Productions	Directors	Sets	Costumes	Lights
The Time of Your Life William Saroyan	Sam Woodhouse	Mark Donnelly	Mary Gibson	Don Childs
Extremities William Mastrosimone	Sam Woodhouse	Don Childs	JoAnn Reeves	Don Childs
Woody Guthrie adapt: Tom Taylor, George Boyd and Michael Diamond, from Woody Guthrie	Bartlett Sher	William Anton and Bartlett Sher	Clare Henkel	Bartlett Sher
Cloud 9 Caryl Churchill	Sam Woodhouse	Nick Reid	Mary Gibson	Don Childs
Baby with the Bathwater Christopher Durang	Douglas Jacobs	Don Childs	Ingrid Helton	Don Childs

San Francisco Mime Troupe

COLLECTIVE LEADERSHIP

PETER SNIDER
Board President

855 Treat St.
San Francisco, CA 94110
(415) 285-1717

FOUNDED 1959
Ronnie Davis

SEASON
Year-round

FINANCES
January 1, 1984–December 31, 1984
Operating expenses: $408,000

AUDIENCE
Annual attendance: 75,000

TOURING CONTACT
Mason-Brune, Mariano & White

PRODUCTIONS 1984

Productions	Directors	Sets	Costumes	Lights
Steeltown book: Joan Holden; music and lyrics: Bruce Barthol and Ed Robledo	Arthur Holden	Alain Schons	Jennifer Telford	David Brune
1985 book: company-developed; music and lyrics: Bruce Barthol and Glen Appell	Brian Freeman	David Brune	Jennifer Telford	El Sol

PRODUCTIONS 1985

Productions	Directors	Sets	Costumes	Lights
Factwino—The Opera book: Joan Holden; music and lyrics: Bruce Barthol	Dan Chumley and Sharon Lockewood	Spain	Jennifer Telford	David Brune
Crossing Borders Steve Most, Michele Linfante and company; music: Ed Robledo; lyrics: Muzuki	Brian Freeman	David Brune and Rinaldo Iturrino	Jennifer Telford	El Sol
Steeltown book: Joan Holden; music and lyrics: Ed Robledo and Bruce Barthol	Arthur Holden	Alain Schons	Jennifer Telford	David Brune

San Jose Repertory Company

JAMES P. REBER
Executive Producer

DAVID LEMOS
Producing Director

ELAINE KNOERNSCHILD
Board President

Box 2399
San Jose, CA 95109-2399
(408) 294-7572

FOUNDED 1980
James P. Reber

SEASON
November–August

FACILITIES
Montgomery Theatre
291 South Market St.
Seating capacity: 500
Stage: proscenium

FINANCES
July 1, 1984–June 30, 1985
Operating expenses: $1,108,014

AUDIENCE
Annual attendance: 62,000
Subscribers: 7,500

AEA LORT (D) contract

PRODUCTIONS 1983–84

Productions	Directors	Sets	Costumes	Lights
The Dining Room A.R. Gurney, Jr.	David Lemos and Peter Buckley	David Lemos and Bill Breidenbach	Marcia Frederick	Barbara Du Bois
The Miracle Worker William Gibson	Tom Ramirez	Ken Holamon	Elizabeth Poindexter	James Brentano
How the Other Half Loves Alan Ayckbourn	Peter Nyberg	Dennis Howes	Barbara Bush	David Percival
Nuts Tom Topor	Peter Buckley	Vicki Smith	Sylvia Muzzio	Mickey White
The School for Scandal Richard Brinsley Sheridan	Julian Lopez-Morillas	Ken Holamon	Marcia Frederick	David Percival
The Tempest William Shakespeare	Dakin Matthews	Ariel Parkinson	Marcia Frederick	Barbara Du Bois
Yup! book: J. Stephen Coyle, David Lemos, Kathryn Nyomen, Roy Zimmerman, Kathryn Garcia; music and lyrics: Roy Zimmerman	David Lemos	David Lemos and Kevin Short	David Lemos	Joseph Driggs

---

PRODUCTIONS 1984–85

Productions	Directors	Sets	Costumes	Lights
What I Did Last Summer A.R. Gurney, Jr.	David Lemos	Vicki Smith	Marcia Frederick	Barbara Du Bois
The Servant of Two Masters Carlo Goldoni	Julian Lopez-Morillas	Ken Holamon	Marcia Frederick	Joseph Driggs
Extremities William Mastrosimone	Tom Ramirez	John B. Wilson	Frances Kenny	Barbara Du Bois
The Country Girl Clifford Odets	Joy Carlin	Ken Holamon	Hope Hanafin	Barbara Du Bois
To Gillian on Her 37th Birthday Michael Brady	David Lemos	Vicki Smith	Karen Mitchell	Kurt Landisman
Amadeus Peter Shaffer	Margaret Booker	Robert Dahlstrom	Marcia Frederick	Barbara Du Bois
Yup! book: J. Stephen Coyle, David Lemos, Kathryn Nyomen, Roy Zimmerman and Kathryn Garcia; music and lyrics: Roy Zimmerman	David Lemos	Steve Snyder	Karen Mitchell	Joseph Driggs
Execution of Justice Emily Mann	Anthony Taccone and Oskar Eustis	Vicki Smith	Eliza Chugg	Derek Duarte
Up the Yup! book, music and lyrics: Roy Zimmerman	David Lemos	Steve Snyder	Karen Mitchell	Joseph Driggs

---

Seattle Repertory Theatre

DANIEL SULLIVAN
Artistic Director

ROBERT L. KING, JR.
Board Chairman

155 Mercer St.
Seattle, WA 98109
(206) 443-2210 (business)
(206) 443-2222 (box office)

FOUNDED 1963
Bagley Wright

SEASON
October–May

FACILITIES
Bagley Wright Theatre
Seating capacity: 850
Stage: proscenium

PONCHO Forum
Seating capacity: 180
Stage: flexible

FINANCES
July 1, 1984–June 30, 1985
Operating expenses: $3,298,924

AUDIENCE
Annual attendance: 219,071
Subscribers: 22,901

TOURING CONTACT
Vito Zingarelli

BOOKED-IN EVENTS
Theatre, music

AEA LORT (B) contract

PRODUCTIONS 1983–84

Productions	Directors	Sets	Costumes	Lights
The Ballad of Soapy Smith Michael Weller; music: Norman Durkee	Robert Egan	Eugene Lee	Robert Blackman	Spencer Mosse
The Adventures of Huckleberry Finn adapt: James Hammerstein and Christopher Harbon, from Mark Twain; music: Ralph Affoumado	James Hammerstein	Robert Dahlstrom	Liz Covey	Arden Fingerhut
Make and Break Michael Frayn	Daniel Sullivan	Hugh Landwehr	Robert Wojewodski	Pat Collins
The Misanthrope Molière; trans: Richard Wilbur	Garland Wright	Paul Zalon	Kurt Wilhelm	Jennifer Tipton
Master Harold . . . and the boys Athol Fugard	Paul Weidner	Ralph Funicello	Sally Richardson	Robert Dahlstrom
As You Like It William Shakespeare; music: Kenneth Benshoof	Daniel Sullivan	Robert Dahlstrom	Kurt Wilhelm	Dennis Parichy

---

PRODUCTIONS 1984–85

Productions	Directors	Sets	Costumes	Lights
Our Town Thornton Wilder	Daniel Sullivan	Karen Gjelsteen	Robert Wojewodski	Pat Collins
Passion Play Peter Nichols	Douglas Hughes	Loren Sherman	Jess Goldstein	Dennis Parichy
I'm Not Rappaport Herb Gardner	Daniel Sullivan	Tony Walton	Robert Morgan	Allen Lee Hughes
The Mandrake Niccolo Machiavelli; adapt: Daniel Sullivan	Daniel Sullivan	Robert Dahlstrom	Kurt Wilhelm	James F. Ingalls, Jr.
The Wedding Bertolt Brecht; trans: Richard Nelson	Daniel Sullivan	Robert Dahlstrom	Kurt Wilhelm	James F. Ingalls, Jr.
'night, Mother Marsha Norman	Amy Saltz	Thomas M. Fichter	Sally Richardson	Robert Peterson
Guys and Dolls book: Jo Swerling and Abe Burrows; music and lyrics: Frank Loesser	Paul Giovanni	Kate Edmunds	Kurt Wilhelm	Dawn Chiang

---

The Second Stage

ROBYN GOODMAN
CAROLE ROTHMAN
Artistic Directors

ROSA I. VEGA
Managing Director

ANTHONY C.M. KISER
Board Chairman

Box 1807
Ansonia Station
New York, NY 10023
(212) 787-8302 (business)
(212) 873-6103 (box office)

FOUNDED 1979
Robyn Goodman, Carole Rothman

SEASON
November–June

FACILITIES
McGinn/Cazale Theatre
2162 Broadway
Seating capacity: 108
Stage: proscenium

FINANCES
July 1, 1984–June 30, 1985
Operating expenses: $460,000

AUDIENCE
Annual attendance: 10,331
Subscribers: 2200

AEA letter of agreement

PRODUCTIONS 1984

Productions	Directors	Sets	Costumes	Lights
Serenading Louie Lanford Wilson	John Tillinger	Loren Sherman	Clifford Capone	Richard Nelson
All Night Long John O'Keefe	Andre Gregory	Adrianne Lobel	Susan Hilferty	James F. Ingalls
Landscape of the Body John Guare	Gary Sinise	Loren Sherman	Jess Goldstein	Kevin Rigdon
Linda Her and the Fairy Garden Harry Kondoleon	Carole Rothman	Andrew Jackness	Mimi Maxmen	Frances Aronson

PRODUCTIONS 1985

Productions	Directors	Sets	Costumes	Lights
Short Eyes Miguel Piñero	Kevin Conway	David Jenkins	V. Jane Suttell	Marc B. Weiss
The Vienna Notes Richard Nelson	Carole Rothman	Andrew Jackness	Shay Cunliffe	Frances Aronson
Juno's Swans E. Katherine Kerr	Marsha Mason	Kate Edmunds	Ann Roth	Frances Aronson

Sister and Miss Lexie
  adapt: Brenda Currin and David Kaplan, from
  Eudora Welty
	David Kaplan	Susan Hilferty	Susan Hilferty	Ken Tabachnick

Shakespeare & Company

TINA PACKER
Artistic Director

ANN OLSON
General Manager

WALTER C. CLIFF
Board Chairman

The Mount
Lenox, MA 01240
(413) 637-1197 (business)
(413) 637-3353 (box office)

FOUNDED 1978
Tina Packer, Kristin Linklater, B.H.
   Barry, John Broome, Dennis
   Krausnick

SEASON
July–September

FACILITIES
Main Stage
Seating capacity: 500
Stage: outdoor

The Salon
Seating capacity: 60
Stage: arena

FINANCES
April 1, 1984–March 31, 1985
Operating expenses: $1,152,786

AUDIENCE
Annual attendance: 115,000

TOURING CONTACT
Eric Pourchot

*AEA LORT (C) and Theatre for Young
   Audiences contracts*

PRODUCTIONS 1983–84

Productions	Directors	Sets	Costumes	Lights
The Comedy of Errors William Shakespeare; music: Bruce Odland	Tina Packer	Bill Ballou	Kiki Smith	Bill Ballou
The Mount: A Turning Point Karen Shreefter	Charlene Bletson		Georgia Carney	

PRODUCTIONS 1984–85

Productions	Directors	Sets	Costumes	Lights
Romeo and Juliet William Shakespeare	Tina Packer and Dennis Krausnick	Bill Ballou	Kiki Smith	Bill Ballou
A Midsummer Night's Dream William Shakespeare	Tina Packer and Kevin Coleman	Bill Ballou	Kiki Smith	Bill Ballou
Edith Wharton: Songs from the Heart Mickey Friedman	Virginia Ness		Deborah Shaw	Thomas Dale Keever
The Custom of the Country Jane Stanton Hitchcock	Tina Packer	Mitz Pratt	Deborah Shaw	Thomas Dale Keever

Soho Repertory Theatre

JERRY ENGELBACH
MARLENE SWARTZ
Artistic Directors

80 Varick St.
New York, NY 10013
(212) 925-2588

FOUNDED 1975
Jerry Engelbach, Marlene Swartz

SEASON
January–June

FACILITIES
Greenwich House
27 Barrow St.
Seating capacity: 100
Stage: modified thrust

FINANCES
July 1, 1984–June 30, 1985
Operating expenses: $135,000

AUDIENCE
Annual attendance: 8,000
Subscribers: 800

BOOKED-IN EVENTS
Dance, music, video, performance art

AEA Funded Nonprofit Theatre code

PRODUCTIONS 1983–84

Productions	Directors	Sets	Costumes	Lights
Under the Gaslight Augustin Daly	Stephen Wyman	Robert E. Briggs	Martha Kelly	David Noling
Wood Painting Ingmar Bergman	Alan Wynroth		Donna Zakowski	Bruce A. Kraemer
Yes Is for a Very Young Man Gertrude Stein	Rob Barron	Dorian Vernacchio	Jeremy Stuart Fishberg	Bruce A. Kraemer
Bertha Kenneth Koch	Steven Brant		Stephanie Kerley	Bruce A. Kraemer
George Washington Crossing the Delaware Kenneth Koch	Steven Brant		Susan Kanaly	Bruce A. Kraemer
The Business of Good Government John Arden	Jerry Engelbach	Tarrant Smith	Mary L. Hayes	Heather Carson
Catchpenny Twist Stewart Parker; music: Shaun Davey	Marlene Swartz	Jerry Engelbach		Bruce A. Kraemer
The Dwarfs Harold Pinter	Jerry Engelbach	Joseph A. Varga	Steven L. Birnbaum	David Noling
Mandrake book adapt and lyrics: Michael Alfreds, from Niccolo Machiavelli; music: Anthony Bowles	Anthony Bowles	Bill Wolf	Paige Southard	David M. Shepherd
Lenz Mike Stott	Alma Becker			

PRODUCTIONS 1984–85

Productions	Directors	Sets	Costumes	Lights
The Crimes of Vautrin Nicholas Wright	Carol Corwen	Marek Dobrowolski	Marek Dobrowolski	Chaim Gitter
Energumen Mac Wellman	Rebecca Harrison	Felix E. Cochren	Gabriel Berry	Dan Kotlowitz
Almos' a Man book adapt, music and lyrics: Paris Barclay, from Richard Wright	Tazewell Thompson	Steve Saklad	Daniel Bolke	Steve Saklad
The Winter's Tale William Shakespeare	Anthony Bowles	Steve Saklad	Gabriel Berry	Dan Kotlowitz

---

South Coast Repertory

DAVID EMMES
MARTIN BENSON
Artistic Directors

TIMOTHY BRENNAN
General Manager

GEOFFREY L. STACK
Board President

Box 2197
Costa Mesa, CA 92628
(714) 957-2602 (business)
(714) 957-4033 (box office)

FOUNDED 1964
David Emmes, Martin Benson

SEASON
September–June

FACILITIES
655 Town Center Dr.
Mainstage
Seating capacity: 507
Stage: modified thrust

Second Stage
Seating capacity: 161
Stage: thrust

SCR Amphitheatre
Seating capacity: variable
Stage: outdoor amphitheatre

FINANCES
September 1, 1984–August 31, 1985
Operating expenses: $3,400,000

AUDIENCE
Annual attendance: 250,000
Subscribers: 22,300

TOURING CONTACT
Kris Hagen

AEA LORT (B) and (D) contracts

PRODUCTIONS 1983–84

Productions	Directors	Sets	Costumes	Lights
Amadeus Peter Shaffer	John Allison	Michael Devine	Martha Burke	Tom Ruzika
The Playboy of the Western World John Millington Synge	Martin Benson	Mark Donnelly	Barbara Cox	Cameron Harvey
Becoming Memories Arthur Giron	Martin Benson	Michael Devine	Louise Hayter	Greg Sullivan
Good C.P. Taylor	David Emmes	Ralph Funicello	Dwight Richard Odle	Tom Ruzika
The Seagull Anton Chekhov; trans: Jean-Claude van Itallie	Sharon Ott	Cliff Faulkner	Shigeru Yaji	Kent Dorsey
Angels Fall Lanford Wilson	Mary B. Robinson	Christopher Idoine	Martha Burke	Paulie Jenkins
A Christmas Carol adapt: Jerry Patch, from Charles Dickens	John-David Keller	Cliff Faulkner	Dwight Richard Odle	Tom Ruzika
Men's Singles D.B. Gilles	Paul Rudd	Mark Donnelly	Kim Simons	Paulie Jenkins
Christmas on Mars Harry Kondoleon	David Emmes	Dwight Richard Odle	Kim Simons	Liz Stillwell
Life and Limb Keith Reddin	Jules Aaron	Mark Donnelly	Barbara Cox	Paulie Jenkins
Sally and Marsha Sybille Pearson	Lee Shallat	Cliff Faulkner	Shigeru Yaji	Brian Gale
Bing and Walker James Paul Farrell	Martin Benson	John Ivo Gilles	Barbara Cox	Liz Stillwell

PRODUCTIONS 1984–85

Productions	Directors	Sets	Costumes	Lights
Saint Joan George Bernard Shaw	John Allison	Michael Devine	Noel Taylor	Tom Ruzika
The Gigli Concert Thomas Murphy	Martin Benson	Susan Tuohy	Barbara Cox	Cameron Harvey
The Show-Off George Kelly	Lee Shallat	Mark Donnelly	Shigeru Yaji	Peter Maradudin
The Importance of Being Earnest Oscar Wilde	David Emmes	Cliff Faulkner	Susan Dennison	Kent Dorsey
The Debutante Ball Beth Henley	Stephen Tobolowsky	Mark Donnelly	Robert Blackman	Tom Ruzika
Master Harold . . . and the boys Athol Fugard	Martin Benson	Cliff Faulkner	Dwight Richard Odle	Cameron Harvey

Productions	Directors	Sets	Costumes	Lights
A Christmas Carol adapt: Jerry Patch, from Charles Dickens	John-David Keller	Cliff Faulkner	Dwight Richard Odle	Tom and Donna Ruzika
Top Girls Caryl Churchill	David Emmes	Cliff Faulkner	Shigeru Yaji	Brian Gale
Shades David Epstein	John Frank Levey	Mark Donnelly	Deborah Slate	Paulie Jenkins
Reckless Craig Lucas	Jan Eliasberg	Cliff Faulkner	Barbara Cox	Tom Ruzika
Salt-Water Moon David French	Martin Benson	Michael Devine	Sylvia Moss	Peter Maradudin
Rum and Coke Keith Reddin	David Emmes	Cliff Faulkner	Susan Dennison	Peter Maradudin

Stage #1

JACK CLAY
Artistic Director

ERNEST E. FULTON
Managing Director

ANGUS G. WYNNE, III
Board President

Box 31607
Dallas, TX 75231
(214) 559-3754 (business)
(214) 824-2552 (box office)

FOUNDED 1979
Jack Clay

SEASON
September–May

FACILITIES
Greenville Avenue Theatre
2914 Greenville Ave.
Seating capacity: 97
Stage: modified proscenium

FINANCES
July 1, 1984–June 30, 1985
Operating expenses: $268,000

AUDIENCE
Annual attendance: 12,300
Subscribers: 600

AEA Small Professional Theatre contract

PRODUCTIONS 1983–84

Productions	Directors	Sets	Costumes	Lights
The Foreigner Larry Shue	Cynthia White	Roger Farkash	Karla Johnson	Tom Korder
Quilters book and lyrics: Molly Newman and Barbara Damashek; music: Barbara Damashek	Jenna Worthen	Roger Farkash	Sally Askins	Tom Korder
Mass Appeal Bill C. Davis	Jack Clay	Chris Rusch	Karla Johnson	Nancy Collings
Standing on My Knees John Olive	Patrick Kelly	Zak Herring	Karla Johnson	Zak Herring
Neutral Countries Barbara Field	David Buxton	Stephen Cowles	Karla Johnson	Dylan Thomas

PRODUCTIONS 1984–85

Productions	Directors	Sets	Costumes	Lights
Curse of the Starving Class Sam Shepard	David Bassuk	Chris Rusch	A. Dale Nally	Susan Takis

PRODUCTIONS 1984–85

Productions	Directors	Sets	Costumes	Lights
Native Speech Eric Overmyer	Cynthia White	Greg Matz	Ruth Fields and Daniela Maretka	Chris Rusch
Angels Fall Lanford Wilson	Patrick Kelly	Chris Rusch	Virginia Linn	Chris Rusch
Courtship and *Valentine's Day* Horton Foote	Jack Clay	Michael O'Sullivan	Rondi Hillstrom Davis	Wayne Lambert
K2 Patrick Meyers	Jenna Worthen	Roger Farkash	Valerie Jo Gruner and Neil Larson	David Opper

Stage One: The Louisville Children's Theatre

MOSES GOLDBERG
Producing Director

DEBRA HUMES
General Manager

BARBARA HOUSE
Board President

721 West Main St.
Louisville, KY 40202
(502) 589-5946 (business)
(502) 584-7777 (box office)

FOUNDED 1946
Sara Spencer, Ming Dick

SEASON
September–May

FACILITIES
Kentucky Center for the Arts: Bomhard Theater
#5 Riverfront Plaza
Seating capacity: 626
Stage: modified thrust

FINANCES
June 1, 1984–May 31, 1985
Operating expenses: $512,385

AUDIENCE
Annual attendance: 82,000
Subscribers: 2,000

TOURING CONTACT
Debra Humes

BOOKED-IN EVENTS
Dance, mime, puppetry

AEA Theatre for Young Audiences contract

PRODUCTIONS 1983–84

Productions	Directors	Sets	Costumes	Lights
Paul Bunyan Curt L. Tofteland	Curt L. Tofteland	Randal R. Cochran	Deborah A. Brothers	
The Glass Christmas Tree book and lyrics: Billy Ed Wheeler; music: Ewel Cornett	Moses Goldberg	Randal R. Cochran	Deborah A. Brothers	H. Charles Schmidt
Our Town Thornton Wilder	Moses Goldberg	Randal R. Cochran	Deborah A. Brothers	H. Charles Schmidt
The Wind in the Willows adapt: Moses Goldberg, from Kenneth Grahame	Moses Goldberg	Randal R. Cochran	Deborah A. Brothers	Randal R. Cochran
The Men's Cottage Moses Goldberg	Moses Goldberg	Deborah A. Brothers	Deborah A. Brothers	H. Charles Schmidt
Aladdin Moses Goldberg	Moses Goldberg	H. Charles Schmidt	Randal R. Cochran	H. Charles Schmidt
Boy Meets Girl Meets Shakespeare Curt L. Tofteland	Curt L. Tofteland			
Mark Twain Catherine Dezseran	Catherine Dezseran			

Productions	Directors	Sets	Costumes	Lights
Jack and the Beanstalk book: Curt L. Tofteland; music and lyrics: Lisa Palas	Curt L. Tofteland	Randal R. Cochran	Deborah A. Brothers	H. Charles Schmidt
Great Expectations adapt: Barbara Field, from Charles Dickens	Moses Goldberg	Randal R. Cochran	Deborah A. Brothers	Randal R. Cochran
Pinocchio Timothy Mason	Moses Goldberg	Randal R. Cochran	Deborah A. Brothers	H. Charles Schmidt
Snow White and the Seven Dwarfs company-adapt; music: Luigi Zaninelli	Nancy Staub	Deborah A. Brothers	Deborah A. Brothers	H. Charles Schmidt
Tom Sawyer book adapt: Richard Stockton, from Mark Twain; music: Sheldon Markham; lyrics: Annette Leisten	Curt L. Tofteland	Randal R. Cochran	Deborah A. Brothers	H. Charles Schmidt
The Brementown Musicians company-adapt; music: Lisa Palas	Moses Goldberg	Randal R. Cochran	Deborah A. Brothers	H. Charles Schmidt
Mother Hicks Susan Zeder	Moses Goldberg	Randal R. Cochran	Deborah A. Brothers	H. Charles Schmidt
Jesse Stuart's Kentucky Catherine Dezseran	Breton Frazier			
Boy Meets Girl Meets Shakespeare Curt L. Tofteland	Curt L. Tofteland			
Choices Catherine Dezseran	Catherine Dezseran and Moses Goldberg			

Stage West

JERRY RUSSELL
Artistic/Managing Director

DAVID B. KNAPP
Board President

Box 2587
Fort Worth, TX 76113
(817) 332-6265 (business)
(817) 332-6238 (box office)

FOUNDED 1979
Jerry Russell

SEASON
October–September

FACILITIES
Mainstage
821 West Vickery
Seating capacity: 149
Stage: thrust

FINANCES
October 1, 1983–Sept 30, 1984
Operating expenses: $252,630

AUDIENCE
Annual attendance: 18,456
Subscribers: 914

AEA Small Professional Theatre contract

PRODUCTIONS 1983–84

Productions	Directors	Sets	Costumes	Lights
Side by Side By Sondheim music and lyrics: Stephen Sondheim, et al.; adapt: Ned Sherrin	Jerry Russell	Mark Walker		Michael O'Brien
What the Butler Saw Joe Orton	Jerry Russell	Mark Walker	Jim Covault	Michael O'Brien
Equus Peter Shaffer	Jim Covault	Mark Walker		Michael O'Brien
The Importance of Being Earnest Oscar Wilde	Jerry Russell	Mark Walker	Jim Covault	Michael O'Brien

PRODUCTIONS 1983–84

Productions	Directors	Sets	Costumes	Lights
The Longest Running, Unproduced Production in the History of Broadway book: Ray Golden and Loretta Lottman; music and lyrics: Ray Golden	Jerry Russell	Michael Murray	Jim Covault	Michael O'Brien
The Dining Room A.R. Gurney, Jr.	Jim Covault	Mark Walker		Michael O'Brien

PRODUCTIONS 1984–85

Productions	Directors	Sets	Costumes	Lights
Once in a Lifetime George S. Kaufman and Moss Hart	Jerry Russell	Mark Walker	Jim Covault	Michael O'Brien
Alphabetical Order Michael Frayn	Jerry Russell	Mark Walker		Michael O'Brien
Chicago book: Fred Ebb and Bob Fosse; music: John Kander; lyrics: Fred Ebb	Jerry Russell	Mark Walker	Jim Covault	Michael O'Brien
Lone Star, and Laundry and Bourbon James McLure	Jerry Russell	Mark Walker		Michael O'Brien
Merrily We Roll Along book: George Furth; music and lyrics: Stephen Sondheim	Jerry Russell	J. Allen Brown	Jim Covault	Michael O'Brien
All My Sons Arthur Miller	Jim Covault	Mark Walker		Michael O'Brien

StageWest

GREGORY BOYD
Artistic Director

MARVIN WEAVER
Managing Director

JANE STEARNS
Board President

One Columbus Center
Springfield, MA 01103
(413) 781-4470 (business)
(413) 781-2340 (box office)

FOUNDED 1967
Stephen E. Hays

SEASON
October–May

FACILITIES
S. Brestley Blake Theatre
Seating capacity: 479
Stage: thrust

Winifred Arms Studio Theatre
Seating capacity: 120
Stage: flexible

FINANCES
July 1, 1984–June 30, 1985
Operating expenses: $1,420,000

AUDIENCE
Annual attendance: 105,000
Subscribers: 9,917

BOOKED-IN EVENTS
Theatre

AEA LORT (C) contract

Note: During the 1983–84 season, Stephen E. Hays served as producing director; during the 1984–85 season, Timothy Near served as artistic director.

PRODUCTIONS 1984–85

Productions	Directors	Sets	Costumes	Lights
The Miser Molière	Ron Lagomarsino	Jeffrey Struckman	Jeffrey Struckman	Barry Arnold
Candida George Bernard Shaw	Donald Hicken	Jeffrey Struckman	Bill Walker	Jeff Davis

PRODUCTIONS 1983-84

Productions	Directors	Sets	Costumes	Lights
Hannibal Blues Bernard Sabath	Thomas Gruenewald	James Leonard Joy	Mariann Verheyen	Barry Arnold
All My Sons Arthur Miller	Timothy Near	Tom Lynch	Jeffrey Struckman	Robert Jared
The Gin Game D.L. Coburn	Ted Weiant	Joseph W. Long	Georgia Carney	Joseph W. Long
Man with a Load of Mischief book: Ben Tarver; music: John Clifton; lyrics: Ben Tarver and John Clifton	Ted Weiant	Jeffrey Struckman	Jeffrey Struckman	Ned Hallick
The Unexpected Guest Agatha Christie	Timothy Near	Jane Clark	Jeffrey Struckman	Ned Hallick

PRODUCTIONS 1984-85

Productions	Directors	Sets	Costumes	Lights
The Rainmaker N. Richard Nash	Timothy Near	Jeffrey Struckman	Jeffrey Struckman	John Gisondi
True West Sam Shepard	James Milton	Jeffrey Struckman	Deborah Shaw	John Gisondi
Ain't Misbehavin' book adapt: Richard Maltby, Jr.; music and lyrics: Fats Waller, et al.	Murray Horwitz	Ron Placzek	Jeffrey Struckman	Jeremy Johnson
The Glass Menagerie Tennessee Williams	Timothy Near	Carolyn Ross	Jeffrey Struckman	Max De Volder
Master Harold . . . and the boys Athol Fugard	Jim O'Connor	Jeffrey Struckman	Kiki Smith	Frances Aronson
The Good Doctor Neil Simon	Stephen Katz	Richard Hoover	Jeffrey Struckman	John Gisondi
A Doll's House Henrik Ibsen; adapt: Kathleen Tolan; trans: Frank Hugus	Timothy Near	Jane Clark	Jeffrey Struckman	Max De Volder

Steppenwolf Theatre Company

GARY SINISE
Artistic Director

STEPHEN B. EICH
Managing Director

LARRY EDWARDS
Board President

2851 North Halsted St.
Chicago, IL 60657
(312) 472-4515 (business)
(312) 472-4141 (box office)

FOUNDED 1976
Terry Kinney, Jeff Perry and Gary
  Sinise

SEASON
September–July

FACILITIES
Steppenwolf Theatre Company
Seating capacity: 211
Stage: thrust

FINANCES
October 1, 1983–September 30, 1984
Operating expenses: $634,864

AUDIENCE
Annual attendance: 55,000
Subscribers: 3,029

*AEA Chicago Area Theatre contract and
  letter of agreement*

PRODUCTIONS 1983–84

Productions	Directors	Sets	Costumes	Lights
The Hothouse Harold Pinter	Jeff Perry	Louis DeCrescenzo	Wendy Oldenburg and Patti Minter	Louis DiCrescenzo
Our Town Thornton Wilder	Ralph Lane		Frank Vybiral	Louis DiCrescenzo
Tracers John DiFusco	Gary Sinise	Deb Gohr		Louis DiCrescenzo
Fool for Love Sam Shepard	Terry Kinney	Louis DeCrescenzo	Glenne Headly	Doug Gould

PRODUCTIONS 1984–85

Productions	Directors	Sets	Costumes	Lights
Stage Struck Simon Gray	Tom Irwin	Kevin Rigdon		Robert Christen
The Three Sisters Anton Chekhov; trans: Lanford Wilson	Austin Pendleton	Gary Baugh	Frank Vybiral	Michael Rourke
Orphans Lyle Kessler	Gary Sinise	Kevin Rigdon	Cookie Gluck	Kevin Rigdon
Coyote Ugly Lynn Siefert	John Malkovich	Kevin Rigdon	Erin Quigley	Kevin Rigdon
Miss Julie August Strindberg; trans: Everett Sprinchorn	James Dardenne	James Dardenne and Kevin Rigdon	Nan Cibula	Kevin Rigdon

The Street Theater

GRAY SMITH
Executive Director

GARY F. KRISS
Board Chairman

228 Fisher Ave.
White Plains, NY 10606
(914) 761-3307

FOUNDED 1970
Gray Smith

SEASON
July–August touring

FINANCES
June 1, 1984–May 31, 1985
Operating expenses: $162,991

AUDIENCE
Annual attendance: 11,000

TOURING CONTACT
Gray Smith

PRODUCTIONS 1983–84

Productions	Directors	Sets	Costumes	Lights

Playground
  company-developed
	Patricia Smith
	  and Sara
	  Rubin			

Workdreams
  adapt: Sara Rubin, from Studs Terkel
	Sara Rubin and
	  Patricia Smith			

PRODUCTIONS 1984–85

Productions	Directors	Sets	Costumes	Lights
Mom, the Brat, and Me Patricia Smith and company	Patricia Smith			

Monsters and Other Strangers
  Martin Henderson, Patricia Smith and
  company
	Martin
	  Henderson
	  and Patricia
	  Smith			

Studio Arena Theatre

DAVID FRANK
Artistic Director

RAYMOND BONNARD
Managing Director

RICHARD BEZEMER
Board President

710 Main St.
Buffalo, NY 14202
(716) 856-8025 (business)
(716) 856-5650 (box office)

FOUNDED 1965
Neal DuBrock

SEASON
September–May

FACILITIES
Seating capacity: 637
Stage: thrust

FINANCES
July 1, 1984–June 30, 1985
Operating expenses: $2,250,000

AUDIENCE
Annual attendance: 140,000
Subscribers: 12,000

BOOKED-IN EVENTS
Theatre

AEA LORT (B) contract

PRODUCTIONS 1983–84

Productions	Directors	Sets	Costumes	Lights
What I Did Last Summer A.R. Gurney, Jr.	David Frank	Patricia Woodbridge	Donna Langman	Robby Monk
Cabaret book: Joe Masteroff; music: John Kander; lyrics: Fred Ebb	Carl Shurr	Gary C. Eckhart	John Carver Sullivan	Robby Monk
Wait Until Dark Frederick Knott	Kathryn Long	Paul Wonsek	Janice I. Lines	Paul Wonsek
The Dresser Ronald Harwood	Geoffrey Sherman	Paul Wonsek	Mariann Verheyen	Michael Orris Watson
Terra Nova Ted Tally	Kathryn Long	John Scheffler	Catherine B. Reich	Robby Monk
Arms and the Man George Bernard Shaw	David Frank	Robert Morgan	Robert Morgan	Brett Thomas
A Place to Stay Richard Culliton	Ron Lagomarsino	Lowell Detweiler	Lowell Detweiler	Curt Osterman

PRODUCTIONS 1984–85

Productions	Directors	Sets	Costumes	Lights
A Midsummer Night's Dream William Shakespeare; music: Terrence Sherman	David Frank and Robert Morgan	Fred Duer	Lorraine Calvert and Mary Nemecek-Peterson	Brett Thomas
Dark of the Moon Howard Richardson and William Berney; music: Terrence Sherman	David Frank and Robert Morgan	Fred Duer	Catherine B. Reich	Brett Thomas
The Doom of Frankenstein Geoffrey Sherman and Paul Wonsek; music: Bob Volkman	Geoffrey Sherman	Paul Wonsek	Bill Walker	Paul Wonsek
Master Harold... and the boys Athol Fugard	Kathryn Long	David Potts	Janice I. Lines	Curt Ostermann
Anything Goes book: P.G. Wodehouse, Guy Bolton, Howard Lindsay and Russel Crouse; music and lyrics: Cole Porter	Carl Schurr	James Joy	John Carver Sullivan	Jeff Davis
I Ought to Be in Pictures Neil Simon	David Frank	Gary C. Eckhart	Janice I. Lines	Brett Thomas
The Glass Menagerie Tennessee Williams; music: Michael Valenti	Donald Driver	Philipp Jung	Janice I. Lines	Michael Orris Watson

Syracuse Stage

ARTHUR STORCH
Producing Artistic Director

JAMES A. CLARK
Managing Director

EDWARD W. McNEIL
Board Chairman

820 East Genesee St.
Syracuse, NY 13210
(315) 423-4008 (business)
(315) 423-3275 (box office)

FOUNDED 1974
Arthur Storch

SEASON
October–May

FACILITIES
John D. Archbold Theatre
Seating capacity: 510
Stage: proscenium

Experimental Theatre
Seating capacity: 202
Stage: proscenium

Daniel C. Sutton Pavilion
Seating capacity: 100
Stage: flexible

FINANCES
July 1, 1984–June 30, 1985
Operating expenses: $1,606,288

AUDIENCE
Annual attendance: 108,675
Subscribers: 9,833

TOURING CONTACT
Barbara Beckos

AEA LORT (C) contract

PRODUCTIONS 1983–84

Productions	Directors	Sets	Costumes	Lights
The Shadow of a Gunman Sean O'Casey	George Ferencz	John Doepp	Sally J. Lesser	Judy Rasmuson
The Show-Off George Kelly	William H. Putch	James M. Fouchard	Arnold S. Levine	Judy Rasmuson
Cyrano de Bergerac Edmond Rostand; adapt: Emily Frankel	Arthur Storch	Victor A. Becker	Jennifer von Mayrhauser	Michael Newton-Brown
'night, Mother Marsha Norman	Claudia Weill	John Doepp	Davelle E. DeMarco	William T. Patton
The Dining Room A.R. Gurney, Jr.	Susan Einhorn	Bob Davidson	Maria Marrero	Victor En Yu Tan
The Double Bass Patrick Suskind	Arthur Storch	Charles Cosler	Maria Marrero	F. Mitchell Dana

PRODUCTIONS 1984–85

Productions	Directors	Sets	Costumes	Lights
Arms and the Man George Bernard Shaw	Arthur Storch	John Doepp	Arnold S. Levine	Gregg Marriner
Clarence Booth Tarkington	Arthur Storch	John Doepp	Arnold S. Levine	Gregg Marriner
Handy Dandy William Gibson	Arthur Storch	Victor A. Becker	Maria Marrero	Judy Rasmuson
Shepard Sets: *Angel City, Suicide in B-flat* and *Back Bog Beast Bait* Sam Shepard; music: Max Roach	George Ferencz	Bill Stabile	Sally J. Lesser	Blu
A Lesson from Aloes Athol Fugard	Josephine R. Abady	David Potts	Carol Kunz	Ann Wrightson
Passion Peter Nichols	Terry Schreiber	Charles Cosler	Maria Marrero	Craig Miller

Tacoma Actors Guild

RICK TUTOR
Artistic Director

RUTH KORS
Managing Director

WILLIAM BECVAR
Associate Artistic Director

KATE HAAS
Board President

1323 South Yakima Ave.
Tacoma, WA 98405
(206) 272-3107 (business)
(206) 272-2145 (box office)

FOUNDED 1978
Rick Tutor, William Becvar

SEASON
October–March (Mainstage); June–
August (Ft. Worden)

FACILITIES
Tacoma Actors Guild
Seating capacity: 298
Stage: flexible

TAG at Ft. Worden
Pt. Townsend, WA
Seating capacity: 275
Stage: modified proscenium

FINANCES
July 1, 1984–June 30, 1985
Operating expenses: $639,094

AUDIENCE
Annual attendance: 40,990
Subscribers: 4,877

BOOKED-IN EVENTS
Children's theatre, storytelling

AEA LORT (D) contract

PRODUCTIONS 1983–84

Productions	Directors	Sets	Costumes	Lights
How the Other Half Loves Alan Ayckbourn	Robert Robinson	Bruce Jackson, Jr.	Leslie Simpson	J. Patrick Elmer
The Glass Menagerie Tennessee Williams	Rick Tutor	Karen Gjelsteen	Julie James	J. Patrick Elmer
The 1940s Radio Hour Walton Jones	Rick Tutor	Stephen Packard	Rose Pederson	William C. Strock
A Raisin in the Sun Lorraine Hansberry	William Becvar	Stephen Packard	Leslie Simpson	William C. Strock
The Incredible Murder of Cardinal Tosca Alden Nowlan and Walter Learning	Richard Owen Geer	Jennifer Lupton	Sally Richardson	James Verdery
Mass Appeal Bill C. Davis	Rick Tutor	Scott Weldin	Rose Pederson	J. Patrick Elmer

PRODUCTIONS 1984–85

Productions	Directors	Sets	Costumes	Lights
The Rainmaker N. Richard Nash	Rick Tutor	Silas Morse	Rose Pederson	J. Patrick Elmer
Stage Struck Simon Gray	Rick Tutor	Stephen Packard	Anne Thaxter Watson	J. Patrick Elmer
Season's Greetings Alan Ayckbourn	Robert Robinson	Jennifer Lupton	Rose Pederson	James Verdery
Splittin' Hairs Rebecca Wells	Rick Tutor	Bill Forrester	Rose Pederson	J. Patrick Elmer
84 Charing Cross Road adapt: James Roose Evans, from Helen Hanff	William Becvar	Bill Forrester	Rose Pederson	Claudia Gallagher
Dracula adapt: Richard Sharp, from Bram Stoker; music: Todd Barton	Richard Owen Geer	Bruce Jackson	Sarah Campbell	James Verdery

The Theater at Monmouth

RICHARD SEWELL
Artistic Director

KATE PENNINGTON
Managing Director

MARJORIE L. SEWELL
Board President

Box 385
Cumston Hall
Monmouth, ME 04259
(207) 933-4371 (business)
(207) 933-2952 (box office)

FOUNDED 1970
Richard Sewell, Robert Joyce

SEASON
May–October

FACILITIES
Cumston Hall
Main St.
Seating capaicity: 249
Stage: thrust

FINANCES
January 1, 1984–December 31, 1984
Operating expenses: $137,375

AUDIENCE
Annual attendance: 18,000
Subscribers: 750

TOURING CONTACT
Kate Pennington

BOOKED-IN EVENTS
Children's theatre, music

AEA Small Professional Theatre contract

PRODUCTIONS 1984

Productions	Directors	Sets	Costumes	Lights
A Midsummer Night's Dream William Shakespeare; adapt Richard Sewell	Richard Sewell	Richard Sewell	Richard Sewell	Richard Sewell
The Comedy of Errors William Shakespeare	Ted Davis	Raymond Pellerin	Deborah Shippee-O'Brien	Elizabeth Townsend
Twelfth Night William Shakespeare	Richard Sewell	Raymond Pellerin	Deborah Shippee-O'Brien	Elizabeth Townsend
Hamlet William Shakespeare	Richard Sewell	Raymond Pellerin	Hillary Derby	Elizabeth Townsend
Cyrano de Bergerac Edmond Rostand	Ted Davis	Raymond Pellerin	Hillary Derby	Elizabeth Townsend
Ruckus at Machias Richard Sewell	Richard Sewell	Raymond Pellerin	Deborah Shippee-O'Brien	Elizabeth Townsend

PRODUCTIONS 1985

Productions	Directors	Sets	Costumes	Lights
Jane Eyre adapt: Ted Davis, from Charlotte Bronte	Ted Davis	Richard Sewell	Hillary Derby	David Kaye
The Importance of Being Earnest Oscar Wilde	Richard Sewell	Richard Sewell	Hillary Derby	David Kaye
The Doctor in Spite of Himself Molière	Richard Sewell	Richard Sewell	Hillary Derby	David Kaye
The Rivals Richard Brinsley Sheridan	Ted Davis	Richard Sewell	Hillary Derby	David Kaye
The Tempest William Shakespeare	Richard Sewell	Richard Sewell	Hillary Derby	David Kaye
Twelfth Night William Shakespeare; adapt: Richard Sewell	Richard Sewell	Richard Sewell	Deborah Shippee-O'Brien	

Theatre by the Sea

TOM CELLI
Artistic Director

JANET WADE
Managing Director

ANNE HUGHES
Board President

Box 927
Portsmouth, NH 03801
(603) 431-5846 (business)
(603) 431-6660 (box office)

FOUNDED 1964
Pat and C. Stanley Flower

SEASON
October–May

FACILITIES
125 Bow St.
Seating capacity: 263
Stage: thrust

FINANCES
June 1, 1984–May 31, 1985
Operating expenses: $979,856

AUDIENCE
Annual attendance: 72,000
Subscribers: 4,914

BOOKED-IN EVENTS
Children's theatre, music, dance,
puppetry

AEA LORT (C) contract

PRODUCTIONS 1983–84

Productions	Directors	Sets	Costumes	Lights
Passion of Dracula Bob Hall and David Richmond	Tom Celli	Bob Phillips	Kathie Iannicelli	David Weiss
The Diary of Anne Frank Frances Goodrich and Albert Hackett	Peter Bennett	Kathie Iannicelli	Kathie Iannicelli	Michael Orris Watson

She Loves Me
  book: Joe Masteroff; music; Jerry Bock; lyrics:
  Sheldon Harnick
	Derek Wolshonak	Mark Pirolo	Kathie Iannicelli	David Weiss

Equus Peter Shaffer	John Fogle	Mark Pirolo	Mark Pirolo	Michael Orris Watson
Good Evening Peter Cooke and Dudley Moore	Malcolm Morrison	Kathie Iannicelli	Kathie Iannicelli	Harry Sangmeister
Betrayal Harold Pinter	Richard E. Hughes	Bob Phillips	Alice Fogel	Harry Sangmeister

Stop the World, I Want to Get Off
  book, music and lyrics: Leslie Bricusse and
  Anthony Newley
	John Montgomery	Kathie Iannicelli	Kathie Iannicelli	Harry Sangmeister

PRODUCTIONS 1984–85

Productions	Directors	Sets	Costumes	Lights

Ain't Misbehavin'
  book: Murray Horwitz and Richard Maltby, Jr.;
  music and lyrics: Fats Waller, et al.
	John Montgomery	Jack Doepp	Susie Smith	David Lockner

The Imaginary Invalid Molière; adapt: Henri van Laun	Larry Carpenter	Gary English	Barbara Forbes	David Lockner
A Christmas Carol adapt: Peter DeLaurier, from Charles Dickens	Peter DeLaurier	Kathie Iannicelli	Kathie Iannicelli	David Weiss
Agnes of God John Pielmeier	Richard E. Hughes	Mark Pirolo	Lisa Micheels	Michael Orris Watson
Painting Churches Tina Howe	Tom Celli	Gary English	Lisa Micheels	David Lockner
Fool for Love Sam Shepard	Peter Bennett	James P. Murphy	Lisa Micheels	Charles Greenwood
You Can't Take It with You Moss Hart and George S. Kaufman	Tom Celli	Mark Pirolo	Lisa Micheels	Charles Greenwood

Theater for the New City

GEORGE BARTENIEFF
CRYSTAL FIELD
Artistic Directors

HARVEY SEIFTER
Managing Director

SHEILA KEENAN
Administrator

162 Second Ave.
New York, NY 10003
(212) 254-1109

FOUNDED 1970
George Bartenieff, Crystal Field,
   Lawrence Kornfeld, Theo Barnes

SEASON
Year-round

FACILITIES
Cino Theater
Seating capacity: 150
Stage: proscenium

Waring Theater
Seating capacity: 99
Stage: flexible

Stanley Theater
Seating capacity: 50
Stage: flexible

FINANCES
July 1, 1984–June 30, 1985
Operating expenses: $360,000

AUDIENCE
Annual attendance: 60,000

TOURING CONTACT
Sheila Keenan

BOOKED-IN EVENTS
Theatre, music, dance

AEA Showcase code

PRODUCTIONS 1983–84

Productions	Directors	Sets	Costumes	Lights
Self Crystal Field	Crystal Field	Tony Angel	Edmund Felix	
Flo and Max Toby Armour	Aileen Passloff			
Iris Charles Choset	Lee Alan Morrow			
That's How I Was Toilet Trained Donald Kavares	Larry Locke			
The Inferno Susan Mosakowski	Susan Mosakowski			
Puzzles Argenta	Norman Briski			
Eden to Armageddon Walter Corwin	Dale Engele	Tony Angel		
The Dreamkeeper Speaks John Patterson	John Patterson			
Speech Avram Pratt	Avram Pratt			
Mud Maria Irene Fornes	Maria Irene Fornes		Gabrielle Berry	Anne Militello
Success and Succession Ronald Tavel	Michael Hillyer			Craig Kennedy
Hollywood Hell Michael Musto	John Albano			
Art Follows Reality Daryl Chin	John Albano			
The Martha Play Patricia Coby	Saskia Hegt			
Kareer Suicide Stephen Holt	Bob Plunkett			
Delicate Feelings Rosalyn Drexler	George Ferencz	Bill Stabile		Blu
Sticky Buns Bloolips	Bette Bourne			
The Panel Kenneth Bernard	John Albano			
Pow Wow and Dance Concert The Thunderbird American Indian Dancers	Louis Mossie			
Greek Fire Rod Faber	Jacques Schwat			
Tropical Fever in Key West Robert Heide	Sebastian Stuart			

PRODUCTIONS 1983–84

Productions	Directors	Sets	Costumes	Lights
Realism in Our Time Daryl Chin	Larry Qualls			
Play with an Ending Kenneth Bernard	John Vaccaro			
Zones of the Spirit Amlin Gray	Sharon Ott			
Afamis Notes H.M. Koutoukas	Crystal Field			
Disco is Just a Fad, But the Party Lasts Forever Rome Neal	Rome Neal			
On That Day Ralph Pezzullo	Linda Chapman			
Positions Herbert Leibman	Valeria Wasilewski			
The Last of Hitler Joan Schenkar	Joan Schenkar			
The Story Behind the Twentieth Century Bruce Mulholland	Bruce Mulholland			
Journey Into Happiness Franz Xaver Kroetz	Achim Nowack			
Without Heroes Alice Eva Cohen	Karen Ludwig			
Death in the Organization David Schanker	Harvey Seifter			
Stuff As Dream Fred Curchak	Fred Curchak			
Nostalgia for the Future steve ben israel	steve ben israel			
Flowers That Bloom Mimi Stern-Wolf	Mimi Stern-Wolf			
Clown Shorts Jan Greenfield	Jan Greenfield			

PRODUCTIONS 1984–85

Productions	Directors	Sets	Costumes	Lights
Hamletmachine Heiner Müller	Uwe Mengel	Jody Culkin		
The Conduct of Life Maria Irene Fornes	Maria Irene Fornes	Tim Baumgartner	Sally J. Lesser	Anne Militello
My Foetus Lived on Amboy Street Ronald Tavel	Ronald Tavel	Ronald Kajiwara	Jane Aire	Craig Kennedy
Smoking Newports and Eating French Fries Sebastian Stuart	Sebastian Stuart	Randy Benjamin	Russ Morrison	Anne Militello
Fever of Unknown Origin Stephen Holt	Martin Worman	Robert Croonquist		
Act and the Actor Daryl Chin	Daryl Chin and Larry Qualls	Larry Qualls		
On the Lam Georg Osterman	John Albano	Bill Wolf		
The Tree Artist book: Rosalyn Drexler; music: David Tice	Crystal Field	John Paino and Jo Anne Basinger	Edmond Felix	Craig Kennedy
Transients Welcome Rosalyn Drexler	John Vaccaro		Tavia Ito	
Walden book: Henry David Thoreau; music: Charles Choset	Roger Sullivan	Frank Shifreen		Harry Rubeck
The Wits of the Court Beauties Terry Talley	Lester Malizia	Jeffrey Wallach		
The Flats Ray Dobbins	John Stolzberg	Scott Caywood		Manny Cavaco
Everywoman Walter Corwin	Walter Corwin	Tony Angel	Bosa Washburn	Robert M. Sudderth
The Major General's Memoirs William Russell	Lawrence Sacharow	Warren Jorgenson	Marianne Powell-Parker	Vivien Leone
We Shall Not All Sleep Jamie Leo	Jamie Leo			

Productions	Directors	Sets	Costumes	Lights
From Behind the Moon Ralph Pezzullo	Linda Chapman	John Paino		Manny Cavaco
In Between Bina Sharif	Bina Sharif			
Songs from the Sea Harvey Perr	Harvey Perr			
The Grandpa Chronicle Robert Morris	Robin Saex	David Birn		Nancy Collings

Marsyas
    Timothy Flannery
	Timothy
	    Flannery
		Jo Anne
		    Basinger		

Scrapers in the Sky
    Elie Pressmann
	Harvey
	    Pressmann
				Alvin Ho

Theatre IV

BRUCE MILLER
Artistic Director

PHIL WHITEWAY
Managing Director

JANE ROSENTHAL
Board Chairman

6 North Robinson St.
Richmond, VA 23220
(804) 353-1048 (business)
(804) 359-0498 (box office)

FOUNDED 1975
Bruce Miller, Phil Whiteway

SEASON
October–May

FACILITIES
Theatre at First Church
3000 Grove Ave.
Seating capacity: 80
Stage: thrust

Broad Street Theatre
5410 Broad St.
Seating capacity: 500
Stage: proscenium

FINANCES
July 1, 1984–June 30, 1985
Operating expenses: $507,354

AUDIENCE
Annual attendance: 241,250
Subscribers: 3,434

TOURING CONTACT
Ford Flannagan

AEA Guest Artist contract

Productions	Directors	Sets	Costumes	Lights
Do Lord Remember Me James de Jongh	Bruce Miller	Bruce Miller	John Glenn	Bill Jenkins
Children of a Lesser God Mark Medoff	Bruce Miller	Terrie Powers	John Glenn	Bill Jenkins
The Shadow Box Michael Cristofer	W.R. Hutchinson	Terrie Powers	John Glenn	Bill Jenkins
I'm Getting My Act Together and Taking It on the Road book and lyrics: Gretchen Cryer; music: Nancy Ford	John Glenn	Terrie Powers	Blair Rochester	Bill Jenkins
The Emperor's New Clothes book, music and lyrics: Judy Bain and Bill Roper	John Glenn	Blair Rochester	Kathryn Szari	

Santa's Enchanted Workshop
    book, music and lyrics: Richard Giersch
	Bruce Miller	Terrie Powers	Joan V.
			    Brumbach	

The Shoemaker and the Elves
    book and lyrics: Bruce Miller; music: Richard Giersch
	Bruce Miller	Terrie Powers	Joan V.
			    Brumbach	

PRODUCTIONS 1983–84

Productions	Directors	Sets	Costumes	Lights
Beauty and the Beast book and lyrics: Blair Rochester; music: Richard Giersch	Bruce Miller	Bruce Miller	John Glenn	
Hugs and Kisses book and lyrics: Bruce Miller and Terry Bliss; music: Richard Giersch	Bruce Miller	Terrie Powers	John Glenn	
The Jamestown Story book and lyrics: Ford Flannagan; music: K. Strong	Ford Flannagan	Terrie Powers	Cheryl Craddock	
Bound for Freedom book and lyrics: Bruce Miller; music: traditional	John Glenn	Terrie Powers	John Glenn	

PRODUCTIONS 1984–85

Productions	Directors	Sets	Costumes	Lights
Equus Peter Shaffer	Bruce Miller	Terrie Powers	Ann McDow and Terrie Powers	Bill Jenkins
To Gillian on Her 37th Birthday Michael Brady	John Glenn	Terrie Powers	Blair Rochester	Bill Jenkins
Bosoms and Neglect John Guare	Kenneth Campbell	Terrie Powers	John Glenn	Bill Jenkins
The Diviners Jim Leonard, Jr.	Gary C. Hopper	Terrie Powers	Elizabeth Weiss Hopper	Bill Jenkins
The Family Richard Kinter	Bev Appleton	Terrie Powers	Regi Clemon	Bill Jenkins
A Little Night Music book: Hugh Wheeler; music and lyrics: Stephen Sondheim	Bruce Miller	Ann E. Gumpper	Tom Hammond	Bill Jenkins
Charley and the Pirates book and lyrics: Jody Smith; music: Ron Barnett	Bruce Miller	Terrie Powers	Kathryn Szari	
Santa's Christmas Miracle book, music and lyrics: Richard Giersch	John Glenn	Terrie Powers	Joan V. Brumbach	
Babes in Toyland book: Bruce Miller; lyrics: Glen McDonnough; music: Victor Herbert	Bruce Miller	Terrie Powers	Kathryn Szari	
Snow White and the Seven Dwarfs book and lyrics: Ford Flannagan; music: David Montgomery	John Glenn	Terrie Powers	John Glenn	
The Ugly Duckling book, music and lyrics: Richard Giersch	Ford Flannagan	Terrie Powers	John Glenn	
Hugs and Kisses book and lyrics: Bruce Miller and Terry Bliss; music: Richard Giersch	Bruce Miller	Terrie Powers	John Glenn	
First Ladies book and lyrics: Drina Kay and Doug Jones; music: Carol Gulley	John Glenn	Terrie Powers	John Glenn	
Booker T. book and lyrics: Lenny Brisendine; music: Carol Gulley	John Glenn	Terrie Powers	John Glenn	
Shake Hands with Shakespeare Bruce Miller	Bruce Miller	Terrie Powers	John Glenn	

Theater of the Open Eye

JEAN ERDMAN
Producing Artistic Director

AMIE BROCKWAY
Artistic Director

RICHARD HEEGER
Managing Director

DAN BERKOWITZ
Board President

270 West 89th St.
New York, NY 10024
(212) 769-4141 (business)
(212) 769-4142 (box office)

FOUNDED 1972
Jean Erdman, Joseph Campbell

SEASON
October–June

FACILITIES
Mainstage
Seating capacity: 120
Stage: modified proscenium

FINANCES
July 1, 1984–June 30, 1985
Operating expenses: $195,000

AUDIENCE
Annual attendance: 9,500
Subscribers: 100

TOURING CONTACT
Richard Heeger

BOOKED-IN EVENTS
Theatre, dance

AEA letter of agreement

PRODUCTIONS 1983–84

Productions	Directors	Sets	Costumes	Lights
Anna adapt: Viveca Lindfors, from Anna Oldstotter-Wing; music: Patricia Lee Stotter	David Man	Johniene Papandreas	Franne Lee	Toni Goldin
3rd Annual Holiday Dance Festival	Muna Tseng		various	Jon Garness
Under Heaven's Eye . . . 'til Cockcrow J.E. Franklin	Thelma Carter	Ernest Allen Smith	Lynn P. Hoffman	Robert R. Strohmeier
Presque Isle Joyce Carol Oates; music: Paul Shapiro	Sallie Brophy	Thomas Stoner	Linda Vigdor	Matt Ehlert
Scapin Molière; adapt: Amie Brockway; music: Paul Shapiro	Amie Brockway	Adrienne J. Brockway	David Mickelson	Adrienne J. Brockway

PRODUCTIONS 1984–85

Productions	Directors	Sets	Costumes	Lights
Scapin Molière; adapt: Amie Brockway; music: Paul Shapiro	Amie Brockway	Adrienne J. Brockway	David Mickelson	Adrienne J. Brockway
4th Annual Holiday Dance Festival	Muna Tseng	Ronald Kajiwara and Robert Lanzner	various	Jon Garness and Whitney Quesenbery
A Cricket on the Hearth adapt: Amie Brockway, from Charles Dickens	Amie Brockway	Adrienne J. Brockway	Michael S. Schler	Adrienne J. Brockway
She Also Dances Kenneth Arnold; music: Nikki Stern	Amie Brockway	Adrienne J. Brockway		
The Dream of Kitamura Philip Kan Gotanda	Jean Erdman	Adrienne J. Brockway	Eiko Yamaguchi, Isamu Noguchi and Ralph Lee	Victor En Yu Tan
Miss Julie August Strindberg; trans: Harry Carlson; music: Michael Bacon	Kent Paul	William Barclay	Adrienne J. Brockway	Phil Monat
The Coach with the Six Insides adapt: Jean Erdman, from James Joyce; music: Teiji Ito	Jean Erdman	Dan Butt and Milton Howarth	Gail Ryan	Kathryn Reid

Theatre Project Company

FONTAINE SYER
Artistic Director

DIANE HOLT
General Manager

CHARLES H. WALLACE
Board Chairman

4219 Laclede St.
St. Louis, MO 63108
(314) 531-1301

FOUNDED 1975
Fontaine Syer, Christine E. Smith

SEASON
September–April

FACILITIES
New City School
5209 Waterman St.
Seating capacity: 240
Stage: proscenium

FINANCES
July 1, 1984–June 30, 1985
Operating expenses: $315,000

AUDIENCE
Annual attendance: 62,849
Subscribers: 1,157

TOURING CONTACT
Connie Lane

BOOKED-IN EVENTS
Dance, theatre, mime

AEA Small Professional Theatre
contract

PRODUCTIONS 1983–84

Productions	Directors	Sets	Costumes	Lights
Much Ado About Nothing William Shakespeare	Wayne Salomon	Bill Schmiel	Elizabeth Eisloeffel	Glenn Tonsor
Lone Star and *Laundry and Bourbon* James McLure	Fontaine Syer	Suzanne Sessions	Wanda Whalen Curth	Glenn Tonsor
Beauty and the Beast adapt: Brian Hohlfield	Courtney Flanagan	Hunter Crabtree	John Gutoskey	Glenn Tonsor
Translations Brian Friel	Fontaine Syer	Bill Schmiel	Kim Gruner	Christine E. Smith
American Buffalo David Mamet	John Grassilli	Mel Dickerson	Joyce Kogut	Christine E. Smith
Angels Fall Lanford Wilson	Fontaine Syer	Bill Schmiel	Elizabeth Eisloeffel	Christine E. Smith
Star Odyssey John Contini	Debra L. Wicks	Pook Pfaffe	Kim Gruner	
Rikki-Tikki-Tavi Brian Hohlfield	Courtney Flanagan	Pook Pfaffe	Kim Gruner	
Waiting on the Levee Sue Greenberg	John Grassilli	Bill Schmiel	Lanette Marquardt	
The Five Freedoms Revue Sue Greenberg	Courtney Flanagan	Hunter Crabtree	Kim Gruner	
Life on the Mississippi Ray Fanning	Courtney Flanagan	Pook Pfaffe	Lanette Marquardt	

PRODUCTIONS 1984–85

Productions	Directors	Sets	Costumes	Lights
Jacques Brel Is Alive and Well and Living in Paris adapt: Eric Blau and Mort Shuman; music: Jacques Brel	Fontaine Syer	Mel Dickerson	Joyce Kogut	K. Dale White
K2 Patrick Meyers	William Grivna	Bill Schmiel	Joyce Kogut	Peggy DePuy
The Wizard of Oz adapt: Frank Gabrielson, from L. Frank Baum	Debra L. Wicks	Frank Bradley	John Gutoskey	K. Dale White
The Birthday Party Harold Pinter	Wayne Salomon	Mel Dickerson	Joyce Kogut	Peggy DePuy
Antigone Jean Anouilh	Lynne Green	Bill Schmiel	Elizabeth Eisloeffel	Katherine J. Cardwel
The Last Meeting of the Knights of the White Magnolia Preston Jones	John Grassilli	Suzanne Sessions	Caroline DeMoss	Christine E. Smith
Give Me Liberty Pamela Sterling	Pamela Sterling	Frank Bradley	Laura Hanson	

Productions	Directors	Sets	Costumes	Lights
The Wondrous Adventures of Marco Polo Sue Greenberg	Debra L. Wicks	Frank Bradley	Laura Hanson	
Waiting on the Levee Sue Greenberg	Sue Greenberg	Bill Schmiel	Lanette Marquardt	
The Canterbury Tales adapt: Pamela Sterling, from Chaucer	Pamela Sterling	Hunter Crabtree	Leo Cortez	

Theatre Three

NORMA YOUNG
Artistic Director

JAC ALDER
Executive Producer/Director

MICHAEL C. BARLERIN
Board Chairman

2800 Routh St.
Dallas, TX 75201
(214) 651-7225 (business)
(214) 871-3300 (box office)

FOUNDED 1961
Norma Young, Jac Alder

SEASON
September–August

FACILITIES
Seating capacity: 241
Stage: arena

FINANCES
September 1, 1984–August 31, 1985
Operating expenses: $1,063,957

AUDIENCE
Annual attendance: 66,198
Subscribers: 3,774

TOURING CONTACT
Jac Alder

BOOKED-IN EVENTS
Theatre, dance

AEA LORT (D) contract

PRODUCTIONS 1983-84

Productions	Directors	Sets	Costumes	Lights
Rosencrantz and Guildenstern Are Dead Tom Stoppard	Norma Young and Jimmy Mullen	Charles Howard	Patty Greer McGarity and Danealia Maretka	Shari Melde
For Colored Girls who have Considered Suicide/ When the Rainbow is Enuf Ntozake Shange	Laurence O'Dwyer	Charles Howard	Michael Pittman	Michael Murray
The School for Wives Molière	Norma Young and Kurt Kleinmann	Charles Howard	Patty Greer McGarity	Michael Murray
Charlotte Sweet book: Michael Colby; music: Gerald Jay Markoe	Jac Alder	Charles Howard	Mary Therese D'Avignon	Shari Melde
The Wake of Jamey Foster Beth Henley	Laurence O'Dwyer	Charles Howard	Karla J. Johnson	Michael Murray
Second Threshold Philip Barry	Charles Howard	Charles Howard	Karla J. Johnson	Michael Murray
The Actor's Nightmare and *Sister Mary Ignatius* *Explains It All for You* Christopher Durang	Jac Alder	Charles Howard	Charles Howard	Michael Murray
A Day in Hollywood/A Night in the Ukraine book and lyrics: Dick Vosburgh; music: Frank Lazarus	Laurence O'Dwyer	Harland Wright	Cheryl Denson	Shari Melde

PRODUCTIONS 1984–85

Productions	Directors	Sets	Costumes	Lights
Angry Housewives A.M. Collins and Chad Henry	Laurence O'Dwyer	Charles Howard	Rick Tankersley	Shari Melde
Outside Waco Patricia Griffith	June Rovenger	Charles Howard and Harland Wright	Cheryl Denson	Peter Metz
Arms and the Man George Bernard Shaw	Jac Alder	Charles Howard	Mary Therese D'Avignon	Michael G. Moynihan
Foxfire Hume Cronyn and Susan Cooper	Charles Howard	Cheryl Denson	Susie Thennes	Ken Hudson
Quartermaine's Terms Simon Gray	Charles Howard	Peter Metz	Susie Thennes	Ken Hudson
You're Gonna Love Tomorrow adapt: Paul Lazarus; music and lyrics: Stephen Sondheim	Jac Alder	Michael G. Moynihan and Jac Alder	Alice Camille McClellan	Ken Hudson

TheatreVirginia

TERRY BURGLER
Artistic Director

EDWARD W. RUCKER
General Manager

LEE P. DUDLEY
Board President

Boulevard and Grove Aves.
Richmond, VA 23221
(804) 257-0840 (business)
(804) 247-0831 (box office)

FOUNDED 1955
Virginia Museum of Fine Arts

SEASON
October–May

FACILITIES
Seating capacity: 500
Stage: proscenium

FINANCES
July 1, 1984–June 30, 1985
Operating expenses: $1,193,000

AUDIENCE
Annual attendance 71,100
Subscribers: 8,000

BOOKED-IN EVENTS
Film, music, performance art

AEA LORT (C) contract

Note: During the 1983-84 and 1984-85 seasons, Tom Markus served as artistic director.

PRODUCTIONS 1983–84

Productions	Directors	Sets	Costumes	Lights
Shine--The Horatio Alger Musical book: Richard Seff and Richard Altman; music: Roger Anderson; lyrics: Lee Goldsmith	Darwin Knight	Charles Caldwell	Susan Tsu	Richard Moore
Macbeth William Shakespeare	Tom Markus and Terry Burgler	Joseph A. Varga	Bronwyn Caldwell	Lynne M. Hartman
A Christmas Carol adapt: Tom Markus, from Charles Dickens	Terry Burgler	Charles Caldwell	Julie Keen	Lynne M. Hartman
A Perfect Gentleman Herbert Appleman	Tom Markus	Charles Caldwell	Bronwyn Caldwell	F. Mitchell Dana
Mass Appeal Bill C. Davis	Terry Burgler	James Burbeck	Julie Keen	Lynne M. Hartman
Sleuth Anthony Shaffer	Josephine R. Abady	Charles Caldwell	Bronwyn Caldwell	Lynne M. Hartman
The Dining Room A.R. Gurney, Jr.	Tom Markus	James Burbeck and Charles Caldwell	Julie Keen	Lynne M. Hartman
At This Evening's Performance Nagle Jackson	Nagle Jackson	Elizabeth K. Fischer	Emelle Holmes	Richard Moore

Productions	Directors	Sets	Costumes	Lights

Final Touches
  Kenneth O. Johnson
	Tom Markus	Charles Caldwell	Bronwyn
			  Caldwell
				Lynne M.
				  Hartman

The Mistress of the Inn
  Carlo Goldoni; adapt: Freyda Thomas and
  David Carlyon
	Tom Markus	Charles Caldwell	Julie Keen	Lynne M.
				  Hartman

A Christmas Carol
  adapt: Tom Markus, from Charles Dickens
	Terry Burgler	Charles Caldwell	Bronwyn
			  Caldwell
				Lynne M.
				  Hartman

Greater Tuna Jaston Williams, Joe Sears and Ed Howard	Darwin Knight	David Crank	Lana Fritz	Terry Cermak

Cloud 9
  Caryl Churchill
	Tom Markus	Charles Caldwell	Bronwyn
			  Caldwell
				F. Mitchell Dana

A Raisin in the Sun
  Lorraine Hansberry
	Terry Burgler	Charles Caldwell	Julie Keen	Lynne M.
				  Hartman

Under Milk Wood
  Dylan Thomas
	Robert
	  Lanchester
		Elizabeth K.
		  Fischer
			Susan Rheaume	Richard Moore

Crimes of the Heart Beth Henley	Charles Towers	Charles Caldwell	Candace Cain	Dirk Kuyk

Theatre West Virginia

JR WEARS
General Director

R.C. GALLAGHER
Board President

Box 1205
Beckley, WV 25802
(304) 253-8317 (business)
(304) 253-8313 (box office)

FOUNDED 1961
Local citizens

SEASON
June–September

FACILITIES
Cliffside Amphitheatre
Grandview State Park, Beaver
Seating capacity: 1,288
Stage: proscenium

FINANCES
October 1, 1983–September 30, 1984
Operating expenses: $411,500

AUDIENCE
Annual attendance: 108,000
Subscribers: 800

TOURING CONTACT
Johanna Young

BOOKED-IN EVENTS
Theatre, music, dance

Productions	Directors	Sets	Costumes	Lights

Hatfields and McCoys
  book and lyrics: Billy Edd Wheeler; music:
  Ewel Cornett
	John S.
	  Benjamin
		T.P. Struthers	Susi Kwast	Mark Shickel

Honey in the Rock
  book: Kermit Hunter; music: Jack Kirkpatrick
  and Ewel Cornett
	John S. Arnold	T.P. Struthers	Susi Kwast	Mark Shickel

Dracula adapt: Ted Tiller, from Bram Stoker	John S. Arnold	Sandy Marks	Susi Kwast	Mark Shickel

Productions	Directors	Sets	Costumes	Lights

Hatfields and McCoys
  book and lyrics: Billy Edd Wheeler; music:
  Ewel Cornett
	John S. Arnold	Thomas P.
		  Struthers
			Susi Kwast	Joseph Marley

PRODUCTIONS 1984–85

Productions	Directors	Sets	Costumes	Lights
Honey in the Rock book: Kermit Hunter; music: Jack Kirkpatrick and Ewel Cornett	Ken Lambert	Thomas P. Struthers	Susi Kwast	Joseph Marley
Fiddler on the Roof book: Joseph Stein; music: Jerry Bock; lyrics: Sheldon Harnick	JR Wears	W. James Brown	JR Wears	Joseph Marley
The Near Sighted Knight and the Far Sighted Dragon book, music and lyrics; Eleanor and Ray Harder	Sharon Fenwald	JR Wears	JR Wears	

Theatreworks/USA

JAY HARNICK
Artistic Director

CHARLES HULL
Managing Director

JUDITH O'REILLY MACK
Board Chairman

131 West 86th St.
New York, NY 10024
(212) 595-7500 (business)
(212) 595-7508 (box office)

FOUNDED 1961
Jay Harnick, Robert K. Adams

SEASON
October–March

FACILITIES
Promenade Theatre
Broadway and 76th St.
Seating capacity: 381
Stage: thrust

Town Hall
123 West 43rd St.
Seating capacity: 1,500
Stage: proscenium

FINANCES
October 1, 1983–September 30, 1984
Operating expenses: $1,546,000

AUDIENCE
Annual attendance: 1,000,500
Subscribers: 6,347

TOURING CONTACT
Ken Arthur

BOOKED-IN EVENTS
Theatre, dance, opera, puppetry

AEA Theatre for Young Audiences contract

PRODUCTIONS 1983–84

Productions	Directors	Sets	Costumes	Lights
Play to Win book and lyrics: James de Jongh and Charles Cleveland; music: Jimi Foster	Regge Life	Tom Barnes	Mary L. Hayes	
Rapunzel book and lyrics: David Crane and Marta Kauffman; music: Michael Skloff	Paul Lazarus	Mavis Smith	Mary L. Hayes	
First Lady book: Jonathan Bolt; music: Thomas Tierney; lyrics: John Forster	John Henry Davis	Jack Stewart	Martha Hally	
The Amazing Einstein book: Jules Tascal; music: Thomas Tierney; lyrics: Ted Drachman	Andy Cadiff	Tom Barnes	Martha Hally	
Sara Crewe book: Mary Anderson; music: Shelly Markham; lyrics: Carrie Maher	William Koch	Richard B. Williams	Carol H. Beule	
Freedom Train Marvin Gordon	Bob Wright	Hal Tine	Ben Benson	

Productions	Directors	Sets	Costumes	Lights
Lady Liberty book and lyrics: John Allen; music: Joe Raposo	David Holgrive	Tom Barnes	Martha Hally	
When the Cookie Crumbles, You Can Still Pick Up the Pieces company-developed	Jay Harnick and Bob Gainer	Tom Barnes	Martha Hally	
Teddy Roosevelt book: Jonathan Bolt; music: Thomas Tierney; lyrics: John Forster	John Henry Davis	Phillipp Jung	Debra Stein	
Look to the Stars book and lyrics: John Allen; music: Joe Raposo	Greg Gunning	Hal Tine	Carole H. Beule	
Play to Win book and lyrics: James de Jongh and Charles Cleveland; music: Jimi Foster	Regge Life	Tom Barnes	Mary L. Hayes	
Rapunzel book and lyrics: David Crane and Marta Kauffman; music: Michael Skloff	Paul Lazarus	Mavis Smith	Mary L. Hayes	
First Lady book: Jonathan Bolt; music: Thomas Tierney; lyrics: John Forster	John Henry Davis	Jack Stewart	Martha Hally	
The Amazing Einstein book: Jules Tasca; music: Thomas Tierney; lyrics: Ted Drachman	Andy Cadiff	Tom Barnes	Martha Hally	

Theatre X

JOHN SCHNEIDER
FLORA COKER
Associate Artistic Directors

MORRIS MEYER
Managing Director

HOWARD G. TAYLOR
Board President

Box 92206
Milwaukee, WI 53202
(414) 278-0555 (business)
(414) 272-2787 (box office)

FOUNDED 1969
Conrad Bishop, Linda Bishop, Ron Gural

SEASON
September–July

FACILITIES
Black Box Theater
Lincoln Center for the Arts
820 East Knapp St.
Seating capacity: 135
Stage: flexible

FINANCES
September 1, 1984–August 31, 1985
Operating expenses: $83,900

AUDIENCE
Annual attendance: 12,500

TOURING CONTACT
Morris Meyer

BOOKED-IN EVENTS
Theatre, modern dance, performance art, installations, club acts

Productions	Directors	Sets	Costumes	Lights
Nam John Schneider and Mark Baker	John Schneider			
For the Sake of the Argument, Imagine It's the 4th of May Croxton	Ritsaert ten Cate			
Firebreaks John Kishline	John Kishline			
Half My Father's Age John Wood	Ritsaert ten Cate			

PRODUCTIONS 1983–84

Productions	Directors	Sets	Costumes	Lights
An Interest in Strangers John Schneider	John Schneider			
Acts of Kindness John Schneider	John Schneider and Marcie Hoffman			
Not I, That Time and *Footfalls* Samuel Beckett	Marcie Hoffman			
The Milwaukee Project John Schneider	John Schneider and Susie Bauer			
I Used to Like This Place Before They Started Making All Those Renovations John Schneider	John Schneider			

PRODUCTIONS 1984–85

Productions	Directors	Sets	Costumes	Lights
Fall of the Amazons Heinrich von Kleist; adapt: Eric Bentley	John Schneider and John Kishline	John Storey	Sam Fleming	John Kishline
My Werewolf John Schneider	John Schneider and Eric Hill	David Rommel	Sam Fleming	David Rommel
An Interest in Strangers John Schneider	John Schneider	John Kishline		David Rommel
The Living End Moe Meyer	Moe Meyer	David Rommel	Mary Piering	David Rommel
I Used to Like This Place Before They Started Making All Those Renovations John Schneider	John Schneider	John Kishline		David Rommel
Faust: An Entertainment John Kishline	John Kishline	John Kishline	John Kishline	John Kishline

Trinity Repertory Company

ADRIAN HALL
Artistic Director

E. TIMOTHY LANGAN
Managing Director

BRUCE G. SUNDLUN
Board Chairman

201 Washington St.
Providence, RI 02903
(401) 521-1100 (business)
(401) 351-4242 (box office)

FOUNDED 1963
Adrian Hall

SEASON
Year-round

FACILITIES
Upstairs Theatre
Seating capacity: 560
Stage: flexible

Downstairs Theatre
Seating capacity: 297
Stage: thrust

FINANCES
July 1, 1984–June 30, 1985
Operating expenses: $2,413,000

AUDIENCE
Annual attendance: 160,000
Subscribers: 19,300

TOURING CONTACT
E. Timothy Langan

BOOKED-IN EVENTS
Theatre, music, dance

AEA LORT (C) contract

Productions	Directors	Sets	Costumes	Lights
Billy Bishop Goes to War John Gray and Eric Peterson	Richard Jenkins	Eugene Lee	William Lane	John F. Custer
Bus Stop William Inge	George Martin	Robert D. Soule	William Lane	John F. Custer
Galileo Bertolt Brecht	Adrian Hall	Eugene Lee	William Lane	Eugene Lee
The Wild Duck Henrik Ibsen	Adrian Hall	Eugene Lee	William Lane	John F. Custer
A Christmas Carol adapt: Adrian Hall and Richard Cumming, from Charles Dickens	William Radka	Robert D. Soule	William Lane	John F. Custer
Fool for Love Sam Shepard	David Wheeler	Robert D. Soule	William Lane	John F. Custer
Cloud 9 Caryl Churchill	Philip Minor	Robert D. Soule	William Lane	John F. Custer
Amadeus Peter Shaffer	Patrick Hines	Robert D Soule	William Lane	John F. Custer
Crimes of the Heart Beth Henley	Paul Benedict	Robert D. Soule	William Lane	John F. Custer
Jonestown Express James Reston, Jr.	Adrian Hall	Eugene Lee	William Lee	Eugene Lee

Productions	Directors	Sets	Costumes	Lights
Beyond Therapy Christopher Durang	Philip Minor	Robert D. Soule	William Lane	John F. Custer
What the Butler Saw Joe Orton	Peter Gerety	Robert D. Soule	William Lane	John F. Custer
Terra Nova Ted Tally	Peter Gerety	Robert D. Soule	William Lane	John F. Custer
Passion Play Peter Nichols	Adrian Hall	Eugene Lee	William Lane	Eugene Lee
Tartuffe Molière; trans: Richard Wilbur	Richard Jenkins	Robert D. Soule	William Lane	John F. Custer
A Christmas Carol adapt: Adrian Hall and Richard Cumming, from Charles Dickens	Timothy Crowe	Robert D. Soule	William Lane	John F. Custer
Misalliance George Bernard Shaw	Philip Minor	Eugene Lee	William Lane	John F. Custer
And a Nightingale Sang . . . C. P. Taylor	Peter Gerety	Robert D. Soule	William Lane	John F. Custer
The Country Wife William Wycherly	Tunc Yalman	Robert D. Soule	William Lane	John F. Custer
Master Harold . . . and the boys Athol Fugard	Patrick Hines	Robert D. Soule	William Lane	John F. Custer
Present Laughter Noel Coward	Philip Minor	Robert D. Soule	William Lane	John F. Custer

Victory Gardens Theater

DENNIS ZACEK
Artistic Director

MARCELLE McVAY
Managing Director

CAROL EASTIN
Board President

2257 North Lincoln Ave.
Chicago, IL 60614
(312) 549-5788 (business)
(312) 871-3000 (box office)

FOUNDED 1974
Cecil O'Neal, Cordis Fejer, David
Rasche, Warren Casey, Stuart
Gordon, Roberta Maguire, June
Pyskacek, Mac McGinnes

SEASON
September–June

FACILITIES
Mainstage
Seating capacity: 195
Stage: thrust

Studio
Seating capacity: 60
Stage: flexible

FINANCES
July 1, 1984–June 30, 1985
Operating expenses: $547,119

AUDIENCE
Annual attendance: 48,000
Subscribers: 3,600

TOURING CONTRACT
Marcelle McVay

AEA Chicago Area Theatre contract

PRODUCTIONS 1983–84

Productions	Directors	Sets	Costumes	Lights
Turntables Jeff Berkson and John Karraker	Dennis Zacek	Jeff Bauer	Marsha Kowal	Chris Phillips
Home Samm-Art Williams	Chuck Smith	Patrick Kerwin	Kate Bergh	Michael Rourke
Butler Country Dean Corrin	Sandy Shinner	Jeff Bauer	Kerry Fleming	Rita Pietraszek
Scheherazade Marisha Chamberlain	Dennis Zacek	Nan Zabriskie	Marsha Kowal	Rita Pietraszek
Eminent Domain Percy Granger	Dennis Zacek	Nels Anderson	Virgil Johnson	Rita Pietraszek
Crossing Niagara Alonso Alegria	Pamela Hoxsey	Carl Forsberg	Carl Forsberg	Carl Forsberg
Dreams of Flight (from a bird in a cage) Brian Richard Mori	Jonathan Wilson	Greg Weber	Greg Weber	Greg Weber

PRODUCTIONS 1984–85

Productions	Directors	Sets	Costumes	Lights
The Fifth Sun Nicholas Patricca	Dennis Zacek	Rick Paul	Patricia Hart	Rita Pietraszek
Tab for Stardom Jeff Berkson, Denise DeClue and John Karraker	Dennis Zacek	Jeff Bauer	Ellen Gross	Chris Phillips
Levitation Timothy Mason	Sandy Shinner	Jeff Bauer	Marsha Kowal	Rita Pietraszek
Master Harold . . . and the boys Athol Fugard	Chuck Smith	Nan Zabriskie	John Brooks	Patrick Kerwin
The God of Isaac James Sherman	Dennis Zacek	Nels Anderson	Nan Zabriskie	Robert Shook
Symphony Pastorale/Fugue Bob Barnett	Jim Corti	Carl Forsberg	Carl Forsberg	Carl Forsberg
The Sovereign State of Boogedy Boogedy Lonnie Carter	Dennis Zacek	James Dardenne	Glenn Billings	Paul Miller
Young Psycho-Vivisectionists Meet Marilyn Monroe Steven Ivcich	Steven Ivcich and Sandy Shinner	Paul Miller	Sheila Myrcik	Paul Miller

Virginia Stage Company

CHARLES TOWERS
Artistic Director

DAN J. MARTIN
Managing Director

STEPHEN C. LAMPL
Board President

108 East Tazewell St.
Norfolk, VA 23510
(804) 627-6988 (business)
(804) 627-1234 (box office)

FOUNDED 1979
Community members

SEASON
October–April

FACILITIES
Mainstage
Seating capacity: 700
Stage: proscenium

Second Stage
Seating capacity: 150
Stage: arena

FINANCES
July 1, 1984–June 30, 1985
Operating expenses: $972,000

AUDIENCE
Annual attendance: 46,000
Subscribers: 5,000

BOOKED-IN EVENTS
Theatre, dance, music, lectures

AEA LORT (C) contract

PRODUCTIONS 1983–84

Productions	Directors	Sets	Costumes	Lights
Island book: Brent Nicholson; music and lyrics: Peter Link; additional lyrics: Joe Bravaco and Larry Rosler	Peter Link	Joe Ragey	Anne-Marie Wright	Spencer Mosse
Betrayal Harold Pinter	Charles Towers	Joe Ragey	Carrie Curtis	Charles Towers
Artichoke Joanna Glass	Jamie Brown	Joe Ragey	Carrie Curtis	Joe Ragey
The Night of the Iguana Tennessee Williams	Charles Towers	Joe Ragey	Anne-Marie Wright	Joe Ragey
A Lesson from Aloes Athol Fugard	Bill Partlan	Joe Ragey	Carrie Curtis	Tina Charney
The Dining Room A. R. Gurney, Jr.	Jamie Brown	Joe Ragey	Anne-Marie Wright	Joe Ragey
True West Sam Shepard	Charles Towers	Joe Ragey	Carrie Curtis	Christoper Furth

PRODUCTIONS 1984–85

Productions	Directors	Sets	Costumes	Lights
Amadeus Peter Shaffer	Charles Towers	Joe Ragey	Martha Kelly	Joe Ragey
Husbandry Patrick Tovatt	Jamie Brown	Joe Ragey	Candice Cain	Joe Ragey
Taking Steps Alan Ayckbourn	Alex Dmitriev	Joe Ragey	Candice Cain	Joe Ragey
The Mound Builders Lanford Wilson	Charles Towers	Joe Ragey	Candice Cain	Spencer Mosse
Morocco Allan Havis	Christopher Hanna	Michael Miller	Candice Cain	Steve Pollock
Crimes of the Heart Beth Henley	Charles Towers	Charles Caldwell	Candice Cain	Dirk Kyuk

Walnut Street Theatre Company

BERNARD HAVARD
Executive Director

MARY BENSEL
General Manager

EDWIN P. ROME
Board President

825 Walnut St.
Philadelphia, PA 19107
(215) 574-3550 (business)
(215) 574-3586 (box office)

FOUNDED 1983
Bernard Havard

SEASON
November–March

FACILITIES
Mainstage
Seating capacity: 1,052
Stage: proscenium

Studio Theatre
Seating capacity: 99
Stage: proscenium

Second Stage
Seating capacity: 85
Stage: flexible

FINANCES
June 1, 1984–May 31, 1985
Operating expenses: $4,540,400

AUDIENCE
Annual attendance: 215,767
Subscribers: 15,161

TOURING CONTACT
Andrew Lichtenberg

BOOKED-IN EVENTS
Theatre, music, dance, opera, lectures,
conferences, film

AEA LORT (A) contract

PRODUCTIONS 1983–84

Productions	Directors	Sets	Costumes	Lights
A Flea in Her Ear Georges Feydeau; adapt: Suzanne Grossmann and Paxton Whitehead	Donald Ewer	Mark W. Morton	Susan E. Hirschfeld	William B. Duncan
Oliver! book, music and lyrics: Lionel Bart	Charles Abbott	W. Joseph Stell	Sigrid Insull	William B. Duncan
Mornings at Seven Paul Osborn	Malcolm Black	Paul Wonsek	Martha Kelly	William B. Duncan
A Perfect Gentleman Herbert Appleman	Tom Markus	Charles Caldwell	Bronwyn J. Caldwell	F. Mitchell Dana
The Taming of the Shrew William Shakespeare	David Chambers	Michael C. Smith	Marie Anne Chiment	Arden Fingerhut

PRODUCTIONS 1984–85

Productions	Directors	Sets	Costumes	Lights
Do Black Patent Leather Shoes Really Reflect Up? book: John R. Powers; music and lyrics: James Quinn and Alaric Jans	Joe Leonardo	James Maronek	Nancy Potts	John Hastings
Chekhov in Yalta John Driver and Jeffrey Haddow	John Driver	Loren Sherman	Nan Cibula	James Ingalls
The Music Man book, music and lyrics: Meredith Wilson	Charles Abbott	Mark W. Morton	Kathleen Blake	Gregg Marriner
Another Part of the Forest Lillian Hellman	Fred Chappell	Ursula Belden	Susan Hirschfeld	William B. Duncan
Quartermaine's Terms Simon Gray	Malcolm Black	Paul Wonsek	Martha Kelly	Paul Wonsek
The Elocution of Benjamin Franklin Steve J. Spears	Andrew Lichtenberg	David Felix	Kevin Pothier	Robert Lyons
A Midsummer Night's Dream William Shakespeare	Gregory S. Hurst	Karen Gerson	Karen Gerson	Jane Reisman

The Whole Theatre

OLYMPIA DUKAKIS
Artistic Director

LAURENCE FELDMAN
Managing Director

ROBERT PEACOCK
Board Chairman

544 Bloomfield Ave.
Montclair, NJ 07042
(201) 744-2996 (business)
(201) 744-2989 (box office)

FOUNDED 1973

SEASON
October–April

FACILITIES
Seating capacity: 199
Stage: proscenium

FINANCES
July 1, 1984–June 30, 1985
Operating expenses: $985,905

AUDIENCE
Annual attendance: 35,000
Subscribers: 4,218

TOURING CONTACT
Ellen Williams

BOOKED-IN EVENTS
Theatre

AEA LORT (D) contract

PRODUCTIONS 1983–84

Productions	Directors	Sets	Costumes	Lights
Nobody Starts Out to Be a Pirate book and lyrics: Fred Tobias; music: Stanley Lebowsky	Arnold Mittelman	Loren Sherman	Galen M. Logsdon	Rachel Budin
A Soldier's Play Charles Fuller	Douglas Turner Ward	Felix E. Cochren	Judy Dearing	Allen Lee Hughes
Alterations Leigh Curran	Tom Brennan	Paul Dorphley	Sigrid Insull	Carol Rubinstein
Talley's Folly Lanford Wilson	Olympia Dukakis	Richard Harmon	Richard Harmon	Richard Moore
Blithe Spirit Noel Coward	Stuart Howard	Michael Miller	Sam Fleming	Richard Moore

---

PRODUCTIONS 1984–85

Productions	Directors	Sets	Costumes	Lights
Of Mice and Men John Steinbeck	Apollo Dukakis	Michael Miller	Sigrid Insull	Rachel Budin
Absurd Person Singular Alan Ayckbourn	Robert Moss	Rick Dennis	Michael Krass	David Noling
Ghosts Henrik Ibsen; trans: Rolf Fjelde	Austin Pendleton	Michael Miller	Sigrid Insull	Carol Rubinstein
The Sorrows of Frederick Romulus Linney	Tom Brennan	Reagan Cook	Sigrid Insull	Carol Rubinstein
The Middle Ages A. R. Gurney, Jr.	Porter Van Zandt	Philipp Jung	Andrew B. Marlay	Richard Moore

Williamstown Theatre Festival

NIKOS PSACHAROPOULOS
Artistic/Executive Director

BONNIE MONTE
Artistic Associate

WILLIAM H. EVERETT
Board President

Box 517
Williamstown, MA 01267
(413) 597-3377 (business)
(413) 597-3400 (box office)

FOUNDED 1955
Nikos Psacharopoulos, trustees of
Williamstown Theatre Festival

SEASON
July–August

FACILITIES
Mainstage
Seating capacity: 479
Stage: proscenium

Other Stages
Seating capacity: 96
Stage: flexible

FINANCES
December 1, 1983–November 30, 1984
Operating expenses: $877,623

AUDIENCE
Annual attendance: 47,000

*AEA Council on Resident Stock Theatre
contract*

PRODUCTIONS 1984

Productions	Directors	Sets	Costumes	Lights
The Tale of the Wolf Ferenc Molnar	Nikos Psacharopoulos	Hugh Landwehr	Jess Goldstein	Pat Collins
The Devil's Disciple George Bernard Shaw	Stan Wojewodski, Jr.	Douglas Stein	Dunya Ramicova	William Armstrong
Uncle Vanya Anton Chekhov; trans: Ronald Hingley	Jeff Bleckner	Andrew Jackness	Jess Goldstein	Paul Gallo
Vieux Carré Tennessee Williams	Austin Pendleton	Kevin Rupnik	Susan Hilferty	Roger Meeker
Peer Gynt Henrik Ibsen	Nikos Psacharopoulos	John Conklin	Dunya Ramicova	Peter Hunt
Richard Cory A. R. Gurney, Jr.	Steven Schacter	John Hutman	John Hutman	Christina Giannelli
Slides George Shea	Geraldine Fitzgerald	John Hutman	John Hutman	Christina Giannelli
Real Dreams Trevor Griffiths	Trevor Griffiths	John Hutman	John Hutman	Christina Giannelli
Daniela Frank Alonso Alegria	Jack Hofsiss	John Hutman	John Hutman	Christina Giannelli

PRODUCTIONS 1985

Productions	Directors	Sets	Costumes	Lights
Undiscovered Country Arthur Schnitzler; adapt: Tom Stoppard	Nikos Psacharopoulos	David Jenkins	Jennifer von Mayrhauser	Arden Fingerhut
La Ronde Arthur Schnitzler	David Trainer	John Conklin	Dunya Ramicova	Paul Gallo
The Royal Family George S. Kaufman and Edna Ferber	Edward Payson Call	Hugh Landwehr	David Murin	William Armstrong
Tonight at 8:30 Noel Coward	Ellis Rabb	Hugh Landwehr	Dunya Ramicova	Stephen Strawbridge
The Glass Menagerie Tennessee Williams	Nikos Psacharopoulos	Andrew Jackness	Jess Goldstein	Pat Collins
To Whom It May Concern music and lyrics: Carol Hall	Geraldine Fitzgerald	Philip Baldwin	Philip Baldwin	Christina Giannelli
Citizen Tom Paine Howard Fast	James Simpson	Philip Baldwin	Philip Baldwin	Christina Giannelli
Not About Heroes Stephen MacDonald	Dianne Wiest	Philip Baldwin	Philip Baldwin	Christina Giannelli
Song book, music and lyrics: Don Black and Andrew Lloyd Webber	Richard Maltby, Jr.	Philip Baldwin	Philip Baldwin	Christina Giannelli
Pantomime Derek Walcott	Kay Matschullat	Philip Baldwin	Philip Baldwin	Christina Giannelli

The Wilma Theater

JIRI ZIZKA
Artistic Director

BLANKA ZIZKA
Executive Director

MICHAEL SCHOLNICK
Board President

2030 Sansom St.
Philadelphia, PA 19103
(215) 963-0249 (business)
(215) 963-0345 (box office)

FOUNDED 1973
Linda Griffith, Liz Stout

SEASON
October–July

FACILITIES
Seating capacity: 100
Stage: flexible

FINANCES
September 1, 1983–August 31, 1984
Operating expenses: $347,658

AUDIENCE
Annual attendance: 16,572
Subscribers: 2,680

AEA letter of agreement

PRODUCTIONS 1983–84

Productions	Directors	Sets	Costumes	Lights
Marat/Sade Peter Weiss	Jiri Zizka	Jiri Zizka	Ramona Broomer	McLarence Dieckerson
A Life in the Theater David Mamet	Peter Wallace	S. M. R. D. Theatricals	Lisa Youndt	Jay Madara
The Picture of Dorian Gray adapt: Jiri Zizka, from Oscar Wilde	Jiri Zizka	Scott Roper	Nancy Miller	James Leitner
Mirror House (An Evening of One-acts):				
The Lover, Harold Pinter	Blanka Zizka	John Musall	John Musall	James Leitner
Words, Donald Drake	Tim Moyer	John Musall	John Musall	James Leitner
Don't Walk Around Stark Naked, Georges Feydeau	Jiri Zizka	John Musall	John Musall	James Leitner

---

PRODUCTIONS 1984–85

Productions	Directors	Sets	Costumes	Lights
Beyond Therapy Christopher Durang	Jiri Zizka	S. M. R. D. Theatricals	Christina Kingsley	George Black
The Suicide Nikolai Erdman	Jiri Zizka	S. M. R.D. Theatricals	John Musall	George Black
The Hairy Ape Eugene O'Neill	Blanka Zizka	Jiri Zizka	John Musall	James Leitner
Happy End book and lyrics: Bertolt Brecht; music: Kurt Weill	Jiri Zizka	Philip Graneto	John Musall	James Leitner
Beyond Therapy Christopher Durang	Jiri Zizka	Philip Graneto	John Musall	James Leitner

Wisdom Bridge Theatre

ROBERT FALLS
Artistic Director

JEFFREY ORTMANN
Executive Director

DIANE GOLDIN
Board President

1559 West Howard St.
Chicago, IL 60626
(312) 743-0486 (business)
(312) 743-6442 (box office)

FOUNDED 1974
David Beaird

SEASON
September–July

FACILITIES
Mainstage
Seating capacity: 196
Stage: proscenium

Studio
1560 West Howard St.
Seating capacity: 40
Stage: proscenium

FINANCES
August 1, 1984–July 31, 1985
Operating expenses: $1,199,050

AUDIENCE
Annual attendance: 60,000
Subscribers: 6,000

AEA Chicago Area Theatre contract

PRODUCTIONS 1983–84

Productions	Directors	Sets	Costumes	Lights
In the Belly of the Beast: Letters from Prison adapt: Robert Falls, from Jack Henry Abbott	Robert Falls	Robert Falls	Dale Calandra	Michael S. Philippi
Kabuki Medea adapt: William Mark Streib and Lou Anne Wright, from Euripides	Shozo Sato	Shozo Sato	Shozo Sato	Michael S. Philippi
Billy Bishop Goes to War John Gray and Eric Peterson	David Colacci	Michael S. Philippi	Sara Davidson	Michael S. Philippi
Life and Limb Keith Reddin	Robert Falls	Michael S. Philippi	John Murbach	Michael S. Philippi
Careless Love John Olive	Robert Falls	Michael S. Philippi	Marjory Jakus	Michael S. Philippi

---

PRODUCTIONS 1984–85

Productions	Directors	Sets	Costumes	Lights
Terra Nova Ted Tally	Robert Falls	Michael S. Philippi	Nanalee Raphael-Schirmer	Michael S. Philippi
Kabuki Medea adapt: William Mark Streib and Lou Anne Wright, from Euripides	Shozo Sato	Shozo Sato	Shozo Sato	Michael S. Philippi
Hamlet William Shakespeare	Robert Falls	Michael Merritt	Michael Merritt	Michael Merritt
In the Belly of the Beast: Letters from Prison adapt: Robert Falls, from Jack Henry Abbott	Robert Falls	Robert Falls	Dale Calandra	Michael S. Philippi
Painting Churches Tina Howe	Doug Finlayson	Michael S. Philippi	Sara Davidson	Michael S. Philippi
You Can't Judge a Book by Looking at the Cover: Sayings from the Life and Writings of Junebug Jabbo Jones, Vol. II John O'Neill, Barbara Watkins and Steven Kent	Steven Kent		Curtis King	Ken Bowen

The Wooster Group

ELIZABETH LeCOMPTE
Artistic Director

LINDA CHAPMAN
General Manager

RON VAWTER
Board President

Box 654, Canal Street Station
New York, NY 10013
(212) 966-9796 (business)
(212) 966-3651 (box office)

FOUNDED 1967
Richard Schechner

SEASON
Year-round

FACILITIES
The Performing Garage
33 Wooster St.
Seating capacity: 100
Stage: flexible

FINANCES
July 1, 1984–June 30, 1985
Operating expenses: $350,000

AUDIENCE
Annual attendance: 18,000

TOURING CONTACT
Linda Chapman

BOOKED-IN EVENTS
Experimental theatre, music, dance

PRODUCTIONS 1983–84

Productions	Directors	Sets	Costumes	Lights
L. S. D. (Parts 1, 2, 3) company-developed	Elizabeth LeCompte	Jim Clayburgh and Elizabeth LeCompte		Ken Kobland
North Atlantic Jim Strahs	Elizabeth LeCompte	Jim Clayburgh and Elizabeth LeCompte		
Hula company-developed	Elizabeth LeCompte			
Swimming to Cambodia Spalding Gray				

PRODUCTIONS 1984–85

Productions	Directors	Sets	Costumes	Lights
L. S. D. (. . . Just the High Points) company-developed	Elizabeth LeCompte	Jim Clayburgh and Elizabeth LeCompte		Ken Kobland
Swimming to Cambodia Spalding Gray				
Miss Universal Happiness Richard Foreman	Richard Foreman and Jim Clayburgh	Richard Foreman and Jim Clayburgh		

Worcester Foothills Theatre Company

MARC P. SMITH
Executive Producer/Artistic Director

JOHN W. CURTIS
Board Chairman

Box 236
Worcester, MA 01602
(617) 754-3314 (business)
(617) 754-4018 (box office)

FOUNDED 1974
Marc P. Smith

SEASON
September–May

FACILITIES
22 Front St.
Seating capacity: 200
Stage: thrust

FINANCES
June 1, 1984–May 31, 1985
Operating expenses: $78,000

AUDIENCE
Annual attendance: 3,100

BOOKED-IN EVENTS
Theatre, music

PRODUCTIONS 1983–84

Productions	Directors	Sets	Costumes	Lights
How He Lied to Her Husband George Bernard Shaw	Jack Magune	Patrick J. Mahoney	Deborah Bock	Patrick J. Mahoney
The Twelve Pound Look James M. Barrie	Jack Magune	Patrick J. Mahoney	Deborah Bock	Patrick J. Mahoney
Lamentations on a High Hill Marc P. Smith	Marc P. Smith	Patrick J. Mahoney	Beth Rontal	Patrick J. Mahoney

PRODUCTIONS 1984–85

Productions	Directors	Sets	Costumes	Lights
Whacko, George! Allison Spitz	Jack Magune			
Brigadier General Dyer Explains the Amritsar Incident William Novick	Jack Magune			
First Night Jack Neary	Nancy Kindelan			

WPA Theatre

KYLE RENICK
Artistic Director

WENDY BUSTARD
Managing Director

BETTY ANN BESCH SOLINGER
Board President

519 West 23rd St.
New York, NY 10011
(212) 691-2274 (business)
(212) 206-0523 (box office)

FOUNDED 1977
Howard Ashman, Craig Evans, Edward
    T. Gianfrancesco, Kyle Renick,
    Stephen G. Wells, R. Stuart White

SEASON
September–June

FACILITIES
Seating capacity: 98
Stage: proscenium

FINANCES
July 1, 1984–June 30, 1985
Operating expenses: $385,000

AUDIENCE
Annual attendance: 11,000
Suscribers: 843

AEA letter of agreement

PRODUCTIONS 1983-84

Productions	Directors	Sets	Costumes	Lights
The Alto Part Barbara Gilstrap	Zina Jasper	Edward T. Gianfrancesco	Don Newcomb	Craig Evans
La Brea Tarpits Alan Gross	Stephen Zuckerman	James Fenhagen	Mimi Maxmen	Phil Monat
Thin Ice Jeffrey Haddow	Dann Florek	Tom Schwinn	Don Newcomb	Phil Monat
Mr. & Mrs. Kevin Wade	David Trainer	David Gropman	David Murin	Paul Gallo

PRODUCTIONS 1984-85

Productions	Directors	Sets	Costumes	Lights
Feathertop book adapt: Bruce Peyton, from Nathaniel Hawthorne; music and lyrics: Skip Kennon	Susan H. Schulman	Edward T. Gianfrancesco	David Murin	Craig Evans
The Incredibly Famous Willy Rivers Stephen Metcalfe	Stephen Zuckerman	James Fenhagen	Mimi Maxmen	Richard Winkler
The Hitch-Hikers adapt: Larry Ketron, from Eudora Welty	Dann Florek	Edward T. Gianfrancesco	Don Newcomb	Phil Monat
Out of Gas on Lovers Leap Mark St. Germain	Elinor Renfield	Edward T. Gianfrancesco	Don Newcomb	Craig Evans

Yale Repertory Theatre

LLOYD RICHARDS
Artistic Director

BENJAMIN MORDECAI
Managing Director

222 York St.
New Haven, CT 06520
(203) 436-1587 (business)
(203) 436-1600 (box office)

FOUNDED 1966
Robert Brustein

SEASON
September–May

FACILITIES
Mainstage
1120 Chapel St.
Seating capacity: 487
Stage: thrust

University Theatre
222 York St.
Seating capacity: 684
Stage: proscenium

FINANCES
July 1, 1984–June 30, 1985
Operating expenses: $1,850,143

AUDIENCE
Annual attendance: 84,200
Subscribers: 7,615

AEA LORT (C) contract

PRODUCTIONS 1983-84

Productions	Directors	Sets	Costumes	Lights
Major Barbara George Bernard Shaw	Lloyd Richards	Michael H. Yeargan	Dunya Ramicova	Peter Maradudin
A Raisin in the Sun Lorraine Hansberry	Dennis Scott	Robert M. Wierzel	Richard F. Mays	Jennifer Tipton
Richard II William Shakespeare	David Hammond	Derek McLane	Catherine Zuber	Robert M. Wierzel
Winterfest IV: Chopin in Space, Philip Bosakowski	James Simpson	Michael H. Yeargan	Candice Donnelly	William B. Warfel
The Day of the Picnic, Russell Davis	Tony Giordano	Peter Maradudin	Charles H. McClennahan	Tom Roscher

PRODUCTIONS 1983–84

Productions	Directors	Sets	Costumes	Lights
The Sweet Life, Michael Quinn	Robert Alford, III	Andrew Carter	James D. Sandefur	William J. Buck
Night Is Mother to the Day, Lars Noren; trans: Harry G. Carlson	Goran Graffman	Richard F. Mays	Catherine Zuber	Robert M. Wierzel
Ma Rainey's Black Bottom August Wilson	Lloyd Richards	Charles H. McClennahan	Daphne Pascucci	Peter Maradudin
The Road to Mecca Athol Fugard	Athol Fugard	Elizabeth Doyle	Derek McLane	William B. Warfel

PRODUCTIONS 1983–84

Productions	Directors	Sets	Costumes	Lights
Tartuffe Molière; trans: Richard Wilbur	Walton Jones	Kevin Rupnik	Dunya Ramicova	William B. Warfel
Henry IV, Part 1 Wiliam Shakespeare	David Hammond	Timothy Averill	Susan Condie Lamb	Jennifer Tipton
A Play of Giants Wole Soyinka	Wole Soyinka	James D. Sandefur	Claudia Marlow Brown	Mary Louise Geiger
Winterfest V:				
Between East and West, Richard Nelson	John Madden	Basha Zmyslowski	Rusty Smith	David Alan Stach
Faulkner's Bicycle, Heather McDonald	Julian Webber	Pamela Peterson	Scott Bradley	Mary Louise Geiger
Rum and Coke, Keith Reddin	Bill Partlan	Clare Scarpulla	David Peterson	Donald Holder
Vampires in Kodachrome, Dick Beebe	Evan Yionoulis	Charles E. McCarry	Arnall Downs	Donald Holder
What the Butler Saw Joe Orton	Andrei Belgrader	Michael H. Yeargan	Candice Donnelly	William B. Warfel
Talley's Folly Lanford Wilson	Dennis Scott	Susan Condie Lamb	Claudia Marlow Brown	Mary Louise Geiger
Fences August Wilson	Lloyd Richards	James D. Sandefur	Candice Donnelly	Danianne Mizzy

CHRONOLOGY
INDICES

THEATRE CHRONOLOGY

The following is a chronological list of founding dates for the theatres included in this book. Years refer to dates of the first public performance or, in a few cases, the company's formal incorporation.

1896
Hudson Guild Theatre

1915
Cleveland Play House

1925
Goodman Theatre

1928
Berkshire Theatre Festival

1933
Barter Theatre

1934
Paper Mill Playhouse

1935
Oregon Shakespearean
    Festival

1937
Old Globe Theatre

1946
Stage One: The Louisville
    Children's Theatre

1947
Alley Theatre
La Jolla Playhouse

1949
The Emmy Gifford Children's
    Theater
New Dramatists

1950
Arena Stage

1951
Circle in the Square

1954
Court Theatre
Milwaukee Repertory Theater
New York Shakespeare
    Festival

1955
Honolulu Theatre for Youth
TheatreVirginia
Williamstown Theatre Festival

1956
Academy Theatre
Philadelphia Drama Guild

1957
Detroit Repertory Theatre

1959
Dallas Theater Center
San Francisco Mime Troupe

1960
Asolo State Theater
Cincinnati Playhouse in the
    Park

1961
The Children's Theatre
    Company
Theatre West Virginia
Theatreworks/USA
Theatre Three

1962
Great Lakes Theatre Festival
Pioneer Memorial Theatre

1963
Center Stage
Fulton Opera House
Goodspeed Opera House
The Guthrie Theater
New Jersey Shakespeare
    Festival
Periwinkle Productions
Seattle Repertory Theatre
Trinity Repertory Company

1964
Actors Theatre of Louisville
The American Place Theatre

Hartford Stage Company
Missouri Repertory Theatre
O'Neill Theater Center
PCPA Theaterfest
South Coast Repertory
Theatre by the Sea

1965
A Contemporary Theatre
Cumberland County Playhouse
East West Players
The Julian Theatre
Long Wharf Theatre
Looking Glass Theatre
Studio Arena Theatre

1966
Arizona Theatre Company
BoarsHead: Michigan Public
    Theater
Body Politic Theatre
INTAR
Living Stage Theatre Company
New Stage Theatre
The Repertory Theatre of St.
    Louis
Yale Repertory Theatre

1967
CSC: City Stage Co.
Magic Theatre
Mark Taper Forum
StageWest
The Wooster Group

1968

AMAS Repertory Theatre
Berkeley Repertory Theatre
The Changing Scene
Ford's Theatre
Omaha Magic Theatre
Ontological-Hysteric Theatre
Playhouse on the Square
Repertorio Español

1969

Alliance Theatre Company/
   Atlanta Children's Theatre
Circle Repertory Company
Folger Theatre
Free Street Theater
The Odyssey Theatre
   Ensemble
Theatre X

1970

American Theatre Company
The Empty Space
Mabou Mines
Manhattan Theatre Club
New Federal Theatre
The Salt Lake Acting Company
The Street Theater
The Theater at Monmouth
Theater for the New City

1971

Cocteau Repertory
Dell'Arte Players Company
Ensemble Studio Theatre
Interart Theatre
Music-Theatre Group/Lenox
   Arts Center
The Old Creamery Theatre
   Company
Playwrights' Center
Playwrights Horizons

1972

The Acting Company
Alabama Shakespeare Festival
Eureka Theatre Company
GeVa Theatre
Indiana Repertory Theatre
Intiman Theatre Company
McCarter Theatre Company
New American Theater
New Playwrights' Theatre
Theater of the Open Eye

1973

Florida Studio Theatre
The Hippodrome State Theatre
L. A. Public Theatre
The Whole Theatre Company
The Wilma Theater

1974

American Jewish Theatre
At the Foot of the Mountain
Berkeley Shakespeare Festival
Clarence Brown Company
George Street Playhouse
Germinal Stage Denver
Illusion Theatre
The Independent Eye
L. A. Theatre Works
Northlight Theatre
The People's Light and
   Theatre Company
The Philadelphia Company
Portland Stage Company
Roadside Theater
Syracuse Stage
Victory Gardens Theater
Wisdom Bridge Theatre
Worcester Foothills Theatre
   Company

1975

American Stage Festival
Attic Theatre
Bilingual Foundation of the
   Arts

Caldwell Playhouse
Fairmount Theatre of the Deaf
The Hartman Theatre
Long Island Stage Company
New Arts Theatre
Pittsburgh Public Theater
The Road Company
Soho Repertory Theatre
Theatre IV
Theatre Project Company

1976

Alaska Repertory Theatre
American Theatre Arts
Arkansas Repertory Theatre
California Theatre Center
The CAST Theatre
Dorset Theatre Festival
Empire State Institute for the
   Performing Arts
The Great-American Theatre
   Company
Illinois Theatre Center
Nebraska Theatre Caravan
One Act Theatre Company of
   San Francisco
PlayMakers Repertory
   Company
San Diego Repertory Theatre
Steppenwolf Theatre Company

1977

Actors Theatre of St. Paul
Coconut Grove Playhouse
Horse Cave Theatre
Pan Asian Repertory Theatre
Pennsylvania Stage Company
WPA Theatre

1978

Ark Theatre Company
A Traveling Jewish Theatre
Center for Puppetry Arts
Crossroads Theatre Company
The Group Theatre Company
The Harold Clurman Theatre

River Arts Repertory
Round House Theatre
Shakespeare & Company
Tacoma Actors Guild

1979

The American Stage Company
The Back Alley Theatre
Chocolate Bayou Theater
   Company
Delaware Theatre Company
Merrimack Regional Theatre
New York Theatre Workshop
Perseverance Theatre
The Second Stage
Stage #1
Stage West
Virginia Stage Company

1980

American Repertory Theatre
Capital Repertory Company
Denver Center Theatre
   Company
L. A. Stage Company
San Jose Repertory Company

1982

The Huntington Theatre
   Company
Philadelphia Festival Theatre
   for New Plays

1983

Mirror Repertory Company
Walnut Street Theatre
   Company

1984

Lamb's Theatre Company

1985

Los Angeles Theatre Center

INDEX OF NAMES

B

Babe, Thomas, 157, 231, 242
Babier, Brian, 219
Bacon, Michael, 275
Badger, Mary, 112
Bagdasian, Harry M., 209
Bagley, Ben, 113, 210
Baierlein, Ed, 156
Bailey, Brian, 184
Bailey, Bruce, 76, 77
Bailey, R. S., 188, 189
Bain, Judy, 273
Baitz, Jon Robin, 184
Baizley, Doris, 127, 128
Baker, August, 120
Baker, Clifford Fannin, 84, 85, 98
Baker, Don, 248
Baker, Edward Allan, 147
Baker, Georgia, 105, 209
Baker, Jonathan D., 121
Baker, Margaret, 247
Baker, Mark, 281
Baker, Paul, 135
Baker, Word, 135, 136
Bakkom, James, 243
Baldwin, Philip, 204, 288
Baley, Deborah, 233
Balfior, Joseph, 144, 145
Ball, Jenny, 88
Ball, William, 114
Ballance, Jack, 200
Ballif, Ariel, 237
Ballou, Bill, 256
Banks, Christina, 184
Bannan, Paul, 150
Bannon, Paul W., 122
Baral, Vicki, 144, 182, 183, 184
Barbano, Karen, 177
Barber, Philip, 192
Barber, Roy, 249
Barbour, W. Lansing, 93, 215
Barclay, Paris, 257
Barclay, Susan E., 185
Barclay, William, 151, 157, 170, 229, 275
Barkla, Jack, 97, 121, 164
Barlerin, Michael C., 277
Barnes, Peter, 220
Barnes, Robert, 100, 227
Barnes, Theo, 271
Barnes, Tom, 87, 181, 280, 281
Barnett, Bob, 157, 283
Barnett, Gina, 146
Barnett, Ron, 274
Barr, Nancy, 184
Barranger, Milly S., 240
Barreca, Christopher, 126
Barrie, James M., 95, 128, 143, 200, 237, 292
Barron, Rob, 257
Barroso, Luis Q., 117, 118
Barrows, Eddy, 168
Barry, B. H., 256
Barry, Ellen, 208
Barry, Paul, 208, 209
Barry, P. J., 80, 186
Barry, Philip, 83, 108, 277
Bart, Lionel, 87, 286
Bartenieff, George, 271
Barthol, Bruce, 252
Bartlett, Bridget, 112, 113
Bartlett, Dewey F., Jr., 95

Bartlett, Jeffrey W., 121
Bartlett, Reid, 155
Barton, John, 233
Barton, Todd, 268
Bartow, Arthur, 209
Bartsch, Hans, 227
Basinger, Jo Anne, 272, 273
Bassuk, David, 259
Bates, Kathy, 81
Battelle, Anthony, 117
Battley, Wade, 130
Bauer, Beaver, 106, 148, 191
Bauer, Irvin S., 187
Bauer, Jeffrey, 111, 112, 214, 284
Bauer, Susie, 282
Baugh, Gary, 112, 214, 264
Baum, L. Frank, 114, 117, 276
Baumgartner, Tim, 272
Baxter, Cash, 100, 228
Baxter, Ernest, 89
Bay, Howard, 199
Beaird, David, 290
Beals, Howard P., Jr., 136, 137
Beals, Teri, 136
Bean, Patti, 122
Beasley, Karen Keech, 215
Beattie, Kurt, 78
Beatty, John Lee, 108, 125, 126, 151, 158, 187, 192, 193
Beaty, Anita, 76
Beck, Carl, 202
Becker, Alma, 89, 205, 206, 257
Becker, Ken, 254
Becker, Victor A., 86, 145, 267
Becket, George, 104
Beckett, Samuel, 78, 79, 91, 100, 155, 156, 164, 174, 189, 190, 194, 195, 238, 246, 249, 282
Beckos, Barbara, 267
Becvar, William, 268
Bedell, Todd, 167
Beebe, Dick, 294
Beecroft, Jeffrey, 148, 151
Beer, Lenny, 183
Beesley, Christopher, 81, 97, 121
Beethem, Jaye, 103
Behan, Brendan, 186
Behling, Robert, 184
Beilke, Bill, 250
Belden, Ursula, 157, 193, 238, 286
Belgrader, Andrei, 90, 294
Belgreier, Bernett, 178
Belknap, Allen R., 151
Bell, Barbara A., 129
Bell, David H., 152
Bell, Neal, 222, 242
Belleville, Brad, 107
Belli, Keith, 84
Belling, Edward, 87
Benbow, Claudia, 92
Bender, Joanne, 174
Benedetti, N. J., 93, 94
Benedict, Paul, 182, 283
Benedikt, Michael, 156
Benham, Suzanne, 152
ben israel, steve, 272
Benjamin, John S., 279
Benjamin, Randy, 272
Benmussa, Simone, 164
Bennett, Allan, 110
Bennett, Butch, 187

Bennett, Frank, 112, 113
Bennett, John, 202
Bennett, Michael, 211, 212
Bennett, Peter, 238, 270
Bennett, Sid, 88
Bennett, Stephen, 184
Bennett, Terry A., 133
Bennett, Tim, 117
Bensel, Mary, 286
Benshoof, Kenneth, 254
Benson, Ben, 280
Benson, Martin, 258, 259
Benson, Susan, 139
Bentley, Eric, 98, 104, 133, 282
Berendes, David, 216
Berendes, Rita, 216
Berezin, Tanya, 125
Bergh, Kate, 284
Berglund, John, 91, 92
Bergman, Ingmar, 238, 257
Berkoff, Steven, 184
Berkowitz, Dan, 275
Berkson, Jeff, 214, 284
Berlin, Brenda, 179
Berlin, Irving, 159, 173
Berlin, Pamela, 115, 146, 171, 242
Berliner, Charles, 127, 128, 182
Berlinger, Robert, 194, 218
Berman, Norman L., 103, 125, 200, 213
Berman, Paul, 119
Bermel, Albert, 90, 91, 207
Bernard, Kenneth, 271, 272
Berne, Eric, 107
Berney, William, 134, 174, 266
Bernhardt, Melvin, 166
Bernstein, Douglas, 192
Bernstein, Jeff, 141
Bernstein, Leonard, 87, 158, 202, 233, 237
Bernstein, Mark D., 235
Berry, Gabriel, 89, 176, 177, 190, 257, 271
Berry, Wendell, 80
Bertlotto, Caterina, 99
Berwick, Danny, 120
Bessoir, Robert, 88, 185
Bethke, Scott, 249
Betts, Nancy, 138
Beule, Carole H., 280, 281
Beuttler, G. Auguste, 146
Bevan, Edward, 173
Bewley, David, 91
Bezemer, Richard, 266
Bicat, Nick, 173
Bick, Kristine, 238
Bickerstaff, Jimmy A., 214
Bieber, Cathy, 172
Biedenstein, Larry, 246
Bier, Susan, 204
Bierman, A. K., 179
Bigelow, Dennis, 225
Bihr, Jeffrey, 161
Bildner, Albert, 89
Bill, Don, 119
Bill, Mary, 161
Billig, Etel, 172
Billig, Steve S., 172
Billings, Glenn, 284
Billings, Jim, 104
Billington, Ken, 195, 240
Bingham, Sallie, 79, 90, 169
Birch, Patricia, 144
Birkenhead, Susan, 128

Birn, David, 273
Birnbaum, Rhonda, 220, 221
Birnbaum, Steven L., 257
Birturk, Ricia, 121
Bishop, Andre, 241
Bishop, Conrad, 125, 174, 175, 281
Bishop, John, 125, 221
Bishop, Linda, 174, 281
Bishop, Neal, 181
Black, Bill, 126, 127
Black, Don, 288
Black, George, 234, 289
Black, Malcolm, 286
Black, Patti Carr, 210
Blackman, Mark, 219
Blackman, Robert, 90, 138, 183, 193, 194, 212, 218, 228, 254, 258
Blackwell, Vera, 194, 211
Blackwood, Barbara, 88
Blahnik, Jeremy, 184
Blair, Tom, 198
Blake, Kathleen, 195, 286
Blakeny, Blanche, 133
Blanche, Michele Jo, 184
Blase, Linda, 136, 169
Blau, Eric, 247, 276
Blau, Frances, 127, 128
Bleckner, Jeff, 288
Blessing, Lee, 80, 81, 122, 173, 221, 222
Bletson, Charlene, 256
Bliss, Matthew, 242
Bliss, Terry, 274
Blitzstein, Marc, 78, 85, 142, 148, 163, 242
Block, Richard, 79
Bloodgood, William, 97, 106, 145, 225
Bloom, Mark, 173
Bloom, Michael, 236
Bloom, Mitchell S., 208, 209
Bloom, Sidney S., 235
Blount, Roy, Jr., 79, 80
Blu, 177, 266, 271
Blue, Adrian, 149
Board, John L., 239
Boarman, Eileen, 187
Bobcean, Janet, 141
Bobrick, Sam, 169, 216
Boccaccio, 76
Bock, Deborah, 129, 292
Bock, Jerry, 86, 227, 270, 280
Boddy, Claudia, 237
Boderite, Gisela, 156
Boehlke, Bain, 121
Boerner, Ted, 160
Boesing, Martha, 102
Boesing, Paul, 102
Bogart, Anne, 201
Bogdanov, Michael, 151
Bohlin, Ted, 196
Boily, Deborah H., 122
Bolang, Anders, 113
Bolding, Betsy L., 97
Bolger, T. Michael, 197
Bolinger, Don, 134
Bolke, Daniel, 257
Bolt, Jonathan, 128, 280, 281
Bolt, Robert, 199, 208, 237
Bolton, Guy, 159, 164, 266
Bonafede, Bruce, 80
Bond, Edward, 173
Bond, Tim, 162

INDEX OF TITLES

About TCG

Theatre Communications Group is the national organization for the nonprofit professional theatre. Since its founding in 1961, TCG has developed a unique and comprehensive support system that addresses the artistic and management concerns of theatres, as well as institutionally based and freelance artists nationwide.

TCG provides a national forum and communications network for a field that is as aesthetically diverse as it is geographically widespread. Its goals are to foster the cross-fertilization of ideas among the individuals and institutions comprising the profession; to improve the artistic and administrative capabilities of the field; to enhance the visibility and demonstrate the achievements of the American theatre by increasing public awareness of the theatre's role in society; and to encourage the development of a mutually supportive network of professional companies and artists that collectively represent our "national theatre."

TCG's centralized services today encompass some twenty-five programs, including casting and artist referral services; management and research services; publications; literary services; conferences; and a wide range of other information and advisory services. These programs facilitate the work of thousands of actors, artistic and managing directors, playwrights, literary managers, directors, designers, trustees and administrative personnel, as well as a constituency of over 250 theatre institutions across the country.

Theatre Communications Group, Inc.
355 Lexington Ave.
New York, NY 10017
(212)697-5230

Peter Zeisler, Director
Lindy Zesch, Associate Director

BOARD OF DIRECTORS
Lloyd Richards
President
Emily Mann
Vice President
John Jensen
Secretary/Treasurer
Lyn Austin
Colleen Dewhurst

John Dillon
Charles Fuller
Spalding Gray
John Guare
David Hawkanson
Rosetta LeNoire
Romulus Linney
Mako
Des McAnuff
Hugo V. Neuhaus, Jr.
David Ofner
Robert J. Orchard

Sharon Ott
Harold Prince
Barbara Rosoff
Stanley Silverman
Daniel Sullivan
Fontaine Syer
Jennifer Tipton
William P. Wingate
Robert Woodruff
Peter Zeisler